THE INTERNATIONAL HORSEMAN'S DICTIONARY

To Jenny —
Many Happy Days of Riding.

Love,

Uncle Steve

Christmas
1977

CHARLES STRATTON

THE INTERNATIONAL HORSEMAN'S DICTIONARY

THE DIAL PRESS
New York 1975

Originally published in Great
Britain by The Hamlyn Publishing
Group Limited, Feltham, Middlesex

© Copyright 1975 The Hamlyn Publishing Group Limited

Library of Congress Catalogue Card Number: 75–8650

ISBN 0–8037–3763–7

First Dial printing, 1975

Manufactured in Great Britain

Introduction by Janet Hodgson

This is an invaluable reference book for all who are connected with or interested in horses, for the enlightenment of old and young, novice and experienced. The most experienced horseman will always tell you that even after a lifetime with horses, there is still more to learn and *The International Horseman's Dictionary* contains much useful specialized information, thus supplementing knowledge already acquired.

Obviously much thought and research has gone into compiling the Dictionary and just a glimpse at the first dozen entries gives an insight into the scope covered. It is generously illustrated with photographs and line drawings to expand the written text, and items of additional interest are the tables of results (show-jumping championships, Olympic Games, flat races in both Britain and the United States, etc.). No one is more qualified to supply such information than Charles Stratton, better known perhaps as a horseshow commentator, but also having experience in the administrative side of horsemanship, with the British Show Jumping Association and the National Equestrian Centre at Stoneleigh, and as chef d'équipe with British show-jumping teams abroad.

Through the media, particularly television, equestrianism has increased immensely in popularity, thus enhancing the demand for such an informative book. It will appeal to the enthusiast in that it covers such subjects as show-jumping and eventing — its personalities, both horses and riders; competitions, their definitions and conditions; the leading events in both fields (such as Badminton, Burghley, Royal International Horse Show, Horse of the Year Show) and the history behind them and their organizers. All the major breeds of the world are included and considerable coverage is given to various aspects of horsemanship in the United States.

Items on racing include the background to national and international classics and their winners both on the flat and over fences, including some such famous names as Arkle, Brigadier Gerard, Mill Reef and Nijinsky, and the races they won. All aspects of hunting are covered, both the types of hounds used in each specific field of hunting and the definition of the terms involved. There are also lists of the foxhounds, harriers and staghounds in the British Isles with the country they hunt and of foxhounds in the United States and the country they hunt. Dressage and polo, with their smaller following, are given their due attention. Conformation and unsoundness are covered with equal care. The points of the horse are taken in detail, while an accurate description of unsoundness is enlarged on by discussing the most likely causes. The days of the head groom, with his comprehensive knowledge built up over a lifetime with horses, are past, making such ready information as provided here invaluable to today's owner/rider/groom.

The International Horseman's Dictionary is a fascinating book not only for its wealth of useful information but also for its coverage of the more obscure aspects of equestrianism, which nevertheless provide interesting and intriguing reading. Any dictionary must be a source of reference rather than a book to read from cover to cover and as such this book will be of permanent value.

Anatomy of the horse.

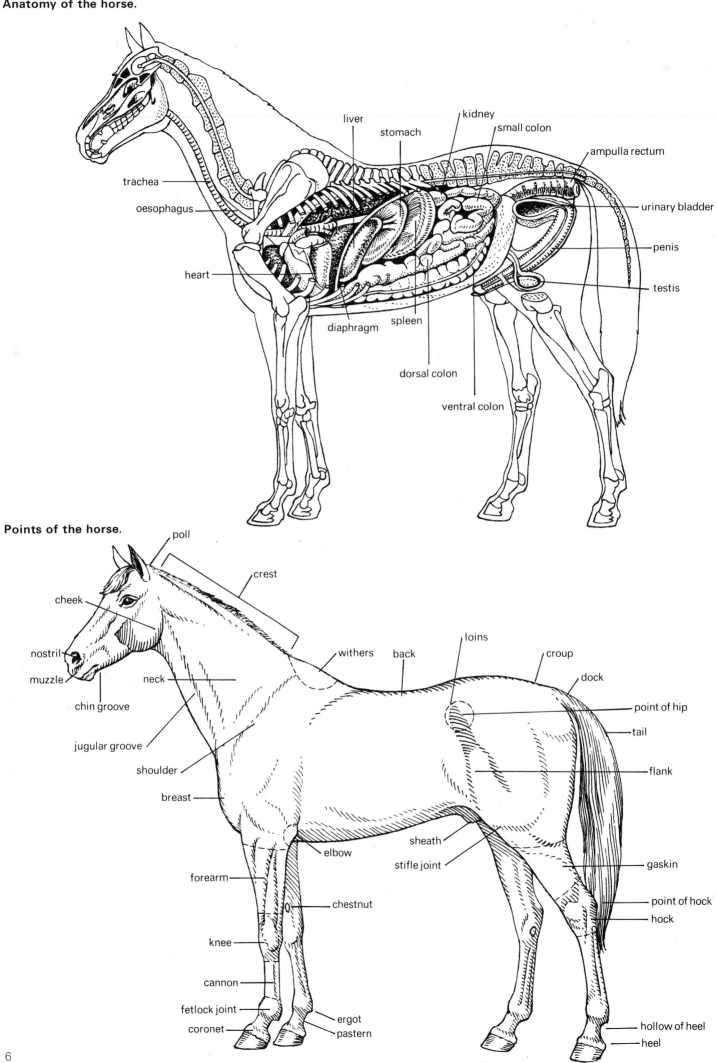

liver

stomach

kidney

small colon

ampulla rectum

trachea

oesophagus

urinary bladder

penis

heart

testis

diaphragm

spleen

dorsal colon

ventral colon

Points of the horse.

poll

crest

cheek

nostril

muzzle

chin groove

neck

jugular groove

shoulder

breast

forearm

chestnut

knee

cannon

fetlock joint

coronet

ergot

pastern

withers

back

loins

croup

dock

point of hip

tail

flank

sheath

stifle joint

gaskin

point of hock

hock

elbow

hollow of heel

heel

a. aged.

Abergavenny, 5th Marquess of, (born 1914) The Queen's representative at Ascot since 1972, having been a trustee since 1952, the Marquess of Abergavenny is a member of the Jockey Club and a former amateur rider. He is a director of Massey Ferguson and of Lloyds Bank, two firms which have done much to sponsor English racing.

He is chairman and a past master of the Eridge Foxhounds, and a former president of the British Horse Society and the British Show Jumping Association. His home, Eridge Park, has been the venue of two European Junior Championships, and at the horse trials held there by the British Horse Society from 1961 to 1972 final selections were made for Olympic, World and European teams.

accident In dressage, combined training and show-jumping, if a horse or rider is unable to complete the course because of an accident, both are eliminated as no change of horse or rider is permitted.

account for *hunting* (of hounds) to kill a fox.

accumulator competition a show-jumping competition in which the course consists of five to seven obstacles of progressive size and difficulty.

Points are awarded as follows:

first obstacle cleared	1 point
second obstacle cleared	2 points
and so on, to seventh obstacle cleared	7 points

The maximum points are 15, 21 or 28, according to whether five, six or seven obstacles are included in the course. No points are awarded for obstacles knocked down.

Refusals, disobediences, etc. are penalized as follows:

fall of horse and/or rider	8 penalty points
first refusal or disobedience	3 penalty points
second refusal or disobedience	6 penalty points
third refusal or disobedience	elimination
every second or part of a second in excess of the time allowed	$\frac{1}{4}$ penalty point

In the event of equality of points for first place, the whole course is jumped again, and the winner is the competitor who scores the greatest number of points in the shortest time.

acey-deucey *racing* with one stirrup leather longer than the other; a style of riding sometimes adopted by jockeys in the United States to help them maintain their balance on sharp bends, so that on a left-hand course they would ride with the right stirrup shorter than the left, and vice versa.

acid firing See under FIRING.

acting master a person appointed temporarily to organize a hunt, whether for a day because the master is away, or for a longer period pending the appointment of a master.

added money the portion of the prize money for a race contributed by the race fund or by sponsors, etc., as opposed to the portion made up of the entry fees paid by the racehorse owners. Also called ADDED PURSE.

added purse See ADDED MONEY.

adjustable head collar a type of head collar having an adjustable head strap, noseband and throat strap. Also called YEARLING HEAD COLLAR.

advanced class a national combined training competition in Britain which, depending on the schedule, may be restricted to horses in Grade I or Grades I and II, or may be open to all grades. In such classes the dressage test is of elementary standard. No obstacle in the show-jumping phase exceeds 3 feet 11 inches in height or 5 feet 11 inches in spread at the highest point and 9 feet 2 inches at the base, and the test is carried out at a speed of 382 yards per minute. The cross-country course is no less than 2 miles and no more than $2\frac{1}{2}$ miles long, with eight to ten obstacles per mile, and no obstacle exceeds 3 feet 11 inches in height.

aerborn sheet See ANTISWEAT RUG.

African horse sickness an infectious virus disease of equine animals occurring mainly in Africa, the Middle East and South America, though there was an outbreak in southern Spain in 1966. The virus is spread by a biting nocturnal insect and may be carried by a horse for up to three months before it develops. In its mild form the disease may consist only of a fever and sickness, but in its most acute form the heart is affected, the breathing becomes laboured, swellings appear on the head and neck, and there is a discharge from the nose. It develops very quickly, and death soon occurs. A vaccine has been developed but it has not proved completely effective against the disease, and there is a ban on horses entering Britain from countries where African horse sickness is prevalent.

against the clock *show-jumping* decided by time, as a competition or jump-off, the winner being the competitor with the least number of faults in the fastest time.

Aga Khan Trophy a trophy awarded since 1926 to the winning teams in the Prix des Nations at the Dublin International Horse Show.

aged (of a horse) seven years old or over.

Agricultural Hall At the five-day show held in 1876 at the Agricultural Hall in Islington, competitors in the show classes were allowed to enter for the leaping classes for no extra fee. This is the first record of horses jumping indoors in Britain.

Agrippin rubber tread a rubber tread inserted into stirrup irons to help the rider keep his feet in position.

A.H.S.A. American Horse Show Association.

aid 1. any of the signals used by a rider to convey instructions to his horse. **2.** any of the means by which these signals are produced; the body, hands, legs and voice are classed as NATURAL AIDS, while whips, spurs, etc., are known as ARTIFICIAL AIDS.

Aintree a racecourse near Liverpool in Lancashire; the famous home of the Grand National Handicap Steeplechase. Racing had been organized by a local landowner at Maghull, some ten miles away, when, in 1829, a rival committee headed by William Lynn, a local innkeeper, established racing at Aintree. Seven years later a steeplechase, which was won by Capt. Becher on The Duke, was held there, followed in 1837 by the Grand Liverpool Steeplechase, the race which came to be recognized as the first Grand National. The winner was again The Duke, though on this occasion he was not ridden by Capt. Becher. In 1839 racing was taken over by a committee which included Lord George Bentinck and Lords Eglington, Derby, Sefton and Wilton. The first race under this management was over a distance of 4 miles with twenty-nine jumps, and attracted eighteen starters. It was during this race that Capt. Becher fell at a high fence with double rails and a wide ditch on the landing side, the fence known ever since as BECHER'S BROOK. The early Grand National

Aintree. General view.

Aintree. Mrs Mirabel Topham, whose family owned the racecourse until it was sold at the beginning of 1974.

courses consisted of an enormous variety of obstacles, including stone walls, and areas of plough. In 1843 the race became a handicap known as the Liverpool and National Steeplechase and then, four years later, it was finally renamed the Grand National Handicap Steeplechase. Among the other steeplechase races held at Aintree are the Topham Trophy, named after the famous Topham family which owned the racecourse for many years, the Mildmay Memorial Chase and the Foxhunters' Chase. A number of flat races are also held there, including the Liverpool Spring Cup, first run in 1848, and the Liverpool Autumn Cup, first run in 1856.

Aintree breastplate See under BREASTPLATE.

air any of the movements, other than the normal gaits of walk, trot and canter, performed by horses trained in the classical manner; any of the high school movements of the horse, such as passage, piaffe.

air above the ground any of various high-school movements, such as the ballotade, capriole, courbette, croupade or levade, performed with the forelegs or with the forelegs and the hind legs off the ground. Also called SCHOOL JUMP.

A.I.T. Area International Trial.

Akhal-Teke an ancient breed of hardy saddlehorse developed in the region of Turkmenistan in the Soviet Union. It has a majestic appearance, with light but strong bone, and the breed has been used very successfully for racing and dressage. The colours vary considerably; there are bays, greys and others, but the most prized colour is golden dun. As in the Karabakh, the coat takes on a characteristic metallic sheen in sunlight. Another distinctive feature of the breed is the exceptionally short mane and tail.

albino The albino is a colour type more than a breed of horse, which has been fostered in the United States since the foundation of the American Albino Horse Club in 1937. At birth the albino has pure white hair, pale skin and pale, translucent blue eyes. Like all other albino creatures it is lacking in pigmentation, and because of this suffers from some weaknesses. For this reason it is not popular with many people.
   It is possible to breed an albino, for the two genes do stay true to type and colour. The breeding is believed to stem from a cross between the Arab and Morgan horses.

all on *hunting* the expression used, generally by the whipper-in, to let the huntsman know that all the hounds are up with the pack.

all-round cow horse a horse which is good at performing all the duties required of it by a cowboy, such as cutting and roping.

also-ran *racing* any unplaced horse in a race.

alter to castrate or geld a horse or colt.

Alter-Real a breed of saddle-horse from the Alentejo province of Portugal, where it has been bred for several centuries. A short close-coupled horse, the Alter-Real has a deep wide chest, a short arched neck and a relatively small head. The legs are well placed under the body, and the upper legs are particularly thick. It is a highly strung animal, full of energy, with an extravagant, very showy action.

Alter-Real. A Portuguese breed, the Alter-Real is a popular riding horse and has proved particularly suitable for haute école.

Alycidon, with Doug Smith up.

Alycidon (by Donatello II out of Aurora. Donatello II was unbeaten in all his races in France, except the Grand Prix de Paris, before being sold to England.) Foaled in 1945, Alycidon was bred and owned by Lord Derby and trained by Walter Earl. As a two-year-old he was backward; he ran only twice and was unplaced on each occasion. The following season, after being unplaced in the Christopher Wren Stakes at Hurst Park, he won the Classic Trial Stakes at Thirsk, came third in the Chester Vase and won the Royal Standard Stakes at Manchester. He was third in the King Edward VII Stakes at Ascot, but went on to win the Princess of Wales Stakes at Newmarket and the St George Stakes at Liverpool. In the St Leger he was second, and in his final race of the season, the King George VI Stakes at Ascot, he came first. He remained in training as a four-year-old and was unbeaten in his five races: the Ormonde Stakes at Chester, the Corporation Stakes at Doncaster, the Gold Cup at Ascot, the Goodwood Cup and the Doncaster Cup.

He was then retired to stud, where he sired 235 foals, including Meld and Alcide, winner of the St Leger and the King George VI and Queen Elizabeth Stakes.

amateur 1. *dressage, combined training, show-jumping* any person aged eighteen or over who does not attempt to make a profit through competition and who does not engage in any activities which would make him a professional rider under the rules of the F.E.I. For Olympic and Regional Games he also has to satisfy the definition of an amateur set out in the rules of the International Olympic Committee. If the amateur status of a competitor entered in the Olympic or Regional Games is in doubt, the final decision rests with the National Olympic Committee.

Amateurs who are owners may not sell more than three competition horses a year, unless authorized to do so by their national federation.

An amateur who wishes regularly to ride horses owned by someone else must apply for permission to his national federation. If a horse is ridden by an amateur, prize money is always paid to the registered owner of the horse; if an amateur rider owns the horse he is allowed to receive the prize money.

An amateur who wishes to compete internationally has to obtain an authorization annually from his national federation. **2.** See JOCKEY.

amble 1. a lateral gait, as used by pacers in harness racing but somewhat slower. **2.** (Western US) a slow leisurely walking pace.

American head collar an extremely hard-wearing head collar. It has a throat strap but no browband, and the head strap is adjustable.

American Horse Shows Association Founded in 1917 by Reginald Vanderbilt, the American Horse Shows Association became the national federation and the governing body of equestrian sport in the United States in 1937. It is now the governing body for over 1000 horse shows a year.

American Quarter Horse The Quarter Horse was originally found in the eastern states of America among the colonial seaboard settlements. The breed resulted from crossing Spanish horses, which had been brought to the country some time previously, with good English stallions. The horse gained its name from the fact that the early settlers cut race tracks, usually a quarter of a mile long, in the forests — hence 'Quarter Horse'. They stood about 15 h.h., were compact and of chunky build, with very strong muscular quarters, with which they were able to develop tremendous thrust and great pull through their shoulders and haunches, making them brilliant performers over a short distance.

Gradually, with the development of longer, round

American Quarter Horse.
Clover Drift, a young stallion, demonstrates two of the qualities which have made the breed so invaluable for cattle work: speed and agility.

race tracks, the Quarter Horse was banished to the western states. Over the years it developed a protective instinct toward other animals, and with it a shrewd capacity to anticipate their actions and the ability to stop or turn suddenly or do a dashing sprint to head an animal off. Thus the Quarter Horse became an invaluable partner to the cattle-man on the ranch, and today the breed is found all over the world where there are cattle, even in Africa and Australia.

In recent years there has been a return to short-distance racing, and the Quarter Horse has re-established itself as a brilliant performer, attracting some of the richest prize money.

American Saddle-Horse a breed of saddle-horse whose development traces back over 400 years to the days of the early settlers. As there were no indigenous horses in America, English amblers and pacers — and, later, English Thoroughbreds — together with oriental and continental breeds were imported. The pioneers required a fast hardy horse that was comfortable to ride for long periods, and by a process of careful selective breeding they developed the KENTUCKY SADDLE-HORSE, the parent breed of the American Saddle-Horse, although the English Thoroughbred Denmark, imported in the 1840s, is regarded as the official founder of the present breed.

On average 15.3 h.h. and usually bay, brown or chestnut in colour, the breed is characterized by a high leg action, high head carriage and high tail carriage, produced by nicking. Now bred almost entirely for showing, American Saddle-Horses are known as three- or five-gaited saddlers; the THREE-GAITED SADDLER is trained to perform at the walk, trot and canter, and customarily has a hogged mane, and tail close clipped at the top and pulled rather thin, while the FIVE-GAITED SADDLER performs at the walk, trot, canter, slow gait and rack, and is distinguished by a flowing mane and tail.

Andalusian This Spanish breed owes its origin to the monks of three different monasteries who took a keen interest in horse breeding and zealously guarded the purity of the breed. The original stallions were probably imported from Arabia, where the pasture and climate were very similar, although the present-day examples of the breed have none of the Arabian's characteristics.

The old monastery at Jerez still has a stud farm in front of it, retaining its original name *Salto al Cielo* ('Leap into Heaven'). The breed was successfully hidden from Napoleon's invading forces, and later fetched very high prices when sold to breeders who had been less successful.

The Andalusian is a strong, deep-bodied horse, with a good front and strong quarters, and a low, smooth action. It has an excellent temperament, making it a good and attractive ride. The colour is usually grey, either flea-bitten or spotted.

angle-cheek Pelham a pelham bit formerly used by the army, and designed to suit as wide a variety of mouths as possible. The mouthpiece is smooth on one side and serrated on the other and so can be changed to suit the horse. There are two pairs of cheek slots, thus enabling the position of the reins also to be changed.

Anglo-Norman The original strong and powerful Norman horse was crossed with Danish and Mecklenburg carthorses. In the eighteenth century Arabs, English Thoroughbreds and half-breds were used extensively, and at the end of the nineteenth century the Norfolk trotter was also introduced.

There are now two main types: the heavy draught horse, which contains a lot of Percheron blood, and the lighter animal, which contains much Thoroughbred blood and is very popular and successful in show-jumping and combined training events.

angoras chaps made of goatskin with the hair left on.

Animal Health Trust a charitable organization founded in 1942 with the object of carrying out scientific research into the causes, prevention and treatment of disease in all types of domestic animals. It has four separate research stations, including the EQUINE RESEARCH STATION at Newmarket, which deals with diseases affecting the horse.

Anne, H.R.H. The Princess, *GB* (born 1950) Princess Anne has always had an interest in horses, having been a member of the Pony Club, and also a founder member of the National Equestrian Centre. She has competed in dressage and show-jumping, but it is in combined training that her main interest lies, and in this she has been considerably helped by her trainer, Alison Oliver, and on occasions also by Lars Sederholm.

The first combined training horse on which Princess Anne competed was Lt Col. Miller's Purple Star. In 1969 the Princess started riding the home-bred 16.2 h.h. chestnut gelding, DOUBLET, winning a novice competition at Windsor. In 1971 the pair entered their first three-day event at Badminton, where they were a very creditable fifth, and on this showing they were selected as individuals for the European Championships at Burghley in September of the same year. There, after a very good dressage test they led the field, never to be headed, and won the European Championship by a margin of thirty-eight penalties from their nearest rival. Unfortunately, Doublet went lame in spring 1972, and they were therefore out of consideration for the Olympic Games in Munich. In 1974 Princess Anne, riding Goodwill, competed as an individual in the World Three-Day Event Championships at Burghley and finished twelfth.

Ansell, Col. Sir Michael Picton, (born 1905) A regular soldier in the 5th Royal Inniskilling Dragoon Guards, Sir Michael was a keen enthusi-

H.R.H. Princess Anne. Crowds gather at the Trout Hatchery as the Princess, riding Doublet, splashes through the water during the 1971 European Three-Day Event Championship at Burghley.

Col. Sir Michael Ansell, director of the Royal International Horse Show and the Horse of the Year Show, and president of the British Equestrian Federation.

ast for all equestrian sport before the Second World War. He took part in hunting, polo and racing, and represented Great Britain in international show-jumping competitions.

After being partially blinded as a result of war injuries, he decided to take on an administrative role in show-jumping, and it is largely due to his efforts that show-jumping is such a popular sport today, both nationally and internationally. From 1944 to 1964 he was the chairman of the British Show Jumping Association, and from 1964 to 1966 he was its president. He was primarily responsible for the organization of the National Championships at the White City in London in 1945 and for the reopening of the International Horse Show in 1947, of which he was appointed director in 1951. Again, it was largely due to him and to Capt. Collings that the Horse of the Year Show was started in 1949, a show of which he has been the director since its inception.

He was honorary director of the British Horse Society from 1952 to 1963, when he was appointed the first chairman of the society, a position he held until 1972. He then became president and chairman of the newly formed British Equestrian Federation.

A Member of Honour of the F.E.I., he was appointed a C.B.E. in 1951 and was knighted in 1968, both for services to show-jumping.

ante-post betting *racing* the placing of bets on a race, at an agreed price, before the day of the race, as opposed to starting-price betting.

anticast roller See ARCH ROLLER.

antilug bit a snaffle bit designed for use on horses which tend to hang to one side. The mouthpiece is jointed, but not in the centre, the longer piece being on the side to which the horse hangs. The shorter piece is curved back. This is also a particularly useful bit for horses which tend to veer to one side when jumping.

antisweat rug a sheet of open cellular cotton mesh used to help horses cool off after exercise without becoming cold. The cotton mesh traps small, insulating pockets of air next to the skin, thus preventing too rapid a reduction in the body temperature. Also called AERBORN SHEET.

antler one of the solid deciduous, usually branched horns of a stag. See also TINE.

anvil 1. a heavy iron block with a smooth flat face, usually of steel, on which horseshoes are shaped. **2.** (Western US) a horse, especially one which is shod, which strikes the forefeet with the hind feet.

Appaloosa It is thought that the original stock, like that of so many other breeds, came to America from Spain. The name was then derived from a breed developed in the Palouse district of Idaho by the Nez Percé Indians, who were excellent horse-breeders and developed animals of high quality. In recent years the breed has become very popular and now rates among the top five in the United States.

The Appaloosa Horse Club describes the markings as follows: Most animals are white over the loins and hips, with dark round or oval spots. The spots vary in size from specks to areas three or four inches in diameter. Sometimes spotting occurs all over the body, but is most marked on the hindquarters. Others are white over the hips without the dark spots, and still more are mottled all over. Other characteristics are the whiteness of the eye, and the mottled or muddy appearance of the skin, which also has an overall pink and grey splattering, particularly noticeable around the muzzle and nostrils. The hooves are generally marked with black and white striping.

appointment card a card sent out by the hunt secretary to members, farmers and subscribers telling them of the time, date and place of forthcoming meets.

apprentice *racing* a youth who is being trained as a jockey and serves an indentured apprenticeship of five to seven years.

apron a covering made of strong horsehide worn by farriers to protect the front of the body. It usually has a pouch in the middle for carrying nails and reaches below the knees, but is divided in order to give complete freedom of movement to the legs.

apron-faced having a large white mark on the face.

Arab It is claimed that the Arab as a breed was in existence at the time of Mohammed and that it flourished in the courts of the Hashemite princes as long ago as the seventh century. The pure-bred desert Arab is now found only in a few royal studs. However, the breed occurs in many parts of the world, particularly in the western United States, Britain and Poland.

The average size is between 14 and 15 h.h., but there are no height restrictions within the breed. The most usual colours are grey, chestnut and bay: the brighter and more distinct the colour, the more favourable. The Arab has many characteristics which easily distinguish it from other breeds: the high carriage of both the head and the tail; the quick, almost dancing action at all paces; and, above all, the extreme beauty of the head, which is small and wedgeshaped, with large prominent eyes and small alert ears. The coat and skin are very fine, and the legs have little or no feather. The Arab has a dense quality of bone, hard feet and great muscular strength. It is renowned for its endurance and ability to carry considerable weight over a long distance.

The Arab Horse Society of Great Britain was founded in 1918, and now has some 200 studs registered with it. The American breed society is the Arabian Horse Club Registry of America, Inc.

Archer, Frederick, (1857–1886) Born at Prestbury in Gloucestershire, Fred Archer was apprenticed at the age of thirteen to Matthew Dawson, who had stables at Middleham, Russley Park and Heath House, Newmarket, and rode his first winner, Atholl Daisy, the following year at Chesterfield.

During his career he rode a total of 2748 winners, with no less than 246 victories in 1885. He was champion jockey from 1874 to 1886. He won the Derby on five occasions: in 1877 on Silvic, in 1880 on Bend Or, in 1881 on Iroquois, in 1885 on Melton and in 1886 on Ormonde. He also won the St Leger six times and the Oaks four times.

arch-mouth Pelham a pelham bit having a mouthpiece with an upward curve, which gives the tongue plenty of room and allows the bit to lie across the bars of the mouth.

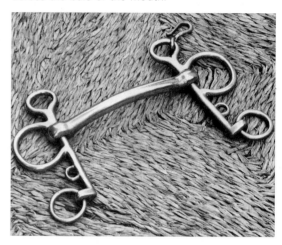

arch roller a type of stable roller in which the pads are connected by a metal arch to prevent the horse rolling over. The arch also serves to remove all pressure from the horse's spine. In the ADJUSTABLE ARCH ROLLER the pads are hinged so that they automatically adjust to the angle of the horse's back. Also called ANTICAST ROLLER.

Ardennes a very hardy breed of horse originating in the Forest of Ardennes in north-east France and south-east Belgium. In France the breed has remained relatively pure; the animal stands between 14.2 h.h. and 15.2 h.h. and is thickset, short, stocky and close to the ground. It has tremendous muscle and a good bone structure, and is widely used on agricultural holdings. In Belgium, on the other hand, the breed was crossed with the Brabant to produce

Far right
arch-mouth Pelham bit. The upward curve of the mouthpiece allows the bit to lie across the bars of the mouth, rather than resting on the tongue.

Right
Arab. Grojec, the famous Polish-bred stallion owned by Lady Anne Lytton.

Far right
Ardennes. A robust French draught horse, but gentle and docile, the Ardennes is much used for farm work.

career was unfortunately brought to a premature end in 1966, when he broke a pedal bone in the King George VI Chase at Kempton. At first it was hoped that it would be possible to race him again after long and intensive treatment, but he developed severe arthritis and was put down in June 1970. In his memory a statue was erected at Cheltenham Racecourse with money raised by the Racegoers' Club.

1961 Lough Ennel Maiden Plate, Mullingar – third
    Greystones Flat Race, Leopardstown – fourth
1962 Bective Hurdle, Navan – first
    Rathconnell Handicap Hurdle, Naas – first
    Balbriggan Handicap Hurdle, Baldoyle – unplaced
    New Handicap Hurdle, Fairyhouse – fourth
    Wee County Handicap Hurdle, Dundalk – first
    The President's Handicap Hurdle, Gowran Park – first
    Honeybourne Chase, Cheltenham – first
1963 Milltown Chase, Leopardstown – first
    Broadway Chase, Cheltenham – first
    Power Gold Cup, Fairyhouse – first
    John Jameson Gold Cup, Punchestown – first
    Donoughmore Maiden Plate (Flat), Navan – first
    Carey's Cottage Chase, Gowran Park – first
    Hennessy Gold Cup, Newbury – first
    Christmas Handicap Chase, Leopardstown – first
1964 Thyestes Chase, Gowran Park – first
    Leopardstown Chase – first
    Gold Cup, Cheltenham – first
    Irish Grand National, Fairyhouse – first
    Carey's Cottage Handicap Chase, Gowran Park – first
    Hennessy Gold Cup, Newbury – first
    Massey Ferguson Gold Cup, Cheltenham – third
1965 Leopardstown Chase – first
    Gold Cup, Cheltenham – first
    Whitbread Gold Cup, Sandown – first
    Gallagher Gold Cup, Sandown – first
    Hennessy Gold Cup, Newbury – first
    King George VI Chase, Kempton – first
1966 Leopardstown Chase – first
    Gold Cup, Cheltenham – first
    Hennessy Gold Cup, Newbury – second
    S.G.B. Chase, Ascot – first
    King George VI Chase, Kempton – second

artificial aids See under AID.

artzel a white mark on the forehead of a horse.

arve a word of command to agricultural horses directing them to turn left. See also GEE.

Ascot a racecourse at Ascot, about twenty-five miles west of London, owned by Queen Elizabeth II and administered by the Ascot Authority, a non-profit-making body headed by the Marquess of Abergavenny. Racing was first held there in 1711 at the behest of Queen Anne, who presented a plate on 11th August, but after her death in 1714 no races were held there for six years. Until after the Second World War Ascot was used only four times a year, and, although the course now has twenty-five days' racing every year, including, since 1965, steeplechase and hurdle race meetings, it is still these four days in June which constitute the course's main meeting and main attraction – Royal Ascot. The colourful pageantry of the royal procession down the course – a tradition first started by George IV in 1825 – and the famous

the BELGIAN ARDENNES, a quiet, stocky animal, averaging 15.1 h.h. to 15.3 h.h., and much closer in type to the Brabant than to the original Ardennes stock. The most common colours of both breeds are bay, chestnut, roan and sorrel.

Area International Trial one of a series of major show-jumping competitions designed to find potential international horses. The competitions are allocated by the B.S.J.A., usually on the basis of one a year to each county, though in exceptional circumstances a second one may be held if the county is very large. Entry is restricted to Grade A horses, and the winner of each trial becomes eligible for the Olympic Trial held annually in August at the British Timken Show, and also for the King George V Gold Cup, if the rider is a man, or the Queen Elizabeth II Cup, if the rider is a woman.

arena the area in which a horseshow or show-jumping competition is held.

Arkle (by Archive out of Bright Cherry) Bred by Mrs Baker at Malahow and foaled in 1957 at the Ballymacoll Stud in County Meath, Arkle was sold in August 1960 to the Duchess of Westminster for 1150 guineas. He was trained by Tom Dreaper at Killsallaghan, near Dublin. During a truly remarkable career, Arkle won no less than twenty-eight of his thirty-five races (for details see below), winning a total of £75,207 in prize money. His array of extravagant, fanciful and sometimes bizarre fashions, as well as the race programme itself, which includes the Ascot Gold Cup and the Queen's Vase, have combined to make Royal Ascot one of the most important meetings in the racing calendar and one of the world's great social occasions.

Ascot Gold Cup a horserace over 2 miles 4 furlongs (2½ miles), held annually at the Royal Ascot meeting since 1807, except from 1941 to 1944, when it was run at Newmarket. (For results see page 235.)

as hounds ran *hunting* the distance covered in a hunt by the hounds.

asking the question asking a horse to make a big effort, i.e. to accelerate in a race or to take a jump in a combined training or show-jumping competition, particularly when a horse is being pushed to its limit.

Association of British Riding Clubs Affiliated to the British Horse Society, the Riding Clubs movement was formed in the 1950s to encourage the weekend rider. There are branches in many towns, and some large firms have their own clubs. Membership is open to both riders and non-riders who are interested in learning more about the horse. In addition to holding riding classes, competitions and shows the clubs also organize such things as lectures, film shows and discussions. At the end of the riding season championships are held annually at the National Equestrian Centre.

association saddle the regulation saddle for all major rodeo contests since 1920. It is built on a modified Ellenberg tree, medium in height, with a fourteen-inch swell and a five-inch cantle; it has small round skirts, three-quarter rigged, with a flank rig set further back than on a regular rigged saddle.

at bay 1. the stand made by a hunted stag which is cornered to face the hounds (to stand at bay). **2.** the position of the hounds thus kept off (kept at bay).

at fault *hunting* (of hounds) having lost the scent of the quarry.

Atherstone girth.
Generally made of baghide leather, it is shaped at the elbows to prevent chafing.

Atherstone girth a baghide girth cut and shaped to give freedom of movement at the elbows and thus prevent chafing.

at stud (of a stallion) available to serve mares for

a fee. The stallion may be able to travel to mares, but more often he will be at a stable and the mares will be brought to him.

Australian cheeker a device for keeping the bit up in the mouth and preventing the horse from putting its tongue over it. Made of rubber, it is shaped like an inverted Y; the two arms are placed over the bit rings on either side of the mouth, while the central band lies on the horse's nose and is held in position on the headpiece. Since pressure is exerted on the nose, it also acts as a restrainer. Also called AUSTRALIAN NOSEBAND.

Australian loose-ring cheek snaffle See FULMER SNAFFLE.

Australian noseband See AUSTRALIAN CHEEKER.

Australian Simplex pattern safety iron a type of stirrup iron in which the lower part of the outer side curves forward, so that in the event of a fall the foot is easily released.

automatic timing an electrical apparatus used for timing show-jumping events. The horse breaks a ray as it goes through the start, thus triggering off the mechanism which starts the clock, and when it goes through the finish the horse breaks another ray, which stops the clock.

autorisation spéciale a pink card which a rider must obtain from his national federation giving him permission to compete in an international equestrian event, whether for dressage, combined training or show-jumping. The card is collected by the organizing show.

autumn double the Cesarewitch Stakes and the Cambridgeshire Stakes.

Avelignese a small sturdy horse bred in mountainous districts all over Italy. Between 13.3 h.h. and 14.3 h.h. and commonly sorrel or palomino in colour, it is very muscular and particularly sure-footed, enabling it to negotiate mountain passes even in the most extreme climatic conditions. Horses of this breed have been used extensively for agricultural work and as pack animals.

away from you *hunting* the expression used to warn people that there is a ditch or similar hazard on the landing side of an obstacle. See also TO YOU.

axletree a bar fixed crosswise under a vehicle, with an arm at each end to which a wheel is attached.

axletree arm one of the rounded spindles at each end of the axletree upon which a wheel rotates.

axletree box one of the metal cylinders for grease or oil, fitted to the axletree arms and fixed firmly in the wheel stock.

b. 1. bay (def. 1). **2.** brought down.

babbler *hunting* a hound which throws its tongue too much, either because it has become separated from the rest of the pack or because it is uncertain of the scent.

back to place a bet on a horse.

back at the knee See CALF-KNEED.

backer a person who places a bet on a horse.

back for a place *racing* to bet that a horse will finish in the first three in a race (in Great Britain) or in the first two (in the United States).

back for a show (US) *racing* to bet that a horse will finish in the first three in a race.

back gammon board the seat on the roof of a coach at the rear. See also GAMMON BOARD.

backhander a polo stroke in which the player galloping forwards hits the ball back in the opposite direction.

back jockey the top skirt of a Western saddle; the uppermost broad leathers joining behind the cantle.

back line *polo* a goal line; a line marking out the total length of the field of play.

back stretch the straight on the opposite side of a racecourse to the winning post and stands.

back to win *racing* to bet that a horse will win a particular race.

Badge of Honour an award presented by the International Equestrian Federation (F.E.I.) to riders taking part in Prix des Nations competitions. The bronze badge is awarded to riders who have competed in five Prix des Nations; the silver for competing in twenty-five; and the gold for taking part in fifty Prix des Nations competitions. Competing in an Olympic Games is regarded as equivalent to taking part in five Prix des Nations.

Badminton Horse Trials a three-day event competition held annually since 1949 at Badminton House in Gloucestershire, the home of the Duke of Beaufort. It always takes place in April, with the dressage on the first day, the speed and endurance tests on the second day and the show-jumping on the third day. Since its inception Badminton has become the classic of the combined training season and a proving ground for the world's greatest riders. (For results see page 228.)

bag fox a fox kept temporarily in captivity until it is required for a hunt. It is then released at a specified time — usually just before a meet or draw — and place. The practice of using bag foxes is very much frowned upon.

Bahram (by Blandford out of Friar's Daughter) Foaled in 1932, Bahram was bred at the Aga Khan's stud at the Curragh in Ireland and was trained at Newmarket by Frank Butters. With his first race as a two-year-old — the National Breeders' Produce Stakes at Sandown, which he won by a neck from stable companion Theft — there began a career which was always to see him in first place in the winner's enclosure, for he was never beaten. That year he went on to win the Rous Memorial Stakes at Goodwood, the Gimcrack Stakes at York, the Bowcawen Stakes and the Middle Park Stakes at Newmarket.

Far right
Badminton Horse Trials.
A smiling Lucinda Prior-Palmer after her victory in 1973 which won her the coveted Whitbread Trophy.

Right
Badminton Horse Trials.
The cross-country phase and a competitor takes the Normandy Bank in fine style.

Bahram. Triple Crown winner in 1935, he was unbeaten on the racecourse.

In 1935 his first race was the 2000-Guineas, which he won by two and a half lengths, again from Theft. His next race was the Derby, which he won by two lengths. Bahram then went to Royal Ascot, where he won the St James' Palace Stakes by half a length, and from there to Doncaster for the St Leger, in which he beat Solar Ray by five lengths, thus winning the Triple Crown. Freddie Fox had become his regular jockey, but because of injury was unable to ride him in the St Leger and was replaced by Charlie Smirke.

The following year Bahram was retired to stud at Newmarket, and at the beginning of the war was sold to an American syndicate. However, he did not prove an immediate success, and in 1946 he was sold on to an Argentinian syndicate. He died in 1956.

bake to ride a horse in such a way as to make it over hot.

bald face Western name for a horse with a white facial marking extending round one or both eyes.

Balding girth a leather girth shaped to prevent chafing. The leather is split in three and at each end the two outer pieces are crossed over the centre strip to reduce the width of the girth at the elbows.

balked *racing* (of a horse) obstructed or prevented from coming through by another horse as, for example, by one which has fallen or run out. Also BAULKED.

ball a means of administering medicine to horses, formerly in much greater general use than today. Medicinal agents are mixed with linseed meal and honey, treacle or soft-soap and beaten into a paste which is then rolled into a ball about three-quarters of an inch in diameter and folded in fine paper or put in a gelatine capsule. To administer the ball, the top of the horse's tongue should be pulled gently to one side of the mouth and the ball should be passed along the roof of the mouth and then released. The jaw should be held closed and the horse watched to make sure the ball passes down the gullet.

ballotade an air above the ground in which the horse half rears, then jumps forward, drawing the hind legs up below the quarters, and lands on all four legs.

Balls Bridge the headquarters of the Royal Dublin Society and the permanent show ground of the Dublin Spring and Dublin International Horse Shows.

Banbury mouthpiece a mouthpiece consisting of a rounded bar which is tapered in the centre and is fitted into slots in the cheekpieces. While allowing the horse to mouth the bit, it prevents him taking hold of it because there is little room for the tongue. The Banbury mouthpiece may be used as a curb or pelham.

band (Western US) a group of horses.

bang-tail (Western US) a mustang.

bank to jump or attempt to jump on to and then off a bank, wall or similar obstacle, rather than jumping over it.

Barb The Barb has frequently been crossed with Arabs and other horses from the east, so that there are now very few true Barbs to be found. The breed, formerly known as the BARBARY HORSE, originated in North Africa, in Morocco, Algeria and Tunisia, an area noted for its horses. It has many similarities to the Arab, but its main quality is an amazing turn of speed over a short distance, coupled with tremendous endurance at a slower rate. Being a desert horse, it is very hardy in constitution. The maximum height for the breed is 15 h.h. It has flat shoulders with a rounded chest, a relatively long concave head with small well-set ears, and a flowing mane and tail.

barding a protective covering of leather or padding used in the Middle Ages to protect warhorses. It reached almost to the ground and covered the body, head and neck.

bareback riding 1. the act of riding a horse without saddle or blanket on its back. **2.** one of the five standard rodeo events. The rider has no bridle, saddle, stirrups or reins, only a simple leather BAREBACK RIGGING, equipped with a handhold much like a suitcase handle. The rider must remain mounted for eight seconds; he may spur freely, but must use only one hand. He is judged on how hard the horse bucks and how well he rides.

barème any of the three tables of rules set by the International Equestrian Federation under which show-jumping competitions are judged:
BARÈME A The result is decided by totalling the jumping faults and any time faults incurred for exceeding the time allowed.
BARÈME B For each obstacle knocked down ten seconds are added to the time taken for the round. This is used only if the length of the course exceeds 700 metres.
BARÈME C For each obstacle knocked down the number of seconds added to the time taken for the course is determined by the length of the course.

bar firing See under FIRING.

Barnum device a schooling device consisting of a leather headpiece, which is strapped to the bit ring on the offside and extends three parts of the way down the nearside. A cord is arranged through the ring of the bit and through the ring of the headpiece so that it will pull the bit upwards and tighten on the head, should the horse attempt to resist. A rubber bit should always be used, as a steel one may damage the mouth.

barouche a heavy four-wheeled carriage with a high seat on the outside for the driver, and seats inside for two couples facing each other. Introduced in about 1800, it became a fashionable carriage for the summer season, but could not be used in bad weather, as it had a hood for the rear half only. It was generally drawn by a pair, but could also be driven to four horses.

barrage *show-jumping* a jump-off.

barrel the part of the horse's body between the forearms and the loins.

barrier 1. See STARTING GATE. **2.** (in a rodeo arena) the barrier behind which the roper's or steer wrestler's horse waits until the stock is far enough out of the chute. The BARRIER FLAGMAN then lowers his flag and at the same time pulls a rope which releases the horse from the barrier.

bar shoe a type of horseshoe with a metal piece welded across the heel, put on horses which have weak heels or damaged quarters and designed to give additional support, placing more pressure on the frog and thus relieving sidebones or corns.

bastard strangles See under STRANGLES.

basterna a type of sedan chair used in ancient Rome; it was supported on poles between two horses, one in front and one behind.

bat a stick or riding whip.

bat wings leather chaps which are buckled on to protect the rider's legs, differing from shotgun chaps, which are slipped on like trousers.

baulked See BALKED.

bay 1. a dark-skinned horse having a dark-brown to a bright, reddish- or yellowish-brown coat, with a black mane and tail, and, usually, black markings on the limbs. **2.** the noise made by a hound, especially when hunting; a deep prolonged bark.

St Leger. In 1910, as a four-year-old, he won the Biennial Stakes at Newmarket, the Chester Vase, the Gold Cup at Ascot and the Dullingham Plate at Newmarket, and was beaten by only a neck in his final race, the Goodwood Cup. His total winnings came to over £44,500.

As a sire he was very successful; he was champion in 1917 and 1918, and his progeny included Gay Crusader and Gainsborough, winners of the Triple Crown in 1917 and 1918, respectively. It was a great loss to English bloodstock when he died at the early age of eleven.

bayo coyote (south-western US) a dun horse with a black dorsal stripe.

bay roan See under ROAN.

bay tine Also BEZ TINE. See under TINE.

b.d. brought down.

B.D.S. British Driving Society.

beagle one of a breed of small hounds used for hunting hares.

beaning the act or practice of disguising an unsoundness in a horse. If, for example, an unscrupulous dealer wished to sell an animal which was lame in the near-fore but sound in the other legs, he would insert a piece of metal or a sharp stone between the shoe and the hoof of the off-fore so that the horse, feeling pain equally in both front legs, would appear to go sound.

bearing rein a leather rein running from one of the rings on the bit to a BEARING REIN POST, a vertical pole attached to the pad, used to promote a high head carriage in harness horses.

beat up a pig (in pigsticking) to advance in a line beating the bushes in order to make the pig leave them.

Beaufort phaeton a type of phaeton, very similar in design to the mail phaeton, except that it was able to seat six people instead of four, and was therefore useful for conveying house guests about in the country. It was named after the Duke of Beaufort for whom it was first built. See also MAIL PHAETON.

Bayardo (by Bay Ronald out of Galicia) Foaled in 1906, Bayardo, a lop-eared colt, was owned by an Australian, A. W. Cox, who for racing purposes adopted the name of Mr Fairie, and was trained by Alec Taylor at Malton in Yorkshire. As a two-year-old he ran seven times and was unbeaten, winning the New Stakes at Goodwood, and the Buckenham Stakes, Rous Memorial Stakes, Middle Park Plate and Dewhurst Stakes, all at Newmarket. After an unsuccessful start to the following season – he was fourth in the 2000-Guineas and unplaced in the Derby – he went on to win all of the eleven races in which he was entered, including the Eclipse Stakes at Sandown, the St Leger and the Doncaster Stakes at Doncaster, the Champion Stakes at Newmarket, the Limekiln Stakes at Liverpool and the Liverpool

Above
Belmont Park. An enormous crowd watches a blanket finish to the 1942 Toboggan Handicap, which was won by Omission (No. 4) from Overdrawn.

Beaufort, the Duke of (born 1900) The Duke was appointed Master of the Horse in 1936, an appointment he still holds, and he has been the master or joint master of the family pack of fox-hounds since 1924. He is the president of the Royal International Horse Show and was formerly a president of the British Horse Society and also of the British Show Jumping Association. He has always had a tremendous interest in the horse, and it is largely due to his enthusiasm and encouragement that combined training has been so successful in Britain. Since 1949 his home has been the setting of one of the most important events in the combined training calendar — the Badminton Horse Trials.

Becher's Brook See under AINTREE.

bed down to make a bed for a horse, either by spreading clean bedding on the floor of its box or stall after mucking out, or by turning the existing bedding and removing any droppings.

bed-eating a habit developed by some horses, especially at night, of eating their bed. Since it can result in flatulence and overweight, the habit is considered harmful. It can be cured either by putting a muzzle on the horse or by using wood shavings rather than straw as a bedding material.

B.E.F. British Equestrian Federation.

behind the bit (of a horse) refusing to take hold of the bit and liable to shake its head.

Belgian Ardennes See under ARDENNES.

Belgian Heavy Draught Horse See BRABANT.

bell In show-jumping competitions a bell is rung by the judges to indicate to the competitor (a) that he may start or continue his round; (b) that he must stop, as, for example, when an obstacle has to be rebuilt because the horse, in refusing, has knocked it down; or (c) that he is eliminated.

belling the harsh resonant cry of the stag during the mating season.

bellyband a leather strap which encircles the belly and the pad of a harness horse.

Belmont Park a racecourse for flat racing and steeplechasing at Elmont on Long Island, New York. Opened in 1905 by Augustus Belmont and James Keene, the course quickly became the scene of some of the finest racing in the United States. From 1915 to 1958 it was the home of the Futurity Stakes, and the principal races held there now are the Belmont Stakes, the Jockey Club Gold Cup and the Metropolitan Handicap.

Belmont Stakes a race over a distance of $1\frac{1}{2}$ miles for three-year-old horses; the third leg of the American Triple Crown. It was first run in 1867 at Jerome Park, where it was held until 1889. It was then transferred to Morris Park until 1904, and since then has been held at Belmont Park, Elmont, Long Island, New York, except between 1963 and 1967, when it was run at Aqueduct. Prior to 1874 the race was run over a distance of $1\frac{5}{8}$ miles; from 1890 to 1892 inclusive, and in 1895, 1904 and 1905, the distance was $1\frac{1}{4}$ miles; in 1893 and 1894 it was $1\frac{1}{8}$ miles, and from 1896 to 1903 and 1906 to 1925 the distance was $1\frac{3}{8}$ miles. (For results see pages 251–252.)

bending race See under GYMKHANA.

bending tackle the equipment used on a horse in training to produce a good head carriage. One of the best-known types is the DISTAS BENDING TACKLE, consisting principally of a bridle, side reins, and a roller with a backstrap and dock. The bridle has a facepiece and an elastic noseband and is fitted with a small pulley on each side of the poll, a Jodhphor-type curb and a Wilson bit. The roller, which is adjustable on both sides, is fitted with rings at the bottom of each pad and under the belly so that, if necessary, a martingale can be used. On the backstrap at the dock end is a strong piece of elastic with two rings. The side reins pass straight from the inner rings of the bit to the larger of these two rings. Two lengths of cord — one on each side — are attached to the links on the curb and then passed inside the inner rings, up the side of the head and through the pulleys. One of the cords is threaded through the smaller ring on the backstrap, and the two cords are then tied together.

Once the horse has become used to the tackle, he can be driven on long reins, which are attached to the outside rings of the bit.

Bensington Driving Club the earliest known driving club in the British Isles. It was founded in 1807, and was so called because the members used to drive from London to Bensington (pronounced and now called Benson) in Oxfordshire. On other occasions for a shorter drive they went to Bedfont, near Hounslow.

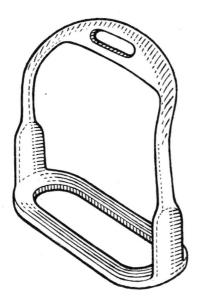

bent-top iron.

bent-top iron a type of stirrup iron in which the top is curved away from the rider's instep, thus preventing damage to it or to the boot, especially if the boot is fully home in the iron.

bet 1. a wager on a horse in a race, usually of money. **2.** to make a wager.

bet across the board See COMBINATION BET.

bets on an expression meaning that all bets become binding since the horses in a race have been placed under starter's orders.

bet the limit to place a bet for the maximum stake that the bookmaker will accept.

betting 1. the quotation of the prices of horses in a certain race. **2.** the placing of a bet on a horse.

betting forecast the suggested odds (given by a newspaper or press agency) at which the horses will start in a particular race.

betting shop a licensed bookmaker's establishment, not on a racecourse, which takes bets on horseraces, etc.

between hay and grass between winter and spring, i.e. when the hay has been finished but the grass has not grown enough for grazing.

B.H.S. British Horse Society.

bib martingale a running martingale having a triangular leather centrepiece between the two arms.

bicycling (Western US) the act of drawing the spurs along the sides of a bucking horse, first with one foot and then with the other, as in riding a bicycle.

bighead a bone disease caused by eating poisonous plants, which results in an enlargement of the horse's head.

big race the principal race of the day at any race meeting.

bike (US) a sulky used in trotting races.

billet 1. a strap attaching the girth to the saddle. **2.** the excrement of foxes.

bird-eyed (of a horse) inclined to shy at imaginary objects.

biscuit Western name for the horn of a saddle.

biscuit straight (of a hound) standing up well on its feet with its head up in the air.

bishop to file down or otherwise alter the appearance of a horse's teeth in order to give a false indication of its age. If, for example, the black grooves in the tables of the incisors have disappeared with age, they can be reproduced using a hot iron. However, the deception is easy to detect since the enamel round the depressions is destroyed by the burning.

bit a device, normally of metal or rubber, attached to the bridle and placed in the horse's mouth in order to control the pace and direction of the horse and to regulate the position of its head. Depending on the type of bit, this is achieved by exerting pressure on one or more of the following parts of the head: the corners of the mouth, the bars of the mouth, the tongue, the roof of the mouth, the poll, the curb groove, or the nose. The four basic classes of bit are the curb, the gag, the Pelham and the snaffle.

bitch fox (US) a vixen.

bitless bridle any of various bridles used without bits, pressure being exerted on the nose and the curb groove, as opposed to the mouth. See also BLAIR BRIDLE, HACKAMORE, SCAWBRIG BRIDLE, W. S. BITLESS PELHAM.

bl. black.

black (of a horse) having a black coat, mane and tail, with, possibly, white markings on the face and/or limbs.

black harness See under BLACK SADDLER.

black saddler a saddler who specializes in making BLACK HARNESS, the items of saddlery used on horses which are driven rather than ridden. See also BROWN SADDLER.

blacksmith an artisan who works in iron; a farrier.

Blair bridle a bitless bridle in which the cheekpieces are sufficiently long to produce pressure on the nose in order to restrain the horse.

blaze a white facial marking which is broad between the eyes and extends the full length of the face to the muzzle.

blemish any scar left by an injury or wound, or any other unsightly disfigurement which does not affect the horse's health or performance.

blind 1. a leather hood used to cover the eyes of a pack mule while it is being loaded. **2.** *hunting* not properly visible; obscured, especially by foliage and vegetation, as the countryside in early autumn.

blind bucker (Western US) a horse which bucks indiscriminately into anything when ridden.

blinder a sack or cloth put over the head of an awkward horse while it is being mounted or shod.

blind switch (US) *racing* the situation in which a horse about to make its run is blocked in by other horses and prevented from doing so.

blacksmith. The process of shoeing a horse.

Right
1. taking off the old shoe.

Far right and below left
2. and 3. trimming and rasping the hoof.

Below right
4. trying the new shoe cold.

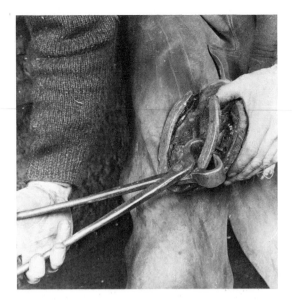
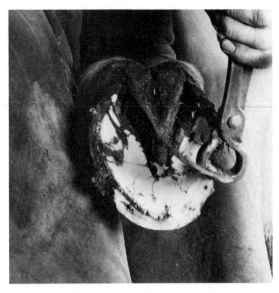
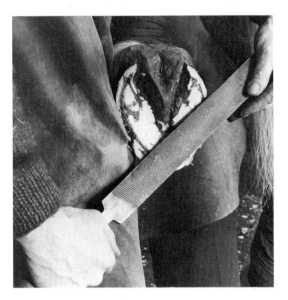

Blink Bonny (by Melbourne out of Queen Mary) Foaled in 1854, Blink Bonny bred, owned and trained by W. I'Anson at Malton, Yorkshire, created two records; she was only the second filly to win both the Derby and the Oaks in the same year (1857), and she was the only filly both to win the Derby herself and also to produce a Derby winner (Blair Atholl, by Stockwell, who won in 1864).

blinkers a pair of leather eye-shields attached to the bridle, used to prevent a horse from seeing sideways or backwards so that it will not be distracted. Frequently used in racing, blinkers are not allowed in combined training, dressage or show-jumping competitions. Also called HOOD.

blood The amount of blood in a horse's body constitutes approximately one-eighteenth of its total body weight.

blood horse an English Thoroughbred.

blooding a hunting ceremony of obscure origin, in which blood from the dead quarry is smeared by the huntsman on the cheeks of newcomers to the hunting field.

bloodstock Thoroughbred horses, especially race and stud animals.

bloom the gloss and shine of a horse's coat; a sign of a healthy animal.

blow a stirrup (US) to lose a stirrup. If this happens in a rodeo contest the rider is disqualified.

blow away *hunting* to send the hounds after a fox by blowing a given signal on the hunting horn.

blow out *hunting* to recall the hounds from a covert by use of the hunting horn when the covert has been drawn blank or the hounds have lost the fox.

blow up (US) to start bucking.

blue dun a black-skinned horse whose body colour is black, evenly distributed but lacking in intensity so that it produces an overall bluish cast. The mane and tail are black, and there may be a dorsal stripe. See also YELLOW DUN.

blue eye See WALL EYE.

Blue Peter (by Fairway out of Fancy Free) Foaled in 1936, Blue Peter was bred and owned by Lord Rosebery and trained by Jack Jarvis. As a two-year-old he ran only twice; he was unplaced in his first race, the Imperial Produce Stakes at Kempton, but was second in the Middle Park Stakes at Epsom. The following season he was unbeaten, winning the Blue Riband Trial Stakes at Epsom, the 2000-Guineas at Newmarket, the Derby at Epsom and the Eclipse Stakes at Sandown. Because of the outbreak of war, the St Leger was abandoned, and

Right
5. applying the shoe hot.

Far right
6. nailing on the new shoe.

Below left
7. nails being rung off.

Below right
8. rasping the hoof.

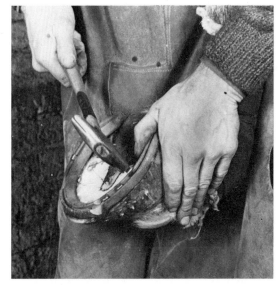

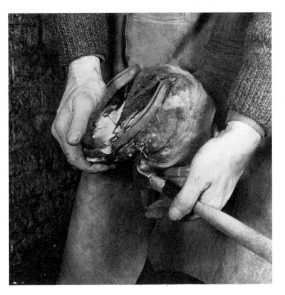

Right
Blue Peter, with Eph Smith
up, being led in by Lord
Rosebery after winning the
Derby in 1939.

Far right
body brush. A girl groom
demonstrates the correct use
of the body brush and
currycomb.

Blue Peter was deprived of the chance to try for
the Triple Crown.

His most successful offspring was Ocean Swell,
winner of the 1944 Derby. Blue Peter died at Lord
Rosebery's stud at Mentmore near Buckingham, in
1957.

blue roan See under ROAN.

blue-ticked hound an American hound, having a
white coat splashed and speckled with black,
giving an overall mottled blue appearance.

bobbery pack See MIXED PACK.

bobtailed (of a horse) having a very short docked
tail.

body brush a short-bristled, tightly packed brush
used, generally after the dandy brush, to remove
dust and scurf from a horse's coat. It should be
applied with pressure and worked in large circular
movements, as it also helps to stimulate the horse's
circulation. It is mainly used in conjunction with a
currycomb.

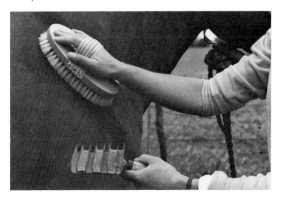

Right
bog spavin.

Far right
bootjack.

bog rider a cowboy whose job is to rescue cattle which have got stuck in mud or marshland.

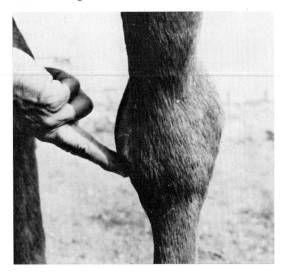

bog spavin a soft non-painful synovial swelling on the inside and slightly to the front of the hock joint. It is similar to a windgall.

boil over (Western US; of a horse) to start bucking.

bola a device consisting of two or more ropes joined together, each with a small stone or iron ball attached to the end, used by cowboys in South America for throwing at and entangling steers to bring them down.

bolt 1. (of a horse) to gallop away uncontrollably. **2.** *hunting* to force a fox out of an earth or drain.

bolter a horse which is in the habit of bolting with its rider.

bona fide hunter any horse certified by a master of hounds as having been regularly and fairly hunted during the season.

Right
bone spavin.

bone spavin a hard bony swelling on the inside lower edge of the hock joint. It involves the small cuneiform bone and the upper part of the inner small metatarsus, sometimes extending to other bones of the hock at its inner and lower aspect. The condition is caused by injury or strain. It is acutely painful and is usually accompanied by chronic or recurrent lameness.

bonnet a person employed by a horse dealer to assist in selling a horse by expounding its merits to the prospective buyer. Also called CHAUNTER.

Bontecou, Fred, the first rider from the United States to win the King George V Gold Trophy at the International Horse Show. He achieved this in 1926, riding Canadian-bred Ballymacshane.

bookie a bookmaker.

bookmaker a professional betting man who is licensed to accept the bets of others on horses, etc. Also called TURF ACCOUNTANT.

boot hook one of a pair of metal hooks which are passed through the two webbing loops on the inside of a top boot to pull it on.

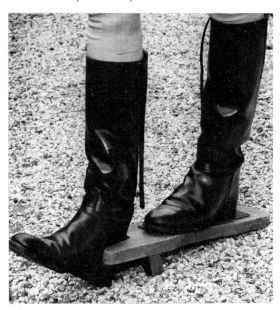

bootjack a device used to hold a boot by the heel while the foot is drawn out of it.

bore (of a horse) to lean on the bit.

bosal the noseband of a hackamore used in training broncos.

Bosnian pony a breed of large, strong and intelligent pony found in Yugoslavia, especially in the Balkans, and used principally as a pack animal. It was originally a heavy mountain breed, considerable improvements being made by the Turks with the introduction of Eastern blood.

bottom *hunting* a fence with a deep and unjumpable ditch or brook close to it.

bottom weight the horse in a handicap race carrying the lightest weight.

Boulonnais Bred originally in the Boulogne district of France in the days of the Crusaders, the Boulonnais is a strong draught horse. The breed was very much improved by the introduction of Arab and Barb stallions, and proved popular as a coach horse because of its good action and tremendous stamina. Today it is still used in agriculture, and Boulonnais blood has been the dominating factor in most French draught horses for many years. It is an extremely elegant animal, between 16 and 17 h.h., and is unique in having a harmony of unbroken lines, with a graceful rounding of its muscular parts.

box 1. to transport a horse from one place to another by rail, or in a horsebox or trailer. **2.** the driver's seat on a horse-drawn coach or carriage, usually made at an angle, so that the coachman was in a semi-standing position.

box in *racing* to prevent a horse from making its run by blocking its path.

box seat a passenger seat to the left of the driver's seat on a coach or carriage.

br. brown.

Brabançon See BRABANT.

Brabant, the massive draught horse of Belgium, here being used for shrimping.

Brabant a breed of very large heavy draught horse from Belgium. Usually over 16 h.h., the Brabant has a small head, a compact muscular body and short, immensely strong legs with a lot of feather. One of the largest and most powerful breeds of draught horse, it is also noted for its docile temperament and willingness to work, and has been used to improve other breeds of draught horse. Also called BELGIAN HEAVY DRAUGHT HORSE; BRABANÇON.

bradoon. Also BRIDOON. See SNAFFLE BIT.

brake In a coach or carriage this is operated by a hand lever or a foot pedal which causes a block to be released and press on the rear wheels of the vehicle.

bran the by-products of grain processing, a useful feedstuff, which when freshly ground and dampened acts as a mild laxative. It acts on the membrane lining of the intestines, causing a slight irritation which increases the secretions and quickens the passage of the contents. It should not be overfed.

brass-mounted head collar an elaborate type of head collar having a rounded throat piece, and a browband attached to the head strap, which is adjustable on both sides.

break 1. to train a horse for whatever purpose it may be required; to school a horse. **2.** (of a horse) to change from one gait to another. **3.** *hunting* (of a fox) to leave a covert or wood. **4.** *racing* (of a horse) to leave the starting stalls at the beginning of a race.

break down (of a horse) to lacerate the suspensory ligament or fracture a sesamoid bone, so that the back of the fetlock drops to the ground.

breaking the barrier (of a contestant in a rodeo) to break the barrier across the pen before it is released; an action which incurs a penalty.

break in two (Western US; of a horse) to begin to buck.

break out (of a horse) to begin to sweat suddenly, as before the start of a race or at a meet.

break range (Western US; of a horse) to leave the home range when it is out to graze.

break up *hunting* (of hounds) to eat the carcass of the fox which has been hunted and killed.

breast girth See BREASTPLATE.

breast high See under SCENT.

breastplate a device, usually of leather, attached to the saddle to prevent it from slipping back on the horse. Also called BREAST GIRTH.
 The most common type, used especially for hunting, consists of three leather straps arranged in a Y-shape from a central ring, with a cross band between the two arms. The long central strap, secured to the girth by means of a loop, is passed between the forelegs, and the arms are attached to the D-rings on the saddle, one on each side.
 The AINTREE BREASTPLATE, used mainly in racing, consists of two straps, one of which passes across the breast and is secured to the girth straps on each side of the saddle, the other passing over the withers. For racing webbing, elastic or lightweight

Brigadier Gerard, ridden by Joe Mercer, on his way to the start of the 1972 King George VI and Queen Elizabeth Stakes and the fifteenth successive win of his racing career.

Far right
Breton, a light draught horse, bred originally in the Black Mountains.

leather, often lined with sheepskin across the breast to prevent chafing, is used.

breeching a broad leather band passing round the quarters of a harness horse and fastened to the shafts, designed to help take the weight of the vehicle and to hold it back when going down hill.

breeder 1. the owner of a mare which gives birth to a foal. **2.** the owner of a stud-farm where horses are bred.

breeders' certificate a certificate required in the United States in order to register a foal with a breed society. The certificate has to be obtained from the owner of the stallion at the time of service.

breeze in (US) to win a race very easily.

Breton a light draught horse originally bred in the Brittany region of France. The Breton is a hardy animal able to exist on the rather sparse vegetation and to survive the severe winters of Brittany. The breed has become popular throughout Europe because of its characteristic alertness, good looks and stamina, and has also been used with success in North Africa where it has been crossed with local horses to produce a hardy agricultural animal

with great stamina.

bridle the part of a horse's saddlery or harness which is placed about the head. All bridles — there

Akhal-Teke, an ancient
breed from the Soviet Union.

American Saddle-Horse,
a breed whose development
goes back over 400 years.

Andalusian, a popular Spanish breed of riding horse with a notably good action.

Anglo-Norman, a French breed, which has become popular as a riding horse and has proved to be very successful across country and in show-jumping.

are several varieties — have the following basic components: a headpiece and throat lash, a browband, a noseband, cheekpieces and reins. See also DOUBLE BRIDLE, PELHAM BRIDLE, SNAFFLE BRIDLE.

bridle hand the hand in which the reins are carried when riding or driving, usually the left hand.

bridoon Also BRADOON. See SNAFFLE BIT.

Brigadier Gerard (by Queen's Hussar out of La Paiva) Foaled in 1968, Brigadier Gerard was bred by John Hislop, owned by his wife and trained by Major Dick Hern at West Ilsley in Berkshire. Probably the greatest English-bred colt of all times, 'The Brigadier', as he was known, became immensely popular and captured the imagination of the racing public. During his short three-year racing career he ran on eighteen occasions and was beaten only once — by the American-bred Roberto in the Benson and Hedges Gold Cup at York in 1972. He won a total of over £253,000 in the following races:

1970   Berkshire Stakes, Newbury
      Champagne Stakes, Salisbury
      Washington Single Stakes, Newbury
      Middle Park Stakes, Newmarket
1971   2000-Guineas, Newmarket
      St James' Palace Stakes, Ascot
      Sussex Stakes, Goodwood
      Goodwood Mile, Goodwood
      Queen Elizabeth II Stakes, Ascot
      Champion Stakes, Newmarket
1972   Lockinge Stakes, Newbury
      Westbury Stakes, Sandown
      Prince of Wales Stakes, Ascot
      Eclipse Stakes, Sandown
      King George VI and Queen Elizabeth Stakes, Ascot
      Queen Elizabeth II Stakes, Ascot
      Champion Stakes, Newmarket.

At the end of the 1972 season he was retired to stud.

bring down *racing* to cause another horse to fall by falling in front of it or otherwise impeding it. A horse may be brought down on the flat if it is severely bumped, sometimes as a result of very close bunching.

brisket the lowest part of the chest.

British Driving Society a society, formed in 1957 and affiliated to the British Horse Society, for people interested in driving horses, ponies or donkeys. It has some 1400 members, and organizes a wide variety of activities, including driving marathons, rallies and competitions.

British Equestrian Federation Formed in 1972 as the co-ordinating body between the British Horse Society and the British Show Jumping Association, the Federation's main purposes are: to liaise with the government on all matters concerning equestrianism; to deal with the International Equestrian Federation on all matters concerning the international field, with other national federations, and with the organizing bodies of the Olympic Games, continental championships and other international events; to appoint a board of management for the National Equestrian Centre; and to act as the body to which both the B.H.S. and the B.S.J.A. can appeal or refer for advice.

The Federation consists of a chairman/president, and eight members: four each from the British Horse Society and the British Show Jumping Association, including the chairman of each body.

British Equestrian Olympic Fund a fund, administered by the British Horse Society, to finance British equestrian teams competing abroad, both at the Olympic Games and other international events. The fund is made up of donations, proceeds from the sale of Christmas cards, badges and similar items, grants and a percentage of the money given to sponsored competitions.

British Equine Veterinary Association a body of practising veterinary surgeons whose object is to promote the veterinary and allied sciences in relation to the welfare of the horse.

British Horse Society the body responsible, under the British Equestrian Federation, for equestrian activities in the United Kingdom. Registered as a charity, it was founded in 1947, on the amalgamation of the Institute of the Horse and the National Horse Association of Great Britain, and now has over 17,000 members. The role of the society is to encourage high standards of horsemanship and the proper care of horses and ponies, to protect the interests of horses and riders, to promote and develop riding as a recreation and sport, and to foster the interests of horse and pony breeding.

Membership is open to anyone over the age of seventeen, and the society provides a wide range of services, designed not only to stimulate interest in the horse, but also to help those who own or ride horses to gain the maximum enjoyment.

Its administrative headquarters are at the National Equestrian Centre, near Kenilworth, Warwickshire, and from there it operates through a network of county and regional representatives and committees and through various other affiliated bodies, such as the Pony Club, which represent specific spheres of activity. Among the many organizations which are associated with the British Horse Society are the British Driving Society, the British Show Jumping Association, and the Riding for the Disabled Association, as well as numerous breed societies and trade organizations.

The society operates a nationwide scheme to inspect riding schools and approve those which meet the required standard, and provides tuition and courses for riding instructors, as well as a system of recognized professional qualifications and examinations. It is also responsible for the organization of the horse trials at Badminton and Burghley, and for the Royal International Horse Show.

British Jumping Derby a major British show-jumping championship, held annually at the All-England Jumping Course, Hickstead, and open to international riders. The Derby was first held in

Far right
British Jumping Derby. Hartwig Steenken on Kosmos, August 1973.

29

1961 and is modelled on the original Jumping Derby held in Hamburg. (For results see page 227.)

British Show Jumping Association an association formed in 1923 as the result of dissatisfaction among regular show-jumping competitors because there were no rules or standards laid down. The first meeting was held at the International Horse Show at Olympia between civilian and military competitors, and as a result the association was incorporated under the Companies Act in 1925.

It is the governing body of show-jumping in Great Britain, and has its headquarters at the National Equestrian Centre near Kenilworth in Warwickshire.

The objects laid down in 1923 are still the same today, namely:

1. To improve and protect the standards of show-jumping.
2. To encourage the improved breeding of horses for show-jumping.
3. To provide for the representation of Great Britain in international competitions, both at home and abroad.
4. To prescribe the type, height and general standard of obstacles.
5. To hold or assist in holding show-jumping competitions and shows and exhibitions in which show-jumping competitions are held.
6. To make rules for the manner and system of judging and awarding points and to promote the universal acceptance of such rules.
7. To define the meaning of terms commonly used in connection with show-jumping.
8. To arrange for the registration of horses.
9. To ensure that horses entered for any competition are the bona fide property of the exhibitor at the time of entry.
10. To keep a record of the results and the winning horses in show-jumping competitions.
11 To admit persons to membership on such terms and conditions and subject to such payment as from time to time be determined.

brocket a two-year-old male deer.

bronc a bronco.

broncho See BRONCO.

bronco an unbroken or imperfectly broken mustang in the western United States. Also BRONCHO; also called BRONC.

bronco-buster (US) a person who breaks and trains broncos. Also called BRONC-BUSTER.

bronc saddle a saddle used in breaking broncos,

having a wide undercut fork with built-in swells, and a deep dished cantle.

bronc stall a narrow stall providing enough room for a horse to stand, but not to rear or kick, used for broncos so that they can be handled and calmed by the trainer.

Broome, David, *GB* (born 1940) David Broome started riding as a child and competed successfully in junior show-jumping competitions before graduating to adult competitions in 1957.

He is the only rider to have won the European Championship three times: in 1961 at Aachen with Oliver Anderson's Sunsalve; in 1967 at Rotterdam with John Massarella's Mister Softee; and in 1969 at Hickstead, again with Mister Softee. He is also one of only a handful of riders to have won the King George V Gold Trophy at the Royal International Horse Show in London on three occasions: in 1960 with Sunsalve; in 1966 with Mister Softee; and in 1972 with Mrs P. Harris's Sportsman.

David Broome has competed in four Olympic Games: Rome in 1960, winning the individual bronze medal with Sunsalve; Tokyo in 1964; Mexico in 1968, winning the individual bronze medal with Mister Softee; and Munich in 1972. In 1970 he became the first British rider to win the World Championship, achieving this at La Baule with Douglas Bunn's Beethoven. The same year he was awarded the O.B.E. for his services to show-jumping. In 1973, along with a number of other British riders, he turned professional.

broom tail (Western US) a wild horse.

brougham a squarish four-wheeled closed carriage with a driver's seat on the outside. The first, a two-seater, which could be drawn by one horse, was built for Lord Brougham in about 1839. Early broughams were very heavy, but in spite of much ridicule soon became extremely popular, and, as well as the original two-seaters, four-seater versions to be drawn by a pair were also built. A warm carriage in winter, the brougham could be ventilated and cooled in summer by opening the windows.

brought down See BRING DOWN.

browband the part of a bridle which lies across the horse's forehead below the ears. Usually a plain leather strap, it may, however, have a coloured silk or plastic covering. In racing, the colours may be those of the owner. Also called FRONT.

brown harness See under BROWN SADDLER.

National in 1931 and 1933, respectively, were sired by him.) Foaled in Ireland in 1924, Brown Jack was sold as a yearling to Marcus Thompson of Tipperary, who a year later sold him to the well-known trainer, Charlie Rogers. After the horse had run twice as a three-year-old, he was purchased by Wiltshire trainer Aubrey Hastings for Sir Harold Wernher, and with that started a racing career which was to span from 1927 until his retirement in 1934.

His first outing in England was in the Southampton Hurdle at Bournemouth in 1927, when he finished third. He then went on to win five races before the end of November: the Juvenile Hurdle at Wolverhampton; the Charlton Musgrove Hurdle at Wincanton; the Juvenile Hurdle at Cardiff; the Three Year Old Hurdle at Nottingham; and the Abbeystead Hurdle at Liverpool — all over 1½ miles. In 1928 he won the Handicap Hurdle at Leicester, which made him eligible for the Champion Hurdle at Cheltenham, a race he won by one and a half lengths, finishing very strongly up the hill. This ended his career over hurdles, for it was then decided to race him on the flat.

He won the White Lodge Stakes at Windsor and the Queen's Plate at Kempton, before being entered for the Ascot Stakes, which he won by two lengths, ridden by Steve Donoghue. He then won the Hwfa Williams Memorial Handicap at Sandown. The next year, 1929, he won the Queen Alexandria Stakes at Ascot (2¾ miles), a race he was to win every year from 1930 to 1934. In addition to other successes, he won the Doncaster Cup in 1930, the Chester Cup and the Ebor Handicap in 1931, the Prince Edward Handicap in 1932, and the Rosebery Memorial Plate in 1933. After his last win at Ascot in 1934, it was decided to retire him and he was sent to Sir Harold Wernher's estate in Leicestershire. He was put down in 1948.

In winning races at seven consecutive Royal Ascot meetings, Brown Jack set a record. He is remembered at Ascot by a bronze statuette and by a race which has been named after him.

brown saddler a saddler who specializes in BROWN HARNESS, the items of saddlery used on horses which are ridden rather than driven. See also BLACK SADDLER.

brow tine See under TINE.

brush the tail of a fox.

brushing the act of striking the inside of one leg, near to or on the fetlock joint, with the opposite hoof or shoe, usually as a result of faulty conformation or action, lack of condition, or tiredness. Also called CUTTING.

B.S.J.A. British Show Jumping Association.

B.S.P.S. British Show Pony Society.

buck 1. (of a horse) to leap into the air with the back arched, coming down with the forelegs stiff and the head low in order to unseat the rider or dislodge the pack. **2.** the male fallow deer.

buckaroo (US) **1.** a cowboy. **2.** a bronco-buster.

bucker a horse that bucks.

bucket elimination See under GYMKHANA.

buck eye 1. a prominent eye. **2.** a horse with prominent eyes.

buckhound a hound used for hunting bucks.

bucking rein a single rope attached to the hackamore of a bucking horse and used by the rider to

Brown Jack, with Steve Donoghue in the saddle. He created a record by winning races at Royal Ascot for seven consecutive years, including five wins in the Queen Alexandra Stakes.

Brown Jack (by Jackdaw out of Querquidella. Jackdaw won the Alexandra Palace in 1912, but made his name mainly as a sire of jumpers: both Grackle and Kellsboro' Jack, who won the Grand

Right
Burghley Horse Trials.
A French competitor, Lt de Croutte on Jacky de la Brosse, having problems on the cross-country course in the 1962 European Three-Day Event Championship, which was held at Burghley.

retain his balance. In rodeo competitions the rider must hold the rope in the same hand all the time.

buckjump to buck.

buck-kneed See CALF-KNEED.

Budenny one of the most recently developed breeds of saddle-horse. It was originally produced for the Russian cavalry in the Rostov district of the Soviet Union by crossing Don mares with thorough-bred stallions and then inbreeding the produce. Standing about 16 h.h. and bay or chestnut — both colours often have an attractive golden bloom — the Budenny is an elegant powerful horse with a neat head and very strong legs. Noted for its speed and stamina, the breed also shows great jumping ability and has already established a remarkable record in the fields of steeplechasing and show-jumping.

bulldog (US) a trotting horse which stays well.

bulldogging See STEER WRESTLING.

bulldogging horse (US) a Western horse used for steer wrestling.

bullfinch a cross-country or natural obstacle consisting principally of a hedge or brush which is too high to jump clear and has to be pushed or scrambled through.

bullhides heavy leather chaps.

bumper *racing* an amateur rider, especially in Ireland.

Burghley Horse Trials a three-day event held annually in September since 1961 at Burghley House, Stamford, Lincolnshire, the home of former Olympic athlete, the Marquess of Exeter. The Burghley Horse Trials replaced the Harewood Horse Trials and are now firmly established as the major autumn event of the British combined training season. In 1966 and again in 1974, Burghley was the site of the World Three-Day Event Championships, and in 1962 and 1971 the European Championships were held there. (For results see page 228.)

burr the protuberance at the base of a stag's horn next to the skull.

burst *hunting* the part of a hunt when the hounds are actually in close pursuit of a fox.

bush track (US) an unofficial race meeting.

butcher a rider who is rough and heavy with his hands.

butterfly snaffle See SPRING-MOUTH SNAFFLE.

buttermilk horse (Western US) a palomino.

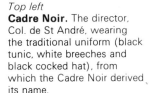

Top left
Cadre Noir. The director, Col. de St André, wearing the traditional uniform (black tunic, white breeches and black cocked hat), from which the Cadre Noir derived its name.

Top right
Byerley Turk, the first of the founding sires of the English Thoroughbred.

Bottom left
Campolino, a close relative of the Mangalarga, found mainly in the areas surrounding Rio de Janeiro.

Bottom right
Budenny, a mare and foal. A fairly recent breed, developed in the Rostov district of the Soviet Union, it was obtained by crossing Don mares with Thoroughbred stallions and then inbreeding the produce.

by sired by.

bye-day an extra meet held by a hunt, usually during the Christmas holidays or to compensate for days lost through bad weather.

Byerley Turk the earliest of the three founding sires of the English Thoroughbred. He was said to have been captured from the Turks at the siege of Vienna in 1686 by Captain Byerley of the Carabineers, who brought him to England in 1689 and the following year rode him as his charger at the Battle of the Boyne. He was then sent to stud at Middridge Grange in County Durham and later at Goldsborough Hall in Yorkshire. Although he covered only a few well-bred mares, he produced some good progeny. See also DARLEY ARABIAN, GODOLPHIN ARABIAN.

C. the symbol used on race programmes, etc., to show that a horse has previously won a race on that particular course.

caballada a band of saddle horses which have been broken, but which at the time are not under saddle.

caberlach a stag with abnormal antlers which, instead of being branched, are shaped like the horns of an antelope. Also called SWITCH.

cabriolet a light high two-wheeled hooded carriage with two seats and a platform at the rear for the groom to stand on. Introduced in about 1815, it was regarded as the carriage of the married couple of rank but limited wealth, although it was also described as a very pleasant bachelor's carriage, when perfectly appointed. It was drawn by a single horse, which had to be of great size and beauty, with good legs and feet, and superlative action in its slow paces.

cade foal a foal reared by hand.

Cadre Noir the corps of riding instructors at the famous cavalry school at Saumur in France. The town had a long history as an equestrian centre even before the cavalry school was established there in the late eighteenth century. The Cadre Noir, which was formed at the end of the Napoleonic Wars, teaches riding in the best French classical tradition.

calf horse a specially trained horse used for calf roping.

calf-kneed having forelegs which, when viewed from the side, are concave in outline. Also termed BACK AT THE KNEE, BUCK-KNEED.

calf roping a rodeo event in which the object is for the rider to rope a calf, and then quickly dismount and tie the calf by three legs. The contestant completing within the shortest time wins.

calkin one of a pair of projections on the underside of a horseshoe, usually made by doubling the ends over, to provide grip and prevent the horse, especially a draught horse, from slipping, or to raise the heel of a horse that has faulty conformation or is inclined to forge. Also CAULKIN; also called CALK.

call-over the naming of the horses in a race, especially an important one, when the latest betting odds on each horse are given.

Cambridgeshire Stakes a horserace over 1 mile 1 furlong held annually at Newmarket since 1839, except in 1940, when it was run at Nottingham. It was one of the first major races to have a handicap. (For results see page 236.)

camera patrol equipment for the filming of a race while it is in progress. The film is studied by the stewards if there is an inquiry or if an objection is raised. It was first used on English racecourses in 1960 at Newmarket.

camp to stand with the fore and hind legs spread as far apart as possible. Originally, harness horses were trained to camp so that they would not begin to move off when people were getting into or out of the vehicle, and the stance is still considered particularly desirable in show hackneys and, in the United States, in show hacks.

Campolino a Brazilian breed of horse founded during the nineteenth century by Cassiano Campolino as a direct result of his efforts to improve the Mangalarga. An extremely hardy animal, the Campolino makes a good riding horse.

Canadian Horse In the second half of the seventeenth century many different types of horse were taken to Canada from France, and within a hundred years a very definite type of Canadian draught horse had been bred. The horse was a hardy, general-purpose animal, very much resembling the French Percheron, and was found mainly in the area around Quebec. However, it soon became so popular that it spread throughout Canada and the United States.

After the British defeated the French in Canada, the horses were crossed with English breeds and went out of fashion. Nevertheless, a stud book was started at the end of the nineteenth century, and some ten years later a breeders' association was formed and two types were developed — one as a draught animal and the other a riding horse. They are now found mainly in the area around Quebec, where the hunter type is flourishing.

canker a morbid growth of the horn of the hoof, affecting the sensitive sole and the frog. Small, greyish-white, spongy, sprouting growths appear on the underside of the hoof, which bleed at the slightest touch and emit a foul-smelling discharge. Canker is most common among horses kept in dirty wet stables or on marshy ground; it can also develop as a result of injury.

cannon bone the stout solid bone extending between the knee and the fetlock. For strength it should be short, and from the side should have a broad, flat appearance.

can-opener (Western US) a spur.

canter one of the gaits of the horse; a pace of three-time, in which the hoofs strike the ground in the following sequence: near hind, near fore and off hind together, off fore (leading leg); or off hind, off fore and near hind together, near fore (leading leg). See also COLLECTED CANTER, EXTENDED CANTER.

cantle the upward curving hind part of a saddle.

cantle board 1. to ride slackly, so that the lower part of the back touches the cantle of the saddle. **2.** to spur a bucking horse all the way back to the cantle.

cap *hunting* the fee payable by a visitor for a day's hunting, so called because the money is collected in a cap by the hunt secretary.

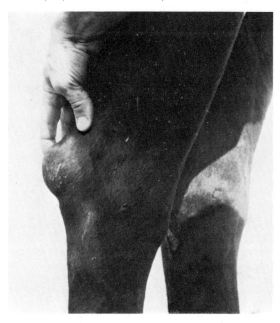

capped hock a swelling on the point of the hock, which results from bruising of the bursa, usually caused by repeated knocks against a hard surface, as when the horse lies down on or gets up off a slippery or inadequately covered stall or loosebox floor. Although unsightly, a capped hock is not an unsoundness.

Caprilli, Federico, *Italy* (1868–1907) Caprilli has often been referred to as the 'father of show-jumping', for while at the Italian Cavalry School, he spent much time working on the theory that it was better for a rider to sit forward and slightly out of the saddle while a horse was jumping, maintaining a firm contact with the horse's mouth

Far right
capped hock, a swelling at the point of the hock.

Far right
capriole, the most difficult of the airs above the ground, being demonstrated at the Spanish Riding School.

and allowing the horse to balance itself. This was contrary to the current practice, which was for the rider to sit back in the saddle at an obstacle. After leaving the Cavalry School Caprilli put his method to the test on his students, and very shortly a considerable improvement in their standard was noticed. Gradually his methods were universally adopted.

capriole a high-school movement in which the horse half rears with the hocks drawn under, then jumps forward and high into the air, at the same time kicking out the hind legs with the soles of the feet turned upwards, and then lands collectedly on all four legs; the most difficult of the airs above the ground. Also called GOAT LEAP.

card See RACE CARD.

carnival (US) a horse which bucks in a very spectacular manner.

carousel a display with a musical accompaniment in which horsemen, usually dressed in period costume, execute a series of complicated figures in formation. Also CARROUSEL.

carry See under TENT PEGGING.

carry a good head *hunting* (of hounds) to run fast and bunched together, rather than spread out, when the scent of the fox is very good.

carrying a scent *hunting* (of a stretch of country) having a good scent of the fox.

cart any two-wheeled vehicle.

carted (of a rider) run away with by his horse.

carted stag a deer which is raised in captivity and kept for hunting. On the day of a hunt it is taken to the meet in a deercart, released, hunted and then recaptured for future use.

cartwheel a spur with a rowel which has long points radiating from the axle.

cast 1. (of a horse) to lose a shoe. **2.** *hunting* (of hounds) to attempt, whether on their own initiative or directed by the huntsman, to regain the scent at a check.

casting the act of throwing a horse to the ground in order to carry out various operations or other veterinary treatments.

The simplest method is by using SIDE-LINES. A strong but soft rope, about 25 yards long, is doubled, and the free ends are threaded through the looped end to form a noose, which is placed round the horse's neck just above the shoulders. Each end is then passed between the forelegs — one to the left and the other to the right — and taken round the respective hind pastern from outside to inside, up to and across the shoulder and through the loop round the neck. When the ends are pulled the animal is cast; in doing this the head must be kept well back. The hind feet are then pulled forwards and upwards close to the chest and secured by a hitch round the pasterns. The forelegs are made fast by passing the rope round each pastern and tying it to the corresponding hind pastern.

Special hobbles of leather are also made. These are put round the pastern of each leg and linked together by means of loops, through which a chain or rope is passed. When the chain is pulled the legs are drawn together and the animal is thrown.

castor See CHESTNUT (def. 2).

catch hold (of a horse) to pull continually while being ridden.

catchweight *racing* the random or optional weight carried by a horse when the conditions of a race do not specify a weight; except in matches, this does not occur now.

cat foot the round and upright pad common to most English foxhounds.

caulkin See CALKIN.

cavalcade a procession of people on horseback or in horse-drawn vehicles.

cavalletti a series of small wooden jumps used in the basic training of any type of riding horse in order to encourage the horse to lengthen his stride, to help improve his balance and to loosen up and strengthen his muscles. Each cavalletto consists of a pole eight to ten feet long resting on X-shaped cross pieces at each end. By turning the cross pieces the height of the pole can be raised or lowered.

cayuse (Western US) an Indian horse or pony.

C.C. Clerk of the Course.

C.C.I. Concours Complet International.

C.C.I.O. Concours Complet International Officiel.

C.C.N. Concours Complet National.

C.D.I. Concours de Dressage International.

C.D.I.O. Concours de Dressage International Officiel.

cee-spring See C-SPRING.

cert See CERTAINTY.

certainty *racing* a horse regarded as certain to win a particular race. Also CERT.

Cesarewitch Stakes a horserace over 2 miles 2 furlongs ($2\frac{1}{4}$ miles), held annually at Newmarket since 1839. Between 1939 and 1941 the distance was changed to 2 miles 24 yards. Like the Cambridgeshire Stakes, the Cesarewitch was one of the first races to have a handicap. (For results see page 236.)

chaff meadow hay or green oat straw cut into short lengths for use as a feedstuff. It is usually fed mixed with oats, etc. A horse which is particularly

Below
cavalletti.

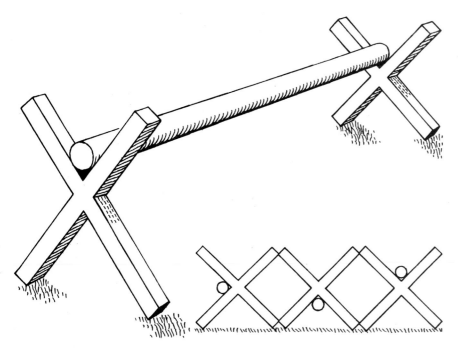

hungry should also be given hay, as chaff eaten too quickly can easily cause colic.

chalk jockey a jockey whose name is chalked on the racecourse runners-and-riders board, i.e. a jockey too little known for the course to have his name painted on the board.

Chambon martingale.

Chambon martingale a type of martingale which, like the continental martingale, originated in France and is used for schooling purposes. The main strap from the girth divides at the breast into two long arms. Each arm is taken upwards, passed through a ring on a pad which extends across the poll, and then clipped to the appropriate bit ring.

chambrière a short-handled whip with a broad lash, invented in the seventeenth century by Antoine de Pluvinel to help with the dressage schooling of horses. It was used by a groom on the ground to encourage the action of the hind legs.

chamfrain armour for a horse's head, used in medieval times. Also CHANFRON.

champ to mouth and chew on the bit with impatience.

Champion Hurdle Challenge Cup the major hurdle race in England, run annually since 1927 during the National Hunt Festival over a distance of 2 miles 200 yards. (For results see page 248.)

Champion Stakes a horserace over 1 mile 2 furlongs (1¼ miles), held annually at Newmarket since 1877. (For results see page 237.)

chanfron See CHAMFRAIN.

change foxes *hunting* (of hounds) to change to another fox from the one hunted — especially liable to happen in a covert if a fresh fox jumps up. The huntsman is able to tell whether it is a fresh fox, since the hounds will go off with a much louder cry, and the older and more experienced hounds will drop back and not work with such enthusiasm.

change leads (of a horse) to change the leading leg while galloping or cantering. See also FLYING CHANGE.

change of leg a movement in cantering when the horse is brought back to the walk for a definite pace or two, the canter then being restarted with the horse leading with the other leg.

channel the groove which runs the entire length of the saddle, between the panels, giving clearance between the tree and the back of the horse.

Chapot, Frank Davis, *US* (born 1932) A veteran of five Olympic show-jumping teams, in Stockholm, Rome, Tokyo, Mexico and Munich, Frank Chapot rode Trail Guide when the American team won the silver medal in Rome (1960), and in Munich (1972), where the team again won the silver medal, he rode White Lightning. At the Pan-American Games of 1959 in Chicago and of 1963 in São Paulo he was in the gold medal team, on the first occasion riding Diament, and on the second riding San Lucas. Frank Chapot has had a large number of successes, both in America and Europe. He became the only member of the United States team to have been placed in a Men's European Championship when he was second at Lucerne in 1966, riding San Lucas, and in 1974, riding Main Spring, he was equal third in the Men's World Championship at Hickstead.

His wife, MARY MAIRS (born 1944), has also competed both in the United States and Europe. In 1963 at São Paulo she made history when, riding Tomboy, she became the first American and the first woman to win an individual gold medal in the Pan-American Games. In 1968 on White Lightning she became the first American to win the Queen Elizabeth II Cup at the Royal International Horse Show in London. She competed at the Olympic Games of 1964 in Tokyo and of 1968 in Mexico.

chaps full-length seatless leather riding trousers which fit over ordinary trousers, originally worn for protection by cowboys.

charger 1. a horse ridden in battle. **2.** any riding horse used by the army.

Charles James See CHARLEY.

Charley a fox.

chase steeplechase. Also 'CHASE.

chase-me-Charlie See under GYMKHANA.

chaser any horse used for steeplechasing, as opposed to flat racing.

chaugan a game played in the East during the sixth century B.C. It was a kind of tennis on horseback, and is said to be the forerunner of polo.

chaunter See BONNET.

check *hunting* a halt or stoppage caused when the hounds lose the scent.

cheek 1. to take hold of the nearside cheekpiece just above the bit and use it, when mounting, to pull the horse's head towards the saddle, in order to prevent the horse moving off or bucking. **2.** See CHEEKPIECE.

cheekpiece 1. the part of the bridle to which the bit is attached. **2.** the side of a curb or pelham bit. The total length of the cheekpiece is normally equal to that of the mouthpiece, although it extends further below than above the mouthpiece. The severity of a bit is proportionate to the length of the cheekpieces, i.e. the longer the cheekpieces, the greater the leverage and therefore the severity of the bit. **3.** the part of a snaffle bit which acts on the horse's cheek; this may be the straight side of the ring, as in the D-cheek snaffle, an extended form of it, as in the normal cheek snaffle, or a separate unit of the bit, as in the Fulmer snaffle. Also called CHEEK.

Avelignese. Found in the mountainous districts of Italy, it is a very muscular and sure-footed breed, which has been used extensively for carrying packs and working on farms.

Balls Bridge. The Irish Army Pipes and Drums lead a parade of visiting teams round the arena during the international horseshow.

Ascot. Queen Elizabeth II making her traditional drive up the course in an open landau before the start of racing at the Royal Ascot meeting.

Badminton. Christopher Robert clears the Baby Elephant trap.

Beagles. The Brighton and Storrington Beagles at Devil's Dyke on the South Downs.

cheek snaffle any snaffle fitted with cheekpieces. In the normal cheek snaffle the cheeks are attached to the ring and the mouthpiece.

cheer on to encourage hounds by the use of the voice.

chef d'équipe the manager of an equestrian team responsible for making all the arrangements, both on and off the field, for a national team competing abroad. The chef d'équipe may or may not be a riding member of the team.

Cheltenham gag a gag bit having a jointed mouth-piece and eggbutt rings.

Above
1963: Mill House, ridden by Willie Robinson, heading for victory.

Right
Cheltenham Gold Cup.
1967: Woodland Venture, with Terry Biddlecombe up, inches forward at the last fence to take the lead from Stalbridge Colonist, ridden by Stan Mellor.

41

Above
Cheltenham Gold Cup.
The Gold Cups of 1933 and 1934, which were won by the Hon. Dorothy Paget's great steeplechaser Golden Miller, who also won the race in 1932, 1935 and 1936 — an all-time record.

Far right
children's riding pony.
The 12.2 h.h. Cusop Pirouette, owned by Dr and Mrs Gilbert Scott and ridden by Anne Pollard.

Cheltenham Gold Cup one of the major steeplechases of the National Hunt season, held annually since 1924 during the National Hunt Festival at Cheltenham, over a distance of 3 miles, 2 furlongs, 76 yards. (For results see page 249.)

Cheltenham Racecourse a racecourse situated at Prestbury Park, close to the town of Cheltenham in Gloucestershire and about a hundred miles from London. Flat racing was first held there in 1815, and 1834 saw the first running of the Cheltenham Grand Annual Steeplechase, held on that occasion over natural obstacles. After the First World War one of the few really important steeplechases in England was the National Hunt Steeplechase, which was run at Cheltenham. The Gold Cup was inaugurated in 1924, followed three years later by the Champion Hurdle Challenge Cup. The racecourse became very popular and was soon the major steeplechasing course in the country, a position it still enjoys today, with its new stands and redesigned course. The National Hunt Festival is held there annually in March.

Cheshire cradle a type of cradle consisting of a padded metal bar which runs the length of the horse's neck. It is attached by straps to the underside of a head collar, and at the other end is joined to a curved padded metal bar which runs horizontally across the breast and is held in place by straps buckled on each side to a roller.

Cheshire martingale a type of standing martingale, closely resembling the running martingale in appearance, except that the arms terminate in hooks or buckles which are fastened to the rings of the bit.

Chester Cup a handicap horserace over a distance of 2 miles, 2 furlongs, 77 yards, first run at Chester in 1824. (For results see page 237.)

Chester Racecourse a racecourse in Cheshire, about 20 miles from Liverpool and 180 miles from London. The course is on an area known as the Roedee or Roodeye, a strip of land on the bank of the River Dee, just below the ancient city walls of Chester, where sports of all kinds took place for many centuries. Although it was decided in 1511 that horseracing should be held there, it was not until 1540 that the first official meeting took place. The course is administered by the city council and is the scene of a number of important events in the flat-race season, including the Chester Cup and the Chester Vase.

Chester Vase a horserace over 1 mile, 4 furlongs, 53 yards, first run at Chester in 1907. Originally it was for both three- and four-year-olds, but since 1959 entry has been restricted to three-year-olds. (For results see page 238.)

chestnut 1. a horse having a gold to dark reddish-brown coat, usually with a matching or slightly lighter or darker mane and tail, or sometimes with a flaxen mane and tail. **2.** a small horny growth on the inside of a horse's leg. On the forelegs it is found just above the knee, and on the hind legs below the hock. Also called CASTOR.

chestnut roan See under ROAN.

Cheyenne roll a leather flange extending over and to the rear of the cantle.

children's riding pony Britain is unique in having nine different breeds of native pony, and, while these breeds are excellent for riding, crossed with polo pony stallions and small Thoroughbred stallions, they have made first-class miniature hunters.

The Children's Riding Pony is a very popular class at all shows in the country. At most shows the class is divided as follows: not exceeding 12.2 h.h.; exceeding 12.2 h.h. and not exceeding 13.2 h.h.; exceeding 13.2 h.h. and not exceeding 14.2 h.h. There is a very strong and thriving market for these ponies, and any which do not make the grade in the show ring are used as general utility ponies.

chime (of hounds) to give tongue in unison when on the line.

china eye See WALL EYE.

choking a partial or total obstruction of the gullet. The horse stands in a crouching position, with the hind legs forward under the body and the head and neck extended. Saliva flows from the mouth, the nose is pointed up and straight out, and the back of the head seemingly pulled backwards and down. The action of the neck muscles every now and again gives the impression the animal is trying to eject whatever is causing the blockage.

chop 1. *hunting* (of hounds) to kill a fox without a chase. **2.** *coaching* to hit the horses on their quarters with a whip.

chucker See CHUKKA.

chuck-line rider (Western US) any person who is out of work and rides through the country accepting free hospitality and meals.

chukka one of a maximum of eight periods of play in a polo match. A bell is rung at the end of $7\frac{1}{2}$ minutes' play, and the chukka ends either when the ball goes out of play or when the umpire considers it to be fair to both sides. An interval of three minutes is allowed between each chukka and five minutes at half time. Although no change is permitted during play, ponies may be changed after each chukka; a pony normally plays two chukkas in each game. Also CHUCKER.

Churchill Downs a racecourse opened in 1875 at Louisville, Kentucky. The programme of the first meeting included the Kentucky Derby and the Kentucky Oaks, two races which have been run there ever since.

In 1908 the Mayor of Louisville introduced a law declaring bookmaking illegal. Pool betting, however, was considered legal, and the parimutuel was introduced, which gradually became the only betting system allowed throughout the United States.

chute (US) **1.** a narrow, fenced lane leading from one corral to another. **2.** an enclosure in which horses and cattle are kept before being released into a rodeo arena.

cinch a type of girth used in the United States. It is made of horsehair, lampwick or leather, and is fastened by rings rather than a buckle.

cinch binder (Western US) a horse which rears on its hind legs, loses its balance and falls over backwards.

cinch up (US) to fasten the girth on a horse.

circle-cheek bit a bit used, like the anti-lug bit, to keep a horse straight. The jointed snaffle mouthpiece is attached to the cheekpieces — set within the rings — rather than to the rings themselves, which are very large and swivel slightly, thus producing a squeezing effect.

classic any of the five chief English flat races for three-year-old horses: the Derby, the Oaks, the St Leger, the 1000-Guineas and the 2000-Guineas.

classic age the age at which horses are eligible for the classics, namely, three years.

clean bred having a pedigree of pure blood; purebred.

clean ground *hunting* land which has not been fouled by stock or stained with manure, and so has a good scent for hunting.

clean-leg any breed of horse which does not have a large amount of long hair or feather on the legs, such as the Cleveland Bay, Percheron or Suffolk Punch, as distinct from the Ardennes, Clydesdale or Shire.

clear round *show-jumping* a round in which the competitor has completed the course without incurring either jumping or time faults.

cleft See under FROG.

clench the pointed end of a nail which protrudes through the hoof after a horse has been shod, and is then hammered over and downwards against the hoof. Also called CLINCH.

Clerk of the Course 1. the person appointed to have overall control of and responsibility for a particular racecourse. **2.** a course builder.

Clerk of the Scales 1. *racing* the licensed official on a racecourse who is responsible for the jockeys' weighing out and in and for the draw for places in flat races. He also has to ensure that the jockeys are wearing the correct colours and to supply the starter and judge with a full list of starters, notifying them of any colour changes. **2.** *show-jumping* (in competitions in which weight has to be carried) the person responsible for seeing that competitors weigh in at the correct weight.

Cleveland Bay The Cleveland Bay has been found in the Cleveland district of north-eastern Yorkshire for the past 200 years and has remained free of outside influence, except for the introduction of some Thoroughbred blood at about the end of the eighteenth century.

The Cleveland Bay Horse Society is one of the oldest breed societies. It was formed in 1884, when the Cleveland was in danger of disappearing because of the continual crossing with Thorough-

Churchill Downs racecourse at Louisville, Kentucky, the home of the Kentucky Derby.

breds to produce a faster and lighter carriage horse. When the breed is crossed with other smaller breeds it transmits its own size, hardiness and depth of bone. It is a powerful, active, clean-legged horse, between 16 and 16.2 h.h., with an efficient but not extravagant or high action. The colour is invariably bay and no white markings are allowed, except for a small white star on the forehead. The Cleveland should have 10 inches of bone below the knee and be 82 inches round the girth.

The United States has its own Cleveland Bay Society, and in recent years the breed has been exported to many countries throughout the world.

click See CLUCK.

climber a jockey who sits too upright and is too high in the saddle.

clinch See CLENCH.

clipping the act of trimming part or all of a horse's coat, usually by means of a clipping machine, in order to prevent the horse's becoming overheated at exercise and to facilitate drying and grooming its coat. Except in the case of greys, which are sometimes clipped at intervals throughout the year to keep the coat clean, clipping is usually carried out in autumn, after the winter coat has grown, and then repeated as necessary until the horse's summer coat begins to appear.

close season the period when no races are held, in Britain the close season for flat racing is approximately from November to March.

close shoeing a method of shoeing in which the horseshoe is set slightly under the wall of the foot.

clothing bib a device secured under a horse's chin to prevent the horse from biting and tearing its rugs. It consists of a rectangular piece of strong leather attached to the underside of a head collar by means of three straps which pass through the rings on the noseband and held in place by a nose strap.

cloud-watcher (Western US) a horse with an excessively high head carriage.

cluck a sound made with the tongue by a rider, driver or handler, in order to encourage his horse to go faster. Also called CLICK.

Clydesdale The breed originated in the area of Scotland now known as Lanarkshire, and it is the draught horse of Scotland. At the time of the Industrial Revolution the need arose for animals of greater height and substance. This was achieved by selective breeding within the native breed, and by crossing with Flemish stallions. The resultant animal proved equally suitable for haulage or farm work.

The Clydesdale combines weight, size, strength and activity with a docile temperament and good wearing qualities in respect of the feet and legs; it is particularly important to have a good large foot. The Clydesdale should have close movement, with the forelegs planted well beneath the shoulders, and the legs should hang straight from the shoulder to the fetlock joint. There must be no openness at the knee and no tendency for the knees to knock together. The hind legs must be planted close together, and the points of the hocks should turn inwards rather than outwards. The forehead should be open and broad between the eyes, the muzzle wide, the nostrils large; the neck should be long and well arched, the withers high and the back should be short with well-sprung ribs. The ideal colour is dark brown, with a clearly defined white stripe on the face, dark forelegs and white hind shanks. Today there are sometimes blacks and chestnuts.

clipping.

Top left
clipped out.

Top right
hunt clip.

Bottom left
trace clip.

Bottom right
blanket clip.

The Clydesdale Society was formed in 1877. The breed is still very popular and has been exported to many countries, including the United States, where the breed society is the Clydesdale Breeders Association of the U.S.

coachdog a dog, especially a Dalmatian, trained to run between the wheels of a horse-drawn vehicle, formerly in order to guard against attacks from highwaymen.

coach fellow (US) one of a team of four coach-horses.

coach-horn a simple straight brass instrument without keys, formerly used by coach guards to clear the road and warn people of the coach's arrival. Modern horns vary between 4 feet and 4 feet 6 inches in length, but early coach-horns were only about 3 feet long. Also called POST-HORN.

Coaching Club a driving club whose members are all owners of four-in-hand coaches. Founded in 1871, it is the oldest club of its kind in Britain. The first meet was held at Marble Arch on 27th June 1871, and some twenty coaches were present Meets were formerly held on the Thursday evening of the Richmond Royal Horse Show and in Hyde Park on the Saturday before the Royal International Horse Show. At the centenary celebrations at Hampton Court Palace in July 1971, fourteen coaches were present and Prince Philip was the guest of honour.

coaching crop the whip used by a coachman when driving a team. The stock, which is usually made of holly wood, has a considerably longer thong than an ordinary driving whip, so that the coachman is able to reach all the horses in the team, including the leaders.

coaching marathon a competition held at horse and agricultural shows for teams of four horses or ponies drawing a coach. Each team is judged for conformation and turnout and then goes on a drive of several miles, before returning to the show ground for the final judging.

coachman a person who drives one or more horses.

coachman's elbow the salute given by a coachman; with the elbow raised he lifts the whip to face level across the body.

Coakes, Marion, See MOULD, MARION JANICE.

coast on one's spurs (Western US) to ride with the spurs locked in the cinch or under the shoulders of the horse.

coat casting Horses cast their coat twice a year, in the spring and in the autumn. The exact time will vary according to whether they were early or late foals, and it will also be affected by the climatic conditions.

cob The cob is a type rather than a breed. It is a short-legged animal, no more than 15.1 h.h., which has the bone and substance of a heavy-

cob. The show cob Jonathan.

weight hunter, and is capable of carrying a substantial weight. For this reason and because it is easier to mount than a full-grown hunter, the cob is traditionally regarded as an old gentleman's horse. It is well proportioned and has a low, free action and tremendous jumping ability. Its main characteristic is its large rounded quarters, which, before docking became illegal in Britain, were often set off by a docked tail. The cob is most common in Ireland, Wales and the west of England, where, because of its size, it is extremely handy over banks and through thickly wooded areas.

In Britain the Cob Society is now combined with the Show Hack Society.

cockade a rosette worn on the top hat of a coachman or footman in full livery. In England cockades are worn only by the staff of commissioned officers in the army or navy.

cock fence *hunting* a thorn hedge which has been cut or laid very low.

cockhorse an extra horse which was attached in front of the leaders, in order to help pull a coach up a steep hill. Instead of being driven, it was ridden by a boy called a COCKHORSE BOY.

cockhorse boy See under COCKHORSE.

cock-tailed (of a horse) having a docked tail.

co-favourite one of two or more horses which are equally favoured to win a particular race and are given the same shortest price in the betting odds.

coffee-housing the act of engaging in idle distracting chatter, as when hunting and the hounds are drawing a covert, or when walking the course before a show-jumping competition.

coffin bone See PEDAL BONE.

coffin head a large coarse ugly head in which the jowl is lacking prominence.

cold-jawed (of a horse) having a hard insensitive mouth.

cold line See under LINE.

cold shoeing a method of shoeing horses with preformed shoes which are not heated and shaped immediately before being nailed on.

colic paroxysmal abdominal pains which may accompany any one of a variety of complaints, but are frequently the symptom of flatulence — a collection of gas in the bowel — an obstruction created by a mass of hard food or faeces in the bowel, or of a twisted gut. In many cases colic is attributable to improper feeding or mismanagement. Some of the most common causes are damaged, dirty, musty or fermenting food, sudden changes in diet, too much or too little food, or irregular feeding.

collar the piece of harness which fits round the horse's neck. It is made of heavily padded leather, and the traces are attached to it.

collar work *driving* particularly strenuous work, especially uphill.

collected canter a slow canter but with great impulsion. The shoulders are supple and free, and the quarters very active.

collected trot a slow controlled trot. The neck is raised to give the shoulders greater ease of movement and the hocks are well engaged, maintaining an energetic impulsion, notwithstanding the slower movement. Although its steps are shorter, the horse is lighter and more mobile than in the ordinary trot.

collected walk a slow walk in which the horse moves resolutely forward, with the neck raised and rounded, the head almost in the vertical position and the hind legs engaged. The mobility is greater but the movement is slower than the ordinary walk, the steps being higher but covering less ground.

collecting ring an area situated close or adjacent to a show ring, arena or the start of a cross-country course, where the horses are assembled prior to entering the ring or starting the course. The area may or may not be large enough to include practice jumps. It is supervised by the COLLECTING RING STEWARD, who is responsible for seeing that the competitors enter the ring or start the course promptly and in the correct order.

Colonel Rodzianko gag a gag bit having rollers round the jointed mouthpiece. It is designed for use on its own, as opposed to with a curb bit.

colours the distinctive colours of the silks worn by jockeys when riding in a race. Colours are exclusive to an owner, and in the British Isles have to be registered with Messrs Weatherby and Sons before they may be used. Racing colours may be of any combination of colour and pattern provided they are sufficiently distinguished from those belonging to any other owner. In the United States colours must be registered in the state in which they are worn and are usually, though not necessarily, also registered with the Jockey Club in New York.

colt an ungelded male horse less than four years old.

colt foal See under FOAL.

combination *polo* teamwork as distinct from individual play.

combination bet (US) *racing* a triple bet that a horse will (1) win, (2) be placed, i.e. finish first or second, and (3) show, i.e. finish in the first three. Also called BET ACROSS THE BOARD.

combination class a class held at horseshows in the United States in which horses are first shown in harness and then under saddle. It is limited to the Arabian, Saddle-horse, Shetland and Welsh Pony divisions.

combination obstacle *show-jumping* an obstacle consisting of two or more separate elements which are numbered and judged as one obstacle. The distance between each element and the next should be no less than 24 feet and no more than 39 feet 4 inches; the measurement is taken between the two facing sides at ground level. If a horse refuses or runs out at any of the elements of a combination obstacle, the competitor must return to the first element and jump the whole obstacle again. Faults incurred at each element are totalled together.

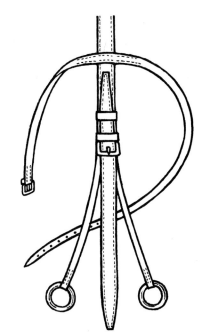

combined martingale a type of martingale having both a central strap which is attached to the noseband, as in a standing martingale, and two arms with rings through which the reins are passed, as in a running martingale.

combined training competition a comprehensive test of both horse and rider, consisting of the following phases: dressage, cross-country and show-jumping, usually, though not necessarily, held in that order. The relative influence on the whole test exerted by the dressage phase is slightly more than the show-jumping, but considerably less than the cross-country; ideally, the ratio should be 3:2:1.

dressage The nature of the dressage test is determined by the degree of difficulty of the whole competition and is related to the quality and standard of preparation of the competitors.

cross-country In advanced and intermediate classes, the course is between 2 and 2½ miles long and contains eight to ten obstacles per mile, the elements of a combination always being numbered and judged as separate obstacles. In novice classes the course is 1 to 1¾ miles long, with sixteen to twenty obstacles in all.

The obstacles are fixed and solid; unlike show jumps, they do not knock down. They must be imposing and, as far as possible, natural in appearance. Each obstacle must be numbered and marked with red and white flags. Sometimes alternative obstacles are also included. These are usually so arranged that the easier obstacle takes more time to negotiate than the more difficult alternative, so that the rider has to decide whether to try to save time or effort.

The minimum time for completing the course is calculated at a speed of 656 yards per minute for open and intermediate classes and 575 yards per minute for novice classes. In novice classes there are no penalty zones, and penalties are given only if, in the opinion of the judges, errors have been made in negotiating an obstacle.

show-jumping The show-jumping test consists of one round over a course of medium-sized obstacles, with at least one double. There is no jump-off. The total distance of the course is no more than 800 yards and the speed required is based on 382 yards per minute for advanced classes or 327 yards per minute for intermediate and novice classes.

Competitors are given penalty points, rather than faults as in normal show-jumping competitions, and these are incurred as follows:

knocking down a red or white flag	2 penalties
first disobedience, knocking down an obstacle, landing on tape of a water-jump or putting one foot or more in water	10 penalties
second disobedience in whole test	20 penalties
fall of horse and/or rider	30 penalties
jumping an obstacle in wrong order, error of course, not rectified	elimination

The penalties accumulated in each phase of the competition are totalled together, the winner being the competitor with the lowest score.

Combined training competitions may be held over one to three days, and are accordingly known as one-day, two-day or three-day events. The three-day event provides the most thorough test of horse and rider, and it is in this form that combined training is included in the Olympic Games. Also called HORSE TRIALS. See also THREE-DAY EVENT.

come-along a rope halter which tightens round the head of the horse when it pulls against the handler but slackens when it obeys.

come apart (Western US; of a horse) to start to buck.

competition horse any horse which, having attained the age of five years, is ridden in national show-jumping or dressage competitions, or three-day events.

Concours Complet National a combined training event in which entry is restricted to nationals who are qualified to compete under the rules laid down by the country's national federation.

Concours de Dressage International a dressage event in which riders from other countries may compete as individuals.

Concours de Dressage International Officiel a dressage event in which teams from other countries may compete.

Concours de Saut International a horseshow which includes show-jumping competitions open to riders from one or more foreign countries. Riders are invited by the host nation and then authorized by their own federation to compete. There is no limit to the number of C.S.I.s a country may hold during a year, providing the show organizers first obtain the permission of their national federation and the International Equestrian Federation.

Concours de Saut International Officiel the official international horseshow of a country, to which foreign show-jumping teams are invited and at which a Prix des Nations is held. No country is permitted to hold more than one C.S.I.O. a year, with the exception of the United States, which is allowed two because of its size.

confidential (of a horse) very quiet, not liable to shy or buck at anything and with which liberties may be taken without upsetting it — a suitable ride for a novice.

Connemara The Connemara pony originated in Ireland, in the part of Connaught to the west of Loughs Carrib and Mask and to the north of Galway Bay, an area which has long been famous for its ponies. The development of the breed is somewhat obscure, but stories tell of rich Galway merchants importing the finest strains of Arabs, some of which are thought to have escaped and joined local herds living on the mountains. The result, after several hundred years, was the Connemara, a breed which combines strength and hardiness of a mountain pony with the speed, agility and beauty of the Arab. Bred in natural conditions, they exist mainly on the scant, rough herbage of the mountains and bogs.

Below
Connemara ponies pictured above Ballyconneely Bay in western Ireland.

The Connemara stands 13 to 14.2 h.h. The predominant colours are grey, black, brown or dun, with occasional roans and chestnuts. The body should be deep and compact, with a well-balanced head and neck and short legs. The bone must be clean, hard and flat, measuring 7 to 8 inches below the knee. The animal should have a free easy action.

The Connemara is a first-class utility pony, equally suitable for carrying a child or average-sized adult and strong enough to do all the work on a holding. It also makes a splendid harness pony, being fast and showy and capable of covering great distances without tiring. The breed society was formed in 1923, and large numbers of ponies have now been exported to Europe and elsewhere. The famous Irish show-jumper, Dundrum, ridden so successfully in the 1960s by Tommy Wade, was out of a Connemara mare.

contact the link which the hands of the rider have with the mouth of the horse through the reins. The contact should always be as light as possible and yet firm.

continental martingale a martingale of French origin used in schooling to obtain the correct positioning and use of the head, neck and back. It consists of a strap which is attached to the girth and ends at the breast in a ring; a second strap, attached at one end to the noseband, is threaded through the ring, passed over the horse's poll and then buckled at the throat.

continental panel See under PANEL.

contract buster (US) a man who makes his living through his ability to sit a bucking horse. He travels the country from ranch to ranch, breaking horses as required.

coper an old name for a horse dealer, nowadays usually applied to one of low repute who may use underhand methods in order to sell a horse. Also called HORSE COPER.

Corinthian class a competition held at horse-shows in the United States for hunters ridden by amateurs, who are members of a particular hunt, in full hunting dress. Both horse and rider are judged for their appearance and turnout.

corn bruising of the sole in the angle between the wall and the heel. A common cause of lameness, the condition is recognizable by a blood-red coloration of the horn, and results from injury or bad shoeing. Hunters are particularly prone to corns because they are often shod with short-heeled shoes.

Cornish snaffle See SCORRIER SNAFFLE.

coronary band one of the sensitive structures of the horse's foot, it is situated in the hollow or semicircular groove which runs round the top and inner aspect of the hoof and is attached to the true skin by its upper margin. The under portion is covered with minute sproutlike projections, which dip into the small orifices of the wall and secrete the horn fibres.

Coronation Coach See STATE COACH.

Coronation Cup a horserace over a distance of 1 mile 4 furlongs (1½ miles), first run at Epsom in 1902, the year of Edward VII's coronation. It was run at Newbury in 1941 and at Newmarket from 1943 to 1945. (For results see page 238.)

coronet a coronary band situated at the top of the hoof of the horse. One of the sensitive structures, it is found in the hollow or semicircular groove which runs round the top and inner aspect of the hoof.

corral a pen or enclosure for animals, usually made of wood and always circular in shape, so that the animals cannot injure themselves.

country *hunting* the area over which a certain pack of hounds may hunt.

couple *hunting* two hounds. Hounds are always counted and referred to in couples, although a single hound is called simply one hound. If a hunt has twenty-five hounds they are referred to as 12½ couple.

couples *hunting* two hound collars joined by a chain and with a lead attached, carried on the saddle by the whipper-in and used, for example, when a couple have lost the others, in order to take them on to rejoin the rest of the pack.

coupling rein See under DRAUGHT REIN.

Far right
courbette. One of the Lipizzaner stallions of the Spanish Riding School demonstrates this spectacular high school movement.

courbette an air above the ground, in which the horse rears to an almost upright position, and then jumps forward several times on its hind legs.

course 1. a racecourse. **2.** *show-jumping* a circuit for which, except in certain special competitions, no distance, track or number of obstacles are prescribed, these being left to the course builder for the competition. **3.** *hunting* (of hounds) to hunt by sight rather than by scent.

course builder the person responsible for designing and building a show-jumping or cross-country course. In show-jumping the course builder will always require a day before the show to build the course and work out changes for other competitions. The judge is responsible for the course overall, and has the right to alter the height, spread or make-up of any obstacle. A cross-country course will take much longer to construct, and the course builder will have to start work several weeks or months before the event. The technical delegate is responsible for the course overall, and may order changes to be made. Also called CLERK OF THE COURSE, COURSE DESIGNER (US).

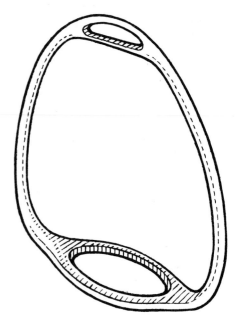

course designer 1. a person who designs a show-jumping or cross-country course and may or may not be responsible for building it as well. **2.** (US) a course builder.

course plan *show-jumping* a plan of the course, drawn up by the course builder for the judges and competitors. The competitors' copy is posted on a notice board in the collecting ring.

The plan, which need not be to scale, shows the approximate position of the obstacles in the ring, the order in which they are to be jumped, the distance of the course and the time allowed, as well as the obstacles, distance and time allowed for the jump-off. The plan must also show if it is necessary to follow a fixed track.

cover (of a stallion) to copulate with a mare.

covered school a covered building used for riding or working horses. It may or may not be fully enclosed and the size will depend on the requirements of the owner. It may only be large enough to train a horse in, or large enough to hold competitions, i.e. dressage and show-jumping. It is particularly useful in the winter when it may not be possible to exercise horses out of doors. Therefore, if it is to be fully enclosed, it should have sufficient lighting. The best floor covering is a mixture of sand and wood shavings on well-drained earth.

covert *hunting* a thicket or small area of woodland.

covert hack See under HACK.

cowboy a man who herds and tends cattle on the ranches in the western United States, doing his work mainly on horseback. Of uncertain derivation, in the days of the Revolutionary War the word 'cowboy' was applied to armed loyalists who rang cowbells to lure farmer patriots with lost cows into the brush, where they later ambushed them. The name was later given to Texas bandits who stole cattle from the Mexicans, often murdering the herders. By the mid-nineteenth century it was being used in Texas to describe a man who handled cattle, but it was not until after the Civil War that it came to signify anyone in the West who tended cattle on horseback.

cowboy boot a high-heeled riding boot worn by cowboys.

Cowboys' Turtle Association the predecessor of the Rodeo Cowboys' Association. Established in 1936, it was the first organization of American rodeo contestants to set standards and guarantee prizes. 'Turtle' refers to the promise made by the first officers of the union to move slowly but surely. The name was changed in 1945.

cow hocks hocks which turn inwards, this being a sign of weakness.

cow horse the horse which a cowboy rides while working cattle. The cow horse must be strong and agile, as well as intelligent, very surefooted and with a good eye. Lightness of foot and quickness of motion fit the cow horse for the work better than any other kind of animal.

cow kick a forward kick with the hind legs by a horse.

cradle a deep collar-like device designed to prevent a horse which has been injured, blistered or fired from biting the affected area.

A cradle is easily made by stringing together at equal intervals ten or twelve rods of wood, which should be about 1½ inches in diameter and of various lengths between 15 and 20 inches, so that they will fit round the horse's neck. See also CHESHIRE CRADLE.

cradle pattern iron a lightweight stirrup iron used in racing. It has a rounded cradle-like shape and is usually made of stainless steel or aluminium.

cramped action a lack of freedom of action in the movements of a horse.

crash helmet hard protective headgear worn especially by jockeys and cross-country riders. Since 1956 it has been compulsory in England for flat-race jockeys to wear a crash helmet.

crawfish (Western US) a horse which tends to pitch backwards.

creep a manger or feeding pen designed to allow a foal to feed without interference from the mare; slats are so spaced as to allow only the foal to reach the food.

crest the ridge along the back of a horse's neck from which the mane grows. It is particularly prominent in stallions and often in geldings which have been castrated late.

crib biting a vice, often associated with wind-sucking, in which the horse bites his crib, the bar of a gate or any other projection, and at the same time swallows air. The habit is often started by boredom. The front portions of the incisor teeth gradually become rounded. Also called CRIBBING.

There are various devices designed to counter the habit. The CRIB STRAP consists simply of a thick leather shield which fits into the gullet and is held in position by an adjustable strap which passes round the nose. The FLUTE BIT is a hollow, perforated mouthpiece which disperses the air as the horse gulps it and prevents it from being sucked in. The MEYERS PATTERN CRIBBING DEVICE, made from vulcanite with a soft rubber centre, is fastened tightly round the gullet with a strap over the poll, and attached to the head collar.

crib strap See under CRIB BITING.

crinet a piece of armour put round the neck of medieval warhorses.

Criollo an Argentinian breed of pony which evolved by a process of natural selection from the Arab and Barb stock originally taken to South America by the Spanish. The horses ran wild on the pampas and only the strongest could survive the extreme climatic conditions and natural hazards. The breed today is noted for its strength and amazing stamina. It stands about 14 h.h. and is usually dun in colour with some white markings.

cronet the hair which grows over the top of the hoof.

crossbreeding the mating of one purebred horse with another of a different breed.

crossed pole *show-jumping* a pole put across an obstacle at right angles to it if the obstacle is not to be jumped in that particular competition. This occurs frequently in a jump-off when only a limited number of the original obstacles are jumped.

cross saddle the general name given to all types of saddle except the side saddle. See also SADDLE.

crouch seat the position of the jockey's body when racing, being bent over the withers in order to lessen the wind resistance, thus giving the horse greater speed. See also SLOAN, JAMES TODHUNTER.

croup the region between the loins and the top of the tail. It should be convex in outline.

croupade an air above the ground in which the horse rears, and then jumps vertically with the hind legs drawn up towards the belly.

crow hop (Western US) a false buck, with the back arched and stiffened knees.

crown See under TINE.

crupper 1. a leather strap, sometimes padded to prevent chafing, which passes in a loop (the DOCK) round a horse's tail and is attached in the case of a HARNESS CRUPPER to the pad, or in the case of a RIDING CRUPPER to the back of the saddle in order to keep the saddle in place, especially on a horse or mule with poor withers. **2.** a piece of armour consisting of two deep plates used in medieval times to protect the whole of the horse's body lying behind the saddle.

cry *hunting* the noise made by hounds when they are hunting their quarry.

C.S.I. Concours de Saut International.

C.S.I.O. Concours de Saut International Officiel.

C-spring a curved spring, shaped like the letter C, which supports the body of a carriage or other vehicle. Also CEE-SPRING.

cub a young fox. Cubs are usually born in April or May in litters of five or six.

cub hunting the hunting of fox cubs, with the aim of introducing young hounds to hunting and of encouraging the fox cubs to leave the covert. It may also have the object of helping to reduce the number of foxes in a certain area. In Britain cub hunting usually takes place from August to October, although its exact starting time will depend upon the date of completion of the harvest. Also called CUBBING.

cup 1. *show-jumping* a metal holder which fits on to the wing of a jump and holds the pole or other supported part of the obstacle in position. **2.** See under TINE.

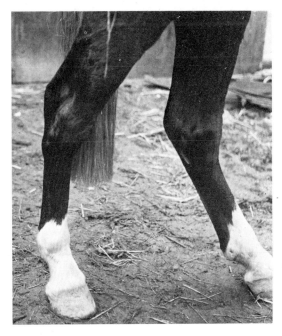

curb a swelling on the lower back part of the hock joint at the point where the small metatarsal bones join the lower row of bones of the hock.

There are two types. The TRUE CURB is the more serious and is caused by strain on the tendons passing over the seat of the curb or by laceration of the calcaneo-cuboid ligament at its attachments. This type of curb is caused by over-exertion and is more likely to occur in a horse with sickle hocks than in one with good conformation. A FALSE CURB is usually the result of a sharp blow and is an effusion of serum under the skin.

curb bit the type of bit used in conjunction with a snaffle bit or, more rarely, with a gag bit in a double bridle. The ordinary form of curb bit consists of two cheekpieces and a mouthpiece with a central port. Each end of the cheekpieces terminates in a ring. The curb reins are attached to the lower pair, and the bridle cheekpieces and curb chain to the upper pair. In the Western United States this type of bit is sometimes used alone. See also BANBURY MOUTHPIECE, WEYMOUTH BIT, WEYMOUTH DRESSAGE BIT.

curb chain a metal chain which is fitted to the eyes of a curb or pelham bit and lies in the groove of the lower jaw, just behind the lip. Pressure on the curb reins increases the leverage, thus tightening the curb chain. The chain, which should be made of broad links in order to avoid cutting, has a central ring through which the lip strap is passed. Less severe forms of curb are made of leather or elastic.

cur dog *hunting* any type of dog other than a hound. Originally care dog, the term was used to describe a dog which looked after sheep.

Curre hound a breed of foxhound developed by Sir Edward Curre by crossing English and Welsh foxhounds. It is characterized by a rough coat, which is usually white.

curricle One of the most fashionable town carriages of the nineteenth century, the curricle had a light open body mounted on C-springs. It was the only English two-wheeled vehicle designed to be drawn by two horses driven abreast.

The most original curricle, built for a famous dandy, Romeo Coates, was made of copper in the shape of a nautilus shell.

currier (formerly) a groom; one who curried or rubbed down a horse.

currycomb a rectangular metal tool with a short wooden handle, used for removing dirt and scurf from a body brush or, more rarely, for removing mud from a horse's coat. It has a flat back, while the front consists of several rows of small metal teeth.

cut to geld or castrate a colt or stallion.

cut a voluntary *hunting* to fall from a horse which has not itself fallen.

cutting See BRUSHING.

cutting horse a horse especially trained for separating selected cattle from a herd. It is the most coveted horse used in cattle herding and many years of hard work and experience are needed to train it to perfection. It understands which animal is to be cut out (selected), and then works it to the side of the herd. The cutting horse has to be very quick and able to spin and turn faster than the cow.

Far right
Dales pony, a native British breed, found chiefly in north-eastern England, where over the centuries it has served in mines, on the land, and in towns as a tradesman's pony.

d. *racing* distance.

daily double *racing* a bet on the totalizator in which the winning horses of two selected races are coupled together: in Great Britain generally the third and fifth races on the card; in the United States often on the first two races.

'Daily Express' National Foxhunter Championship *show-jumping* a national competition in Great Britain for novice horses which have not won a total of £50 in show-jumping competitions. The first two in each preliminary competition qualify to compete in one of the eleven regional finals, the first three or more (depending on the number of competitors) in each of these going forward to the final which is held at the Horse of the Year Show. The aim of the competition, which is named after Foxhunter, the winner of many international competitions for Great Britain, is to find horses of potentially international stature.

daily treble *racing* a bet on the totalizator in which the winning horses of three selected races are coupled together, generally the second, fourth and sixth races.

Dales pony a breed of pony originating in the north-east of England. Its early history is linked with the economic development of that part of the country, where it is largely bred today. Before the advent of the motor car the Dales had no equal. The chief mode of transport, it was used in agriculture, and in the lead and coalmines. It was also common to see the pony in the village high street being used by all the various tradesmen. Large numbers were purchased by the army both as draught and pack animals.

Far right
Dartmoor pony, a native British breed, noted for its kindly reliable temperament.

The Dales is one of the larger English breeds, standing 14 h.h. to 14.2 h.h. Black is the predominant colour, but there are also dark browns and greys. The only acceptable white markings are a star on the nose and white on the hind coronets.

This breed is essentially strong and compact in build, with a small neat pony head, well spaced with small neat slightly incurving ears. The neck is long, elegant and well arched, from well-laid sloping shoulders. The back is short and strong, being well ribbed and deep. The hindquarters should be strong with the tail well set on, and with a good gaskin. The limbs should be set at each corner with good clean flat flinty bone below good flat knees, with strong forearms and clear-cut hocks. The action at the trot should be high, clean and true, moving off all four legs.

dally (Western US) to make a turn round the saddle horn with the rope after a catch has been made.

dam the female parent of a foal.

dandy brush a long-bristled brush for removing the surface dirt or mud from a horse's coat.

dark horse *racing* a horse whose form is little known outside its own stable.

Darley Arabian one of the three founding sires of the English Thoroughbred. About 15 h.h., he was an outstandingly beautiful pure-bred Arabian of the Managhi strain. He was bought in Syria by Thomas Darley, an agent in merchandise abroad and the British Consul in Aleppo, who in 1704 shipped him to England as a four-year-old. He was sent to Aldby Park, Yorkshire, the Darley family seat, and, although he covered only a small number of mares belonging to the family, he established a brilliant line. He was the sire of Flying Childers, the first really great racehorse, and was the great-great grandsire of Eclipse, who was unbeaten in his racing career. See also BYERLEY TURK, GODOLPHIN ARABIAN.

Dartmoor pony From the very earliest times a small pony has roamed the moors in the extreme south-west of England, living on very sparse moorland, most of it over 1000 feet high and swept by winds and gales. Up to 1899, when the Dartmoor Pony Society was formed and a standard of points was introduced, the breed had varied tremendously. Between the wars interest in the Dartmoor grew, but during the Second World War the breed suffered seriously, as Dartmoor was a battle training ground and many ponies were killed by the troops to supplement their rations.

The Dartmoor is an excellent riding pony for children, and is the best possible foundation stock for breeding larger children's ponies. It has a good temperament, is quiet, kind and reliable. The height

Right
Darley Arabian, one of the three founding sires of the English Thoroughbred.

THE DARLEY ARABIAN,
From the Original Painting in the Possession of Henry Darley Esq.r at Aldby Park, Yorkshire

must not exceed 12.2 h.h., and the average is about 11.2 h.h. Bay, black or brown are the colours preferred, although only piebald and skewbald are barred, and excessive white is discouraged. The head should be small and fine, with fairly large eyes, and well set on a strong but not too heavy neck. The back, loins and hindquarters must be strong and muscular, and the legs and feet well shaped. The action should be low and free — a typical hack or riding action.

Dartmoor ponies have been exported all over the world, particularly to the United States.

Dartnall reins a type of riding rein made of soft plaited cotton, which is comfortable to the hand and does not rub the horse.

dash a trotting race run off as one event rather than in heats.

dash board US name for DASHING LEATHER.

dashing leather a leather-covered iron frame attached to a carriage to prevent mud from splashing the passengers or panels. Also called DASH BOARD (US), SPLASHING LEATHER.

Davidson, Bruce, *US* (born 1950) Bruce Davidson, a farmer from Westport, Massachusetts, has ridden since he was a child. He read pre-veterinary science at Iowa State University, and joined the US Equestrian Team in 1970. He competed on Plain Sailing in the three-day event team at the Olympic Games in Munich 1972, where he was a member of the silver medal-winning team, and individually he was placed eighth. In 1974, riding Irish Cap, he was third in the Badminton Horse Trials. Later in the year, riding the same horse, he was a member of the American team which won the World Championship at Burghley, taking the individual title himself.

D-cheek snaffle a bit closely resembling the eggbutt snaffle, but having D-shaped rings, as opposed to oval. Also DEE-CHEEK SNAFFLE.

dead heat *racing* a tie for first, second or third places. If there is a dead heat for first place, the total prize money for the first two places is added together and divided between the two, and similarly with other placings. A bet on a horse which dead-heats is paid to the full odds, but to half the stake.

dead-mouthed (of a horse) having a mouth which is no longer sensitive to the bit.

declaration a statement in writing by an owner, trainer or his representative, made a specified time before a race or competition, that a horse will take part and also giving such other information as may be required.

dee-cheek snaffle See D-CHEEK SNAFFLE.

deep through the girth (of a horse) well ribbed up with a generous depth of girth behind the elbows.

de Gogue martingale a modification of the Chambon martingale in which the arms, instead of being attached to the rings of the bit, are either passed through the rings and joined to the reins (for mounted schooling), or are passed through the rings and then rejoined to the main strap (for schooling from the ground).

den cry (US) the cry of hounds when they have run their fox to ground.

Dennett gig a gig of very light structure which carried two people. It was brought out in the early part of the nineteenth century by a coachbuilder called Bennett, whose name was changed to Dennett because his fashionable West End customers decided that Bennett was too common a name. See also GIG.

Derby a horserace over 1 mile 4 furlongs ($1\frac{1}{2}$ miles) held annually at Epsom since 1780, except from 1915 to 1918 and from 1940 to 1945 when a wartime substitute race was run at Newmarket. The most important horserace in England, the Derby is said to owe its origins to a party given to celebrate the first running of the Oaks, at which the twelfth Earl of Derby and Sir Charles Bunbury were present. It was decided to hold another race at Epsom in the following year, 1780, for three-year-olds and that both colts and fillies should be allowed to run. (Colts carry 9 st. and fillies 8 st. 11 lb.) When the question of choosing a name for the race arose, Lord Derby and Sir Charles Bunbury tossed a coin. The former won and the race was named after him. However, the first time it was run, it was won by Sir Charles's Diomed. (For results see page 239.)

Below
Derby Day. William Powell Frith's famous painting captures brilliantly the holiday atmosphere which is still so much a part of the Epsom scene on Derby Day.

Above
Derby. They're off! The start of the 1971 Derby. Athens Wood (nearest the camera) fortunately came to no harm.

Far right
Derby. The gold trophy awarded in 1974 to Mrs Neil Phillips, whose Snow Knight won by two lengths.

Below
Diamond Jubilee, Triple Crown winner in 1900, with Herbert Jones up.

deviation failure by a competitor to follow the prescribed course in a show-jumping competition, combined training event, etc., or to follow the prescribed course or sequence of movements in a dressage competition. In order to correct a deviation the competitor must return to the point where he went wrong.

Diamond Jubilee (by St Simon out of Perdita II) Foaled in 1897, the year of Queen Victoria's Diamond Jubilee, the horse was owned by the Prince of Wales and trained by Richard Marsh. He was very temperamental and proved extremely hard to train. However, after some unhappy partnerships with a number of jockeys, it was decided to put up Herbert Jones, the lad who had been riding him at excercise, although he had

little experience. Their first race together was the 2000-Guineas of 1900, which they won by four lengths. The combination then went on to win the Derby and the St Leger. By winning the Triple Crown, Diamond Jubilee proved that in spite of his temperament he was a very capable horse.

He was retired to stud at Sandringham. Then, in 1906, he was sold to a South American breeder, and proved very successful in the Argentine, where he eventually died at the age of twenty-six.

Dick Christian a loose-ringed snaffle having a jointed mouthpiece in which the two parts are held together by means of a metal link, as opposed to the normal type of joint. The link, which rests on the tongue, gives greater comfort and also tends to lessen the nutcracker effect.

dicky a seat at the back of a horse-drawn carriage for a groom or servant. Also DICKEY; also called RUMBLE SEAT.

did not finish (of a horse) failed to complete the course by not passing the winning post.

diligence a public stagecoach in parts of Europe, especially France. A very heavy vehicle, it was usually drawn by five horses. The fare varied according to whether the passengers rode inside in comfort or on the outside.

direct rein the natural rein, the action of which is to turn the horse's head to the direction in which the horse is required to move.

dirt track a race track with a covering of sand, cinders or gravel. The first official track of this kind was built in 1819 in the United States at the Union Course, Long Island.

dished foot a horse's foot with hollow walls and a rounded pumiced sole, somewhat similar to but more pronounced than a flat foot. Such feet are very prone to bruising and disease. It is essential when shoeing for the shoe to be well seated on the upper surface next to the sole.

dishing a faulty movement of a horse, in which one or both of the forelegs is thrown outwards and forwards when moving forward.

distaff side the maternal side of a horse's breeding.

Distas bending tackle See under BENDING TACKLE.

Distas bridle See W. S. BITLESS PELHAM.

disunited with the legs used in an incorrect sequence. If a horse is cantering disunited or false the sequence is off hind, near fore and near hind

Don, a hardy active Russian breed, which is also used under saddle.

Canadian Horse, a breed
noted for its agility and
tremendous speed over short
distances.

Clydesdale. A group of
mares and foals.

Döle, a Norwegian breed, related to the English Dales pony. It is medium sized, strong and hardy, and is used principally for agricultural purposes.

Dutch Draught Horse. A stallion with typically massive forequarters and strong, well-placed legs.

together, off fore (leading leg), or near hind, off fore and off hind together, near fore (leading leg).

dividend the amount paid to a person who has backed a winner or placed horse on the totalizator. The total pool, i.e. the total amount staked on all horses, is divided, after certain deductions, among winners in proportion to the amount staked on each ticket.

Dobbin 1. a name for a quiet kindly horse, especially one used for agricultural purposes. **2.** any horse of this kind.

dock 1. the solid fleshy part of a horse's tail, as opposed to the hair. **2.** to cut off a portion of a horse's tail bone. Under the Docking and Nicking Act, 1948, the practice is now illegal in Britain. **3.** See under CRUPPER (def. 1).

doe the female of the deer, hare, rabbit and various other animals.

quarters, the Döle was originally quite a light breed, but with the introduction of heavier agricultural machinery its weight and size were increased by a process of selective breeding. The usual colours are bay or brown.

doll *racing* a light wooden barricade used to mark intersections on the racecourse, in order to keep the horses on the right track, and also to put round an obstacle if for some reason it is not to be jumped.

Don a hardy horse bred in the Don Valley and Black Sea areas of the Soviet Union. The breed was developed during the eighteenth century by the Don Cossacks, who crossed local horses with stallions which they captured in the south. A dual-purpose animal, the Don is used both for agricultural work and as a saddle-horse and was formerly much used by shepherds. Today the breed is also raced very successfully. It has a relatively long body, and on average is about 16 h.h.

dogcart.

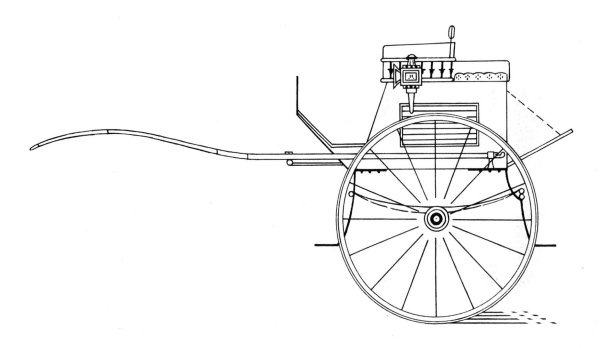

Far right
Steve Donoghue, who rode his first winner in 1904 and retired in 1938 with a total of 1845 wins to his credit.

dog 1. a horse, especially a racehorse, which is sluggish and not keen to work. **2.** a racehorse which is unreliable.

dogcart a light two-wheeled trap drawn by one horse, with seating for four passengers — two facing the front and two behind facing the rear — and a large boot with Venetian slats. Introduced at the beginning of the nineteenth century, it was originally used for carrying sporting dogs and was, therefore, essentially a country vehicle. Numerous variations were subsequently developed, including a spacious four-wheeled version, which could be drawn by two horses, the OXFORD DOG-CART, which was ideal for tandem driving, and the WHITECHAPEL DOGCART (also called the NORFOLK SHOOTING CART), which was probably the most capacious two-wheeled sporting and family carriage.

dog fox a male fox.

doghound a male hound.

Döle a strong hardy Norwegian breed of horse used primarily for agricultural purposes. Now a medium-sized animal with a broad chest and hind-

Donoghue, Stephen, (1884–1945) Born in Warrington, Lancashire, Steve Donoghue served his apprenticeship with John Porter at Kingsclere

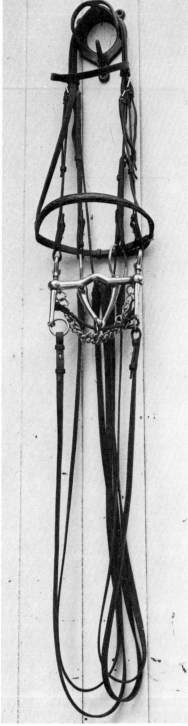

Above and above right
double bridle. Since this is the most advanced form of bridle, it should be used only by horsemen of experience.

in Berkshire and then joined Edward Johnson in France, riding his first winner there in 1904. His first major success in England was in the Cambridgeshire in 1910, which he won on Christmas Daisy. In 1911 he was appointed first jockey to Atty Persse and rode The Tetrarch in all his races. He was champion jockey from 1914 to 1922 and shared the title with Charlie Elliot in 1923. Altogether he rode a total of 1845 winners, including the following Derby winners: Pommern in 1915, Gay Crusader in 1917, Humorist in 1921, Captain Cuttle in 1922, Papyrus in 1923 and Manna in 1925. He won both the Oaks and the St Leger twice. He retired in 1938.

doorman See under FARRIER.

dope to administer drugs to a horse, either to improve or to reduce its performance in a race or competition. Doping is an illegal practice, and in all forms of equestrian sport carries heavy penalties.

doped fox *hunting* a fox which is forced to walk through a strong-smelling liquid when it leaves the place where it is lying, in order to have a good scent and thus ensure a hunt. Also called TOUCHED-UP FOX.

dorsal stripe a continuous black, brown or dun stripe running straight down the back of the horse from the mane to the tail, sometimes extending on to both the mane and the tail.

double 1. the backing of two horses to win in separate races, the winnings of one race being carried on to the second race. If either horse fails to win the bet is lost. **2.** *show-jumping* a combination obstacle consisting of two elements. Also called IN-AND-OUT (US).

double accumulator competition a two-round show-jumping competition in which the first-round points are awarded as for an accumulator competition, with a maximum score of 28 points. In the second round no points are awarded for clearing obstacles, but penalty points are scored for obstacles knocked down and these are deducted from the first round score:

first obstacle knocked down   7 penalty points
second obstacle knocked down 6 penalty points
and so on, to seventh obstacle
knocked down   1 penalty point

In both rounds refusals, disobediences, etc. are penalized as in an accumulator competition. The winner is the competitor with the greatest number of points at the end of the second round. If there is equality of points, the competitor with the fastest time in the second round is the winner.

double bridle the most severe form of bridle, having two bits (a snaffle and a curb bit), which are separately attached, by means of two pairs of cheekpieces, and can be operated independently. The snaffle is placed in the horse's mouth first and below it is the curb bit. To each bit is attached a pair of reins, the snaffle reins being used to raise the horse's head, the curb reins to lower it and to draw in the nose. Also called WEYMOUTH BRIDLE.

double gaited (US) capable of trotting and pacing.

double oxer *show-jumping* a spread fence built in the same way as an oxer, except that behind the brush there is another post and rails, thus increasing the spread. Only one pole should be used at the back, and it should be higher than the brush so that the horse can see it.

Doublet See under ANNE, H.R.H. THE PRINCESS.

doubtful runner *racing* a horse which is not certain to run in a particular race. For instance, the trainer may wait to see the state of the going before deciding whether or not to run the horse.

draft *hunting* to remove a hound permanently from the pack when there is no further use for it.

drag 1. *hunting* an artificial scent made by trailing a strong-smelling material, such as a piece of sacking impregnated with aniseed or a fox's droppings, over the ground. **2.** a private or park coach.

draghound a hound trained to follow a drag.

drag hunt a hunt with a drag or artificial scent.

drag man the person, whether mounted or on foot, who lays the trail for a drag hunt on a prescribed line across country.

dragsman the coachman of a private coach.

drag staff a wooden pole about 3 feet 6 inches long with a spiked metal end which was fitted to the back axle of various early horse-drawn vehicles. It could be let down and pushed into the ground when the vehicle was standing on an incline in order to take some of the strain off the horses and to prevent the vehicle running back. Also called DRAG STICK.

drain *hunting* any underground pipe, ditch or watercourse in which a fox may hide.

draught horse a horse which is used for drawing a vehicle of any size, although the expression is usually confined to breeds of heavy horses. See also HEAVY HORSE.

draught rein one of the main reins of a team or pair which pass from the outside of the bits to the driver's hands. A shorter COUPLING REIN is attached at one end to the draught rein and at the other to the inside of the bit of the partner horse.

draw 1. *hunting* an area to which a huntsman

Below
large dressage arena.

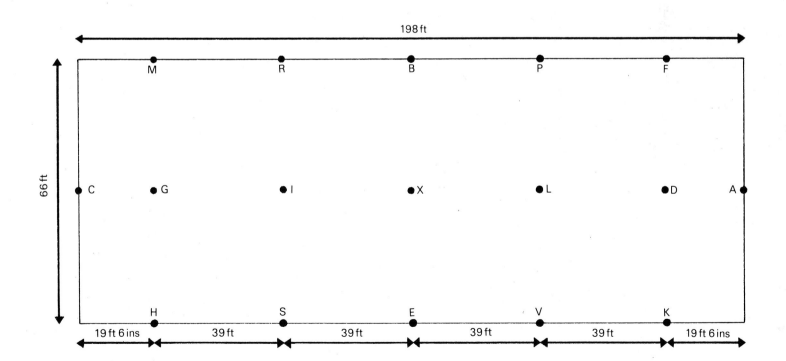

takes the hounds in order to find a fox. **2.** *racing* the drawing of lots to decide in which order the horses should line up at the starting gate. **3.** *show-jumping* the drawing of lots to decide in which order competitors must start in a competition. Under B.S.J.A. rules a draw must be made if the jump-off is against the clock, irrespective of whether there has been a draw for the first round or not.

dray a low loading wagon with no sides, used for carrying heavy loads, such as barrels of beer.

drench a medicine administered to a horse in the form of a drink, usually when it is too bulky to be given as a ball. The ingredients are mixed together in cold or warm water and placed in a special long-necked glass bottle, known as a drenching bottle. The neck of the bottle is inserted in the horse's mouth on the offside and the contents emptied into the mouth slowly and with great caution. This method may also be used to give medicinal draughts or drinks or any liquid dosage.

dressage the art of training the horse beyond the stage of just being useful, making the animal more graceful in bearing, easier to control and more amenable. The finely trained horse is calm, supple, keen and obedient, responding immediately and precisely to the lightest of aids, so that he gives the impression of doing of his own accord whatever is required of him.

The walk should be regular, free and unconstrained; the trot free, supple, regular, sustained and active; and the canter united, light and cadenced. Changes of pace and speed should always be made smoothly but quickly, the cadence of a pace being maintained up to the moment when the pace is changed or the horse comes to a halt. The quarters should never be inactive or sluggish, and at all times, even at the halt, the horse must be on the bit, with the hocks well placed, the neck correctly positioned according to the extension or collection of the pace and the head held steadily in position. Basic dressage is necessary in the training of all horses, but the ideal horse for competitive dressage must have good conformation and should not exceed 16.1 h.h.

Competitive dressage is governed by the Fédération Equestre Internationale (F.E.I.), which has established the following tests: the Prix St Georges (of medium standard); the Reprise Intermédiaire (of advanced standard); and the Grand Prix (of Olympic standard). These, together with the dressage tests designed for use in C.C.I.s and C.C.I.O.s are the only ones admitted in international competition. Tests for national competitions, however, may be issued by the respective national federations.

Under international rules the size of a dressage arena is 22 yards (20 metres) by 66 yards (60 metres). The arena is marked with letters at the sides and the end (see page 63) The jury is situated at the end opposite the entrance, and spectators are always kept at a distance of 22 yards (20 metres) from the arena.

In certain countries, for national competitions at novice and elementary level, a smaller arena, measuring 22 yards (20 metres) by 44 yards (40 metres), is sometimes used. A particular advantage of the smaller arena is that tests can be completed more quickly than in a full-size arena, and this is an important factor, as novice and elementary classes often attract large entries.

Each movement in a dressage test is marked in accordance with the following system:

10 marks	perfection
9 marks	outstanding
8 marks	very good
7 marks	good
6 marks	fairly good
5 marks	sufficient
4 marks	insufficient
3 marks	poor
2 marks	bad
1 mark	very bad
0 marks	unmarkable.

Judging begins as soon as the horse and rider enter the arena at marker A and finishes when they leave the arena at the same point.

dressage saddle a deep-seated saddle designed for use in dressage. Rarely more than sixteen inches long, it has a straight tree, and the bars are extended to the rear so that the leathers hang down the centre of the flap. The flap itself is cut fairly straight, so that the upper leg of the rider lies on the flap, behind the supporting roll on the panel, thus leaving the lower leg free to give better control.

dress chariot an ornate carriage for carrying two people. Introduced about 1840, it was the carriage of the nobleman, and was used for attending important functions. It was usually painted in the family colours and bore the family crest on the door. The coachman, who was dressed in livery, rode on a box seat in front and the two footmen stood on the rear between the C-springs.

Dr Green the new lush grass of spring.

driver 1. any person who drives a horse-drawn vehicle, especially one considered less skilful or practised. **2.** (US) a person holding a licence issued by the American Trotting Association which permits him to drive trotters and pacers in races.

driving apron a knee rug, sometimes tying round the waist, worn by a coachman or driver, and usually by any passengers travelling in an open vehicle. For winter use driving aprons are made of heavy materials, such as boxcloth, while those designed for use in summer are made of light-weight materials.

drop a foal (of a mare) to give birth to a foal.

drop fence a fence in which the ground on the landing side is lower than that on the take-off side.

drop noseband a type of noseband which is fixed around the muzzle below the bit. Normally used in conjunction with a snaffle bit, the main function of the drop noseband is to assist the rider's control of the horse by ensuring that the bit acts correctly on the bars of the mouth (rather than simply the corners), thus making the horse flex correctly and assisting in obtaining correct balance. It is particularly useful in training a young horse not yet ready for a double bridle, and in controlling a horse that pulls as, correctly fitted, it prevents the horse from opening its mouth and thus evading the bit.

droppings the excrement of a horse.

drop side the landing side of a steeplechase obstacle.

drop stirrup a heavy looped leather strap fixed below the stirrup iron in order to facilitate mounting, used especially by women.

Drummond-Hay, Anneli, See WUCHERPFENNIG, ELIZABETH ANN.

dual forecast pool See under FORECAST (def. 2).

dual paternity a term used in the pedigree of a

horse when its dam has been covered by two different stallions during the same season.

dump to shorten a horse's toe by rasping the front wall of the hoof.

dun See BLUE DUN, YELLOW DUN.

Duncan gag a gag bit designed for use with a curb bit, having a plain or twisted mouthpiece with two small eyes, as opposed to rings, for the reins, and short cheeks extending upwards, each terminating in a small eye, through which the rein is passed.

dung-eating the vice and undesirable habit developed by some horses of eating their droppings. As a means of prevention the horse should be muzzled at non-feeding times, but since in some cases the habit results from a mineral or vitamin deficiency, this possibility should also be investigated.

Dutch Draught Horse a comparatively new breed of massive, heavily muscled draught horse developed in the Netherlands. It is a hard, very deep-chested animal with immensely strong forequarters, powerful hindquarters and strong, well-placed legs. It has a very good action with a long easy stride. Breeding is rigorously controlled by the Royal Netherlands Draught Horse Society, and in order to preserve and consolidate the characteristics of the breed only animals of known pedigree and whose conformation meets the required standard are entered in the stud book.

Dutch slip a simple type of head collar, made of leather or tubular web, having only a nose and head strap, both of which are adjustable. It is particularly suitable for foals.

dwell (of a horse) to urinate.

E the symbol on trotting programmes in the United States placed before the names of two or more horses in a race to indicate that they are from the same stable and are running as one number. This shows that there is a common interest between the horses, drivers and owners: it is a precautionary measure to preserve the integrity of the sport and to advise the public of such common interest (specifically for betting purposes).

each way a betting term used in Great Britain to show that a horse has been bet on (1) to win and (2) to finish in the first three.

ear down to stroke one or both of a horse's ears in order to calm, comfort or congratulate the animal.

ear-stripping the act of earing down, usually for a prolonged period a horse which is cold or tired.

earth the underground lair of a fox which it digs below ground level or in the side of a bank.

earth stopper *hunting* a person employed to block up the entrance of an earth once the fox has left it. This is done the night before a meet of the hunt.

Ebor Handicap a horserace over 1 mile 6 furlongs (1¾ miles), held annually at York since 1843, except in 1943 and 1944, when it was run at Pontefract. (For results see pages 239–240.)

Eclipse Stakes a horserace over 1 mile 2 furlongs (1¼ miles), held since 1866 at Sandown Park, except in 1946 when it was run at Ascot. (For results see page 240.)

eggbutt snaffle a snaffle bit with a jointed mouthpiece and egg-shaped rings. The rings are fixed and do not allow for much play in the mouth, so that the horse is unable to avoid the action of the bit. In some cases the rings are slotted, so that the mouthpiece can be fitted in the correct position, and more pressure is exerted on the bars of the mouth than on the corners.

Einsiedler a breed of horse found in Switzerland, used for riding, driving and light agricultural work, and much favoured by the Swiss Army. An elegant animal with a deep chest and alert head, it has an easy action and is an excellent trotter.

elbow *racing* the point on a race track where the course deviates from a straight line.

elimination the excluding of a competitor from further participation in a particular competition. In show-jumping elimination may be incurred for any of the following reasons:
failure to enter the ring when called upon to do so;
jumping an obstacle in the arena before the signal to start is given, even though the obstacle may not be part of the course;
starting before the judges have given the signal;
failure to go through the starting line within forty-five seconds of the signal's being given;
a third disobedience in a round;
showing an obstacle to the horse before the round has started or during the round, after a refusal;
entering or leaving the ring dismounted without having gained permission to do so;
a sixty-second resistance during the round;
taking more than sixty seconds to jump an obstacle, except in the case of a fall;
jumping an obstacle without rectifying a deviation of the course;
jumping an obstacle which does not form a part of the course;
jumping an obstacle in the wrong order;
passing the wrong side of a flag, if the deviation is not corrected;
exceeding the time limit;
jumping an obstacle which has been knocked down, before it has been rebuilt;
starting after an interruption, before the signal to do so has been given;
jumping an optional obstacle (in a jump-off in a puissance, for example) more than once or in the wrong direction;
failure to jump the full obstacle after a refusal or fall at double or combination;
failure to jump out of a closed obstacle in the right direction;
interference with a closed obstacle;
failure to jump each part of a multiple obstacle separately;
failure to cross the finishing line on horseback before leaving the arena;
leaving the arena (horse and/or rider) before the completion of the round;
accepting a whip during the round;
any assistance during the round, considered by the judge to be unauthorized;
failure to have the correct weight when weighing in after the completion of the round;
entering the ring on foot once the competition has started;
dismounting before being given permission to do so by the Clerk of the Scales.

elk lip a wide loose upper lip which overhangs the lower lip.

Empire Pool an indoor sports stadium with a seating capacity of 8000, in Wembley, west London. It has been the home of the Horse of the Year Show since 1959 and of the Royal International Horse Show since 1970.

engaged *racing* (of a horse) entered in a particular race.

English saddle See HUNTING SADDLE.

English show-saddle.

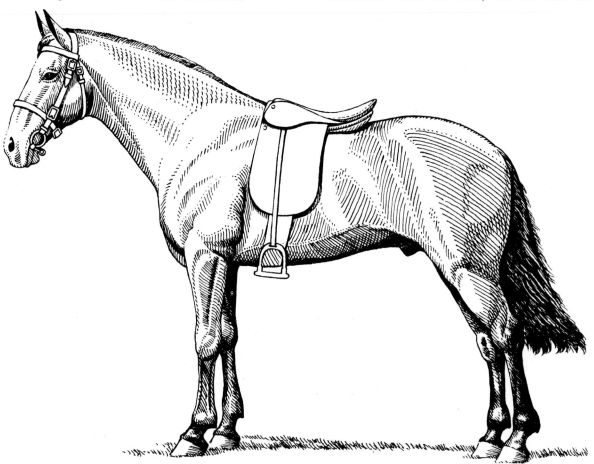

English show-saddle a type of saddle designed purely for use in the show ring to display the conformation of the horse. In order to show the extent of the horse's shoulder the flap is cut in a straight line from the head. The seat is fairly flat and a SKELETON PANEL, a short panel made of thin felt and covered with leather, is used so that the saddle fits closely to the back.

enlarge to set free a carted stag and give it a few minutes' start before laying the hounds on the scent.

enteritis inflammation of the intestinal or bowel lining, which may be set up by bacteria, chemical or vegetable poisons or mouldy or damaged food containing harmful fungi. The symptoms in the early stages are rigours and loss of appetite followed in the acute stages by spasmodic pain and diarrhoea. Enteritis can be a very serious complaint in horses and requires immediate veterinary attention.

'Eohippus' (the 'dawn horse') is the popular name for *Hyracotherium*, the earliest ancestor of the modern horse. It lived some sixty million years ago in the Eocene Epoch, and little was known about it until a complete skeleton was discovered in the United States in 1876. Fossils had earlier been found in Kent, in England, in 1839, but had not at that time been recognized and were thought to belong to a different species. *Eohippus* varied in size between a fox-terrier and a foxhound, with four toes on each forefoot and three on each hind foot. Its teeth were suitable only for eating shrubs and it could not have eaten grass. *Eohippus* is

thought to have originated in North America and then to have migrated to other parts of the world. See also EQUUS, MERYCHIPPUS, MESO-HIPPUS, PLIOHIPPUS.

Epsom a town in Surrey, the site of Epsom Downs racecourse, where the Derby and the Oaks are held. It is probable that racing was started in the early seventeenth century when Epsom became famous as a spa for mineral waters and, in order to attract more people to take the waters, the town council began race meetings on the Banstead Downs. Racing did not become an annual event until 1730 when there were two meetings. The Epsom Grandstand Association, formed in 1828, is responsible for the management of the racecourse.

equestrian 1. of or pertaining to horsemen or horsemanship. **2.** a rider or performer on horseback.

equestrienne a female rider or performer on horseback.

equine 1. of or pertaining to the horse. **2.** a horse.

Equine Research Station See under ANIMAL HEALTH TRUST.

equipage a completely equipped carriage, with horses and attendants.

equirotal phaeton a type of phaeton, invented in 1838 by W. B. Adams, the equirotal was an astonishing vehicle in appearance. It was in fact a combination of two vehicles, a gig in front and a curricle behind, joined by two couplings. The name of the vehicle was taken from the wheels, there being four large ones all the same size. Among its good features were its lack of noise, the fact that it ran lightly and that at all times the driver was directly behind the horses, since his seat moved with the wheels.

Equus The true horse (*Equus*) first appeared in

Above
Exmoor. Hawkwell
Badgeworthy with her foal.
Ponies of this breed are
extremely strong and hardy,
and although small they are
able to carry heavy weights.

North America in the Pleistocene Epoch about one million years ago and thence spread to most other parts of the world. It walked on one toe only, as does the domesticated horse (*Equus caballus*) today and it is still possible to find direct descendants of this animal in Mongolia. Little is known about the horse before the third millennium B.C. when it was first tamed, but most modern breeds are descended from one great migratory stream which in prehistoric times moved south from central Asia to the shores of the Mediterranean. The first records of man's interest in the horse are the vivid paintings on the walls of caves in Spain and in the Sahara. The horse was hunted by prehistoric man for its flesh, rather as deer is hunted today, and, being a swift animal, was not domesticated until many years after the ass, the dog and the ox. The horse was to play a unique role in the development of human civilization – in war, in work and in leisure – and the close and affectionate relationship between man and animal has survived the advent of mechanical transport.

esquire the young wild boar accompanying a singular.

European Junior Championships annual three-day event and show-jumping championships open to competitors from European countries who are under 18 and over 14 years old on the first day of the competition. Both team and individual championships are held, running concurrently in the three-day event and held separately for the show-jumping.

European Three-Day Event Championships a three-day event encompassing concurrent individual and team competitions, held at irregular intervals between 1953 and 1965, and since held every other year. The championship is open to teams of four riders from each European country and to a limited number of individuals. The scores of the three best riders of each team over the three days count in the team championship, and the winner of the individual championship is the rider with the best overall score. The country of the winning team has the right to hold the next championship, but it may not be held in the same country on two consecutive occasions. (For results see page 224.)

evening stables See under STABLES.

evens the betting odds given on a horse when the person who places the bet stands to win the same amount as his stake.

event See STANDARD EVENT.

event horse a horse which competes or is capable of competing in a combined training competition.

e.w. *racing* each way.

ewe neck a neck that is concave between the poll and the withers rather than convex.

Exmoor pony The Exmoor comes from the moors situated in north Devon and west Somerset. Because the moorland it inhabits is high and exposed, the Exmoor pony is extremely strong and hardy. Although small it is capable of carrying heavy weights, and it is not uncommon to see Exmoor ponies being used by farmers for shepherding or out hunting, as they are so sure-footed. They make excellent children's riding ponies.

The Exmoor Pony Society was formed in 1921, and according to its rules mares must not exceed 12.2 h.h. and stallions 12.3 h.h. The prescribed colours are bay, dun or brown, but no white markings or white hairs are permitted. Easily recognizable by its unmistakable mealy muzzle, the Exmoor should have a wide forehead with prominent eyes, and short thick, pointed ears. The body should be deep with a broad chest, medium-length back and powerful loins. The shoulders should be well set back, and the legs must be clean with neat hard feet. In summer the coat is harsh and springy and shines, but carries no bloom in winter.

extended canter a fast but controlled canter, in which the horse lengthens its stride, extending its neck so that the tip of its nose points forwards.

Below
Fairway, Lord Derby's Champion Stakes winner of 1928 and 1929. He was leading sire in 1936, 1939, 1943 and 1944, his most famous sons being Blue Peter and Watling Street.

extended trot a fast but controlled trot. In this movement the horse has to relax its collected shape, lowering the head and neck into a broad extended form. The hind legs take on a driving as opposed to a lifting role, but the movement nevertheless must have rhythm or it becomes a meaningless run.

extended walk a fast walk in which the horse should cover as much ground as possible with each stride, without over-hurrying and without losing regularity of pace. The hind feet should touch the ground ahead of the footprints left by the forefeet. The head and neck should be extended, without the rider's losing contact.

extravagant action an action which is high at the knee and the hock, such as that of the hackney.

f. *racing* fell.

fadge 1. the gait of a horse between a walk and a trot; a slow jog. **2.** to go or ride at a fadge.

Fairway (by Phalaris out of Scapa Flow. Phalaris was a successful middle-distance handicapper. Although Scapa Flow was not a great winner on the racecourse, she was a very successful dam, and her progeny won sixty-three races worth £86,000.) Foaled in 1925, Fairway was owned by Lord Derby and trained by Frank Butler at Newmarket. In his debut as a two-year-old he was unplaced in the Eglington Stakes at York, but won all of his three other races: the Coventry Stakes at Ascot, the July Stakes at Newmarket and the Champagne Stakes at Doncaster. In 1928 he won the Newmarket Stakes, but was then unplaced in the Derby, possibly because he was mobbed by the crowd on the way to the start. He went on to win the Eclipse Stakes at Sandown, the St Leger at Doncaster and the Champion Stakes at Newmarket. He remained in training for one more

Einsiedler. A mare and a
foal.

Finnish Horse. The lighter
specimens of the breed are
used for riding and as
carriage horses, while the
heavier type is used for
draught purposes.

Franches-Montagnes, a
Swiss breed, which is still
used extensively on the land,
particularly in areas that
cannot be reached by tractor.

Friesian. One of the oldest
surviving breeds in Europe,
this Dutch horse is always
black in colour.

season, winning the Burwell Stakes at Newmarket, the Rous Memorial Stakes at Ascot and the Princess of Wales Stakes at Newmarket. He narrowly failed to win his second Eclipse, being beaten by Royal Minstrel, but won the Champion Stakes for the second successive year and wound up his racing career with a win in the Jockey Club Cup at Newmarket.

He was an outstanding success at stud, and was the leading sire in 1936, 1939, 1943 and 1944. He sired the winners of 394 races, worth in total £289,000, including Blue Peter and Watling Street, winner of the 1942 Derby. He was retired from stud in 1945 and died in 1948.

Falabella a breed of miniature pony named after the Argentinian family which developed it during the nineteenth century. At maturity the pony does not exceed 30 inches in height. There are no special colours. The breed is very popular as a pet and is also used in harness.

fall A horse is considered to have fallen when the shoulders and quarters on the same side touch the ground, or the obstacle and the ground. A rider is considered to have fallen when there is separation between him and his horse which necessitates his remounting.

Under A.H.S.A. rules a fall in show-jumping incurs elimination, but under F.E.I. rules the penalty is eight faults, which, as in combined training, are additional to any other faults. A circle in order to retake the track after a fall is not penalized, and the rider should continue the course from a point no nearer the finish than where the fall took place.

false quarter a portion of thin brittle horn in the wall of the hoof, usually on the inner quarter, resulting from a defect in the horn-secreting tissue of the coronet. At the points where the defective horn joins the normal healthy horn of the hoof rifts or furrows may appear which resemble sand cracks.

fancied *racing* (of a horse) thought likely to win a particular race.

fancy matched (of horses in a harness team) having coats of distinctly different colours.

fanning *coaching* the act of lightly using a whip on the horses.

farrier a person who makes horseshoes and shoes horses. He may be a DOORMAN, who prepares the feet, nails the shoes on, and trims the feet and clinches the nails after shoeing, or a FIREMAN, who makes and fits new shoes.

Farriers, Worshipful Company of, an ancient livery company of the City of London, which was founded in the fourteenth century. It still retains an active interest in farriery and runs an apprentice scheme to encourage young men to go into and learn the trade.

fast martingale See STANDING MARTINGALE.

fatty frog See SENSITIVE FROG.

fault *show-jumping* a scoring unit used for recording any knockdown, refusal or other offence committed by a competitor during his round.

In ordinary competitions faults are incurred as follows:

exceeding the time allowed, for each second or part of a second	$\frac{1}{4}$ fault
knocking down an obstacle; landing on the tape or lath of a water jump or putting one foot or more in the water	4 faults
first refusal or disobedience	3 faults

Below
Falabella, a breed of miniature pony developed in the Argentine. The seven-year-old mare Nina, seen here, stands 29 inches high.

second refusal or disobedience   6 faults
fall of horse and/or rider   8 faults
(Faults incurred for a fall are additional to any faults that may be incurred at the same time.)

Jumping and time faults are added together to give the competitor's total for the round. See also ELIMINATION.

fav. *racing* favourite.

favour a leg (of a horse) to avoid putting its full weight on one of its legs. A horse which has an injury to a leg or shoulder will throw as much weight as possible on to the other legs. This is particularly noticeable in steeplechasing when a horse will jump diagonally across a fence rather than straight over it.

favourite *racing* the horse in a particular race having the shortest odds offered against it.

feather 1. the tufts of long hair on the fetlocks of various breeds of horse, such as the Clydesdale or the Shire. **2.** (of a hound) to wave the stern while driving along the presumed line of the scent with nose to the ground; usually an indication that the hound is uncertain that it is on the scent.

feather-edged shoe a type of horseshoe having a narrow inside edge which tapers towards the frog. Usually applied to the hind feet, feather-edged shoes are designed to prevent or minimize damage caused to the fetlocks of the opposite forefeet by brushing.

feather edging the act of driving a vehicle very close to another or close to an obstacle of any kind.

February fox *hunting* the name given during the mating month of February to a dog fox, which may go a long way from home in search of a vixen. It is, therefore, likely to give a straight hunt. Not knowing the surrounding country, it will make for its own territory.

Fédération Equestre Internationale the governing body of international equestrian sport, founded in 1921 by Commandant G. Hector of France, with headquarters at Brussels. The F.E.I. makes rules and regulations for the conduct of the three equestrian sports which comprise the Olympic Equestrian Games, and all national federations are required to comply with these rules and regulations in any international event which may be organized, although national federations may prescribe their own rules for national competitions.

The purposes of the federation are: to be the sole international body concerned with equitation for sporting purposes such as dressage, combined training, show-jumping and any other kind of equestrian sport; to promote the organization of all international equestrian sport; to publish and supervise the application of the rules to be observed at all international equestrian sporting events; and to prepare and approve the rules and programme for championships, regional and Olympic games, and to ensure the technical organization of such events. The official languages of the federation are French and English. Also called INTERNATIONAL EQUESTRIAN FEDERATION.

F.E.I. Fédération Equestre Internationale.

felloe the circular rim of a wheel round which the tyre is fixed. Also FELLY.

Fell pony a hardy breed of pony originating in the north-west of England, including Westmorland, Cumberland and the area bordering on the Lake District. The pony was used for riding by farmers, but was also driven to take them to market or their wives shopping. As they were very strong and could endure long journeys, Fell ponies were also used to haul the lead from the mines to the docks at Newcastle upon Tyne.

The breed society, formed in 1927, lays down the following rules. The height must not exceed 14 h.h., the colours accepted are black, brown, bay or grey, and the only white permitted is a star or a little white on the foot. The head should be small, well chiselled in outline, well set on, with a broad forehead tapering to a nose with large and expanding nostrils. The eyes should be prominent, bright, mild and intelligent. Ears must be neatly set on,

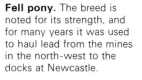

Fell pony. The breed is noted for its strength, and for many years it was used to haul lead from the mines in the north-west to the docks at Newcastle.

well formed and small. The neck should be of proportionate length, giving a good length of rein, strong and not too heavy. The shoulders should be well laid back with a good long blade. A strong back is essential with good outline, a good carcass, thick through the heart, round ribbed from the shoulders to the flank. The Fell should have short and well-coupled hindquarters, square and strong with the tail well set on. Feet should be of good size, round and well formed, with plenty of fine hair at the heels. The mane and tail should be allowed to grow. The action at the walk should be smart and true and at the trot well balanced and round, with good knee and hock action, going well from the shoulders.

felly See FELLOE.

felt pad a simple saddle-like form of thick felt which makes an excellent first saddle for a child. It is close fitting and may have detachable handlebars, a stout leather-covered cane, for the child to hold. The forerunner of the handlebar was the GLOSTER BAR consisting of two shaped and padded bars, which fitted over the top of the thighs. They gave slightly to the movement of the rider and would spring out of position in the event of a fall. Originally designed as a safety device for teaching young children to jump, they are still sometimes used to help the disabled.

fence 1. any obstacle to be jumped in steeple-chasing, cross-country, show-jumping or hunting. **2.** *racing* to jump over an obstacle.

fence cornering (Western US) a style of bucking in which the horse zigzags in a manner resembling the zigzags of the frontier rail fence.

fetlock 1. the joint in a horse's leg between the cannon bone and the long pastern bone. Also called FETLOCK JOINT. **2.** the tuft of hair at the back of this joint.

fiddle head a large plain coarse and ugly head.

field 1. *hunting* the mounted followers of a hunt. **2.** *racing* (a) all the horses running in a particular race. (b) all the horses not individually favoured in the betting.

field master *hunting* the master of the hounds, or someone appointed by him to look after and control the field while the hounds are both drawing and hunting.

Fifinella (by Polymelus out of Silver Fowl) Foaled in 1913, Fifinella was owned by Edward Hulton and trained by Richard Dawson at New-market. Ridden by Steve Donoghue, she won two races as a two-year-old — the Fulbourne Stakes and the Cheveley Park Stakes, both at Newmarket — and as a three-year-old, ridden by Joe Childs, she was beaten by half a length in the 1000-Guineas by Lord Derby's Canyon. In the Derby she ran very lazily but came through at the finish to win by a neck. It was consequently decided to run her again two days later in the Oaks, a race which she won by five lengths. She ran once again in the autumn of 1916 at Newmarket, where she finished third. Fifinella was then retired to stud, but she was not a great success.

She was the last horse to win the Derby and the Oaks in the same year. Her sire, Polymelus, was also the sire of two other Derby winners — Pommern, who won in 1915, and Humorist, the Derby-winner of 1921.

figging the act of putting an irritant, such as ginger, into a horse's anus in order to effect a high tail carriage, thus giving the animal a spirited appearance. Once common, especially at sales, figging is considered cruel and is seldom practised now. Also called GINGERING.

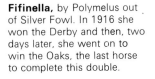

Fifinella, by Polymelus out of Silver Fowl. In 1916 she won the Derby and then, two days later, she went on to win the Oaks, the last horse to complete this double.

Fillis snaffle a bit which is jointed on either side of a low, wide central port, and has separate eyes for the cheekpieces, so that the bit is suspended in the mouth, as opposed to resting in it.

filly a female horse less than four years old.

filly foal See under FOAL.

final horse a horse which is extremely difficult to ride and is therefore kept for the final or championship of a rodeo contest.

fine harness horse an American Saddle-Horse driven to light harness.

finish *racing* A horse is said to finish a race when it passes the winning post mounted, providing, in the case of steeplechase or hurdle race, it has negotiated all the obstacles.

finished alone *racing* an expression used when only one horse finishes a race, the others having fallen or been pulled up, or when a horse wins a race by a very great margin.

Finnish Horse a breed of horse found in Finland and northern Scandinavia, and developed from native ponies, specifically as a general-purpose utility animal, in which agility and strength were considered of greater importance than conformation and appearance. About 15 h.h., the Finnish horse has an excellent constitution and a willingness to work.

fireman See under FARRIER.

fire-wagon (US) a sulky.

firing cauterization; the application of a hot iron or a caustic for curative purposes, used especially to treat sprained tendons or ligaments, sand cracks and bony deposits, such as ringbones, splints or bone spavins. In LINE FIRING (also called BAR FIRING) parallel lines about one inch apart are drawn across the area to be treated, the firing iron penetrating only the superficial layers of the skin, while in PIN FIRING (also called POINT FIRING) the point of the iron is allowed to penetrate the whole thickness of the skin, the tissue or tendon, and, in the case of bony deposits, the bone itself. In ACID FIRING, the hair is removed from the area requiring treatment and sulphuric acid is applied to the skin in small regular circles.

first jockey the principal person engaged by an owner or trainer to ride for him.

first spear the honour in pigsticking of being allowed to plant the first spear or to make the first draw of blood from a wild boar. Also called SPEAR OF HONOUR.

first whipper-in the huntsman's first assistant with a pack of hounds.

fistula a suppurative inflammation characterized by the formation of sinuses through the tissue to the surface of the skin. Fistulas may occur in any part of the body, but most commonly appear on the poll, the condition known as POLL EVIL, or at the height of the withers (known as FISTULOUS WITHERS). In both cases they usually result from an injury, such as a bite or blow, or from badly fitting harness or saddlery.

fistulous withers See under FISTULA.

Fitzwilliam girth a leather and web girth introduced in the nineteenth century and now little used. It consisted of a broad strap, double the width of an ordinary girth, which at each end divided into two, each branch terminating in a buckle. Along the centre of the girth was sewn a narrow strap, also with a buckle at each end, the idea being that should any or all of the buckles on the main strap fail the saddle would still remain securely in place.

five-gaited saddler See under AMERICAN SADDLE-HORSE.

Fjord pony a breed of pony native to Norway. A sturdy, well-muscled animal, it is very adaptable and is widely used for all types of agricultural work. Dun to cream in colour, the Fjord pony has a distinctive dorsal stripe. The legs are sometimes striped, and the upright, often eel-striped mane is customarily trimmed to a crescent shape. Also called FJORDING, NORTHFIELD.

F.K.S.B. Foxhound Kennel Stud Book.

flanchard armour for a horse's flanks, used in medieval times.

flank that part of the horse behind the ribs, below the loins and reaching to the belly.

flapper *racing* a horse which runs at an unauthorized race meeting. Such a horse is never allowed to run under the rules of racing, either on the flat or steeplechasing.

flapping *racing* an unofficial meeting which is not held under the rules of racing.

flat catcher a flashy good-looking horse which is of little practical value.

flat foot a big foot with a very large frog and open weak heel, a condition generally found in carthorses and harness horses. As a rule, the sole is flat rather than concave. Flat feet are usually liable to corns and bruises, and horses with this complaint, therefore, should not be used for excessive roadwork.

flat racing racing in which there are no obstacles for the horses to jump, though the ground may not necessarily be level and may include inclines and declines.

flat-sided (of a horse) having ribs that are not round and well sprung.

flecked (of a horse) having patches of white hair scattered irregularly over any part of the body.

fleshy frog See SENSITIVE FROG.

fleshy sole See SENSITIVE SOLE.

flight *racing* a hurdle.

flighty hound a hound which is unreliable.

float a later version of the governess cart, with two seats facing the front. Designed for use by tradesmen, such as dairymen, it was low and therefore easy to load and unload with goods. Like the governess cart, it could be drawn by a pony.

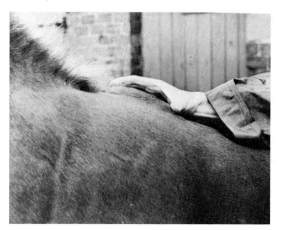

fistula, a permanent running sore on the poll or withers, which begins as a marked swelling.

floorman a bookmaker's runner on a racecourse.

flower rowel a type of rowel shaped like the petals of a daisy.

flute bit See under CRIB BITING.

fly cap a netting cap fitted over a horse's ears and forehead in order to protect it against flies.

fly fence *hunting* an obstacle which can be jumped at the gallop.

flying change a change of leading leg executed at the canter without change of pace. The horse should remain straight and there should be a simultaneous change in the fore and hind legs, so that the legs strike the ground in the correct sequence.

fly whisk a long switch of horsehair bound at one end to a wooden handle used by riders to brush flies off their horses.

foal the young of the horse up to the age of twelve months, usually referred to specifically as a COLT FOAL (male) or a FILLY FOAL (female).

foal head collar a type of head collar resembling the Dutch slip, but slightly more elaborate in that it also has a throat piece.

foal heat a mare's first heat after foaling, usually five to eighteen days after the birth of the foal.

foaling table

DATE OF SERVICE		DUE TO FOAL		DATE OF SERVICE		DUE TO FOAL	
1st	Jan	6th	Dec	2nd	Jul	6th	Jun
8th	Jan	13th	Dec	9th	Jul	13th	Jun
15th	Jan	20th	Dec	16th	Jul	20th	Jun
22nd	Jan	27th	Dec	23rd	Jul	27th	Jun
29th	Jan	3rd	Jan	30th	Jul	4th	Jul
5th	Feb	10th	Jan	6th	Aug	11th	Jul
12th	Feb	17th	Jan	13th	Aug	18th	Jul
19th	Feb	24th	Jan	20th	Aug	25th	Jul
26th	Feb	31st	Jan	27th	Aug	1st	Aug
5th	Mar	7th	Feb	3rd	Sep	8th	Aug
12th	Mar	14th	Feb	10th	Sep	15th	Aug
19th	Mar	21st	Feb	17th	Sep	22nd	Aug
26th	Mar	28th	Feb	24th	Sep	29th	Aug
2nd	Apr	7th	Mar	1st	Oct	5th	Sep
9th	Apr	14th	Mar	8th	Oct	12th	Sep
16th	Apr	21st	Mar	15th	Oct	19th	Sep
23rd	Apr	28th	Mar	22nd	Oct	26th	Sep
30th	Apr	4th	Apr	29th	Oct	3rd	Oct
7th	May	11th	Apr	5th	Nov	10th	Oct
14th	May	18th	Apr	12th	Nov	17th	Oct
21st	May	25th	Apr	19th	Nov	24th	Oct
28th	May	2nd	May	26th	Nov	31st	Oct
4th	Jun	9th	May	3rd	Dec	7th	Nov
11th	Jun	16th	May	10th	Dec	14th	Nov
18th	Jun	23rd	May	17th	Dec	21st	Nov
25th	Jun	30th	May	24th	Dec	28th	Nov

foal head collar.

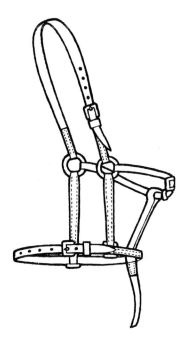

foil *hunting* any kind of scent which obliterates that of the fox, so the hounds are not able to keep hunting. This occurs if a fox crosses a field in which there are cattle or sheep which then cross the line of the fox before the hounds come to it. Also called STAIN.

fold the whip to wrap the thong and lash lightly round the shaft of the whip with a quick movement of the whip hand; the correct way of holding the whip when driving.

footboard the board on a coach upon which the coachman rests his feet.

foot follower *hunting* a person who follows a pack of hounds by any means other than on horseback.

forearm the part of a horse's foreleg between the elbow and the knee.

fore-carriage the front section of the underpart of a four-wheeled carriage, to which the front wheels are attached.

forecast 1. a prediction made in advance of a particular race, generally by a tipster, about which horse will win, or the order in which the horses will finish. **2.** a totalizator bet in racing in which the backer is required to select the horses which finish first and second. In Great Britain, for races with three to six runners, the tote runs a STRAIGHT FORECAST POOL, and the backer must select the first two horses to finish in the correct order. For races with seven to ten runners a DUAL FORECAST POOL is run, and the backer must select two horses to finish first and second in either order.

forehand the part of a horse which is in front of the rider; the head, neck, shoulders, withers and forelegs.

foreleg either of a horse's front legs.

forelock the tuft of hair which grows between a horse's ears and hangs over the forehead.

form the past performances of a horse in racing. An evaluation of form is one method of assessing the chance a horse may have in a given race.

form book a book giving details of the past records of racehorses.

form figures the figures shown on a programme or race card, giving the recent placings of a horse in races.

form fitter any Western saddle which has both a wide undercut fork and cantle to fit the form of the rider.

fothering time feeding time for horses in hunt or farm stables.

Four Horse Club a driving club founded in 1808, the year in which the Earl of Albemarle was admitted to Parliament, when it became fashionable for members not only to acquire the skill of their coachmen, but also to ape their dress, manners and language. One Sunday seven members met at the top of St James's Street and raced their hackney coaches to the north end of Dean's Yard. Also called FOUR-IN-HAND CLUB.

four-in-hand 1. a team of four horses, consisting of two wheelers and two leaders. **2.** a vehicle drawn by four horses.

Four-in-Hand Club See FOUR HORSE CLUB.

fox a carnivorous mammal of the canine family, genus *Vulpes*, having a pointed muzzle, erect ears and a long bushy tail. The common European red fox, which is reddish brown in colour, lives off small animals and birds, and usually hunts for its prey at night.

fox dog (US) a foxhound.

foxhound one of a breed of swift, keen-scented hounds bred and trained for hunting foxes. Standing about twenty-two to twenty-five inches high at the shoulder, the foxhound is characterized by a compact muscular body, with a deep well-developed chest and powerful legs. The coat is short and smooth, and the normal coloration is white with black, tan or biscuit-coloured markings on the head and body, although some hunts, according to the type of country they hunt, breed hounds of a particular colour. There is no set number of foxhounds to a pack and the number varies from one hunt to another. Not all the hounds in a pack will be taken hunting each day. Also called FOX DOG (US).

Foxhound Kennel Stud Book a register dating back to 1856, in which the hounds of a pack may be entered, providing the master is a member of the Master of Foxhounds Association, the body which administers it.

foxhunter 1. a person who takes part in the sport of foxhunting. **2.** a horse kept or used for fox-hunting.

Foxhunter *GB* (bay gelding, 16.3½ h.h.) Foaled in 1941, this world famous show-jumper, owned and ridden by Lt Col. Harry Llewellyn, became a legendary figure. He had his first major success at the International Horse Show at the White City in 1947, and the following year was in the bronze medal team at the Olympic Games in London. Later the same year he won the King George V Gold Trophy at the International Horse Show, a feat he was to repeat in 1950 and 1953. He first travelled abroad to Le Zoute in Belgium in 1947 and then competed virtually all over the world, representing Great Britain on no less that thirty-five occasions. The highlight of his career was in 1952 when he was in the gold medal team at the Olympic Games in Helsinki. Foxhunter died in 1959, and his skeleton now stands at the Royal College of Veterinary Surgeons in London.

Foxhunter Competition See 'DAILY EXPRESS' NATIONAL FOXHUNTER CHAMPIONSHIP.

foxhunting the hunting of the fox in its natural state by a pack of foxhounds, followed by people mounted on horses or on foot. In its modern form foxhunting has been an important institution of British life for nearly 200 years; before that time it was of secondary importance to the hunting of stags and hares. A foxhunt is conducted by the master and a traditional procedure is always followed. Originally reserved for the gentry, foxhunting is now enjoyed by people from all walks of life and in the hunting field all social distinctions are levelled and precedence is given only to the master and the hunt staff. Foxhunting has lost little of its popularity since its heyday in the nineteenth century when it established itself as the most important field sport in Britain.

Foxhunting has also flourished in the United States, which has hunting clubs dating back to the eighteenth century, although it has had to adjust itself to different conditions. For lists of hunts in Great Britain and the United States see pages 219–221 and 222.

Far right
Frederiksborg. Formerly a carriage horse, this Danish breed is now used principally for riding.

Franches-Montagnes a breed of horse developed in Switzerland by crossing native mares with Anglo-Norman stallions. About 15.2 h.h., the breed is immensely strong, compact and very active. It is popular for work on small farms and is also widely used by the Swiss Army for draught purposes. Also called FREIBERGER, JURA.

frank an enclosure for wild boar.

fray (of a stag) to rub the antlers against a FRAYING POST, a tree, post or the like, in order to remove the velvet.

fream the noise made by the wild boar; a grunt.

Frederiksborg a Danish breed of horse used for riding, driving and light agricultural work, and originally established during the reign of King Frederick II for use as a charger. About 15.3 h.h. and almost invariably chestnut in colour, the breed is noted for its good conformation and excellent temperament, and is rapidly becoming one of the most popular riding horses in Europe.

free-for-all horse a trotter capable of trotting or pacing in a fast no-handicap race.

free-legged pacer a pacer which runs without hobbles.

Freeman, Kevin, *US* (born 1941) As a child Kevin Freeman started riding Western style but changed to English style at the age of fifteen. With

Good Mixture he won the United States Three-Day Event National Trials in 1964 and 1966, and the National Intermediate Trials in 1971. In 1963 he was a member of the American gold medal team at the Pan-American Games at São Paulo and the following year he was a member of the silver medal team at the Olympic Games in Tokyo, an achievement he was to repeat in 1968, when he

foxhunting. The Portman Foxhounds fording the River Allen near Witchampton in Dorset.

rode the ex-Argentinian horse Chalan, and in Munich in 1972, riding Good Mixture.

free walk *dressage* a walk in which the reins are stretched to the fullest extent and the horse is allowed complete freedom of the head and neck.

Freiberger See FRANCHES-MONTAGNES.

French bradoon a type of bit resembling the Dick Christian, but having the parts of the mouth-piece joined by a plate, as opposed to a link.

French panel See under PANEL.

fresh *racing* (of a horse) having had a rest from the racecourse.

fresh fox *hunting* the name given to a fox to which hounds suddenly turn their attention, having broken off pursuit of their original quarry.

fresh-legged (of a young horse) showing no signs of having been hard worked.

friendly event any combined training, dressage or show-jumping event which does not have international standing, but which includes one competition or more open to competitors from one other nation, who attend individually with the per-mission of their national federation. In such events the competition open to foreign riders must be held under the rules of the F.E.I.

Friesian The Friesian, one of the oldest surviving horses of Europe, is found in the Friesian district of the Netherlands. From fossils found in excavations it has been discovered that a heavy horse was present in this district over 3000 years ago. The horse was thick set, strong and heavy, and so later answered the requirements of warfare in medieval times. The rich pastures of Friesland were ideal for the development of the breed. How-ever, in the eighteenth century trotting races became very popular in Holland. Breeders began to con-centrate on producing a very much lighter horse, and the Friesian dropped in popularity as a horse for general use. Although a stud book society was formed in the nineteenth century, the breed con-tinued to decline until just before the First World War, when there were only three registered stal-lions left. A new society was formed after the war, which has gone from strength to strength, and in 1954 Queen Juliana granted it the prefix *Royal*.

The present Friesian stands about 15 h.h., with an attractive, compact, muscular appearance, and is always jet black in colour. It is still very much in use as a harness horse.

frog the triangular elastic pad of horn occupying the space between the bars in the undersurface of a horse's foot. It runs to a point towards the toe, and at the back, where it is divided by a shallow depression known as the CLEFT, it forms the bulbs of the heels. It contains about forty per cent of moisture, giving it the consistency of indiarubber. Also called HORNY FROG.

frog band a light-coloured, soft, horny structure, which runs round the top and outside of the foot of the horse at the junction of the hoof and the skin and becomes blended with the bulbs of the frog. It has a protective influence on the newly secreted horn and should never be destroyed.

front See BROWBAND.

front jockey the leather on the top of the skirt of a Western saddle, which fits closely round the horn.

front runner *racing* the horse which leads the field and sets the pace.

full (of a horse) not gelded.

full brothers and sisters horses which have the same sire and dam. Also called OWN BROTHERS AND SISTERS.

full mouth the mouth of a horse at six years old, when it has grown all its teeth.

full panel See under PANEL.

Fulmer snaffle a snaffle bit having cheekpieces attached to the jointed mouthpiece, with the rings outside the cheeks. Also called AUSTRALIAN LOOSE-RING CHEEK SNAFFLE.

Furioso a hardy, robust breed of horse developed in Austria-Hungary during the nineteenth century from Furioso, a Thoroughbred stallion imported from England in about 1836, and North Star, a stallion, reputedly with Norfolk Roadster blood, imported in about 1844. Many other English stallions were later used to strengthen the breed. The early Furioso stock was distributed to studs throughout the Austro-Hungarian Empire, so that there are now marked regional variations in size and colour. The principal use of the Furioso is as a saddle-horse but there are heavier types, which in some countries are used for light draught and agricultural work.

furlong *racing* a unit of measurement equal to one-eighth of a mile and frequently used to describe the length of races which are not exact miles or half-miles, e.g. ten furlongs, instead of a mile and a quarter.

furniture any item of harness or saddlery put on a horse.

futchells the timber or iron of the fore-carriage of a horse-drawn vehicle, to which the pole is attached.

Futurity Stakes a race for two-year-old horses over a distance of $6\frac{1}{2}$ furlongs. First run in 1888 at Sheepshead Bay, it was held at Saratoga in 1910, 1913 and 1914. It was then moved to Belmont Park, Long Island, where it has been held ever since, except in 1959 and 1960, and from 1962 to 1967, when it was held at Aqueduct. Up to 1892 and from 1902 to 1904 the distance of the race was $\frac{3}{4}$ mile; from 1892 to 1900 it was $1263\frac{1}{3}$ yards; and from 1925 to 1933 it was approximately $\frac{7}{8}$ mile. (For results see pages 252–253.)

fuzztail running (US) the act of herding and catching wild horses.

gad (Western US) a spur.

gaff (Western US) to spur on a horse.

gag bit a bit used to raise the horse's head. A wide variety of designs exists, but the gag commonly has two holes in each bit ring, and through these the bridle cheekpieces are passed. The cheekpieces, usually of rounded leather, are sewn or joined directly to the reins in order to give the bit the upward action desired. Gags are divided into two basic types: those designed for use on their own, such as the Col. Rodzianko gag and the Chelten-ham gag, and those designed for use with a curb bit, in place of a snaffle in a double bridle, such as the Duncan gag. See also HACK OVERCHEEK, HITCHCOCK GAG.

gag bridle the type of bridle used with a gag bit. The cheekpieces, made of rounded leather, are passed through holes at the top and bottom of the bit rings and attached directly to the reins. The gag bridle is particularly useful for horses which have a low head carriage.

Furioso mares and foals.

Haflinger, the native pony
of Austria, found chiefly in
the Austrian Alps and
Bavaria.

Gainsborough, winner of
the Triple Crown in 1918,
and the sire of Hyperion.

Far right
Garrano, an extremely hardy
Portuguese breed

Gainsborough (by Bayardo out of Rosedrop)
Foaled in 1915, Gainsborough was owned by
Lady James Douglas and trained by Alec Taylor.
His early good looks rather deceived, for as a two-
year-old he won only the Autumn Stakes (6 furlongs) at Newmarket. However, several people
were interested in purchasing the horse, especially
in the United States, but Lady Douglas would not
sell him. His first race in 1918 was in the Severals
Stakes at Newmarket, in which he was unplaced.
He was then entered for the 2000-Guineas and,
ridden by Joe Childs, he won by one and a half
lengths, Lady Douglas thus becoming the first
woman to own a classic winner in her own colours.
He went on to win a wartime Derby run at Newmarket by one and a half lengths from stable companion Blink. He later won the long-distance Newmarket Gold Cup and completed the Triple Crown
by winning the St Leger from another stable companion, My Dear, by three lengths. In his final race,
the Jockey Club Stakes, he was beaten by stable
companion Prince Chamay.

On retiring to stud, Gainsborough became one
of the most successful and influential stallions. His
most famous offspring was Hyperion, and his
blood still has a strong influence on breeding all
over the world. He died in 1945 at the age of thirty.

gaiting strap a strap which runs along the inside
of the shafts of a trotting sulky from front to rear
used to prevent the horse from running sideways.

gall a skin sore usually occurring under the saddle
or girth, caused by dirty, damaged or badly fitting
saddlery.

Galvayne's groove a dark groove in the centre
of the outer surface of the upper corner incisors.
It first appears as a short line at the top of the
tooth when a horse is eight to ten years old. As
the horse grows older, the groove extends downwards and reaches the bottom of the tooth when
the animal is about twenty.

gambler's choice US name for HAVE A GAMBLE.

gammon board the seat on the roof of a coach
at the front. See also BACK GAMMON BOARD.

Garrano a lightly built breed of pony found in the
rich pastures of the mountain valleys in Portugal.
Between 10 h.h. and 12 h.h. and usually dark
chestnut in colour, with a long mane and tail, the
Garrano is extremely hardy and is used mainly for
farm and forestry work.

Garrison finish (US) a fast and spectacular
finish to a race, so named after the famous jockey
Snapper Garrison, who nearly always won his
races in a spectacular manner.

garron any native pony of Scotland or Ireland.

gaskin the part of a horse's hind leg between the
stifle and the hock. Also called SECOND THIGH.

gate 1. the number of people who pay for
admission to any sporting function. **2.** the total
amount of money paid by those people.

gaucho a cowboy of the South American pampas.

gee a word of command to agricultural horses
directing them to turn right. Also HECK. See also
ARVE.

gee up a command to horses, etc., directing them
to move faster.

Gelderland a breed of horse from the Gelderland
province of the Netherlands, used for light

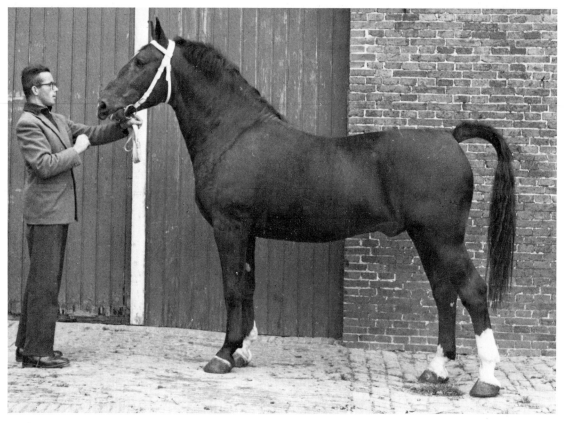

Gelderland. This is a very popular harness breed in the Netherlands.

Far right
general-purpose saddle.

agricultural work, in harness and as a saddle-horse. During the nineteenth century breeders in Gelderland imported numerous stallions of various breeds, including English Thoroughbreds, Norfolk trotters and Holsteins, which they crossed with mares of a very old native breed. The best offspring were interbred and gradually a type became established, which was consolidated by further selective breeding. There were later additions of outside blood and at about the turn of the century Hackney stallions were used, but since then the only new blood has been from Anglo-Normans.

About 15.2 h.h., the Gelderland is a compact, muscular animal with a good lively action. The predominant colours are chestnut, often with white markings, and grey.

gelding a male horse which has been castrated.

general-purpose saddle a type of saddle designed for general use and characterized by a deep seat, sloped-back head and forward supporting rolls for the thighs. The tree — normally a spring tree — is shaped to conform with the line of the horse's back. All bulk under the thighs is eliminated by putting the stirrup bars under the tree instead of on top of it, by reducing the width at the waist of the panel and the length of the points of the tree below the bar, and by sloping the head backwards so that the points are moved forward and clear of the thigh.

gentle to handle a horse, especially a young one, with kindness and understanding in order to gain its confidence.

German snaffle a snaffle bit having a hollow, jointed mouthpiece and loose round rings, used especially for racing, as it is very light. The same type of mouthpiece is also produced with eggbutt rings and is sometimes used in the Fulmer.

German trotter It was only towards the last half of the nineteenth century that trotting became popular in Germany. The first club, the Altona, was formed in Hamburg in 1874, and the first trotting stud was established some ten years later. The German trotter was based on the Orlov trotter, which was imported from Russia, but the standard was considerably raised when horses were imported from the United States, and in more recent years French horses have been introduced. German trotters have an excellent reputation for temperament and tractability. They are often bred on small farms with only one or two mares.

gestation the period between conception and foaling; in horses normally about eleven months. See also FOALING TABLE.

get the offspring of a stallion.

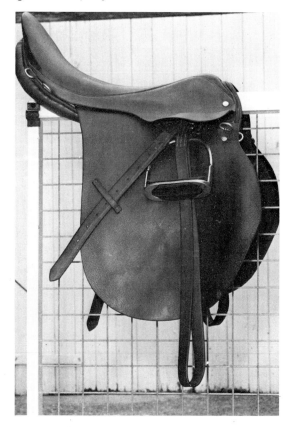

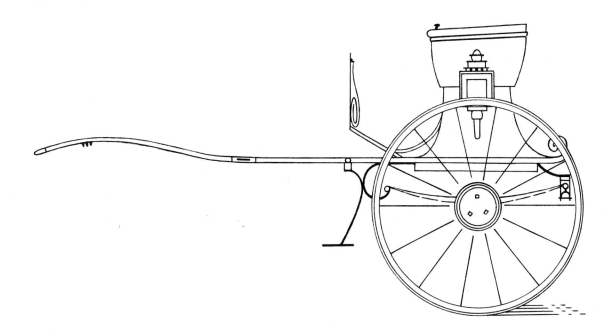

get left *racing* (of a horse) to fail to start with the other horses when the starting gate goes up or the stalls open.

getting up A horse which is lying down stands up by pushing itself on to the haunches with the forelegs and then, extending them slightly in front, raises the hindquarters.

get under (of a horse) to miss its stride and take off too close to an obstacle, in show-jumping, steeplechasing, etc., and thus make an awkward jump, which may result in a fall or in knocking the obstacle down.

gig a light two-wheeled carriage drawn by a single horse. Introduced at the end of the eighteenth century, the gig was much favoured by fashionable ladies for riding in the parks and similar places. The gig required careful construction to avoid an irritating jogging motion arising from the spring of the shafts. However, it became very popular throughout the country and many variations were built. See also DENNETT GIG, LAWTON GIG, LIVERPOOL GIG, STANHOPE GIG, TILBURY GIG.

Gimcrack Stakes a horserace for two-year-olds over a distance of 6 furlongs ($\frac{3}{4}$ mile). Introduced in 1846, it was one of the first major races to be held at York. (For results see page 240.)

gimlet (Western US) to ride a horse in such a manner as will make its back sore.

gingering See FIGGING.

girth 1. the circumference of a horse, measured behind the withers round the deepest part of the body. **2.** a band, usually of leather, webbing or nylon, passed under the belly of a horse to hold the saddle in place. The exact position of the girth around the horse depends very much on the conformation of the withers and the back, but it should be placed far enough back to prevent chafing the elbows. See also ATHERSTONE GIRTH, BALDING GIRTH, FITZWILLIAM GIRTH, THREE-FOLD GIRTH.

girth safe a leather guard which is slipped over

the girth buckles so that they do not damage the saddle flap.

girth sleeve a cover, usually made of sheepskin or rubber, put round a girth to prevent chafing.

girth strap one of the straps on a saddle to which the girth is buckled. There are always two and often three girth straps on each side of the saddle.

give a horse its head to allow a horse greater freedom in running.

give tongue *hunting* (of hounds) to bark or bay when in full cry after a quarry.

give weight *racing* (of a horse) to carry more weight than another horse and thus suffer a proportionately greater handicap.

Gladstone, New Jersey In 1961 Hamilton Farm at Gladstone was made available as a training centre for the United States Equestrian Team by the Brady Security and Realty Corporation. The estate lies in approximately 7000 acres and includes some beautiful wooded countryside.

The stables were built at the beginning of the twentieth century by Wall Street financier James Cox Brady, and provide accommodation for fifty horses on two floors.

The large indoor school is known as Nautical Hall, after the famous American show-jumper. The outdoor arena, which is enclosed by a stone wall, is 350 feet by 280 feet and has a sand mixture surface with an effective watering system. In the 4000 acres available to the teams there are dressage arenas, show-jumping and galloping space, as well as a cross-country course.

glass eye See WALL EYE.

globe cheek Pelham a curb bit used independently of a snaffle. It has a downward and inward action which is produced by pressure on the bars of the mouth, the poll and the curb groove. If the cheekpiece is too long there may be some danger of the horse's becoming overbent.

Gloster bar See under FELT PAD.

Above
Godolphin Arabian, the third of the famous founding sires of the English Thoroughbred.

Far right
Golden Miller, with Gerry Wilson up, winner of five consecutive Cheltenham Gold Cups, from 1932 to 1936, and of the Grand National in 1934.

goal judge See GOAL REFEREE.

goal referee *polo* an official who stands behind the goal and by waving a flag indicates to the umpire whether or not a goal has been scored. If a goal has been scored, the goal referee waves the flag above his head. If not, he waves it in front of his legs. Also called GOAL JUDGE.

go amiss *racing* (of a mare) to come into season when she is due to run in a race.

goat leap See CAPRIOLE.

goat-snatching See KOK-PAR.

go big (US) to go flat out at the start of a trotting race.

Godolphin Arabian one of the three stallions which made such an outstanding contribution to the basis of the English Thoroughbred. Originally called Scham, he was one of eight Barbary horses presented by the Bey of Tunis to Louis XV in 1731. He was about 15 h.h. and brown bay with a white spot on the off hind leg. Because he was said to be vicious, he was later sold, and the story goes that in 1732 an Englishman in Paris on business saw him being used to pull a load of timber which was far too heavy for him. He promptly bought the horse to save him from further cruelty and then brought him back to England, but the horse's viciousness renewed and he was sold again. His new owner was Lord Godolphin. It was in error that Scham was allowed to serve one of his mares, and Lord Godolphin was so angry that the horse was banished from his stud. However: Lath, the foal, showed some fine racing points, with the result that Scham was reinstated at the stud. He proved very successful, his progeny winning many races,

and was renamed the Godolphin Arabian. He died in 1753 at the age of twenty-nine. See also BYERLEY TURK, DARLEY ARABIAN.

go gimpy (of a horse) to move stiffly and sorely.

going the condition of a race track or other ground over which a horse travels. The going may variously be described as 'hard', 'soft', 'firm', 'good', 'heavy' or 'yielding'.

go into the bridle (of a horse) to take hold of the bit firmly.

Golden Horse of the West See PALOMINO.

Golden Miller (by Gold Count out of Miller's Pride) Foaled in 1927, Golden Miller was bred in

County Meath by Laurence Geraghty. In 1930 'The Miller' was purchased as an unbroken three-year-old by Basil Briscoe, who lived near Cambridge, for £500. The horse's first outing was in September of the same year, when he ran unimpressively in a hurdle race at Southwell. He was then sold to Philip Carr, but remained in training with Briscoe. His next race was at Newbury, where he finished a creditable third. The following year he was sold to the Hon. Dorothy Paget.

It was in 1932, as a five-year-old, that Golden Miller began to make his name, winning the Cheltenham Gold Cup, a feat he was to repeat in 1933, 1934, 1935 and 1936 — a truly remarkable record. In 1933 he won the Motre Chase at Hurst Park and the Troytown Chase at Lingfield. In the Grand National that year he fell at the Canal Turn, but won the race the following year, thus completing the Gold Cup and Grand National double. In August 1935 he changed stables and was trained for the remainder of his racing career by Owen Anthony. In 1938 he was beaten by two lengths in the Cheltenham Gold Cup by Macaulay: this was his final race. Out of a total of fifty-five races he had won twenty-nine, and had been ridden by fourteen different jockeys, including Gerry Wilson, Frenchie Nicholson and Fulke Walwyn.

Gold Vase See QUEEN'S VASE.

gone in the wind (of a horse) unsound in the wind. It may mean that the horse is a roarer, a whistler or broken-winded.

gone to ground *hunting* (of a fox) having taken refuge in an earth or a drain.

good hand class a riding competition for children held at horseshows in the United States. The emphasis in the class is on the good use of the hands.

good hound man a person who is keenly interested in breeding and hunting hounds. When hunting he will be up with the hounds, in order to watch them working.

good mouth (of a horse) a soft, sensitive mouth.

good night the expression used at parting after a hunt, no matter how early in the day it may be. Even in cub hunting, which often ends before midday, it is customary for the members of the hunt to bid one another good night.

good rein a correctly positioned head combined with a good neck and shoulders. If a horse has a good rein the saddle fits correctly, thus giving the rider the perfect position.

Goodwood a racecourse in Sussex, on the Duke of Richmond's estate, some sixty miles south-west of London. Racing was first held there in 1801, when the third Duke of Richmond organized hunter races. The course gradually became very popular, especially after Lord George Bentinck took over the management in 1840, for he paid particular attention to the amenities for the public, something which had not previously been considered on racecourses. He was also responsible for introducing the parade of horses in the paddock before each race and the official race card.

Goodwood Cup a handicap horserace over a distance of 2 miles 5 furlongs, instituted in 1812 by the Earl of March and held annually at Goodwood. (For results see page 241.)

goose rump hindquarters which fall away sharply from the highest part towards the tail.

Gordon-Watson, Mary Diana, *GB* (born 1948) Mary Gordon-Watson is the only woman rider to have won the World Three-Day Event Championship, a feat she accomplished at Punchestown, Ireland, in 1970, where she was also a member of the winning British team. A year earlier she had won the European Championship at Haras du Pin in France, and in 1971 she was a member of the winning British team in the European Championships at Burghley. The climax of her career so far came in 1972 at the Munich Olympic Games, where she was a member of the team which won the gold medal, and finished fourth in the individual placings. All her successes have been on her father's Cornishman V, who in 1968 at the Olympic Games in Mexico was ridden by Richard Meade in the gold medal team.

governess cart.

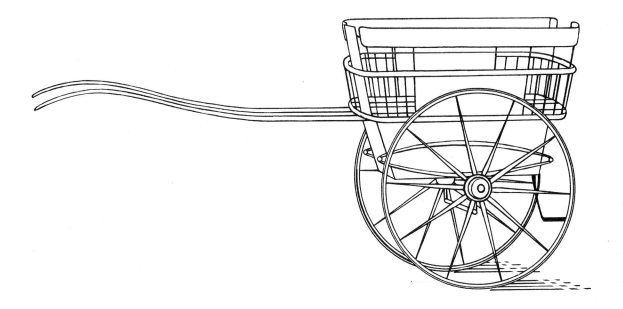

go-round a preliminary round in a rodeo contest. The number of go-rounds varies, depending on the size of the rodeo, between one in a small contest to seven or more in a large rodeo. The winner of each go-round wins a purse and the right to compete for the grand prize at the end of the contest.

go short (of a horse) to be lame or restricted in its action. When first brought out of the stable a horse may go short because of stiffness, which will wear off as soon as it has gone a little way.

go through the field *racing* (of a horse) to come from the back of the field, passing the other runners in the race, and take up a position among the leaders.

governess cart a light low two-wheeled closed trap with seating for four passengers, which was introduced at the beginning of the twentieth century. It was entered by a door at the rear, and was designed to be drawn by a pony. Although not the easiest vehicle to drive, it was very safe and was widely used for transporting children.

gr. grey.

grab the apple (Western US) to catch hold of the saddle horn while riding a bucking horse. Also termed GRAB THE POST, HUNT LEATHER.

grab the post See GRAB THE APPLE.

grading the system of classing animals according to their cash winnings:

combined training
Grade I Any horse which has won a total of £40 or more at official horse trials or three-day events.
Grade II Any horse which has won a total of £15 to £39, inclusive, at official horse trials or three-day events, or any horse which having won less than £15 has represented Great Britain in a C.C.I. abroad or in a C.C.I.O.
Grade III Any horse which has won a total of less than £15 at official horse trials or events.

Only prize money advertised in a schedule is considered in grading; awards for completing the course, etc., do not count.

show-jumping
(GB)
Grade A Any horse which has won £300 or more.
Grade B Any horse which has won £150 to £299, inclusive.
Grade C Any horse which has won less than £150.
Grade JA Any pony which has won £50 or more.
Grade JC Any pony which has won less than £50.

A horse or **pony** may only enter competitions of the

Below
Grand National Handicap Steeplechase. 1972: Graham Thorner and Well To Do, owned and trained by Tim Forster, already set for victory after clearing Becher's Brook on the first circuit.

appropriate grade, and once an animal has been upgraded it can never be downgraded.

(US)
Open Any horse which has won $3000 or more.
Preliminary Any horse which has won less than $1000.
Intermediate Any horse which has won $1000 to $2999, inclusive.

Grainger martingale a type of standing martingale which is attached to the girth in the normal way and divides at the breast into two arms, which are permanently attached to the noseband. It is adjusted by means of a buckle on the main strap.

Grand Circuit the annual calendar of races organized by the American Trotting League. The dates of races held at trotting tracks all over the United States are arranged to fit into a programme running from mid-April to October.

Grand Liverpool Steeplechase See GRAND NATIONAL HANDICAP STEEPLECHASE.

Grand National Handicap Steeplechase a steeplechase over thirty-one fences and a distance of 4 miles 856 yards held at Aintree since 1837, except from 1916 to 1918, when it was run at Gatwick. Formerly called GRAND LIVERPOOL STEEPLECHASE (until 1843), LIVERPOOL AND NATIONAL STEEPLECHASE (until 1847). (For results see pages 249–250.) See also under AINTREE.

Below
Grand National Handicap Steeplechase. The field jumps a formidable Becher's Brook fence in the 1969 running of the Grand National, which was won by twelve-year-old Highland Wedding.

grass yard a run or enclosure for hounds, used especially in warm weather.

graze to feed on growing grass.

grazing a pasture; grassland.

Great Metropolitan Handicap a horserace over 2 miles 2 furlongs (2¼ miles), held annually since 1846 at Epsom. (For results see page 241.)

Great Ovation See under PHILLIPS, CAPTAIN MARK.

great pastern bone See under PASTERN BONE.

green 1. (of a horse) broken but not fully trained; inexperienced. **2.** (US; of a trotter or pacer) not having been raced against the clock.

green-broke (US) a horse which has been ridden only a few times.

green hunter class a competition held at horse-shows in the United States for horses which have not hunted more than one season with a recognized pack of foxhounds and which have not won a first prize in a hunter division of a recognized show prior to 1st January that year.

grey a dark-skinned horse having a coat of black hairs and white hairs. With each successive change of coat the proportion of white hair increases, so that as the horse grows older its coat gradually becomes lighter until it is eventually completely white.

groom 1. any person, male or female, who is responsible for looking after a horse or horses. **2.** to clean the coat and feet of a horse or pony. Any horse kept in a stable should be groomed daily, not only to improve its appearance, but also to help keep the skin in good condition and prevent disease.

grooming kit collectively, the brushes and other items of equipment used to groom a horse; namely, a bodybrush, currycomb, dandy brush, hoof pick, mane and tail comb, sponges (used for wiping the eyes, nostrils, dock and sheath), stable rubber and water brush.

ground (Western US) to let the reins touch the ground after dismounting, so that the horse will stand without having to be tied up.

ground money (in a rodeo) the entry fee and purse money split equally among all the contestants in an event when there is no outright winner.

groy a horse.

guard a liveried attendant on a road coach whose duties were to help the passengers on and off and to blow the coach-horn in order to clear the way.

guard rail 1. *steeplechasing* a thick pole put in front of an open ditch in order to make a horse stand back to jump. **2.** *show-jumping* a pole put in front of an obstacle a few inches off the ground in order to make the jump easier, especially in novice competitions as an encouragement to a horse to jump.

guard's pouch a leather bag with a shoulder strap carried by the guard on a coach. It had a travelling clock set into the side and was used for carrying any tools which might be needed on the journey for making repairs.

guard's seat a slightly raised seat on the nearside at the rear of a coach which was reserved for the guard.

guinea hunter (formerly) a man who acted as a

Above
grooming kit. In the box: sponges, a body brush and a rubber currycomb; in front: a tail bandage, a mane and tail comb and a hoof pick; and below: dandy, water and body brushes, a metal currycomb and a stable rubber.

go-between for dealers, finding out what horses were for sale and their prices and then informing the dealers. Since the horses were sold in guineas, the dealer would retain the pound and give the odd shilling which made up the guinea to the go-between in payment for his services.

gut-twister (Western US) an accomplished bucker.

gymkhana mounted games, usually for children under the age of sixteen. Many of the events, such as musical sacks and sack races, are adaptations of children's party games. Other typical classes include the BENDING RACE in which competitors have to weave quickly in and out of a line of poles; BUCKET ELIMINATION, in which six or seven up-turned buckets are placed in a line to be jumped by the competitors, a bucket being removed with each successive round until only one is left; CHASE-ME-CHARLIE, in which two small jumps are built on opposite sides of the ring and the competitors follow each other in quick succession over the jumps. After each round the jumps are raised, and any competitor whose pony refuses or knocks down an obstacle is eliminated. As well as providing a great deal of fun, events of this kind also help to develop the child as a rider and encourage him to school and exercise his pony.

gyp horse a crossbred with one parent of a heavy breed and the other of a light.

habit the dress worn by a woman riding side-saddle; a long skirt or shaped panel matching the jacket is worn over the breeches and boots.

hack The hack is not a breed but a type of horse, used for ordinary riding as opposed to hunting, etc. Before the age of the motor car there were virtually two types of hack, the COVERT HACK which was ridden generally, as, for example, by a gentleman 'hacking' to the meet of the hounds, where, on arrival, he would change on to his

hunter, and the PARK HACK, which was a far more elegant animal, ridden in such places as Rotten Row in Hyde Park by fashionable people.

Today in England at most major shows there are classes for hacks, and these are really for the park hack, a finely disciplined animal that is able to boast of the best of manners, and in the show ring is always required to give an individual show in order to illustrate the high degree of training. There are normally two classes, one for those animals not exceeding 15 h.h. and the other for those not exceeding 15.3 h.h.

The Show Hack Society is now combined with the Cob Society.

hackamore the oldest and best-known form of bitless bridle. Operated by a single rein, it has long metal cheekpieces, curved so as to embrace the nose by means of a leather strap, which exerts pressure on the nose and the chin groove.

hackney The name 'hackney' was used for many hundreds of years in England to define the general riding horse as opposed to the horse used in battle. It was not until the Hackney Horse Society was formed in 1883 that the hackney was given real prominence, in an attempt to improve the standard of English trotting horses, which were to be found in East Anglia and parts of Yorkshire.

It was at the beginning of the twentieth century that the growing popularity of horseshows led to a demand for very elegant, high-stepping carriage horses. Previously the hackney had been used for drawing military and civilian carriages.

The hackney horse today stands between 14.3 h.h. and 15.2 h.h., the colours accepted being bay, brown, black or chestnut, with some white markings. The head is convex in profile, and the eyes and ears should show its alertness. The head being well set in a neck of average length which should be crested and muscular, the throat and jaw should be clear cut. The back should be of average length with well-sprung ribs and good depth of body, while the shoulder should be flat and laid well back to give great scope for the action of the forelegs; the withers should not be over-fleshy. The limbs should be flat and clean of bone, with short cannons and well-sloped pasterns. The feet should be round and fairly upright.

The action at the walk should be brisk and springy and show the muscles. At the trot the action should be lofty, true, smooth and progressive, with the hind legs propelled well under the body.

During the last eighty years the HACKNEY PONY has been developed and, with its excellent action, has become extremely popular. The height restriction for these ponies is 12 h.h. to 14.2 h.h.

At the beginning of the 1960s hackneys began to be exported abroad, chiefly to the Netherlands and the United States.

hackney pony See under HACKNEY.

hack on *hunting* to ride a horse to a meet rather than transporting it there in a horsebox or trailer.

hack overcheck a twisted gag having rings with very small holes, through which only a cord can be passed, making it an extremely severe bit.

Haflinger The native pony of Austria, the Haflinger is bred chiefly in the Austrian Alps and Bavaria. The breed is thought to have descended from the Alpine Heavy Horse and is naturally very hardy. An excellent pack animal, it is often used in agriculture and forestry. The Haflinger is also noted for its longevity. It stands about 13.3 h.h. and is generally chestnut in colour with a flaxen mane

Above
show hack. Mr and Mrs A. R. Kent's Spring Morning, ridden by their daughter, Mrs Jane McHugh.

Above, far right
half-pass to the right, performed in the dressage test at the 1972 Olympics by the winner of the individual gold medal, Frau Liselott Linsenhoff, riding Piaff.

and tail. It has a fairly long body and a heavy head. The breed is now becoming popular in the British Isles, and increasing numbers have been imported in recent years.

hakma a halter originally used on camels which exerts pressure on the nose rather than on the mouth. Still used in some eastern countries for training, the hakma was undoubtedly the forerunner of the modern hackamore bridle.

half a neck *racing* a measurement used to describe the distance by which a horse has won a race.

half brothers and sisters horses which have the same dam but a different sire.

half halt *dressage* the almost simultaneous action of the rider's hand, seat and legs with the object of increasing the attention and balance of the horse before executing any of various movements or a transition to a lesser pace. More weight is shifted to the quarters to ease engagement of the hind legs and balance on the haunches.

half-hamming a casual manner of riding, adopted especially by cowboys when travelling long distances, in which the rider sits with his weight to one side and with the opposite spur wedged between the girth and the side of the horse.

half-length *racing* one of the measurements of the distance by which a horse may be said to have won a race: half the length of the horse's body and head.

half-pass a dressage movement in which the horse moves obliquely forward on two tracks. The horse's body should remain parallel to the side of the arena, while moving away from it at an angle of fifty degrees. The forehand should slightly lead the quarters, and the stride should be roomy, balanced and even, the horse being full of forward impulsion although moving obliquely.

Right
hackney. Showing his paces, Mrs Ionides's hackney champion Marden Midas, driven by Mrs Haydon.

Facing page, above
harness racing. Flat out round the bend in this trotting race in the Netherlands. Note how the leader, Quicksilver S, has all four legs off the ground.

Facing page, below
harness racing. Harness racing at a track near Long Beach, California.

halter a hemp rope headpiece with lead rope attached, used for leading a horse without a bridle or for tying up in the stable. The lead rope passes through an eye ring, so that as the horse pulls it tightens round the head.

halter-broke (US) broken to be led.

halter-puller a horse which pulls back against the halter when it is being led.

Hambletonian Stakes a classic trotting race for three-year-old horses, held annually since 1926 on the Good Times Track at Goshen, New York.

Hambletonian 10 Abadallah, the grandson of Messenger, was bred to the Charles Kent mare, herself by the imported Norfolk trotter, Bellfounder, to produce Rysdyk's Hambletonian 10. Almost all Standardbred trotters throughout the world show lineage to this horse, and one of the richest trotting races for three-year-olds is named after him.

Hamburg Derby the original show-jumping Derby, first held in 1920. Many other countries now hold similar competitions, including Great Britain, France, Italy and South Africa.

The Hamburg course is 1350 metres long, with seventeen obstacles and a total of twenty-four jumps. It is designed as a typical hunting course, with solid, difficult obstacles, and only horses with considerable stamina as well as jumping ability stand a chance of winning.

There have been two British winners of the Derby: Andrew Fielder with Vibart and Marion Mould with Stroller.

hame either of a pair of curved plated metal pieces attached to the collar of a harness animal. The traces are fastened to the lower end of the hames, which are kept in place round the collar by means of a chain, and the upper end of each hame usually terminates in a TENET, a welded ring through which the reins pass.

hammercloth an ornamental cloth covering the coachman's seat in a state or family carriage.

hand a linear measurement equalling four inches used in giving the height of a horse. The fractions of a hand are expressed in inches. See also HEIGHT, MEASURING STICK.

hand holt one of a series of looped handgrips in the driving reins used for trotters.

hand horse the offside horse of a pair at exercise which is not ridden but led by the rider of the near horse.

handicap *racing* **1.** the weight allocated to a horse in a race. **2.** a race in which the weights to be carried by the horses are worked out by the handicapper in order to give each horse an equal chance of winning.

handicapper an official appointed by the Jockey Club to determine the weights to be carried by the horses in a handicap race so that they all have an equal chance of winning the race.

handled (of a young horse) having been led about on a halter before being broken.

handy (of a horse) supple, agile; able to turn quickly and sharply.

hang (of a horse) to have a tendency to lean to one side when galloping.

hang off *coaching* (of a horse) to lean away from the partner horse.

hang up one's bars to give up coaching.

hang up one's boots (of a jockey) to retire from racing.

Hanoverian Originally descended from the German Great Horse of the Middle Ages, the Hanoverian was introduced to Germany through a combination of oriental, Neapolitan and Spanish stallions. Throughout its long history the breed has been intimately linked with the royal house of Hanover. The close association with British breeders, which had existed for some time, became even closer when George I came to the throne in Britain. Some twenty years later George II founded a stallion depot at Celle, with fourteen black stallions of Holstein descent. Later English Thoroughbreds were used. The depot is still maintained today.

The object has always been to breed a horse that was as strong as possible, so it could be used for agricultural work and at the same time have sufficient 'blood' to give it courage and action for both riding and driving purposes. The Society of Hanoverian Warm Blood Breeders and the Westphalian Stud Book are responsible for conducting the breeding programme.

Hanoverian mouthpiece a Pelham mouthpiece which is jointed on either side of a central port. It has rollers, which act in a similar way to rollers on a snaffle, but, because of the port, put more bearing on the bars of the mouth. If the port is too high, so that it bears on the roof of the mouth, the bit becomes very severe.

hansom a low-hung two-wheeled covered vehicle for two passengers, named after the patentee, J. A. Hansom, a Birmingham architect. It was drawn by one horse, and a driver sat on an elevated seat at the back, the reins passing over the roof. Essentially a town carriage, it was very popular with professional and business men. Hansoms were also used for hire, and were the forerunners of the modern taxicab.

harbour the resting place or refuge of a stag.

harbourer a person with an intimate knowledge of the local countryside employed by a hunt to advise where a warrantable stag is likely to be found on the day of the hunt. By the size and shape of its slots he will be able to give an indication of the stag's size.

hare foot the elongated pad of some foxhounds, especially Fell and American.

hare hunting the hunting of the hare, either on foot with beagles, or mounted with harriers.

Harewood Horse Trials a three-day event held annually in September at Harewood Hall in Yorkshire until 1960, when it was discontinued because of a change in the farming policy. (For results see page 228.)

harness the bridle, collar and other tack used on a horse which is to be driven as opposed to ridden.

harness class any of various show classes for driven horses, such as light and heavy trade turnouts, hackneys, private driving and coster classes.

harness racing a kind of horseracing in which the horses maintain a specified gait, either a trot or a pace, while pulling a two-wheeled sulky in which a driver is seated. The antiquity of this sport is attested by backed clay tablets unearthed in Asia Minor in the 1920s, which contained a comprehensive treatise on training horses to trot while pulling a cart or chariot. These tablets had been made in about 1350 B.C., several hundred years

before horseracing was included in the ancient Greek Olympic Games.

The trotting horse re-emerged from history in the early eighteenth century in the shape of the Norfolk trotter in England, which was primarily bred as a road horse, racing only occasionally. Trotting in the United States started with Messenger, a Thoroughbred exported from England in 1788 as an eight-year-old.

Speed has been the measure of a trotter or pacer's ability since the first recorded mile in less than three minutes was achieved by Yankee at Harlem, New York, in 1806. Harness racing became centred on the rural agricultural fairs in the United States and Canada. It did not prove popular in urban areas until the introduction of the mobile starting gate after the Second World War. This gate allows the horses to line up and move forward one stride to the starting line, no driver being able to gain an advantage by starting ahead of his rivals. It is still used almost exclusively in the United States and Canada. Other countries use standing starts and a system of handicap distances. The sport enjoys great popularity in the United States, where it is watched by some thirty million people every year.

harrier a breed of small hound, originally a cross between a foxhound and a beagle, used principally for mounted hare-hunting. It stands about 16 to 20 inches high at the shoulder.

Harringay Arena an indoor arena owned by the Greyhound Racing Association and situated in north London, which was the home of the Horse of the Year Show from its inception in 1949 until 1958, when the arena was closed down.

Hartwell Pelham a Pelham bit having a ported mouthpiece.

haunches the hips and buttocks of a horse.

haute école See HIGH SCHOOL.

Havana a medium-brown shade of leather made from cowhide.

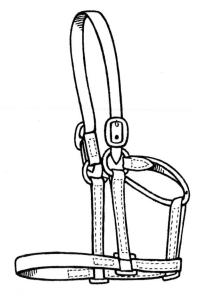

have-a-gamble a timed show-jumping competition in which there are twelve or fourteen obstacles, each carrying a number of points according to their severity. Two obstacles are valued at 10 points, two at 20, two at 30, two at 40, and one each at 50, 60, 70, 80, 90 and 100 points. If there are only twelve obstacles in the course, only one obstacle is valued at 20 and one at 10 points. The points value is scored for each obstacle jumped clear, no points being scored for an obstacle knocked down. The competitor must jump the obstacle valued at 10 points first and may then jump the remaining obstacles in any order, but no obstacle may be jumped more than twice. At the conclusion of one minute the bell is rung and the competitor must then go through the finish in either direction. The winner is the competitor gaining the most points. Also called GAMBLER'S CHOICE (US).

have a leg (of a horse) to have an unsoundness of or a swelling on the leg.

have whip (of a trotter or pacer) to have great speed.

hay grass cut and dried for use as fodder. It forms the bulk of the diet of stabled horses. Ideally it should be hard, sweet smelling, and contain plenty of leaves and flowers or seeds.

hayloft an enclosed area above a stable in which hay and other feedstuffs are stored.

hay net a large bag of rope netting for holding hay for feeding a horse; it is hung in the horse's box or stall from a wall ring. In order to preserve it, the net should be tarred, and it should be hung sufficiently high so that the horse cannot become entangled in it. The advantage of using a hay net is that it cuts wastage to a minimum, and the exact ration of hay to be given to a particular horse can easily be weighed.

head *racing* one of the measurements of the distance by which a horse may be said to have won a race: the length of a horse's head.

head collar a bitless headpiece, usually of leather, for leading a horse which is not wearing a bridle,

or for tying up a horse in a stable. The strongest head collars have brass fittings. Also called HEAD STALL. See also ADJUSTABLE HEAD COLLAR, AMERICAN HEAD COLLAR, BRASS-MOUNTED HEAD COLLAR, DUTCH SLIP, FOAL HEAD COLLAR.

headland a strip of uncultivated land bordering an arable field. Riders should always try to keep to the headland to avoid damaging the plough or growing seeds.

head number the number, corresponding to the number in the programme, displayed on a shield held erect on the crown piece of a trotter's bridle.

head stall See HEAD COLLAR.

heads up *hunting* (of hounds) carrying their heads in the air because they have lost the scent.

head to the wall See TRAVERS.

heavy horse any horse belonging to one of the breeds of large draught horses, such as Clydesdale, Percheron, Shire or Suffolk Punch.

heck See GEE.

heel line the hunting by hounds in the direction from which the fox has come, rather than the direction in which it is going.

height The height of a horse is measured in a perpendicular line from the highest part of the withers to the ground. When the measurement is taken the horse should be standing naturally with its weight evenly placed on all four legs. The ground should be as level as possible; the ideal surface is concrete. See also HAND, MEASURING STICK.

helping (in harness racing) the interfering by one horse with the progress of another.

Helsinki step-fence a cross-country obstacle consisting of a series of steps (normally two or three) cut into sloping ground. The steps are reinforced with rails; if the slope of the ground is not too great two rails may be used for each step, giving the obstacle a much more solid appearance.

Helvetia a kind of leather, yellow in colour, used in the manufacture of nosebands and martingales.

Hickstead The All-England Jumping Course at Hickstead, Sussex, was established in 1960 by Douglas Bunn, who was himself a former international show-jumper. His intention was to set up a permanent show-jumping arena based on continental show grounds, with permanent obstacles. From small beginnings and with very generous sponsorship, it rapidly became one of the most popular show-jumping centres in Great Britain. Many championships have been held there, including the European Junior Championships in 1961 and 1971, the Ladies' European Championship in 1963, the Ladies' World Championship in 1965, the Men's European Championship in 1971 and 1973, and the Men's World Championship in 1974. In 1971 part of the Royal International Horse Show was held there, including the Prix des Nations, the first time the competition had been held outside London. It is also the venue for the British Jumping Derby.

Hickstead has also proved a useful training ground, with its many arenas, and has been used on numerous occasions by the US show-jumping team.

hidebound (of a horse) thin with the skin apparently tight over the ribs and back, usually as a result of worms or a similar complaint.

Highland pony a breed of pony which originated in the Highlands of Scotland and the Western Isles. The Highland pony possesses characteristics which make it almost certain that it is descended from the North European Horse, which probably roamed Scotland when it was attached to Scandinavia. The present-day Highland pony has a lot of foreign blood, much of it Arabian. The breed has four main uses: (1) as a hill pony in deer forests and on grouse moors; (2) for farm work; (3) as a pack pony; and (4) for riding and trekking. The memory of a Highland pony on a mountain or moor where it has once been is quite remarkable. This hardy breed is extremely versatile and its constitution enables it to survive throughout the year on rough hill ground.

Its height varies between 13 h.h. and 14.2 h.h. The head is well carried, attractive and broad between bright and kindly eyes; it is short between the eyes and the muzzle, with wide nostrils. The neck is strong and not short, with a flowing mane and well set back shoulders. The body should have a deep chest, with a slight curve to the back and deep ribs; it should also have powerful quarters with strong thighs and a gaily carried tail. The legs must be flat in bone, with a slight fringe of feather ending in a prominent tuft at the fetlock. The forelegs should be placed well under the weight of the body, with a strong forearm and broad knees. The hocks must be broad, clean, flat and closely set. There are many colours, including grey, black, brown and shades of dun, yellow, cream and mouse. The breed society was formed in 1923.

high school the classical art of equitation. Based on natural leaps and paces, the high school airs were derived from tactics employed by cavalry in combat, and the training of horse and rider which was originally designed for the purely practical purposes of warfare gradually evolved into a refined art, practised as an end in itself. See also AIR. Also called HAUTE ÉCOLE.

hill topper (US) a person who follows foxhounds, either on horse or on foot, by going from one vantage point to another and listening for the cry of the hounds.

hinny the offspring of a stallion and a female donkey.

hippiology the study of horses.

hippodrome 1. a course in ancient Greece or Rome for horseraces and chariot races. **2.** an arena for equestrian and other spectacles.

hippodrome stand a rodeo stunt in which the rider stands up with his feet in straps and leans forwards while the horse is travelling at full speed.

hipposandal an iron-soled bootlike structure which was laced to the feet of horses in ancient Greece and Rome. Even as recently as the 1930s hipposandals of various designs were being experimented with in an attempt to produce a viable alternative to the conventional horseshoe which would not require as much skill in fitting.

hireling a horse which is hired out for riding or driving, usually by the hour or by the day.

hissing a noise made by a groom when he is grooming a horse. It is believed to have a soothing effect on the horse and also helps to prevent any dust being inhaled by the groom.

Hitchcock gag a very severe gag bit sometimes used on polo ponies. It has a jointed mouthpiece with rings and short upward cheeks. The reins are attached to the cheeks, passed upwards through a slip-head below the ears, and then down again and through loops attached to the rings of the bit.

hitch up to harness a horse or horses to be driven.

hit the line (of hounds) to pick up the scent of the quarry.

hobbled stirrups a pair of stirrups linked together by a rope or strap which passes under the belly of the horse. They help to give anchorage to the rider of a bucking horse, though they are not permitted in rodeo contests, as they are considered dangerous should the horse fall.

hobdayed (of a horse) having undergone Hobday's operation.

Hobday's operation a surgical operation performed on the larynx to treat roaring, so called because it was introduced by the distinguished veterinary surgeon, Sir Frederick Hobday.

Far right
Janet Hodgson. With her bay gelding Larkspur she has achieved great success at horse trials in recent years.

Hodgson, Janet (born 1948) The youngest of three daughters of a former master of the Meynell Hunt, Janet Hodgson gained much of her early riding experience in the hunting field. All her major successes in horse trials have been with Larkspur, a 17.1 h.h. Irish-bred bay gelding, foaled in 1962. After a very heavy fall at Badminton in 1971, the pair returned later that year to win the Advanced Class at Chatsworth and then the International Three-Day Event at Boekelo in the Netherlands. In 1972 they won at Burghley, and in 1973 were selected to represent Great Britain in the European Three-Day Event Championship at Kiev, where after a bad fall at the second fence on the cross-country course and in great pain, Janet Hodgson remounted and helped Great Britain to win the team bronze medal. In 1974 they competed as individuals in the World Championship at Burghley, where they finished in fourth place, and Janet Hodgson won the prize for the highest-placed woman rider.

hog back See ROACH BACK.

hogged mane a mane which has been completely shaved off, usually by means of clippers. Also called HOG MANE.

hogget a two-year-old boar.

hog mane See HOGGED MANE.

hog's back *show-jumping* a spread fence in which there are three sets of poles: the first close to the ground; the second at the highest point of the obstacle; and the third slightly lower than the second. The obstacle can be given a more solid appearance by putting another pole, or even a small wall or small brush, under the first pole.

hogster a three-year-old boar.

hoick holloa *hunting* the expression used to attract the attention of the huntsman or to draw the hounds to a holloa.

holding 1. *racing* an expression meaning that the going is soft or heavy and is slowing up the horses. **2.** See under SCENT.

hold up *hunting* to prevent a fox from leaving a covert.

hole the position of a trotter or pacer on the track at the start of a race in relation to the POLE POSITION, the position closest to the rails. For example, if a horse is in the first hole, there is one horse between it and the rails.

holloa *hunting* the cry given by a person to indicate that he has seen a fox. After making the holloa, he should remain still using his hat to point to the direction taken by the fox, until the signal is acknowledged by the huntsman.

to make the breed more compact and shorter-legged, and Yorkshire coach-horse stallions, which produced a high and wide gait, and a good temperament.

As a result the Holstein has become a good horse both for riding and driving, being particularly successful in recent years in show-jumping and three-day events. Probably the most famous Holstein has been Meteor, ridden so successfully by Fritz Thiedemann in the 1950s.

Breeding is administered by the Society of Breeders of the Holstein Horse in Elmshorn, West Germany, which took over responsibility after the closing of the stallion depot at Traventhal.

home straight the straight between the last bend and the winning post on a racecourse. Also called HOME STRETCH (US).

hood 1. a fabric covering which goes over the horse's head, ears and part of its neck, and is used when travelling, particularly in cold weather. **2.** blinkers.

hooded gig See LAWTON GIG.

Far right
hoof.

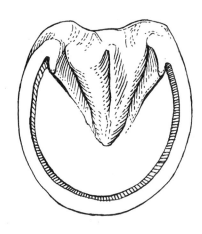

Right
Holstein, a powerful German breed, which has become popular for show-jumping and combined training.

Far right
hoof oil. Stable kit for the care of the legs and feet: a tin of hoof oil, together with a bowl and brush for applying it, leg bandages and a pair of over-reach boots.

Holstein a strong breed of horse, originally bred in the monasteries of Germany, the Holstein traces its history back to the thirteenth century. Regulations for the breed were first laid down in 1719, and updated in 1782. The biggest influences on the Holstein since that time have been the introduction of English Thoroughbred stallions, which helped

hoof 1. the insensitive horny covering which protects the sensitive structures of a horse's foot. **2.** the entire foot.

hoof oil a lubricant for horses' hoofs.

hoof pick a hooked metal instrument used for removing stones and dirt from horses' feet.

hook up to harness a horse or pony to a vehicle of any sort.

hoof pick. The correct way to hold the leg when using a hoof pick.

hook-up stirrup leather See under STIRRUP LEATHER.

hoppled pacer a pacer which is fitted with hopples so that it maintains its gait.

horny frog See FROG.

horse 1. the general term for an equine animal, whether it be a stallion, mare or gelding. **2.** a stallion or uncastrated horse. **3.** to provide a person with a horse to ride. **4.** to ride on horseback.

horse brass a brass ornament originally attached to a horse's harness.

horse-breaker a person who undertakes the initial training of a horse for whatever purpose it is to be used.

horse coper See COPER.

horse course a racecourse.

horse dealer a person engaged in the buying and selling of horses as a business.

horseman 1. a rider on horseback. **2.** a person skilled in the training and management of horses. **3.** a farm labourer who works with horses.

Horse of the Year Show an indoor international horseshow held annually in October since 1949. Originally conceived by Captain Tony Collings and Colonel Sir Michael Ansell, it is organized by the British Show Jumping Association, and until 1959, when it was moved to its present home, the Empire Pool, Wembley, it was held at the Harringay Arena. It lasts for five days (running from Monday to Saturday), with a programme that includes not only major show-jumping competitions, such as the Horse and Hound Cup, the Sunday Times Cup and the Ronson Trophy — the Victor Ludorum — but also includes a series of classes to select the horses of the year, such as the hunter, the hack, the children's riding pony and the police horse of the year. Features of the show are the daily parade of the year's horse personalities and the colourful cavalcade which closes the show on the last night.

horserace a competition for horses ridden by jockeys which takes place on the flat or over obstacles within a given area and over a prescribed distance and under the control of appointed officials.

horseshoe a shaped metal band nailed to the base of the horse's hoof to protect the hoof and prevent

Below
Household Cavalry. An autumnal scene in London as a detachment of the Royal Horse Guards returns to the barracks at Knightsbridge after duty on Horse Guards Parade.

it from splitting. Depending on the nature of the work to be done by a particular horse, the weight of the shoe may be varied; for instance, a heavy draught horse doing a lot of road work will require a very much heavier shoe than a racehorse. See also SHOEING.

horseshow a meeting at which competitions are held to test or display the qualities and capabilities of horses and their riders. As well as the major international shows, which are held over several days, every year in many parts of the world there are numerous small local shows, often lasting no more than half a day. These normally include a number of show-jumping competitions, and there are also classes for the various types of horses that are popular in the area. The horseshow season in Britain is from April to October, although with the increasing number of indoor schools shows are now being held throughout the year.

horse sick (of a field, meadow, etc.) producing only scant, poor-quality herbage as a result of continual grazing by horses.

horse standard See MEASURING STICK.

horse stick See MEASURING STICK.

horse trials See COMBINED TRAINING COMPETITION.

horsing stone See MOUNTING BLOCK.

hostler See OSTLER.

hot-blood a Thoroughbred horse.

Household Cavalry the mounted squadron of the Royal Horse Guards (The Blues) and the Royals which escorts the sovereign and the royal family on state and ceremonial occasions, such as the opening of Parliament.

hovel a doorless shelter put up in a field to provide cover for horses which are kept out. It should contain a manger and hay rack and should have a brick or concrete floor with a suitable covering so that the horses can lie down.

Hucul an ancient breed of strong mountain pony formerly found in the Carpathian Mountains, where it was used as a pack animal. A docile intelligent animal, the Hucul is now used in Poland mainly for work on smallholdings and occasionally for riding.

hug the rail *racing* to keep as close as possible to the inside rail on the course, thereby covering the shortest distance.

hull (Western US) a saddle.

hundred-and-elevens (US) the marks made by spurs on a horse's sides.

hunt button a button with the symbol or lettering of a particular hunt on it. Permission to wear hunt buttons is given by the master or masters of the hunt concerned. There are various kinds of buttons. For example, on a scarlet coat a brass

Hanoverian. A strong
breed, descended from the
German Great Horse.

Highland pony. A mare and
foal.

Hucul, an ancient breed of pony from Poland, which is used mainly in harness.

Iceland pony. A group of ponies pictured in front of Mount Snaefell.

Karabakh, a riding horse
from the Soviet Union.

Konik, a breed used
extensively on farms in
Poland.

landau. Pictured in the Royal Mews, Buckingham Palace, a state landau which was built in 1902.

button is worn and on a black coat a black button with the symbol in white.

hunter a horse bred and trained to be ridden for hunting. The home of the hunter is the British Isles, since it is here that the sport of foxhunting originated. Hunters are recruited from many breeds, but the Thoroughbred is considered the most suitable, for the hunter must above all have good stamina in order to be able to endure many days' hunting during the season from November to March, and has to be able to carry a good weight for a considerable time. Thus it is necessary for it to have deep and well-sprung ribs, allowing room for great heart and lung capacity. Temperament is all-important since, for many hours a day, the hunter is in the company of other horses. The action of the hunter must be free and he must be able to maintain an effortless and rhythmical gallop, with the forelegs sweeping out and skimming the ground, while the drive from the hocks brings the hind legs right underneath the body.

1885 with the object of improving and promoting the breeding of hunters and other horses used for riding and driving. To this end, the society annually offers premiums to the owners of the best available stallions which are calculated to produce up-to-weight hunters. See also PREMIUM STALLION.

hunter steeplechase a steeplechase entry to which is restricted to amateur riders and to horses certified by a master of hounds as having been regularly hunted during the season.

hunter trials a type of competitive event, held by most hunts during the season, in which horses are ridden over a course of obstacles built to look as natural as possible. The course has to be completed within a specified time. The method of judging varies considerably, but is usually based on performance and style.

hunting the sport of following different types of hound, either mounted or on foot, in pursuit of the fox, the stag or the hare. See also CUB HUNTING,

hunter. Roy Trigg riding Miss Griffin's show hunter Aristocrat. At the end of a very successful season in 1974, Aristocrat won the Hunter of the Year Championship at the Horse of the Year Show.

hunter class any of various show classes held at horseshows in Britain for hunters, such as LIGHT-WEIGHT HUNTER, which is open to animals — mares or geldings — capable of carrying up to 12 st. 7 lb; MIDDLEWEIGHT HUNTER, which is for animals capable of carrying over 12 st. 7 lb but not more than 14 st.; and HEAVYWEIGHT HUNTER, which is open to animals capable of carrying more than 14 st. All these classes are restricted to animals aged four years or more and ridden astride, as is the SMALL SHOW HUNTER, a class for animals over 14.2 h.h. but not exceeding 15.2 h.h. There are also hunter classes for women riders, and in these the horses must be ridden side-saddle, as well as in-hand classes for young stock, stallions and brood mares.

Hunters Improvement and National Light Horse Breeding Society a society founded in

HARE HUNTING, FOXHUNTING, STAGHUNTING.

hunting box a house or cottage, in or near the area of a hunt or shoot, which may be occupied by guests or rented out to members during the season. Also called HUNTING LODGE.

hunting cap a velvet-covered protective riding hat, formerly worn in the hunting field only by masters, ex-masters, field masters, hunt secretaries and children, but now generally worn in place of bowlers by women and also to a lesser extent by men.

hunting competition *show-jumping* a competition to test the obedience, handiness and speed of a horse over a twisting course with varied obstacles.

There should be no fixed track to follow, so that the competitor takes the shortest distance between obstacles to save time. Faults are penalized in seconds, which are added to the time taken by the competitor to complete the course. The winner is the competitor with the shortest time total. Also called PARCOURS DE CHASSE.

hunting gate a narrow gate for the use of riders, often found alongside a field gate.

hunting horn a cylindrical instrument, usually 9 to 10 inches long and made of copper with a nickel or silver mouthpiece, used by huntsmen to give signals, both to the hounds and to the field.

hunting lodge See HUNTING BOX.

hunting saddle a shallow-seated rigid-tree saddle, formerly widely used in England for hunting and hacking. Because of the saddle's shape — the shallow seat and the high fore-arch — the weight of the rider is thrown to the back of the saddle, over the loins, restricting the horse's action and placing the rider behind the movement. As the bars and the points on the straight head of the saddle are under the rider's thigh, the saddle tends to be uncomfortable. Moreover, the tree is usually found to be too broad in the waist, again spreading the rider's thighs, and there is no support under the panel to help the rider fix his position correctly in relation to the movement of the horse. Also called ENGLISH SADDLE.

hunting season the period during which a certain animal may be hunted. The dates are as follows:
foxhunting, 1st November to 1st April;
staghunting, 12th August to 12th October;
deer hunting, 10th November to 3rd March.

hunting stock See STOCK.

hunting tie See STOCK.

hunting year the twelve-month period commencing 1st May, the date on which all changes of mastership and hunt staff take effect and subscriptions fall due.

hunt leather See GRAB THE APPLE.

hunt livery the distinctive coat of a particular hunt worn by the staff of the hunt. Although many coats are scarlet, the collar may be of a different colour or have a motif on it. Also called HUNT UNIFORM.

hunt secretary The hunt secretary carries out the normal duties of a secretary, in connection with the hunt, but he is also responsible for maintaining close contact with the farmers and landowners within the area of the hunt, and has the additional task of collecting the cap money at the meet.

hunt servant any salaried employee of a hunt, such as the huntsman, kennel huntsman or whippers-in.

huntsman the man in charge of the hounds during a hunt, whether the master himself, or a huntsman employed by him.

hunt subscription the fee payable by a person who is a member of a hunt. In Britain it becomes due in advance on 1st May each year. The amount varies from hunt to hunt, and will depend on the number of days that are normally hunted each week, not by the individual, but by the pack of hounds.

hunt supporters' club an organized group of people who are interested in hunting. Usually unable to afford to hunt themselves, they help in many ways with the hunt, not least through the raising of money through social events, such as dinners, dances and discussions, in order to purchase equipment for the hunt, such as vans for the hounds and horseboxes. Most hunts in Britain now have their own supporters' clubs.

hunt terrier a small short-legged terrier kept by a hunt and used to bolt foxes from earths, drains or other places which are inaccessible to the hounds.

hunt uniform See HUNT LIVERY.

hurdle one of a series of wattle fences over which horses must jump in hurdle racing.

hurdle race a horserace over hurdles. There must be a minimum of six flights of hurdles in the first $1\frac{1}{2}$ miles and one for every additional $\frac{1}{4}$ mile or part thereof.

Hyperion (by Gainsborough out of Selene. In the short space of two seasons Selene won fifteen of her twenty-two races.) Foaled in 1930, Hyperion was owned by Lord Derby and trained by George Lambton. His debut on the racecourse, as a two-year-old, was in the Zetland Maiden Plate at Doncaster, in which he finished fourth, and his first win came in the New Stakes at Ascot. He dead-heated in the Prince of Wales Stakes at Goodwood, was third in the Boscawer Stakes at Newmarket and won the Dewhurst Stakes, also at Newmarket, finishing the season with a win in the Chester Vase. The following season Hyperion was unbeaten: he won the Derby, the Prince of Wales Stakes at Ascot, the St Leger at Doncaster and the March Stakes at Newmarket. He ran only three times as a four-year-old, recording his only win in the Burwell Stakes at Newmarket.

He was then retired to stud at Newmarket. Hyperion was undoubtedly one of the greatest sires in the history of the turf. When he died his progeny had won 748 races worth over half a million pounds. Among his classic winners were Godiva, winner of the 1000-Guineas and the Oaks, Owen Tudor, Sun Chariot and Sunstream, winner of the 1000-Guineas and the Oaks. Among his other winners were Gulf Stream, Hyperbole, Aureole, High Beam and High Hat. He continued at stud until the age of twenty-nine. He was put down in 1960, and his skeleton now stands in the Natural History Museum in South Kensington, London.

Far right
Hyperion, one of the greatest sires in the history of the turf.

Iceland pony a breed of strong sturdy pony which was developed in Iceland from the ponies taken to the island by the early Norwegian settlers and from the Irish and Scottish stock later taken there by the immigrants from the Western Isles. Between 12 h.h. and 13 h.h. and usually dun or grey, the Iceland Pony is extremely hardy; it is very docile but alert, and noted for its exceptionally keen eyesight. For centuries the ponies were the only means of transport and traction in Iceland, and were not only ridden but were also used for all types of agricultural and haulage work. Also called ICELANDIC PONY.

imperial 1. the top of a carriage, especially of a diligence. **2.** a box or case for luggage carried there.

Imperial Spanish Riding School a classical riding academy situated in the centre of Vienna, in the Hofburg, Josefsplatz. Founded during the fifteenth or sixteenth centuries, it is the oldest riding academy in the world. The building, designed by Fischer von Erlach, was begun in 1729 and completed in 1735. The only coloured decoration in the lofty white hall is a portrait of Charles VI, under whose patronage it was built. The riding area itself measures 55 metres by 18 metres.

Lipizzaner stallions are the only horses used in the school. During the first three to four years of their training the stallions are taught all the classical airs on the ground. The best animals then go on to learn the airs above the ground. It takes a rider four to six years to learn to ride a fully trained horse, and a further two to four years to learn to train his own horse. The traditional uniform worn by the riders consists of a black cocked hat, a brown tail coat, white breeches, and high black boots. On gala occasions a red coat trimmed with gold is worn.

The director of the school for many years was Col. Alois Podhajsky. He was succeeded by Col. Hans Handler who died in 1974.

in-and-out 1. a cross-country or show-jumping obstacle consisting of two elements which are too widely spaced to be jumped as one, but not far enough apart to allow horses to take a stride between jumping the first part and taking the second. **2.** See DOUBLE (def. 2).

in blood (of hounds) having made a kill.

inbreeding the mating of related individuals, such as brother and sister, sire and daughter or son and dam.

independent seat the ability to maintain a firm, balanced position on a horse's back, without relying on the reins or stirrups for support.

Indian broke (US; of a horse) trained to allow

Imperial Spanish Riding School. An intrigued audience watched the Lipizzaners perform a quadrille.

the rider to mount from the offside rather than the nearside, as is more usual.

Indian side (US) the offside of the horse, so called because it was customary for Indians to mount from that side.

indoor polo a form of polo played indoors, with an inflated rubber ball, by teams of three.

indoor show a horseshow which is held in an indoor arena. They are becoming increasingly popular, and can be held throughout the year. Among the best-known indoor shows in the world are those held at Madison Square Garden in New York and at the Empire Pool, Wembley, in London.

in foal (of a mare) pregnant.

in full cry *hunting* (of a pack of hounds) in strong pursuit of the quarry and giving tongue.

in hand led, as opposed to being ridden or driven.

in-hand class any of various show classes, such as young stock, breed or condition classes, in which the animals are led, usually in a show bridle or head collar, but otherwise without saddlery (except in the case of draught horses which are often shown in their harness), and are judged principally for conformation and/or condition.

in high (US, of a trotter or pacer) moving as fast as possible; flat out.

inside car a type of jaunting car in which the

passengers sit facing each other rather than back to back.

Institute of the Horse an institute formed in 1925 as an authoritative centre for information relating to the training and management of the horse. In 1947 it was amalgamated with the National Horse Association of Great Britain to form the British Horse Society.

intermediate class a combined training competition in Britain restricted to horses in Grade II, or Grades II and III, depending on the schedule. In such competitions the dressage test is of novice or preliminary standard. No obstacle in the show-jumping phase exceeds 3 feet 11 inches in height or 5 feet 11 inches in width at the highest point and 9 feet 2 inches at the base, and the test is carried out at a speed of 327 yards per minute. The cross-country course is no less than 2 miles but no more than $2\frac{1}{2}$ miles long, with eight to twelve obstacles per mile, and no obstacle exceeds 3 feet 9 inches.

international calendar a calendar published annually in December by the International Equestrian Federation, giving the dates of all the international dressage, combined training and show-jumping events to be held in the coming year.

international competition horse any horse which, having attained the age of five years, is ridden in international or official international

Below
Piero d'Inzeo, winner of the King George V Gold Cup on three occasions, seen here riding The Rock.

show-jumping or dressage competitions, three-day events, or friendly shows.

International Equestrian Federation See FEDERATION EQUESTRE INTERNATIONALE.

in the book accepted for or entered in the General Stud Book.

in the clear (of a record set by a trotter or pacer) made without the assistance of a pacemaker or windbreak.

in the plate mounted and sitting in the saddle.

in whelp (of a hound bitch) pregnant.

Inzeo, Lt Col. Piero d', *Italy* (born 1923) Piero is the elder of the famous Italian show-jumping brothers, and has been competing successfully in international competitions for over twenty years. He has competed in every Olympic Games since the Second World War, and although he has won silver and bronze medals, the gold has always eluded him. In the 1952 Olympic Games at Helsinki he competed in both the show-jumping and the three-day event. In 1959 in Paris, riding Uruguay, he won the European Championship and has also been second twice and third once. One of only a few people to win the King George V Gold Trophy on three occasions, his triumphs were in 1957 with Uruguay, and 1961 and 1962 with The Rock, the horse with which he had so many famous victories.

Inzeo, Major Raimondo d', *Italy* (born 1925) Because of his interest in horses, Raimondo, the younger brother of Piero d'Inzeo, left Rome University and joined the Carabinieri in 1950. In 1948 at the Olympic Games in London he competed in the three-day event, and has since been a regular member of the Italian show-jumping team, winning the individual gold medal in Rome in 1960 with Posillipo. Twice World Champion, he first won the title in 1956, riding Merano in Aachen, and retained it in 1960, riding Gowran Girl in Venice. In addition to those already mentioned, his most successful horses have been Bells of Clonmell, Bellevue and Fiorello, the horse on which he was a member of the bronze medal team at the 1972 Olympic Games in Munich.

Irish martingale See IRISH RINGS.

Irish rings a short leather strap with a ring at each end through which the reins are passed. It is used, especially in racing, to keep the rein pull in the right direction and to stop the reins going over the horse's head in the event of a fall. Also called IRISH MARTINGALE.

irons stirrup irons.

Iroquois (by Leamington out of Maggie B.B.) Foaled in 1878 at the Erdenheim Stud, Philadelphia, Iroquois became the first American-bred colt to win the British Derby. Owned by P. Lorillard, trained by Jacob Pincus and ridden by Fred Archer, he won the Derby in 1881, and in the same year went on to win the St Leger.

Below
Raimondo d'Inzeo, the younger brother of Piero, riding Posillipo. He has competed in every Olympic Games since 1956 as a member of the Italian show-jumping team and has twice won the Men's World Show Jumping Championship.

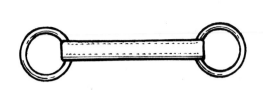
Irish rings.

Isinglass (by Isonomy out of Dead Lock) Foaled in 1890, Isinglass was owned by H. McCalmont and trained by J. Jewitt at Newmarket. He won three races as a two-year-old: the first at Newmarket; then the New Stakes at Ascot; and finally the Middle Park Stakes, again at Newmarket. The following year, 1893, ridden by Tom Loates, he won the Triple Crown, the 2000-Guineas, the Derby and the St Leger, also winning the Newmarket Stakes in the same year. As a four-year-old he won the first running of the Princess of Wales Stakes at Newmarket, and went on to win the Eclipse Stakes at Sandown and the Jockey Club Stakes at Newmarket. He was raced only once as a five-year-old, when he won the Ascot Gold Cup. His total winnings of £57,455 remained a record until 1952.

island fence an obstacle on a cross-country course standing on its own away from any hedge or fence.

Isinglass, winner of the Triple Crown in 1893.

Italian Heavy Draught Horse a breed of heavy draught horse descended from the Breton and found principally in the area around Venice. It is stockily built, standing 15 h.h. to 16 h.h., and is usually sorrel or roan, with a long mane and a lot of feather on the legs. An extremely powerful animal, it has a docile temperament and is particularly noted for its speed in action.

jack a male donkey. Also called JACKASS.

jackpot a rodeo event in which no purse is put up by the organizers, and the prize winners split a part or the whole of the entry fee.

jagger a pony used by a pedlar to carry his goods.

jarvey the driver of a hackney carriage.

jaunting car an open two-wheeled horse-drawn vehicle, popular in Ireland, having room for up to six passengers sitting on each side back to back, with folding footrests above the wheels and a small seat in front for the driver. See also INSIDE CAR.

jelly hound a beagle or a harrier, so called because it was customary to eat hare with red currant jelly.

jenny the female of the donkey and various other animals.

jerked down (Western US; of a horse) pulled to the ground by a steer which has been roped.

jib (of a horse) to refuse to go forward, sometimes moving backwards or sideways instead. In many cases, if the horse is being ridden, it will have to be turned round before it will go forward or, if it is being driven, a groom may have to lead it forward.

jibbah the shield-like formation of the frontal and parietal bones in the skull of the Arab which gives it its distinctive dished profile.

jig 1. an uneasy bouncy, very short-paced trot; a gait sometimes adopted by horses which refuse to walk. **2.** to go or ride at a jig.

jiggle the ordinary gait of a cow horse, averaging approximately 5 m.p.h.

jink (of a wild boar) to turn sharply to the right or left when hard pressed.

jobbing spear a short spear with a bamboo shaft and heavy blade used in pigsticking. It is thrown overhand and used at close range.

job master a person who keeps horses for hire, either for riding or for driving.

jockey 1. *racing* a person engaged to ride a horse in a race. A jockey may be either amateur or professional, but must be in possession of a licence issued by the appropriate turf authority, in Britain the Jockey Club, and which is renewed annually. A professional jockey is anyone who has been paid directly or indirectly for riding in a race, or who, during the last three years, has been paid to work in a licensed trainer's yard, or who has been a groom in any other stable. Any such person is considered to have ridden for hire, and is not eligible to be an amateur. **2.** (formerly) a dealer in horses, especially a disreputable one.

Jockey Club the governing body exercising control over racing and breeding in Britain. Founded in the mid-eighteenth century by a group of wealthy racing enthusiasts, it gradually became recognized as the supreme flat-racing authority, first at Newmarket and eventually throughout the country, laying down clearly defined rules for the proper conduct of the sport. In 1969 the National Hunt Committee, which had previously exercised similar control over steeplechasing, was amalgamated with the Jockey Club, which now assumed responsibility for all forms of racing. The policy of the Jockey Club is administered by three elected stewards, each of whom holds office for three years. Its headquarters are at Newmarket.

Below
jumping lane.

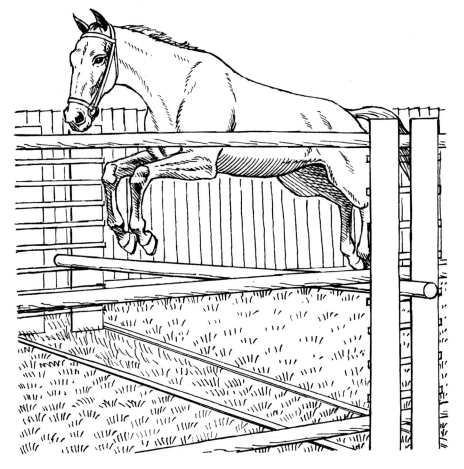

Jockey Club of America the parent body of the American turf, founded by charter on 8th February 1894 as a successor to the Board of Control, which was founded in 1891. The present headquarters are in Park Avenue, New York. The organization is responsible for maintaining the Stud Book and every Thoroughbred racing in the United States has to be registered with it. It also registers racing colours and stable names, and names for horses have to be checked and approved by it.

Jockeys' Association of Great Britain an association whose chief aims are to maintain the highest standards of honour, integrity and courtesy among jockeys, to support and protect the character, status and interest generally of the jockeys' profession, and to work to the best interests of racing in general.

jockeyship the art of riding a horse in a race.

jodhphor polo curb a more severe type of curb chain having a large oval-shape fitting in the centre, which lies between the bones of the lower jaw thereby exerting considerable pressure.

jog 1. a short-paced trot, similar in action to the jig. **2.** to go or ride at a jog. Also called JOG-TROT.

John Player Trophy an international show-jumping challenge trophy instituted in 1961 and presented by John Player and Sons at the Royal International Horse Show. (For results see page 227.)

jointed Pelham a Pelham bit having a jointed mouthpiece similar to that of a jointed snaffle.

joint-master one of two or more people who share the mastership of a pack of hounds. See also MASTER.

jowl the space in front of the throat and between the jawbones of a horse.

July racecourse See under NEWMARKET.

jump *driving* (of a wheeler) to break from a trot to a canter because it feels that the vehicle it is pulling is beginning to overtake it.

jumper any horse trained to compete over jumps, such as a chaser or show-jumper.

jumping course 1. a racecourse with obstacles to be jumped. **2.** a show-jumping course.

jumping lane a long, narrow, high-fenced lane containing a series of obstacles for training a horse to jump. The jumps extend the total width of the lane so that the horse cannot run out, and are usually adjustable in height.

jump jockey a jockey who rides over hurdles or steeplechase fences.

jump-off *show-jumping* a round held to decide the winner of a competition from among the competitors who have tied for first place in a previous round.

The jump-off is always held under the same rules as the first round of the competition. Except in some special competitions, the number of obstacles in the jump-off may be reduced, and those to be jumped may be increased in height and/or width, though the shape and nature of the obstacles must not be changed.

Unless the rules of a competition specifically state otherwise, there are never more than two jumps-off; the conditions laid down in the schedule should always specify the number.

Junqueira See MANGALARGA.

Jura See FRANCHES-MONTAGNES.

Above
Jutland. A stallion showing off his paces. Note the deep broad chest, which is typical of the breed.

Below
Kabardin, a very tough and reliable breed, found in the mountainous regions of the Soviet Union and used principally for riding.

Jutland a breed of hardy heavy horse originating in Denmark, the Jutland was noted as a warhorse more than 700 years ago, and its history goes much further back. There is a certain resemblance between the Jutland and the Schleswig horse of Germany, and it is probable that in the past a number of Jutlands were exported to Germany. During the Middle Ages the Jutlands were in great demand as chargers, since they had good stamina and were able to carry the heavy weight of a knight in full armour. The Jutland has also been an excellent agricultural and draught horse, but is now declining because of the lack of demand for it in the age of mechanical transport.

The Jutland is of medium size, but with a good width of body; it has massive legs, with soft smooth hair. The most common colour is chestnut, but brown, bay, roan, grey or black are also accepted.

Kabardin a breed of horse found in the Caucasus, and developed from local horses crossed with other native breeds from the south and improved with the addition of Arab blood. About 15 h.h. and usually bay or black, the Kabardin has short but very strong stout legs, and is an extremely reliable and sure-footed riding horse, noted for its powers of endurance.

Karabair one of the oldest breeds of horse found in Central Asia, originating in the mountainous regions of Uzbekistan in the Soviet Union. The Karabair is a dual-purpose breed, used both for driving and riding. About 15.2 h.h. and bay, chestnut or grey in colour, it is noted for its tremendous stamina. Karabairs are used extensively as mounts for kok-par, a game which requires horses of great speed and agility.

Karabakh a breed of small mountain riding horse from the Caucasus. Usually about 14.2 h.h., the Karabakh is energetic, with a good action at both the walk and the gallop, and has a good temperament. The face is slightly dished, indicating that there is probably some Arabian blood in its ancestry. The usual colours are dun, chestnut or bay, with a characteristic metallic sheen.

Karacabey a Turkish breed of horse derived from native mares crossed with Nonius stallions, used both for riding and for light agricultural work, and by the Turkish Army as pack animals and remounts. The average height is about 16 hands, and all colours are found.

Kazakh an ancient breed of pony found in Kazakhstan in the Soviet Union. About 14 h.h., the Kazakh is a very hardy animal, used mainly by farmers for herding cattle.

keep a grass field which is used for grazing.

keep on a tight rein to restrain a horse by holding the reins short and thus exerting pressure on the bit.

keep the race (of the winner of a race) to be confirmed in one's position after an objection has been lodged and overruled.

Kelso (by Your Host out of Maid of Flight; ridden by Johnny Longden, Your Host won the Santa Anita Derby in 1950) Foaled in 1957 at A. Hancock's stud in Kentucky, Kelso was owned by Mrs C. du Pont. For his first year in training he was in the charge of Dr J. Lee, and was then transferred to Carl Hanford for the remainder of his racing career.

A backward colt, his first outing was not until the autumn of 1959, when he won at Atlantic City,

Karabair. One of the oldest breeds found in the Soviet Union, it is used both for riding and driving.

Left
Karacabey. A Turkish cavalry squadron mounted on Karacabeys.

Below
Kazakh, an extremely hardy breed, found on the Russian Steppes.

Below right
Kelso, winner of the Jockey Club Gold Cup from 1960 to 1964, inclusive, seen here with Ismal Valenzuela up after his victory in the 1964 Washington International at Laurel Park.

but was second in his two other races. As a three-year-old he ran successfully at meetings at Monmouth and Aqueduct. His first major success came later in the year at Monmouth, where he won the Choice Stakes, following this up with two wins at Aqueduct in the Jerome and the Discovery Handicaps. He then ran in the Lawrence Realization Stakes at Belmont Park, the American equivalent of the St Leger, and gave a sparkling performance to equal the track record. In the Hawthorne Gold Cup at Illinois he won by six lengths. His next victory was at Aqueduct in the two-mile Jockey Club Gold Cup, which he won by three and a half lengths, at the same time breaking the American record for the distance.

In 1961 he won the Handicap Triple Crown at Aqueduct, the Metropolitan, Suburban and Brooklyn Handicaps, and the Whitney Stakes at Belmont Park. He then went on to win the Woodward Stakes, again at Belmont Park, and his second Jockey Club Gold Cup at Aqueduct. In the Washington D.C. International at Laurel Park he was narrowly beaten by T. V. Lark.

Not only did he have two further victories in the Woodward Stakes, winning by four and a half lengths in 1962 and by three and a half lengths in 1963, but he also won the Jockey Club Gold Cup again in 1962, 1963 and 1964. Also in 1964, having finished second on three previous occasions, he faced the starter for his fourth and last Washington International, this time winning from Gun Bow by some four and a half lengths. In 1965 he won the rich Whitney Stakes again, as well as five other races. Although he remained in training as a nine-year-old, he was not successful.

So popular was he with the public in the United States that he was voted Horse of the Year on five occasions — from 1960 to 1964, inclusive — an amazing record. On his retirement from the racecourse he was regularly hunted by his owner.

kennel huntsman a person employed by a hunt which has an amateur huntsman to manage the hounds and to act as first whipper-in on hunting days.

kennel man a person who works in hunt kennels under the supervision of a huntsman or kennel huntsman.

kennels the buildings and yards where a pack of hounds is housed.

Kentucky Derby a race over 1¼ miles for three-year-old horses, first run in 1875 at Churchill Downs, Louisville, Kentucky; the first leg of the Triple Crown. (For results see pages 253–254.)

Far right
Kentucky Derby. The magnificent trophy awarded to the winner of this race, which was first run in 1875.

Below
Kladruber. A magnificent thirteen-in-hand team of Kladruber greys approaches the starting post for the great Pardubice steeplechase in Czechoslovakia.

Kentucky Saddle-Horse See under AMERICAN SADDLE-HORSE.

kept up (of a horse) kept in a stable rather than turned out to grass during the period between the end of one hunting or racing season and the beginning of the next.

kicking strap a broad leather strap used on harness horses which are inclined to kick. It passes over the loins and through a loop in the crupper, and is attached to the shafts on each side by means of a loop. The pressure exerted on the hindquarters by the strap prevents the animal from kicking out with any real force.

Kimblewick a combination of a snaffle and a curb bit, having square as opposed to round eyes so that greater downward pressure can be applied to the poll. An adaptation of a Spanish jumping bit, it was originally made for Fel Oliver, for his show-jumpers, and takes its name from the village where he lives. Several slight variations have been produced under such names as the KIMBERWICK.

Kincsem (by Cambuscan out of Water Nymph) Foaled in 1874 at the Hungarian National Stud, Kisber, Kincsem was a remarkable mare who won fifty-four races (a record) in no less than five different countries.

After her successful career on the turf she was retired to stud, where she produced three fillies and two colts, which were to win forty-one classic races in Germany, Austria-Hungary, Italy, Poland, France and Romania.

King George V Gold Cup a gold challenge trophy depicting St George and the Dragon, which was presented to the Royal International Horse Show by George V in 1911 to be competed for by male show-jumping riders. It was won outright in 1934 by Lt J. Talbot-Ponsonby, who won it twice with Chelsea and then with Best Girl, and was re-presented by him for perpetual competition. (For results see page 227.)

King George VI and Queen Elizabeth Stakes a horserace over a distance of 1 mile 4 furlongs ($1\frac{1}{2}$ miles), held annually at Ascot since 1951 (For results see page 242.)

Kladruber a breed of horse which took its name from the imperial Kladrub Stud in Bohemia, where it was originally bred. Derived from imported Spanish stock, the Kladruber retained the typical Roman nose, heavily crested neck and high action of the parent breed. During the nineteenth century it was in great demand by the Austro-Hungarian court as a carriage horse for state occasions, and, by a process of selective breeding, black and grey became the only two colours of the breed and the height was increased to an average of 17 to 18 hands. The breed today is used mainly for agricultural purposes, and crossbreeds are used for riding.

knack a worthless and worn-out horse.

knacker a person who buys horses for slaughter.

knockdown *show-jumping* the complete or partial displacement of an obstacle by a competitor. A knockdown is considered to have occurred when, through the fault of the horse or the rider,
- (a) any part or the whole of an obstacle is dislodged, even when the dislodged member is arrested in its fall by another part of the obstacle;
- (b) at least one of the ends of the obstacle is dislodged from its support;
- (c) any framework forming an integral part of the obstacle falls. (If the same part is merely touched or displaced, however, there is no penalty.)

When an obstacle or part of an obstacle is composed of several elements placed one above the other in the same vertical plane, the dislodging of the top element alone is penalized, and if an obstacle or part of an obstacle falls after the competitor has gone through the finish no penalties are incurred.

Koechlin-Smythe, Patricia, *GB* (born 1928) Pat Smythe was a regular member of the British show-jumping teams from 1952 to 1962, although she had competed internationally from 1947. She became one of the best-known personalities in show-jumping and competed all over the world. She won the Ladies' European Championship four

King George V Gold Cup, one of the most coveted individual awards in the show-jumping world. It depicts St George slaying the Dragon.

times: in 1957 at Spa; in 1961 at Deauville; in
1962 in Madrid; and in 1963 at Hickstead. At
Stockholm in 1956 she became the first woman
rider to compete in the Olympic Games, when she
was a member of the British bronze medal team.
Her best-known horses were Finality, Tosca, Prince
Hal and Flanagan.

Since her marriage and retirement from active
participation, she has acted as chef d'équipe to
British teams on a number of occasions. In 1956
she was awarded the O.B.E. for her services to
show-jumping.

kok-par a very popular equestrian game of
Central Asia, in which the object is to carry a
stuffed goat through the opponents' goal. The
two opposing teams can be made up of any
number of riders. Also called GOAT-SNATCHING.

Konik a native pony of Poland. About 13 h.h.
and usually bay or dun, the breed is extremely
popular for work on smallholdings, as it is a
strong and active worker and can survive on small
amounts of food.

Kournakoff iron a type of stirrup iron designed to
ensure that the rider's foot is held in the correct
position. The eye through which the leather passes
is set to the inside, as opposed to centrally, and
the sides of the iron slope forwards, while the tread

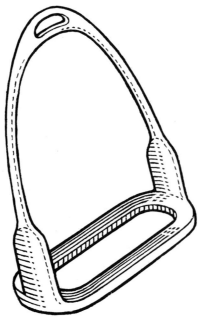

slopes upwards, thus assisting the rider to keep the toe up and the heel down.

Kusner, Kathryn Hallowell, *US* (born 1940) Kathy Kusner started her show-jumping career in 1960. She joined the United States Equestrian Team two years later, and has since been a regular member. She has been the champion rider at the Harrisburg and New York shows, and at the latter in 1962 she won the United States President's Cup. Her successes have in the main been on horses owned by Mr and Mrs Patrick Butler, particularly on Untouchable, and it was on this horse that she made history by becoming the first person to win the Irish Grand Prix in Dublin in two consecutive years, in 1964 and 1965. At Fontainebleau in 1967 she became the first American to win the Ladies' European Championship.

She was one of the first women to be granted a flat-race jockey's licence, and has raced in Chile, Puerto Rico, Germany and South Africa, as well as in the United States.

laced reins a type of riding rein in which a lace is passed over and through the leather in a series of 'V' shapes, in order to provide a better grip.

lad 1. a boy or stableman who works in a stables of any kind. **2.** a girl who works in racing stables.

Ladies' European Show Jumping Championship an individual show-jumping championship for women riders, held annually, except when there is a Ladies' World Show Jumping Championship or occasionally in Olympic years, since 1957. It is open to two competitors from each country, and each rider is allowed to compete with two horses. The championship consists of three competitions, each held on a different day, and there is usually a rest day between the second and third competitions. The winner is the rider with the lowest score overall, one point being awarded for first place in each competition, two for second, and so on. If the rider has two horses, only the score of the better-placed horse in each competition counts. The country of the winning rider has the right to hold the championship the following year, but the competition may not be held for two consecutive years in the same country. (For results see page 225.)

Ladies' World Show Jumping Championship an individual show-jumping championship for women riders, held every fifth year since 1965. It is open to two riders from each country, and each rider may compete with two horses. The championship is spread over three days and is judged in the same way as the Ladies' European Show Jumping Championship, the winner being the competitor with the lowest overall score. Similarly, the country of the winning rider has the right to hold the next championship, but the competition may not be held in the same country on two consecutive occasions. (For results see page 226.)

lady-broke (US; of a horse) thoroughly broken and very quiet; suitable for a lady to ride.

laid in *staghunting* (of tufters) sent into a herd of deer in order to single out the one which is to be hunted.

lame hand a bad unskilful coachman.

laminitis inflammation of the laminae, which lie between the horny wall of the hoof and the pedal bone. The condition, which is acutely painful, since the rigid wall of the hoof allows no room for the swelling, usually affects the forefeet, though the hind feet may also be affected. It may result from any of a variety of causes, including too much corn or heating food, excessive work, especially if the animal is not fit, too much rich pasture and too little exercise, standing for excessively long periods, as when travelling, or, in mares, the retention of afterbirth after foaling. There is marked lameness, and the animal shows an unwillingness to move. If made to do so, it will move along on its heels, with its back arched, the body thrown back so that the weight is on the hind legs, which are pushed well forward under the belly, and the neck and forelegs stretched out in front. The horse will also experience difficulty in lying down and getting up, so that if it does go down it will lie, often flat on its side, for unusually long periods.

If the inflammation continues for any length of time, the laminae between the horn and the bone become detached, the body weight causes the pedal bone to drop down so that the sole of the foot becomes flat or even convex, and distinct ridges form around the hoof.

landau a four-wheeled vehicle with room for four to six passengers on facing seats. It had two doors — one on each side — and a leather hood made in two parts, which could be folded back in summer. It was drawn by two horses, and there was room on the box for the driver and the footman. In use at the beginning of the nineteenth century, it was named after the town in Germany where it was first made.

landing side the opposite side of an obstacle to the take-off side.

lane creeper (in the New Forest) a pony which leaves the forest and finds its way into a village.

large pastern bone See under PASTERN BONE.

lash a length of whipcord or the like forming the extremity of a hunting crop, driving or lungeing whip.

last year's bronco a Western horse which is in its second year of work.

lather (of a horse) **1.** the froth formed in profuse sweating. **2.** to become covered in lather.

Laurel Park Racecourse a racecourse in the state of Maryland, some twenty miles from Baltimore. The first meeting held there was on 2nd October 1911. Since then Laurel Park, as the home of a number of important races, including the Laurel Park International, has become one of the most famous racecourses in the United States. There is accommodation in the stables for 1300 horses, and over seventy days' racing are now held there every year between the beginning of October and the end of December.

law the start of about twelve minutes allowed to a carted stag before the hounds are laid on.

lawn meet *hunting* any meet held at a private house, by invitation of the owner.

Lawton gig a type of gig with a hood and rubber tyres. Named after the coachbuilder who made these improvements, the vehicle was smart in appearance and had good springing. Also called HOODED GIG. See also GIG.

lay against to offer a bet whereby more money is to be won than the stake which has been put down.

lay on to offer a bet whereby less money is to be won than the stake which has been put down.

leader 1. *driving* either of the two front horses of a team. See also WHEELER. **2.** any horse which leads one horse or more, whether being ridden or driven.

leading jockey the jockey who has won the greatest number of races during a specified period of time.

lead rope a short rope used for leading horses.

lead the field *racing* (of a horse) to be ahead of all the other runners in a particular race.

leaper (formerly) a horse that jumps, whether a racehorse or a show-jumper. Also called LEPPER.

leaping competition (formerly) a show-jumping competition. Also called LEPPING COMPETITION.

leather See STIRRUP LEATHER.

leather sole a piece of leather cut to the size and shape of a horse's hoof and used to protect an injured sole. It is put on between the hoof and the horseshoe. Since it will stop the flow of air to the sole, a leather sole should be used only when absolutely essential and the horse will require plenty of exercise to keep its foot in a healthy condition.

Lefèbvre, Janou, See TISSOT, JANOU.

left behind (of a rider) thrown back in the saddle as the horse is jumping.

left-hand course a racecourse which is run in an anticlockwise direction.

leg *racing* **1.** either part of a double bet. **2.** (formerly) a bookmaker on a racecourse, usually a dishonest one.

leg jockey (on a Western saddle) the leather flap which covers the stirrup leather where it issues from the side of the saddle.

leg up the assistance given by another person to the rider when he is mounting a horse.

length *racing* one of the measurements of the distance by which a horse may be said to win a race: the length of a horse's head and body.

lepper See LEAPER.

lepping competition See LEAPING COMPETITION.

levade a high-school movement in which the horse rears, drawing its forefeet in, while the hindquarters are deeply bent at the haunches and carry the full weight.

level weights *racing* (of two or more horses) set to carry the same amount of weight.

l.h. left-hand course.

liberty horse a circus horse which performs without being ridden, driven or led, controlled only by the trainer's voice or whip.

lift *hunting* (of a huntsman) to collect the hounds if they appear to have lost the scent and take them on to a place where the fox is thought to have gone, or to a place where someone has seen it.

lift a leg *racing* (of a horse) to be lame or limping.

light (Western US) to dismount.

light horse any horse, except a Thoroughbred, used or suitable for riding, such as a hack or a hunter.

light mouthed (of a horse) having a sensitive mouth.

light rider (Western US) any person, no matter what his weight, who keeps in balance with the horse, and is able to ride long distances without causing the horse's back to become sore.

Lincoln Handicap a one-mile horserace held annually at Doncaster. Formerly known as the LINCOLNSHIRE HANDICAP, it was first run at Lincoln in 1853 and continued to be held there until 1964, except from 1942 to 1945, when it was held at Pontefract. (For results see page 242.)

line *hunting* the direction in which the fox has gone with the hounds in pursuit. A COLD LINE occurs when the hounds are a long way behind the fox, or when there is very little scent.

line firing See under FIRING.

linseed the seed of flax, used, generally in the form of linseed jelly, oil or tea, as a laxative and to improve the condition and gloss of the horse's coat.

linseed jelly a jelly prepared in the following manner: cover a handful of linseed with cold water and allow to soak for several hours. Add more water, bring to the boil and simmer until the linseed is soft. Remove from heat and allow to cool and set.

linseed oil an oil obtained by pressing linseed. It is produced commercially and can be obtained from corn-chandlers and pharmacies.

linseed tea an infusion made by soaking and then boiling and simmering one pound of linseed in two gallons of water. When the seeds are soft, the water, which is highly nutritious, can be poured off and added to a hot or cold mash. It can also be used to moisten the manger feed, especially if this is of a constipating nature.

Lipizzaner a long-established breed of warm-blooded horse from central Europe, originally developed at the imperial stud at Lipizza, near Trieste, from imported mares and stallions.
The Lipizzaner has a longish, well ribbed-up body, with strong quarters, heavy shoulders and neck with a fine, rather small head, and good clean legs. The predominant colour is grey. When the Spanish Riding School was opened in Vienna in 1735, it was found the Lipizzaner could be trained very successfully in the airs of the high school, and today is practically the only breed used for this

levade, demonstrated in the Spanish Riding School by Col. Hans Handler.

purpose. Lipizzaners also make excellent coach horses.

Lithuanian Heavy Draught Horse a breed of heavy draught horse introduced in Lithuania by crossing the locally bred Zhmud horses with imported Swedish Ardennes. The breed was first officially recognized by the USSR Ministry of Agriculture as recently as 1963. About 15.2 h.h. and usually chestnut in colour — though there are some bays — the Lithuanian has a broad, relatively long body and short thickset legs. The neck is short, and the head is well set on, with a broad forehead. The horse has a good action at both the

walk and the trot, and has a remarkable capacity for work.

litter a number of puppies produced by a hound bitch, or a number of cubs produced by a vixen in one whelping.

Liverpool and National Steeplechase See GRAND NATIONAL HANDICAP STEEPLECHASE.

Liverpool Charlie See under TIPSTER.

Liverpool gig a type of gig named after a coach-builder in Liverpool. Similar to the Lawton gig, it had excellent springing. See also GIG.

Above
Lithuanian Heavy Draught Horse, a four-year-old stallion, Linas. At the age of 3½ he covered 2000 metres with a load of 1500 kilograms in 18 minutes 27 seconds.

Lt Col. Harry Llewellyn and the legendary Foxhunter, winners of so many international show-jumping competitions.

livery 1. the stabling, feeding, exercising, etc., of a horse for pay. **2.** a horse kept at a livery stable. **3.** *US* a livery stable.

livery stable an establishment where privately owned horses are kept, exercised and generally looked after for an agreed charge. Also called LIVERY (US).

Llanero a Venezuelan breed of pony descended from and similar to the Andalusian. Up to 14 h.h., the breed shows great stamina and endurance, and is widely used as a cow pony.

Llewellyn, Lt Col. Henry Morton, *GB* (born 1911) In 1936 Harry Llewellyn was second in the Grand National Steeplechase, riding Ego, and his first love has always been steeplechasing. It was not until after the Second World War that he turned his attention to show-jumping. In 1947 he went to Nice with the first British team to compete abroad after the war, and from that time until he retired Col. Llewellyn competed in more Prix des Nations competitions than any other British rider and won no less than 152 international competitions. The majority of his successes were with Foxhunter, and he will always be remembered for his association with this remarkable horse. See also FOXHUNTER.

lockjaw See TETANUS.

loft See HAYLOFT.

Lokai a Russian breed of horse found in the western valleys and mountains of Uzbekistan, and used for riding and as a packhorse. Considerably influenced by the Arab and the Karabair, the Lokai stands about 15 h.h. and tends to be long in the leg. The hooves are exceptionally strong, and unshod animals are often worked in the mountains. The colours of the breed are bay, chestnut and grey; sometimes the coats are curly.

London a light-brown shade of leather made from cowhide, usually used for saddlery.

long-horse a horse capable of travelling long distances at high speeds.

long pastern bone See under PASTERN BONE.

long reining the act of driving a young horse. Long reins are attached to the bit, and the trainer walks behind the horse. In this way the horse can be schooled without having to carry the weight of a rider.

long rider a Western outlaw, so called because he often had to ride long distances and spend a long time in the saddle in order to avoid capture.

long Tom *racing* a hunting crop carried by the starter's assistant in order to encourage horses to start when the signal is given.

looker a person, especially on the Romney Marshes in Kent, employed to watch the horses and cattle turned out on unfenced marshland.

loose *racing* (of a horse) continuing alone on a racecourse having fallen or unseated its jockey.

loosebox a compartment within a stable in which a horse is housed. Unlike a stall, it is enclosed on four sides so that the horse can be turned loose and has complete freedom of movement. The size of looseboxes varies, but for a fully grown horse should be no less than 12 feet by 12 feet.

lope (Western US) the long swinging stride of a horse; a slow gallop.

lop-eared (of a horse) having ears which tend to hang downwards.

loriner a person who makes the metal parts of saddlery and harness, such as bits, curb chains and stirrup irons. Also, LORIMER.

lunge rein a piece of cotton or nylon webbing, usually about 1 inch wide and 25 feet long, which is attached by means of a buckle and leather strap to one of the side rings on a breaking cavesson, and is used in training horses.

m. mile.

Macken, Eddie *Ireland* (born 1949) A successful junior rider, Eddie Macken was a pupil of the former Ladies' European Champion, Iris Kellett, and on her retirement in 1969 became the stable jockey. He has had many successes with Iris

Lokai. A Russian horse from
Uzbekistan.

Liverpool gig. E. Smith driving Regency Boy to a Liverpool gig.

Eddie Macken (second from left), together with the three other finalists in the 1974 Men's World Show Jumping Championship at Hickstead; (left to right) Hugo Simon (Austria), Hartwig Steenken (West Germany) and Frank Chapot (US).

Richard Meade goes through the lake at Badminton on Laurieston, the horse on which he won the individual gold medal in the 1972 Olympic Games.

Kellett's horses Easter Parade, Oatfield Hills, and Pele, and it was on Pele, a comparative novice eight years old, that he made nearly all the running in the World Show Jumping Championship at Hickstead in 1974. During the championship, when the four finalists rode one another's horses, he finished a very creditable second behind Hartwig Steenken of West Germany.

macs waterproof breeches worn by jockeys in bad weather.

made (of a horse) fully broken or trained for the purpose which it is intended to be used for.

Madison Square Garden a centre in New York containing an indoor arena where horseshows have been held since 1883. Until 1909 the shows were national. In that year the president, Alfred Vanderbilt, invited competitors from overseas to take part.

Magenis snaffle a jointed snaffle having rollers set within, as opposed to around, the mouthpiece.

magpie jump *dressage* a movement occasionally made by a horse when attempting to execute a piaffe; instead of moving each hind leg in turn and in proper diagonal sequence, it uses both hind legs together.

Mahmoud (by Blenheim out of Mah Mahal; Blenheim won the Derby in 1930) Foaled in France in 1933, Mahmoud was owned by the Aga Khan and was sent to England to be trained by Frank Butters at Newmarket. His first win, as a two-year-old in the Exeter Stakes at Newmarket, was followed by further victories in the Richmond Stakes at Goodwood and the Champagne Stakes at Doncaster.

In 1936, in the 2000-Guineas, he was beaten by a short head by Pay Up. Next came the Derby, in which he was ridden by Charlie Smirke. He won by three lengths from the Aga Khan's other runner, Taj Akbar, at the same time setting a record time for the race of 2 minutes 33⅘ seconds, a record which still stands today. He was also only the third grey to win the race, the others being Gustavus in 1821 and Tagalie in 1912. In the St Leger he was

third, and although he failed to win the Triple Crown, he was placed in the first three of the classics for colts.

He was then retired to stud and in 1940 was sold to the United States, where he was an outstanding success, siring such famous winners as Oil Capitol (winner of the Equipoise Mile at Arlington Park and the Flamingo Stakes at Hialeah in 1950), First Flight, Mighty Story, Snow Goose and Vulcan's Forge.

maiden a horse of either sex which to date has not won a race of any distance.

maiden mare a mare which has not had a foal, though she may be carrying one.

maiden race a race in which only horses which have never won a race may be entered.

mail axle a kind of axle used on mail coaches and also on most other horse-drawn vehicles, and generally considered to be the safest. Three nuts were used to hold the wheel in position.

mail coach a coach specially designed for the conveyance of mail. Introduced in Britain in the latter half of the eighteenth century, it was used as a safe way of carrying the mail until the introduction of the railway. Mail had previously been carried by men on horseback, who were easy targets for highwaymen. The coach also carried passengers providing there was room for them.

mail phaeton a high-seated, hooded, pair-horse driving carriage which carried the driver, one passenger and two grooms. Introduced in the reign of George IV, it gradually replaced the mail coach as roads improved and longer journeys were undertaken by train. It was a very comfortable vehicle and was used as much in the town as in the country. In order to help women to enter and alight steps were built. There was ample room for carrying both luggage and feed for the horses.

main bar the central and longest bar on a coach. The main bar is hung on the swingle tree and the traces of the leaders are attached to it.

Mairs, Mary, See under CHAPOT, FRANK DAVIS.

mail coach.

mail phaeton.

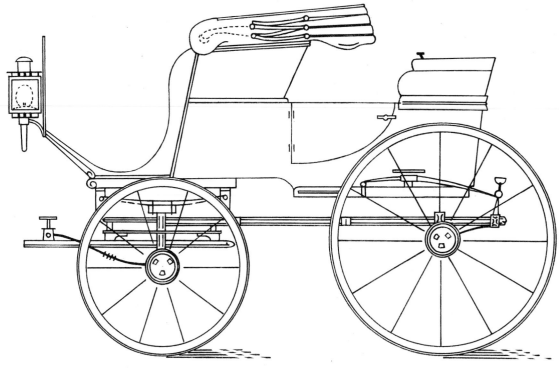

make the running *racing* (of a horse) to go into the lead in a race and set the pace.

making a pack *hunting* the counting of the hounds by the whipper-in when the hounds leave a covert or when there is a check.

mallet See POLO STICK.

Malopolski a breed of horse found in south-west Poland, derived from native ponies crossed with Arab stallions. An elegant animal, the Malopolski is used chiefly as a riding horse, though it is also suitable for farm work.

manada a herd of mares, especially brood mares.

Manchester team three horses driven abreast.

Mancinelli, Graziano, *Italy* (born 1937) A

member of the Italian junior team which won the European Junior Championships in 1952 and 1954, Graziano Mancinelli made his adult international debut in 1957. He won the European Championship in 1963 on Rockette, a full sister of The Rock. He was a member of the show-jumping teams which won the bronze medal at the Olympic Games in Tokyo in 1964 and Munich in 1972. Also in Munich, riding the Irish-bred Ambassador, he won the individual gold medal.

His wife, Nelly Passotti, has also represented Italy in international show-jumping competitions.

mane the long hair growing on the top of a horse's head and down its neck to the withers.

mane and tail comb a small long-toothed metal comb used for cleaning or pulling the mane and tail.

Mangalarga a saddle-horse bred in Brazil and developed by crossing stallions imported from Spain and Portugal with existing stock. Up to 15.2 h.h., the Mangalarga is noted for its peculiar gait, which is something between a trot and a canter. Also called JUNQUEIRA.

Man O'War (by Fair Play out of Mahubah; as a three-year-old Fair Play won the Dwyer Stakes and the Lawrence Realisation. Mahubah was by the English Triple Crown winner Rock Sand.) Foaled in 1917 at Major Belmont's stud at Lexington, Kentucky, Man O'War was purchased by Louis Fenstel, the trainer for S. Riddle, for 5000 dollars, and transferred to his stable in Maryland. Here, because of his size and the rich chestnut colour of his coat, he was nicknamed 'Big Red', a name which was to stay with him throughout his racing career.

At Belmont Park he won his first race as a two-year-old by six lengths, following it up a few days later by winning the important Keene Memorial. He went on to win at Jamaica, Aqueduct and Saratoga, but was then beaten at Saratoga by Upset. Shortly afterwards, however, the result was to be reversed in another race on the same track. His last two races in 1919 were the Hopeful Stakes and the Belmont Futurity, both of which he won.

As a three-year-old he won the Preakness Stakes and the Belmont Stakes, but was not entered in the third leg of the Triple Crown, the Kentucky Derby. He also won the Withers Stakes and the Lawrence Realisation, both at Belmont, the Dwyer Stakes at Aqueduct and the Potomac Handicap at Havre de Grace. His last race was an 80,000-dollar match over $1\frac{1}{4}$ miles at Kenilworth Park in Canada, in which he beat Sir Barton by seven lengths.

On his retirement from the race track, his stud duties were limited to twenty-five mares a year. Among his progeny, however, were such famous horses as the brilliant American Flag, Triple Crown winner War Admiral, and Battleship, winner of the Grand National.

Man O'War died in 1947 at the age of thirty.

mare a female horse aged four years or over.

Market Harborough a device used, like the martingale, to regulate the position of the horse's head. It consists of a strap which is fixed to the girth in the same way as the running martingale and ends at the breast in a ring to which two straps are attached. The straps, which are made of raw-hide or rounded leather, are passed upwards, through the rings of the bit, and attached to the reins by means of a buckle or hook fastener.

mark to ground *hunting* (of hounds) to run a fox to ground and then bay at the entrance to the earth or drain.

martingale a device used to keep a horse's head down, thus giving the rider greater control by making the horse take hold of the bit. It consists of a strap or arrangement of straps, which is fastened to the girth at one end, passed between the forelegs and, depending on the type, attached at the other end to the reins, noseband, or directly to the bit. See also COMBINED MARTINGALE, RUNNING MARTINGALE, STANDING MARTINGALE.

Maryland Hunt Cup a famous American steeplechase, run over timber, over a distance of 4 miles, in Glyndon, Maryland. It was first held in 1894, and is open to amateur riders.

mask the head of a fox.

master the person appointed by a hunt committee to have overall responsibility for the running and organization of the hunt. He is usually a local landowner and a person known and respected in the area. As well as being able to control the field when hunting, he has to obtain permission from local farmers and landowners to hunt over their land. He has to maintain and keep the huntsman, hunt staff, kennels, hounds and horses, supported only by the hunt subscriptions. The appointment lasts for one year.

Master of Foxhounds Association an association founded in 1881 to which all the masters of foxhounds in Britain belong; the governing body of hunting in the British Isles.

Master of Foxhounds Association of America an association founded in New York in 1907 to which the master of each recognized pack of foxhounds belongs; the governing body of foxhunting in the United States.

Mangalarga, a Brazilian breed, noted for its peculiar gait, the *marcha.*

Man O'War, by Fair Play out of Mahubah, with Clarence Kemmer up.

Master of Hounds the master of a pack of hounds of any type except foxhounds.

Master of the Horse the controller of the British royal stables. The office, instituted during the reign of Richard II, was first held by John Russel. The present holder is the tenth Duke of Beaufort, who was appointed in 1936.

match a race between two horses, on terms agreed by their owners, with no prize added.

matinee (US) a trotting race meeting for amateurs, usually held on a Saturday afternoon. No entry fee is paid and the prizes are in kind.

May fox *hunting* a fox hunted in the month of May. Most hunts stop in April, or before, but in some districts it is possible to hunt later in the year, particularly in areas where there is no farming, and these hunts will continue until they have killed a fox in May.

McClellan saddle a deep-seated saddle resembling the Western saddle. Once widely used by the cavalry in the United States, it has since become a popular general-purpose saddle and is particularly suitable for trail riding.

McMahon, Paddy John, *GB* (born 1933) After only one season in junior jumping competitions, Paddy McMahon started competing in adult classes in 1951. It was with Mr Mulholland's Tim II that he had most of his early successes, winning many major national competitions, including the National Championship in 1956, 1959 and 1960. Then, after a period of four years at Fred Hartill's Pennwood Stables, he started riding for Trevor Banks and in 1969, with Hideaway, he was a member of the victorious British team in the Prix des Nations at Barcelona.

In 1970 he returned to the Pennwood Stables at Wolverhampton and immediately struck up a partnership with the 16.2 h.h. bay gelding, PENNWOOD FORGE MILL, which had joined the Hartill stable as a three-year-old in 1967. After a number of major successes at home in 1971, they had their first trip abroad at the end of the season, competing with the British team in the Prix des Nations competitions in Ostend, where they won the Grand Prix, and in Rotterdam. The following year they were short-listed for the Olympic Games but were left out of the final selection. They competed in the Prix des Nations teams in Rome and London, and among their wins at home were the Texaco Championship at the Royal Show, a competition they were to win again in 1973, the British Timken Olympic Trial, and the Ronson Trophy – the Victor Ludorum – at the Horse of the Year Show.

1973 saw the pair in tremendous form; they won the Grand Prix in Madrid, as well as numerous championships at home, before going to Hickstead to win a very hotly contested Men's European Show Jumping Championship. The following week they won the King George V Gold Cup and the Horse and Hound Cup at the Royal International Horse Show, and a fortnight later they jumped two clear rounds to help the British team win the Prix des Nations in Dublin.

Meade, Richard John Hannay, *GB* (born 1938) Richard Meade competed in his first senior combined training event at Tidworth in 1961. He won the Burghley Horse Trials in 1964, riding Barberry, and two years later was second on the same horse in the World Championships, also at Burghley. He competed at the Tokyo Olympics (1964), and at the 1968 Olympic Games in Mexico he was a member of the gold medal team, riding Brigadier Gordon-Watson's Cornishman V. In 1970 he opened the year by winning Badminton with The Poacher and later the same year, again with The Poacher, he was a member of the winning team in the World Championships at Punchestown, Ireland, where he came second in the individual placings. In the European Championships at Burghley in 1971 the pair were again in the winning British team. Riding Major Allhusen's Laurieston at the 1972 Olympic Games in Munich, he won the individual gold medal and was also in the gold medal team. In the 1974 World Championships at Burghley, riding Wayfarer II, he was a member of the British team, which won the silver medal; in the individual placings he was seventh.

measuring stick an instrument for measuring the height of horses consisting of a long wooden stick, marked in hands and inches, with a right-angled sliding arm, usually containing a spirit level. The stick is held upright, with its end on the ground, against the horse, and the arm is adjusted until it lies across the withers; the height can then be read off on the vertical scale. Also called HORSE STANDARD, HORSE STICK. See also HAND, HEIGHT.

measuring wheel an instrument for measuring the length of a cross-country or show-jumping course consisting of a wheel with a handle, attached to which is a clock that shows, either in yards or metres, the distance covered.

meet *hunting* **1.** the place at which the hunt servants, hounds, followers, etc. assemble before a hunt. **2.** the meeting itself.

Meld (by Alycidon out of Daily Double) Bred and owned by Lady Zia Wernher, Meld was foaled in 1952 and was trained at Newmarket by Captain Cecil Boyd-Rochfort. Because she split a pastern in training, she had only two races as a two-year-old; she was second in the Newmarket Foal Stakes and followed this by winning the Quy Maiden Stakes at Newmarket. In 1955 she ran in the 1000-Guineas, the Oaks, the Coronation Stakes at Ascot and the St Leger, winning all four races.

She was then retired to stud. Her best colt was undoubtedly Charlottown by Charlottesville, the winner of the Derby in 1966. He was only the fifth Derby winner out of an Oaks winner.

Mellor, Stanley Thomas Edward, (born 1927) Stan Mellor first started riding as an amateur with

Far right
Meld, ridden by W. H. Carr, winning the 1955 Oaks from Ark Royal (E. Mercer) and Reel In (A. Breasley).

George Owen at Tarporley in Cheshire in 1952, and for the next twenty years he dominated the steeplechasing world, being the first National Hunt jockey to ride over 1000 winners in his career. His 1000th win was on Ouzo at Nottingham on 18th December 1971, and his last ride in England before his retirement – on Arne Folly at Stratford-on-Avon on 2nd June 1972 – gave him his 1035th victory.

Right
Stan Mellor, the first steeplechase jockey to ride 1000 winners.

Far right
'Merychippus'.

He was champion jockey for three consecutive seasons; 1959/60 with 68 winners, 1960/61 with 118 winners and 1961/62 with 80 winners. Among his many wins were the Mildmay Memorial Chase in 1968 on Stalbridge Colonist, the Whitbread Gold Cup in 1962 on Frenchman's Cove, the Mackeson Gold Cup in 1964 on Super Flash, the Hennessy Gold Cup in 1966 on Stalbridge Colonist, the King George VI Steeplechase in 1964 on Frenchman's Cove, the Grand Sefton Chase in 1965 on The Fossa, the Great Yorkshire Steeplechase in 1961 on Chavara and in 1964 on King's Nephew.

On retiring as a jockey he took out a licence to train and now has a yard at Lambourn, Berkshire.

Men's European Show Jumping Championship an individual show-jumping championship for men riders from Europe, held annually since 1957, except in Olympic or Men's World Show Jumping Championship years. Each country is allowed to enter two riders, each with two horses. The championship consists of three competitions held on different days, usually with a rest day between the second and third competitions. The winner is the rider with the lowest overall score, one point being awarded for first place in each competition, two for second, and so on. If the rider has two horses, it is the score of the better-placed horse in each competition which counts in his final score. The country of the winning rider has the right to hold the championship the following year, but the competition may not be held in the same country on two successive occasions. (For results see page 225.)

Men's World Show Jumping Championship an individual show-jumping championship for men riders, held in 1953, 1954, 1955, 1960 and 1964, and since 1966 held every second year after an Olympic Games. It is open to two competitors from each country and is run in the same way as the Men's European Show Jumping Championship, except that after the first three competitions, there is a fourth and final competition for the four leading riders at this stage. In this competition each rider must jump the course on his own horse and then on the horse of each of the other finalists. The winner of the championship is the rider with the least number of faults overall in the final. The country of the winning rider has the right to claim the next championship, but it may not be held in the same country on two successive occasions. (For results see page 226.)

Merely-a-Monarch See under WUCHERPFENNIG, ELIZABETH ANN.

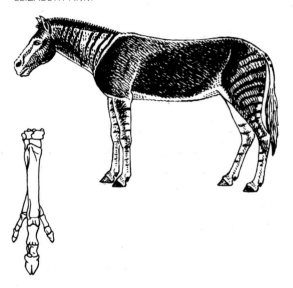

'Merychippus' one of the important stages in the evolution of the horse. *Merychippus*, which lived some fifteen to twenty million years ago during the middle Miocene Epoch, had three toes on each foot but only the middle one reached the ground. Its teeth were adapted for eating grass and in appearance it was in many respects similar to a modern pony. See also EOHIPPUS, EQUUS, MESO-HIPPUS, PLIOHIPPUS.

Far right
'Mesohippus'.

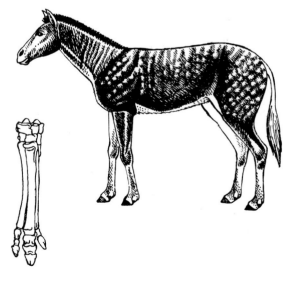

'Mesohippus' one of the important stages in the evolution of the horse. *Mesohippus*, which lived some forty million years ago during the Oligocene Epoch, was twice the size of *Eohippus*, the earliest known ancestor of the modern horse. It had three toes on front and hind feet, and its teeth had undergone considerable changes. See also EOHIPPUS, EQUUS, MERYCHIPPUS, PLIOHIPPUS.

Messenger Foaled in England in 1780, Messenger retired from racing after three seasons, during which he had won ten of sixteen races and had been second twice and third twice. He was exported to the United States in 1788, where, until his death in 1808, he provided the foundation for American trotters.

methody (of a horse's knees) broken through continual falls.

mews a district in an English city or town where horses were stabled. The name was first applied to the royal stables at Charing Cross, which in 1534 were built on the site of the old royal hawk mews. The word is derived from the French *muer*, meaning to moult or shed feathers.

Meyers pattern cribbing device See under CRIB BITING.

Meynell, Hugo (1735–1808) Hugo Meynell has been called by many the 'father of modern fox-hunting'. In 1753, after buying a pack of foxhounds, he proceeded to revolutionize the sport of fox-hunting. During his forty-seven years as master of that area now hunted by the Quorn, he reduced the size, not only of the woods, but also of the horses and hounds, so that much faster hunts took the place of the previously long and slow draw of big woodlands. His system proved popular and was soon adopted in other areas.

M.F.H. Master of Foxhounds.

M.H. Master of Hounds.

middle distance (of a horserace) over a distance of 6 to 8 furlongs.

Middle Park Stakes a race over 6 furlongs for two-year-old colts, held at Newmarket since 1866, except in 1940, when it was run at Nottingham. Formerly called (until 1921) MIDDLE PARK PLATE. (For results see pages 242–243.)

miler a horse which runs in or specializes in races over the distance of 1 mile.

military boot (US) a white canvas boot, sometimes worn by officers' chargers on ceremonial parades.

Below
Mill Reef, with Geoff Lewis up.

Mill Reef (by Never Bend out of Milan Mill. In 1962, as a two-year-old, Never Bend, by Nasrullah, won the Champagne Stakes, the Codwin Stakes and the Futurity Stakes at Belmont Park, and was the Two-Year-Old Champion.) Foaled in 1968, Mill Reef was bred in the United States by his owner, Paul Mellon, and sent to England to be trained by Ian Balding at Kingsclere. As a two-year-old, he ran five times in England, winning all five races: the Salisbury Stakes at Salisbury, the Coventry Stakes at Ascot, the Gimcrack Stakes at York, the Imperial Stakes at Kempton Park and the Dewhurst Stakes at Newmarket, his only defeat coming in France, in the Prix Robert Papin at Maisons-Laffitte, in which he was beaten by a short head by My Swallow.

The following season he won the Greenham Stakes at Newbury, but was beaten by three lengths in the 2000-Guineas by Brigadier Gerard. He was made a hot favourite for the Derby, which he duly won by two lengths from Linden Tree, and then went on to win the Eclipse Stakes at Sandown, beating the French-trained Caro by four lengths. He won the King George VI and Queen Elizabeth Stakes at Ascot, and became the first English-trained horse for twenty years to win the Prix de L'Arc de Triomphe at Longchamp, at the same time breaking the 1½-mile course record in a time of 2 minutes 28·30 seconds.

As a four-year-old Mill Reef won the Coronation Cup at Epsom, but then, after a training setback, he shattered a bone in a foreleg while at exercise, and his brilliant racing career was brought to a premature close. However, he was given the best possible medical care and recovered sufficiently to be able to take up stud duties at the National Stud.

Below
Mill Reef. Owner-breeder Paul Mellon looks with pride at the bronze statue of his famous horse. Standing to his right is the artist John Skeaping.

misfit a horse used for any purpose other than the one for which it was bred, as, for example, a horse bred for racing which is used as a riding horse for hire.

Mister Softee *GB* (chestnut gelding, 16.1½ h.h.) Owned by John Massarella of Yorkshire, and first registered with the B.S.J.A. in 1960. Mister Softee was ridden in early competitions by the owner's brother, Andrew, and by Bobbie Bealby. In 1961 the ride was given to fellow Yorkshireman, C. David Barker, with whom Mister Softee won the first of three European Championships at the White City in 1962. The combination enjoyed a most successful partnership at home and abroad until mid-1965, two of their greatest triumphs abroad being the Grand Prix at Ostend and Rotterdam in 1963. From June to August 1965, Mister Softee was ridden by yet another Yorkshireman, John Lanni, before becoming the mount of David Broome.

It was with David Broome that he had his greatest successes, including two further European Championships — in 1967 at Rotterdam and 1969 at Hickstead — thus becoming the only horse to win this Championship three times. In 1966 he won the King George V Gold Cup, the British Jumping Derby at Hickstead, the Olympic Trial and the Victor Ludorum at the Horse of the Year Show, the only year in which these four major competitions have been won by the same horse and rider. The following year he won the National Championship at home, and the Grand Prix at both Dublin and Rotterdam. He again won the National Championship in 1968, the same year in which he won the individual bronze medal at the Olympic Games in Mexico. He was retired in 1969.

Mitteltrab a form of trot practised in Germany. Both the position of the horse and the speed at which it moves are almost as in a collected trot, but the action, which is delivered with marked cadence, resembles the extended trot.

mixed meeting a race meeting at which both flat and steeplechase or hurdle races are held on the same day.

mixed pack a pack of hounds which includes both dogs and bitches. Also called BOBBERY PACK.

mixed stable a racing stable where both flat race and National Hunt horses are kept.

mochila (Western US) a mail pouch built into the skirt of a saddle in the days of the Pony Express. Later it was simply a large piece of leather which covered the saddle. It had a hole for the horn and a narrow slit for the cantle to pass through, and was attached after the saddle had been put on the horse.

monkey (in betting slang) the sum of £500.

montura (Western US) **1.** a riding horse. **2.** a saddle.

Moore, Ann Elizabeth, *GB* (born 1950) Ann Moore has had a meteoric rise to fame. She won the European Junior Championship at Stoneleigh in 1968 with Psalm and was a member of the winning team in these championships on three occasions: in 1965 in Italy riding Kangaroo; in 1967, again in Italy, riding Hop-a-long Cassidy; and in 1968 with Psalm. In 1968 she also won all three British Young Riders' Championships. In 1971 and 1972 Ann Moore really came into her own with Psalm and the ex-Australian mare, April Love. In 1971, after winning the ladies' competitions at Aachen and Dublin, she went on to win the Ladies' European Championship at St Gallen. The following year she won all over the British Isles, her biggest win coming at the Royal International Horse Show when she won the coveted Queen Elizabeth II Cup. The climax of her riding

career came in Munich at the Olympic Games when, with Psalm, she won the individual silver medal. In 1973, riding Psalm, she successfully defended her Ladies' European title in Vienna, and at the Royal International Horse Show she was equal first in the Queen Elizabeth II Cup.

In June 1974 she announced her retirement from show-jumping.

Morgan a breed of light horse which originated in the United States during the late nineteenth century. The founder of the breed, a 14.2 h.h. bay stallion, known as Justin Morgan after his owner, was foaled in Vermont in about 1890. He proved to be extraordinarily prepotent and, since his conformation and characteristics were much admired, he was used to serve a large number of mares. He was eventually bought by the United States Army, and the Morgan Stud Farm was established.

The Morgan, which stands between 14 h.h. and 15 h.h., has a strong compact muscular body, well-made legs and feet and full mane and tail. The colours accepted by the breed society, the Morgan Horse Club, Inc., are bay, brown, chestnut and black.

morning stables See under STABLES.

Mother Hubbard saddle (Western US) an early improvement on the Mexican saddle. It had a mochila, which at first was detachable, but was later made a permanent part of the saddle. This alteration was carried out in order to give

more comfort to both the horse and the rider.

Mould, Marion Janice, *GB* (born 1947) Marion Mould has had a remarkable show-jumping career with the 14.2 h.h. bay gelding, STROLLER, which was bought for her by her father in 1961. After many successes in junior competitions — they were members of the British team which won the European Junior Championships in Berlin in 1963 — they started competing in adult classes in 1964. From then until the pony's retirement at the end of the 1971 season, they were household names, winning many major championships at home and abroad, and were one of the most widely travelled show-jumping combinations, with competitions as far afield as Olsztyn in Poland, Mexico and Rome. In 1965 they won the inaugural Ladies' World Championship and the Queen Elizabeth II Cup, a win they were to repeat in 1971, and Marion won both the *Daily Express* and the Sportswriters' Sportswoman of the Year awards. In 1967 they won the British Jumping Derby, in 1968 the individual silver medal at the Olympic Games in Mexico, and in 1970 the Hamburg Jumping Derby. The pair's last major success was at the Horse of the Year Show in 1971, when they won the Country Life and Riding Cup.

Marion Mould's husband, David, is a National Hunt jockey.

mount 1. a horse used for riding. **2.** to get up on to the back of a horse.

mounted police policemen who perform their

Morgan, the most popular
general-purpose breed in the
United States.

Murakosi, a breed of fast-moving heavy horse, developed comparatively recently in southern Hungary, where it is used for agricultural work.

Nonius. A Hungarian breed
of horse used for riding and
light agricultural work.

Noriker, a draught horse of
medium size, found in
Austria and southern
Germany.

duties on horseback. In London the mounted branch of the Metropolitan Police traces its history back to 1763 when a small mounted patrol was started by Sir John Fielding. This patrol was incorporated into the Metropolitan Police some seventy years later, and gradually branches were formed in major cities throughout the country. Even in this mechanical age, the mounted policeman is still in great demand, particularly for the control of crowds, since his horse is specially trained to press sideways against groups of people. Moreover, the policeman has a natural vantage point from which to see what is happening further back.

Training for the mounted branch of the Metropolitan Police takes place at Imber Court in Surrey, where the horse and rider spend some six months before being sent out on duty.

mounting block a platform of stone or brick from which to mount a horse. About 2 feet 6 inches to 3 feet high, it is approached by steps. Also called HORSING STONE, PILLION POST.

mount money (Western US) the money paid in a rodeo to a performer riding, roping or bull-dogging in exhibition but not in competition.

mouth See TOOTH.

muck out to clean out a box or stall in which a horse has been stabled, removing the droppings and soiled bedding. Any dry unsoiled bedding should be pushed to the back of the box so that the floor can be cleaned, disinfected and aired before fresh bedding is put down.

mudder (US) a trotting horse which runs well on a muddy track.

mud fever an inflammation of the upper layer of skin, caused by mud and wet. The condition, which occurs mainly in winter, may affect any part of the body which has been splashed with mud,

Above
Marion Mould and the diminutive Stroller.

Right
mounted police. The well-trained police horse still provides one of the most effective means of crowd control and continues to play an active part in the work of police forces all over the world.

137

although the legs, especially if they have been clipped, are most commonly affected. Like cracked heels, it is aggravated by washing off the mud and not drying the skin properly. The hair stands up in patches and the skin becomes covered with scabs. When the scabs come off the hair falls off with them.

mule the offspring of a male donkey and a mare, used extensively as a pack-animal because of its hardiness, sure-footedness and docility. A mule can rarely be bred from.

mule-footed (Western US; of a horse) having round feet.

mule-hipped horse (Western US) one in which the hips slope too much.

muley saddle (Western US) a saddle without a horn.

mullen mouth See under SNAFFLE BIT.

multiple gamblers' stakes *show-jumping* a competition in which obstacles of varying height, numbered only for the purpose of judging, are placed in the ring. A large playing card is placed on the wings of each obstacle to indicate its value. The larger the obstacle the greater the value. For example:

ace	14 points
king	13 points
queen	12 points
knave	11 points, and so on.

After going through the start, the competitor has two minutes in which to jump seven obstacles of his own choice. The obstacles may be jumped in any order and from either direction, and any obstacle may be jumped as many times as the competitor wishes, as long as it is not knocked down. If a competitor jumps more than seven obstacles he is eliminated.

The winner is the competitor gaining the greatest number of points, and, in the event of equality of points, time decides.

Mumtaz Mahal (by The Tetrarch out of Lady Josephine) Foaled in 1921, Mumtaz Mahal was bred at Sledmere by Lady Sykes and purchased as a yearling by the Aga Khan. She was trained by Dick Dawson at Whatcombe. As a two-year-old she won the Spring Stakes at Newmarket, the Queen Mary Stakes at Ascot, the National Breeders' Produce Stakes at Sandown, the Molecomb Stakes at Goodwood, the Champagne Stakes at Doncaster and was just beaten in her last race of the season, the Imperial Produce Stakes at Kempton. The following season she came second in the 1000-Guineas, was unplaced in the Coronation Stakes at Ascot but went on to win the King George Stakes at Sandwich and the Nunthorp Stakes at York.

She was then retired to stud and was the dam of six winners, including Mirza II. It was through the female line that she had such an influence on bloodstock. One of her female progeny, Mah Mahal, was the dam of Mahmoud; another, Mumtaz Begum, produced a number of winners, including Nasrullah, who won the Champion Stakes. Mumtaz Mahal died at the Aga Khan's stud in France during the early part of the Second World War.

Murakosi a comparatively new breed of heavy horse found mainly in the south of Hungary, based on the old MUR INSULANS, a cold-blood horse originally from Yugoslavia, which was improved by the importation of Percherons. Usually over 16 h.h. and chestnut, bay or black in colour, the Murakosi has a short, stocky body with a short neck. It is used mainly for agricultural purposes, as it is of good quality, able to move fast and capable of hauling heavy loads.

Murgese a breed of horse used mainly for light agricultural work but also for riding in the Murge district, near Apulia, Italy, where it has been bred for hundreds of years. The usual colour is sorrel, and the average height is between 15 and 16 hands.

Mur Insulans See under MURAKOSI.

music *hunting* the cry made by hounds when they are hunting.

mustanger (Western US) one who catches mustangs.

Below, right
Left **bar-type muzzle.**
Right **leather muzzle.**

Below
Mumtaz Mahal, with G. Hulme up. Through her daughters she had a great influence on bloodstock.

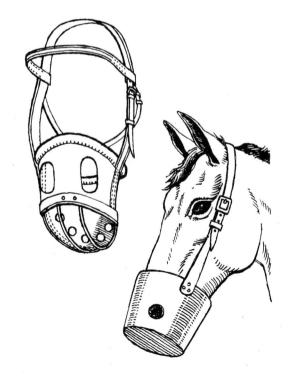

muzzle a device put over a horse's mouth to prevent the horse from biting, or from eating its bedding. The BAR-TYPE MUZZLE is commonly used to prevent horses biting when in the stable. It is bucket-shaped, the sides being made of leather, with holes for the nostrils, and the base consisting of a narrow bar or bars fitted at right angles across the mouth, so that the horse is able to feed. The NET MUZZLE consists of a netting bag which is attached to the noseband. It is used mainly on harness horses which are likely to bite at passers-by. The LEATHER MUZZLE is bucket-shaped, with a solid bottom, which fits against the horse's mouth, and airholes in the sides. It is fitted by means of an adjustable head strap. Since it prevents the horse from eating altogether, it is used mainly to break bed-eating, dung-eating, and similar habits.

nag a horse, especially one of poor quality.

nagbut snaffle.

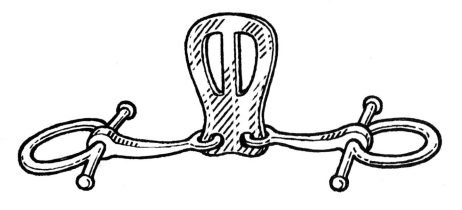

nagbut snaffle a snaffle bit having a jointed mouthpiece with a metal port set in the middle to lie on the tongue and thus prevent the horse from putting it over the bit.

nagsman a professional horseman employed by a riding stable or the like to improve horses, especially those with vices or bad manners.

nap 1. (of a horse) to fail to respond to properly applied aids, as in refusing to go forward or to pass a certain point. In show-jumping competitions and combined training events napping is penalized as for a refusal. **2.** *racing* a good tip.

nappy (of a horse) given to napping.

narrow foot a type of foot similar to the sound foot, except that the heel is higher and the quarters and toe more upright. In a light horse a narrow foot is prone to contraction and navicular disease, while in a heavy horse it is liable to sidebone. The walls and sole are generally strong and hard, but extreme care is needed in shoeing.

National Association of Bookmakers a non-profit making organization whose main object is to protect the interests of bookmakers and persons interested in betting, whether on or off the race-course. It has a network of affiliated associations covering every county in Britain, and is recognized by the government and sporting authorities as representative of and competent to speak for responsible bookmakers throughout the country.

National Equestrian Centre In 1965 the Council of the British Horse Society decided the time had come to move its offices and those of the British Show Jumping Association from their headquarters at Bedford Square, London, to the country. A committee was set up to investigate the possibility of accepting a parcel of land from the Royal Agricultural Society of England on their show ground at Stoneleigh, in Warwickshire, where they had recently established the National Agricultural Centre. The land was accepted as an ideal site for the offices and riding school which would form the nucleus of the National Equestrian Centre.

The first phase of the programme was the building of an office block, which was completed and ready for occupation in May 1967; the second phase was the building of the riding school, which was finished in September 1968 and comprised a riding area measuring approximately 200 feet by

National Equestrian Centre. The indoor arena, which was opened in 1968. It is about 200 feet long and 80 feet wide, and the roof is covered with a filon material to give natural light all day.

80 feet, as well as a lecture room, conference hall, library, first-aid room and canteen. In 1973 a stable block was erected, and the following year a hostel was built to accommodate students attending courses.

For many years since the war it had been obvious there was a worldwide dearth of top-class instructors, mainly as a result of the mechanization of the army. At the same time there had been a tremendous rise in the popularity of riding, and the membership of the British Horse Society alone had increased from 4000 in 1947 to over 15,000 by 1965. It was therefore in response to this situation that the National Equestrian Centre set out to be a university of the horse, providing top-class instructors for riding teachers.

The centre is a joint project between the British Horse Society and the British Show Jumping Association.

national event any combined training, dressage or show-jumping event in which all the competitions are restricted to riders qualified to enter them under the rules of the national federation in the country where the event is held.

national federation the governing body of equestrian affairs in any country affiliated to the F.E.I. For example, the national federation of Great Britain is the British Equestrian Federation.

National Horse Association of Great Britain an association formed in 1922 with the object of furthering the welfare of horses and ponies and the interests of their breeders. In 1947 it was amalgamated with the Institute of the Horse to form the British Horse Society.

National Hunt steeplechasing and hurdle racing.

National Hunt Festival an annual three-day race meeting held, usually in March, at Cheltenham racecourse, Prestbury Park, at which some of the most important steeplechase and hurdle races are run, including the Cheltenham Gold Cup.

National Hunt Steeplechase a four-mile steeplechase for amateur riders, held since 1912 at Cheltenham. (For results see page 250.)

National Hunt Trainers Association an amalgamation formed in 1970 of the Northern and Southern National Hunt Trainers Associations. Its objects are to consider and to promote the interests of all National Hunt trainers and to encourage close liaison with the Jockey Club.

National Trainers' Association a body whose objects are to promote the interests of trainers of horses for flat racing and to enable the views and opinions of all trainers on all racing matters which affect them to be brought before the Turf Authorities for consideration.

Nations' Cup See PRIX DES NATIONS.

native pony any of the mountain or moorland breeds of pony native to the British Isles, namely, the Connemara, the Dales, the Dartmoor, the Exmoor, the Fell, the Highland, the New Forest, the Shetland and the Welsh.

natural aids See under AID.

Navajo blanket a type of blanket pad used under a Western saddle.

nave the hub or stock of a wheel into which the inner ends of the spokes are inserted and through which the axle arm passes.

navicular bone See under NAVICULAR DISEASE.

navicular disease an incurable disease which attacks the NAVICULAR BONE (also called SHUTTLE BONE), a small bone in the hoof, forming part of the joint between the pedal bone and the short pastern bone. The bone is eroded by the disease, becoming pitted with cavities and hollows, and a small growth, known as a spur, often appears at each end of the bone. One of the first visible symptoms is a persistent and obscure lameness, especially in one or both of the forefeet. At rest, the horse will point the diseased foot or feet in order to keep the weight off the heel, and when it moves the animal will take short steps, putting the toes down first. As the disease progresses the shape of the hoof begins to change, becoming short at the toe and deep at the heel, rather like the hoof of a mule or donkey.

near fore the left foreleg of a horse.

near hind the left hind leg of a horse.

nearside the left-hand side of a horse.

neck *racing* one of the measurements of the distance by which a horse may be said to win a race: the length of a horse's head and neck.

neck rein to steer a horse by applying pressure against the neck, rather than on the mouth. For a right-hand turn pressure is applied with the left-hand rein, and vice versa.

neigh the cry of a horse; a whinny.

Nemethy, Bertalan de, *US* (born 1911) Trainer of the United States show-jumping team since 1955, Bert de Nemethy was born in Hungary. After completing his education, he went to the Hungarian Military Academy in Budapest, graduating as a lieutenant in the cavalry in 1932. He later entered the Hungarian Cavalry School and in 1937 was awarded the diploma of riding instructor. He remained at the school, becoming a member of the international show-jumping team, and was trained for the ill-fated Olympic Games of 1940.

Between 1937 and 1940 he represented Hungary in Aachen, Lucerne, Munich, Rome, Florence and Vienna. In 1945 he went to Denmark, and in 1952 emigrated to the United States.

Since his appointment as its coach, the United States team has won half the Prix des Nations competitions in which it has competed and the President's Cup on two occasions.

neronia a triathlon event in ancient Rome introduced by Nero. It included music, wrestling and chariot racing.

Never Say Die (by Nasrullah out of Singing Grass) Foaled in 1951, Never Say Die was bred in the United States at the stud owned by J. A. Bell and was owned by Robert Clark. He was shipped to England as a yearling and went into training with Joe Lawson.

As a two-year-old his only success came in the Rosalyn Stakes at Ascot. The following year, after having been beaten in his first three races, he was ridden in the Derby by Lester Piggott and beat Arabian Night by two lengths. His starting price was 33–1. He gave Piggott his first Derby win and he was only the second American-bred horse to win this race. In his final race, the St Leger, he was ridden by Charlie Smirke and won very convincingly by twelve lengths from Elopement.

Never Say Die was then retired and was presented by his owner to the National Stud.

New Forest pony a breed of hardy pony originating, as its name suggests, in the New Forest area of Hampshire. Its remote ancestry is uncertain but it lives in a region where ponies have always roamed. In the late nineteenth century outside breeds were introduced to the Forest and Arab stallions certainly impressed their stamp on the breed as we know it today. The New Forest is an extremely popular pony and, with the height varying from 12 h.h. to 14.2 h.h., highly suitable for children. Any colour is allowed except skewbald or piebald. The head should be well set on, with the neck a little short from the throat to the chest, but with a well-laid back shoulder which allows plenty of length of rein. The back should be short with strong loins and quarters and the tail well set on. A good forearm and second thigh are essential, with short cannon bones and good feet. The pony should have plenty of bone, though the smaller ponies should be lighter in bone than the larger ones.

The breed society was formed in 1906, and the New Forest pony is now in great demand abroad, particularly in Denmark and the Netherlands. More recently it has been exported to the United States.

Far right
New Forest pony. W. J. Crabb's Burton Starlight.

Below
Never Say Die, owned by R. Clark, trained by J. Lawson and ridden by Charlie Smirke, winning the St Leger in 1954.

Above
New Forest pony. A group
of mares and foals.

Newmarket, the major horseracing centre in Britain. First discovered as a sporting area by James I, who used to hunt there regularly, Newmarket became established as a racing centre in the 1660s, under the patronage of Charles II, who had a palace there and enjoyed race-riding himself. The area, situated partly in Cambridgeshire and partly in Suffolk, was spacious and fairly level, and lent itself ideally to racing.

Today, concentrated in Newmarket and the surrounding area are the headquarters of the Jockey Club, Tattersalls' sales paddocks, the National Stud and the Equine Research Station of the Animal Health Trust, as well as some forty studs and thirty-five racing stables.

There are two racecourses, the JULY and the SEFTON, where some twenty-five days' racing are held every year, the principal races being the 2000-Guineas and the 1000-Guineas, held in the spring, and the Cesarewitch Stakes, the Cambridgeshire Stakes, the Champion Stakes, and the Middle Park Stakes, held in the autumn.

Below
New Zealand rug.

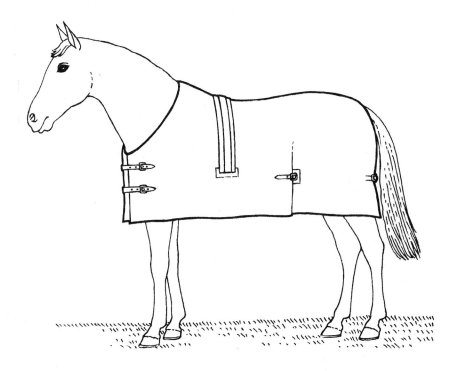

New Zealand rug a stout half-lined rug of water-proof canvas, used to protect a horse which is kept out during the winter, especially if it has been clipped. It is important that the rug fits properly in order to avoid chafing and it must be fixed securely. Some types have straps which fasten near the fore-legs, and some near the hind legs. Both types have a strap which fastens over the breast. A surcingle should not be used, as it would produce constant pressure on the spine and block the free passage of air, thus causing condensation.

n.f.n.f. no foal, no fee.

N.H. National Hunt.

Nijinsky (by Northern Dancer out of Flaming Page; in 1964 Northern Dancer won the Kentucky Derby and the Preakness Stakes in the United States, as well as the richest race in Canada, the Queen's Plate, at Woodbine. Flaming Page was also a winner of the Queen's Plate). Nijinsky was foaled in 1967 in Ontario, Canada, and was sold as a yearling to Charles Engelhard of Toronto, who sent him to Ireland to be trained by Vincent O'Brien.

His debut on the racecourse was at the Curragh in 1969, when he won the Erne Maiden Stakes. Following three further wins on the same course in the Railway, the Anglesey and the Beresford Stakes, he was sent over to England for the Dewhurst Stakes at Newmarket, a race he was to win easily and which was to mark the beginning of his very successful partnership with Lester Piggott.

His first race as a three-year-old was in the Gladness Stakes, which he won by two and a half lengths. He then went for the 2000-Guineas, which he won by two and a half lengths from Yellow God. Next came the Derby, and strong opposition from across the English Channel. Nijinsky, however, was first past the post, two and a half lengths in front of French-bred Gyr. Ridden by Irish jockey Liam Ward, he won the Irish Sweeps Derby from Meadowville, returning to England for his next outing, the King George VI and Queen Elizabeth Stakes at Ascot, in which he beat Blakeney by two lengths. In the St Leger he again beat Meadowville to win the Triple Crown. This, however, was to be his last victory, for in the Prix de l'Arc de Triomphe he was beaten by French Derby-winner Sassafras, and in the Champion Stakes at Newmarket by Lorenzaccio.

Many people were anxious to buy Nijinsky for stud, but Charles Engelhard decided he would be syndicated to America and would go to stud in Kentucky, where his American mares were stabled.

nobble to interfere with a horse in any way which could jeopardize his chances of winning a race.

no foal, no fee a stud term meaning that if a mare is found not to be in foal after being covered, no fee will be charged for the service of the stallion.

nominator the person in whose name a horse is entered to run in a race.

Nonius a Hungarian breed of horse named after its founder — said to have been a French-bred stallion by a half-bred English stallion out of a Norman mare — which was captured by the Hungarian cavalry during the Napoleonic Wars. The height varies between 14.2 h.h. and 16 h.h., and the usual colours are bay, black or brown. The breed makes a very good riding horse and is also used for light agricultural work.

non-starter a horse which having been entered for a race does not actually run in it.

non-stayer a horse which only has limited power of endurance and may not be able to complete the distance of a longer course.

Norfolk, 16th Duke of (1908–75) One of the great patrons of English racing, the Duke was the Queen's representative at Ascot until his retirement in 1971. He was a member, trustee and steward of the Jockey Club, and was vice-chairman of the Turf Board from 1965 to 1968. He owned many successful racehorses, including Sovereign Lord, winner of the Gimcrack Stakes at York in 1961.

He was former president of the British Horse Society and of the British Show Jumping Association, and in 1960 allowed his home, Arundel Park, to be used as the training headquarters of the British Olympic show-jumping team.

Norfolk shooting cart See under DOGCART.

Noriker a breed of draught horse originating in the ancient Roman province of Noricum (a region roughly corresponding to the part of Austria south of the Danube), and now found in Bavaria and parts of Austria. The horse is of medium size, capable of pulling heavy loads and of travelling long distances. It is deep through the heart and short on the leg, and has a long and sure action. The most common colours are chestnut or brown. Also called NORIC HORSE.

normal jumping competition a show-jumping competition in which normal jumping ability is the main factor tested, although speed may be introduced to find the winner in either the first or the second jump-off.

Competitions of this type are judged under Table A, with time either to count or recorded for penalties. The course is built to test the ability of the horse to jump a variety of obstacles, but unless specified in the schedule the actual number and nature of the obstacles is left to the course builder and the judge.

Far right
Northlands, a Norwegian breed, used both for riding and draught work.

Below
North Swedish Horse, an extremely strong draught horse. used in the forests of Sweden for pulling logs.

Northfield See FJORD PONY.

Northlands a Norwegian breed of hardy pony, probably originally imported from Russia and subsequently bred by farmers for riding and use on smallholdings. By the end of the Second World War, the Northlands pony was almost extinct. However, interest in the breed has since revived, and the numbers are now increasing.

North Swedish Horse a breed of heavy draught horse, descendant of an ancient Scandinavian breed, standing about 15 h.h. and having a deep muscular body, sturdy, relatively short legs and a flowing mane and tail. The usual colours are bay, and brown with black points. The breed is noted for its strength and docile temperament.

nose *racing* the shortest measurement of distance by which it is possible for a horse to win a race.

nosebag a bag for feeding horses, fitting over the mouth and held in place by a strap which passes over the head, used especially on agricultural and working horses.

noseband the part of a bridle which lies across the horse's nose and to which a standing martingale is attached. It consists of a leather strap, which is slotted through the headpiece so that it can be tightened in order to prevent it from sagging or becoming too low, and is normally passed between the cheekpieces and the horse's head. Sheepskin-covered nosebands are becoming increasingly common. They were first used on trotting horses in the United States as an anti-shying device, but away from the racecourse they have little use, except possibly to prevent chafing of the nose.

notifiable diseases There is a legal obligation to notify the police or the Ministry of Agriculture, Fisheries and Food if a horse develops any of the following diseases: anthrax, Epizootic lymphangitis, glanders and farcy, mange and rabies.

not yet run *racing* (of a racehorse) in training but not yet having competed in a race.

novice class a combined training competition in Britain restricted to horses in Grade III. In such a class the dressage test is of novice or preliminary standard. No obstacle in the show-jumping phase exceeds 3 feet 9 inches in height or 5 feet in spread at the highest point and 8 feet at the base, and the test is carried out at a speed of 327 yards per minute. The cross-country course is no less than 1 mile but no more than 1¾ miles long, with a total of sixteen to twenty obstacles, and no obstacle exceeds 3 feet 6 inches in height.

Novokirghiz a breed of horse, first officially

recognized by the USSR Ministry of Agriculture in 1954, which was developed in the state of Kirghizia in the Soviet Union by crossing the native Kirghiz with the Don. Averaging 15.1 h.h., the breed is characterized by a long body with comparatively short legs and extremely hard hoofs, and is used as a saddle-horse and for herding cattle. Reared in herds on the mountain pastures, the horses have tremendous stamina and large, well-developed lungs, so that they are particularly suitable for work at high altitudes.

nowhere *racing* (of a horse) not placed in the first three of a race.

numbers In all forms of racing each horse in a race is given a number and this is displayed on a number cloth, which is put on the horse's back, beneath the saddle. In horse trials, the rider wears a large number cloth on his chest and back, and in show-jumping and showing classes the competitor wears a small cardboard number on his back, which is attached by a string tied round the waist.

numnah a pad placed under the saddle in order to prevent undue pressure on the horse's back. It is cut to the shape of the saddle, but is slightly larger, and may be made of sheepskin, felt or cloth-covered foam rubber. In competitions in which a certain weight has to be carried a numnah may be included in that weight.

nursery handicap a flat race confined to two-year-old horses.

nutcracker a horse which has a habit of grinding its teeth.

Oaks a race over 1 mile 4 furlongs for three-year-old fillies, held annually at Epsom since 1779, except from 1915 to 1918 and from 1940 to 1945, when it was run at Newmarket. One of the five classics, it takes its name from a property near Epsom owned by the twelfth Earl of Derby where the idea

of the race was originally conceived. (For results see page 243.)

oats The best oats are short and plump with a sweet taste and sweet flowery smell, and thin smooth skins that slip easily through the fingers. Oats which are mouldy, sprouting or damaged in any way should not be fed to horses as they may cause illness.

objection *racing* An objection may be made against any of the placed horses in a race, and must be heard by the stewards at the meeting where the objection was raised.

objection overruled *racing* the refusal by the stewards at a race meeting to allow an objection which may have been made against a horse or jockey.

objection sustained *racing* the acceptance by the stewards at a race meeting of an objection which may have been made against a horse or jockey.

odd feet a condition occurring most commonly in racehorses in which one foot is larger than the other three. There is no disease; it is caused by a particular shoe being pulled off more than the others and by constant reshoeing.

odds the betting quotation on a horse in a particular race.

off fore the right foreleg of a horse.

off hind the right hind leg of a horse

offside the right-hand side of a horse.

oily bronc (Western US) a bad horse.

Oldenburg The Oldenburg was bred on the natural grassland plains of the Oldenburg region of Germany in the seventeenth century. Its development was due largely to the work of Count Anton Gunther, one of whose stallions, Kranich, was particularly outstanding and left his stamp on the

Oldenburg. The Crown Equerry, Col. Sir John Miller, driving a team of Oldenburgs.

Olympia. These two photographs, taken before 1910, show the elaborate decor which adorned the arena during the International Horse Show.

Below
General view.

Below right
The royal box, occupied on this occasion by King Edward VII and Queen Alexandra.

breed. In the ensuing years, with the introduction of other breeds, especially Cleveland Bays, the Oldenburg became much heavier, and was used both as a coach-horse and in agriculture. However, since the Second World War, the tendency has been to crossbreed with Thoroughbreds and Hanoverians in order to produce a lighter horse which can also be ridden. The breeding policy is organized by the Society of Breeders of the Oldenburg Horse, which has its headquarters in Oldenburg.

Olympia an exhibition hall in Kensington, London, which was the home of the International Horse Show from 1907 until the outbreak of the Second World War.

abandoned at the last minute, and they were first included at Stockholm in 1912, when the host nation were the winners of the Prix des Nations show-jumping and of the team and individual medals in the three-day event. (For results see pages 229–234.)

Olympic Games and International Equestrian Fund the former name of the British Equestrian Olympic Fund.

Olympic Trial a major British show-jumping championship held annually, usually at the British Timken Show, over an Olympic-standard course. Entry is restricted to qualified horses and those specially invited by the British Show Jumping

Olympic Games The inclusion of the equestrian events in the Olympic Games as they are today was largely due to the efforts of Count Clarence von Rosen, Master of the Horse to the King of Sweden, who proposed they should be included in the Games of 1908 in London. It was agreed that the Olympic equestrian events should be held in conjunction with the International Horse Show at Olympia. However, although eighty-eight entries from eight nations were received, the idea was

Association's selection committee.

one-paced (of a horse, particularly a steeplechaser) able to race only at a given speed.

one-sided mouth the mouth of a horse that is unresponsive on one side, usually because the bar of the bit has caused a sore or tenderness on that side of the mouth, which has subsequently healed and become hard and insensitive.

on its toes (of a horse) eager and anxious to move on.

on terms *hunting* (of hounds) able to keep hunting steadily because there is a strong scent.

on the bit (of a horse) taking a definite feel on the reins.

on the leg (of a horse) too long in the leg; a fault normally associated with a lack of depth in the body.

on the rails *racing* (of a horse) running close to the rails marking the extreme edge of the race track.

open country *hunting* a tract of country free from woods.

opening meet *hunting* the first meet of the regular hunting season.

opera board a heavy wooden board built at the rear of early broughams to act as a bumper.

opportunity race a steeplechase or hurdle race in which only jockeys entitled to claim an allowance may ride.

Below
Olympic Games. The victorious British three-day event team at Munich in 1972: (from left to right) Mark Phillips, Mary Gordon-Watson, Richard Meade and Bridget Parker.

Pierre Jonquères d'Oriola, individual gold medallist at the Olympic Games in 1952 and 1964, seen here after winning the Men's World Show Jumping Championship at Buenos Aires in 1966.

Oriola, Pierre Jonquères d', *France* (born 1920) Pierre Jonquères d'Oriola started his show-jumping career in 1946, and has probably been the most successful French show-jumper since the Second World War. He is the only person to have won two individual gold medals for show-jumping in the Olympic Games — at Helsinki in 1952, riding Ali Baba, and at Tokyo in 1964, riding Lutteur B. In 1966 he won the World Championship at Buenos Aires, having been placed in the first four on three previous occasions. He was decorated with the Legion of Honour (Chevalier) by President de Gaulle in 1967.

Orlov a Russian breed of trotting horse developed in the 1770s by Count Alexis Grigorievich Orlov. Usually black or grey — though there are also bays and chestnuts — and about 16.1 h.h., the Orlov has a fine Arab-like head and a substantial frame. As well as for trotting racing, for which it became famous, the breed has been used to draw coaches and carriages and also to improve various breeds of draught horse.

Orssich cavesson.

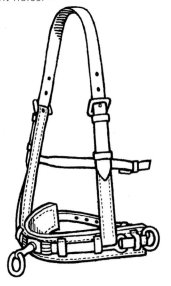

Orssich cavesson a breaking cavesson having a metal plate which is hinged at the nose, on either side of a central projecting ring. The driving rings are fitted at the end of the plate on each side of the noseband, and the central ring is mounted on a swivel so that the lunge rein can be worked more easily.

ostler a person who takes care of horses, especially at an inn or hotel. Also called HOSTLER.

ostrich snaffle a combination of the Fillis and the French bradoon having the same cheek and suspended action as the Fillis and the mouthpiece of the French bradoon. It was formerly a very popular racing bit, especially in the United States.

others *racing* those horses taking part in a race which are not shown in the betting odds by name.

outfit 1. a ranch with all its equipment and employees. **2.** the personal equipment of a cowboy.

outing a horserace.

outlaw (Western US) a horse which is particularly vicious and untameable.

out of born of.

out of blood (of a pack of hounds) not having had a kill for some time.

outrider (US) a person in hunt uniform who leads the horses past the grandstand in the parade before the race.

outside *racing* (of a horse) running furthest away from the inside rails.

outside assistance any form of help given to a competitor during his round which, whether solicited or not, may, in the opinion of the judges, advantageously affect his performance. If, for example, a competitor in a show-jumping or combined training competition were unsure of the sequence in which the obstacles were to be jumped and were directed by a spectator after the signal to start had been given, this would constitute outside assistance, and the competitor would be eliminated.

outsider a racehorse which is given long odds in the betting and is thought to have little chance of winning the race.

over at the knee having a forward bend or curve to the knees. This may be caused by excessive work, but is probably in the conformation of the horse and will count against it in the show ring.

over bent carrying the neck in an exaggeratedly arched position, with the head bent and the chin tucked into the breast.

overcarted (of a horse) harnessed to an excessively large or heavy cart or wagon.

overcheck a leather or cord rein running from the bit to a hook on the pad of a hackney. Used to keep the horse's head in the correct position, it is released when the horse is standing. Also called TOP REIN.

overland route (US) the longest way round a trotting track. A horse may be forced by the other horses to race on the outside and thus take the overland route.

overraced (of a horse) having been raced too frequently and become stale.

overreach 1. (of a horse) to strike with the hind shoe the heel or quarter of the foot in front, or to tread on one foot with another, thus causing an injury to the top of the foot. **2.** the injury itself. Also called TREAD.

override 1. to exhaust a horse by excessive riding. **2.** *hunting* to ride too close to the pack when it is running.

overweight *racing* extra weight carried by a horse. A horse carries more weight than it was set to carry when the jockey is unable to make the necessary weight; i.e. a horse is said to be carrying 2 lb overweight.

owlhead (Western US) a horse which is impossible to train.

own a line *hunting* (of hounds) to hunt and speak with certainty.

own brothers and sisters See FULL BROTHERS AND SISTERS.

owner *racing* the person in whose name a horse runs, irrespective of whether that person is the sole owner of the horse or is a member of a syndicate.

oxbow (Western US) a type of stirrup which is oval and made of wood.

oxer *show-jumping* a spread fence consisting of a post and rails in front of a brush fence. The brush should be lower than the top pole.

Oxford dogcart See under DOGCART.

pace a lateral gait in two time, in which both the hind leg and the foreleg on the same side are moved forward together.

pacemaker *racing* a horse which takes the lead and sets the speed for the race. It is quite usual in a major race over a long distance for a trainer to run two horses, one which he fancies will win and the second one to act as a pacemaker for the first.

pacer a horse trained to race in harness at the pace, as opposed to the trot. Also called WIGGLER.

pad the foot of a fox.

pad a fox to track a fox by following its footprints.

paddock 1. a grassy enclosure near a stable or house in which horses can be turned out. The most suitable type of fencing for a paddock is post and rails, since, unlike barbed wire, for example, the horses are unlikely to injure themselves should they run into it or brush against it. **2.** *racing* the enclosure at a racecourse in which the horses are paraded and then saddled up and mounted before a race. It is supervised by a PADDOCK STEWARD, the official responsible, among other things, for giving the signal for the jockeys to mount and for sending them down to the start on time.

paddock sheet a light, shaped cover, sometimes made up in the owner's colours, put on a horse when it is parading in the paddock before a race.

paddock steward See under PADDOCK (def. 2).

pad groom (formerly) a groom employed to ride a lady's hunter to the meet or to ride the second horse.

pad horse (formerly) a horse used for riding on the road.

Page, Michael Owen *US* (born 1938) In 1956 Michael Page won the United States Junior Combined Training Medal. His first international three-day event was in 1959 at the Pan American Games in Chicago, where, riding Grasshopper, he was first in the individual placings and a member

of the team which came second. In 1963, again with Grasshopper, he won the individual and was a member of the winning team at the Pan American Games in São Paulo. Four years later, riding Foster, he was again in the winning team and was third in the individual placings at Winnipeg. With the same horse he won an individual bronze medal and a team silver medal at the 1968 Olympic Games in Mexico.

Paint horse See PINTO.

palfrey a small light saddle-horse, as distinguished from a warhorse.

palisade a cross-country obstacle consisting of a row of vertical spars surmounted by a top rail, and with a series of proplike poles on the take-off side. For the fence to be safely and correctly built the spars should not extend above the top rail, and the poles should be close enough together to prevent a horse from putting a foot between them.

palm-headed (of a stag) having palmate tops to the antlers.

palomilla a milk-white or cream-coloured horse with a white mane and tail.

Palomino 1. (US) a 'colour-breed' characterized by a golden coat with a flaxen mane and tail. In order that it may qualify for inclusion in the breeding registry, one of the parents must be included in the Palomino Horse Breeders' Association listing, and the other must be of Arabian, Quarter Horse or Thoroughbred blood lines. The animal must also have a specific hue of coat as well as good markings; for instance, white markings on the legs must not extend beyond the knees or hocks, and not more than fifteen per cent of the hairs in the mane and tail may be dark. No rules are laid down as to conformation, except that the height must be between 14 and 16 hands.

The origin of the Palomino, which is now used for parades and similar spectacles, is unknown but probably goes back to the Arab. Breeding was encouraged in Spain, where one was given to Juan de Palomino, and it is likely that this is how the name originated. Also called GOLDEN HORSE OF THE WEST. **2.** (GB) any horse having a golden coat and a flaxen mane and tail.

pancake (Western US) an English riding saddle.

panel the padded area of a saddle lying under the saddle flap and extending below the cantle on either side; the part of the saddle which fits against the horse's back. It may be made of felt covered

Far right
panel. The side view, showing also the straps to which the girth is attached and a girth safe, which is pulled down over the buckles to prevent damaging the flap.

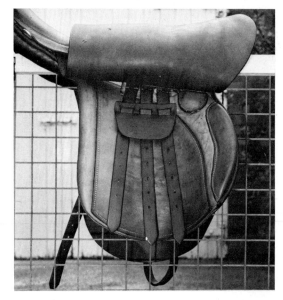

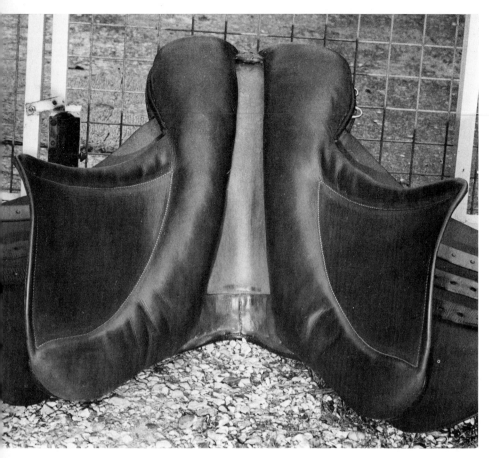

Above
panel. A continental panel
with knees and thigh rolls.

Far right
parrot mouth.

the passengers from all except rain directly in front. Although it appeared to be light it ran heavily. It had no space for luggage and only sufficient room for one groom on the rumble behind. Mainly a ladies' carriage, it was of elegant appearance and could be seen in either town or country. In the country it was often to be found at the side of a covert if the hounds were meeting.

parliamentary horse a horse capable of a fast trot used for drawing a mail coach. Under an act of parliament it was illegal for mail coach horses to be driven at the gallop, but provided one of the team was trotting the law was considered not to be broken. A horse which was able to maintain a fast trot, therefore, was an invaluable asset to the owner of a mail coach.

with leather, or of leather, linen or serge stuffed with wool. There are four main types of panel in use: the FULL PANEL, which is quilted at the side, with a slight knee roll, and corresponds exactly in shape to the flap; the SHORT PANEL (also called RUGBY PANEL), which is completely cut away at the bottom so that the rider's legs are in closer contact with the horse; the SAUMUR PANEL (also called FRENCH PANEL, WITHNEY PANEL), which is forward cut with a sewn-in knee roll and often has an additional knee roll on the outside, under the flap; and the CONTINENTAL PANEL, which is similar to the Saumur, but is narrower at the waist and has a thigh roll.

parabola the arc made by a horse from the point of take-off to the point of landing as it jumps an obstacle.

parallel bars a type of spread obstacle, used both in cross-country and show-jumping courses, consisting of two parallel sets of posts and rails with a spread between. For reasons of safety, only a single rail or pole is used in the second part, since more than one could make the obstacle trappy and dangerous if a horse should fall between the two parts.

parcours de chasse See HUNTING COMPETITION.

parimutuel the American and continental equivalent of the totalizator.

park coach a privately owned four-wheeled closed carriage, popular in the nineteenth and early twentieth centuries, having seats for two or four passengers inside, and on the outside a box seat for the driver and one other passenger and a high rear seat for two servants. Also called DRAG.

park hack See under HACK.

park phaeton a type of low-hung phaeton, drawn by ponies or horses up to 15.2 h.h. It had a hood which completely protected the driver and

parrot mouth a congenital deformity in which the upper jaw is much longer than the lower jaw and overlaps it in front. The teeth become elongated, and in time injury occurs to the bars or gums of the upper jaw.

passage one of the classical high school airs; a spectacular elevated trot in slow motion. There is a definite period of suspension, as one pair of legs remains on the ground, with the diagonal opposites raised in the air. The horse progresses slowly, with rhythmical steps, covering little more than one foot of ground with each stride.

pass on the inside *racing* (of a horse) to overtake another horse by passing between it and the rails.

pastern the part of a horse's limb between the fetlock joint and the hoof.

pastern bone either of two bones of the pastern, the SHORT PASTERN BONE (also called SMALL PASTERN BONE), the lower or second phalanx, which lies partly within the foot, above the pedal bone, and the LONG PASTERN BONE (also called GREAT PASTERN BONE, LARGE PASTERN BONE), the upper or first phalanx, which lies between the short pastern bone and the cannon bone.

pastern joint the joint between the short pastern bone and the long pastern bone.

patchy See under SCENT.

patrol judge (US) one of a number of officials positioned at strategic points on the course in order to see that races are fairly run.

Peacock safety iron a pattern of safety iron used especially for children, in which the tread and one

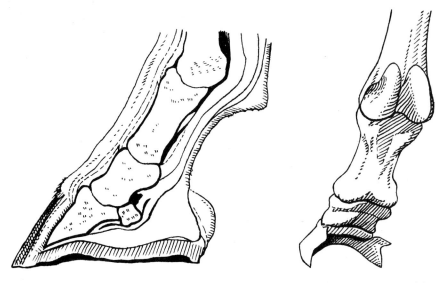

side are made of metal, while the other side (the outer side) consists of a strong rubber ring stretched between a hook (at the top) and a stud (near the tread). In the event of a fall, the rubber band becomes detached and releases the foot, so that the rider will not be dragged.

pedal bone the terminal phalanx in the foot of a horse, enclosed in the hoof. Shaped rather like the hoof itself, it in fact occupies only a relatively small proportion of the interior, at the front and sides. At the back of the bone are two wings, one on each side, and to these are attached the lateral cartilages, which occupy most of the rear portion of the hoof cavity. The bone itself, which does not lie parallel to the ground, but with the front slightly lower than the wings, is full of tiny fissures to accommodate the ramifications of nerves and blood vessels. Also called COFFIN BONE.

pedestrian crossing a cross-country obstacle built like a parallel bars, but with staggered gaps in the rails. It is not necessary for the gaps to be wide enough for a horse to walk through.

Pelham bit a bit designed to reproduce the action of the double bridle, that is, to produce with only one mouthpiece the combined effects of a snaffle bit and a curb bit. The basic shape is similar to that of the Weymouth bit, except that on each side, at the point where the mouthpiece is joined to the cheek, there is an additional ring to which the second pair of reins is attached, the other pair being attached, as in the Weymouth, to the rings at the bottom of the cheeks. Mouthpieces of various patterns are used, but possibly the most common is the normal mullen mouthpiece of metal, vulcanite or flexible rubber, which lies across the tongue.

Pelham bridle the type of bridle used with a Pelham bit. It normally has two pairs of reins, pressure being applied on the corners of the mouth when the snaffle rein is used, and on the poll and curb groove when the curb rein is brought into use. On the other hand, it is possible to adapt the Pelham for use with only one pair of reins, by using a leather couplet to link the snaffle ring to the curb ring.

penalty *racing* an additional weight handicap carried by a horse, usually imposed when it has won a race since the weights for the race were published.

penalty zone *combined training* one of the rectangular areas on the cross-country or steeple-chase course of a three-day event in which refusals, falls, etc., are penalized. Each penalty zone extends 10 metres in front of the obstacle and 20 metres beyond it, to a width of 10 metres on each side of the boundary flags marking the limit of the obstacle. The zone may be marked with sawdust, by pegs, or any other means which will not interfere with the competitors.

The penalties incurred within a zone are as follows:

first refusal, run out or circle	20 penalties
second refusal, run out or circle at the same obstacle	40 penalties
fall of horse and/or rider at obstacle	60 penalties
third refusal, run out or circle at the same obstacle;	
second fall of horse and/or rider at obstacles in the steeplechase course, or	
third fall of horse and/or rider at obstacles in the cross-country course;	
error of course not rectified;	
omission of obstacle or red and white flag;	
retaking an obstacle already jumped;	
jumping an obstacle in the wrong order	elimination

Pennwood Forge Mill See under MCMAHON, PADDY JOHN.

perch a long timber pole or iron rod which links the front and rear wheels in certain four-wheeled carriages, mainly all those which are fitted with C-springs.

Percheron a breed of heavy horse originating in the small La Perche district in north-west France, where it has been bred for centuries. The Percheron has been very popular in all parts of the world as a draught horse for agriculture. Before the age of the motor vehicle it was used for drawing stage-coaches in France and later buses in Paris.

Noted for its docility, the Percheron possesses great muscular development, combined with style and activity. The stallions stand not less than 16.3 h.h. and the mares 16.1 h.h., and the average weight of stallions is 18 to 20 cwt and of mares 16 to 18 cwt. The head should be wide between the eyes, with medium-sized and erect ears, and a deep cheek curved on the lower side, but not too long from the eyes to the nose. The neck should be strong and have a full arched crest. A wide chest is necessary with deep well-laid shoulders. The back should be strong and short, with exceptionally wide hindquarters and good length from the hips to the tail. Strong arms are necessary, with big knees. There should also be full second thighs and broad hocks. Limbs must be as clean and as free as possible of hair. In action the Percheron must be straight and bold, with a long free stride, hocks well flexed and kept close. The only colours accepted are grey or black, with the minimum amount of white hair. The British Percheron Horse Society was formed in 1918.

Peruvian Stepping Horse a Peruvian saddle-horse descended from the stock originally taken into the country by the Spanish. Usually between 14 h.h. and 15.2 h.h., it has a distinctive action and is capable of covering great distances at speed, causing little tiredness to the rider. The predominant colours of the breed are chestnut and bay.

Below
Nelson Pessoa, the leading Brazilian show-jumper, riding Gran Geste down the bank at Hickstead.

Pessoa, Nelson, *Brazil* (born 1935) Nelson Pessoa made his Olympic debut at the Stockholm Games in 1956. He won the European Show Jumping Championship at Lucerne in 1966 and the following year was a member of the Brazilian team which won the gold medal in the Pan-American Games at Winnipeg. He has had numerous victories all over Europe, and has won the Hamburg Jumping Derby four times and the British Jumping Derby twice. His most successful horses have been Gran Geste, Huipil, Cangaceiro and Nagir; on Nagir he won the Grand Prix at Aachen in 1972. Since 1961 he has been based in Europe.

Peterborough Royal Foxhound Show an annual foxhound show first held at Peterborough in 1877, and now firmly established as the major foxhound show in the British Isles. Since the amalgamation of the Peterborough Agricultural show in 1966, it has been held at the East of England Show at Alwalton, a few miles outside Peterborough.

Entry is restricted to hounds belonging to packs, and exhibitors all wear hunt uniform. Doghounds and bitches are judged separately and there are classes for unentered novices, unentered couples, entered novice couples, two couples, stallion hounds and brood bitches, as well as overall awards for champion doghound and champion bitch.

Petite Etoile (by Petition out of Star of Iran) Owned by the Aga Khan and trained by Noel Murless, Petite Etoile, a grey, was foaled at the Curragh in Ireland in 1956. Her debut as a two-year-old was at Manchester in the Prestwick Stakes, in which, ridden by Lester Piggott, she was an inauspicious second, beaten by eight lengths by the only other runner. Her next race — and first success — was the Star Stakes at Sandown. Later that season she was to have another win on the same course — in the Rose Stakes.

Her first race the following year was in the Free Handicap at Newmarket. Ridden by Australian jockey George Moore in the Aga Khan's colours, she won by three lengths. Her first classic win was at Newmarket, where, ridden by Doug Smith, she beat Rosalba by one length in the 1000-Guineas. Her next race was the Oaks at Epsom, with Lester Piggott, which she won by one and a half lengths. She then went on to win the Yorkshire Stakes at York, the Sussex Stakes at Goodwood and the Champion Stakes at Newmarket, thus ending the season unbeaten.

In 1960 Petite Etoile's first outing was in the Victor Wild Stakes at Kempton Park, which she won. Then came the Coronation Cup and the long-awaited confrontation with Parthia and Above Suspicion. Sweeping both aside, she won by one and a half lengths. Her only other race that year was the King George VI and Queen Elizabeth Stakes, in which she was beaten by half a length by Aggressor.

It was decided to keep her in training as a five-year-old, a policy which was to pay off, for of her six races she won four: the Coronation Stakes at Sandown; the Coronation Cup at Epsom; the Rous Memorial Stakes at Ascot; and the Scarborough Stakes at Doncaster.

She was then retired to stud at the Curragh, but was not a success.

peytrel the part of a medieval warhorse's armour which protected the breast — it consisted of three deep curved plates with a glancing knob to deflect lance blows. Also POITREL.

Above
Petite Etoile, with
Australian jockey George
Moore up.

Right
H.R.H. Prince Philip
playing polo on Smith's
Lawn in Windsor Great Park.
It was largely due to his
enthusiasm that polo became
so popular in the British Isles
after the Second World War.

Far right
piaffe, performed here by a
member of the Imperial
Spanish Riding School.

Philip, Prince, Duke of Edinburgh A keen
equestrian, Prince Philip was for many years a
leading polo player. He was president of the British
Horse Society in 1956, and is a founder member of
the National Equestrian Centre. Since 1964 he has
been president of the International Equestrian
Federation. He has taken a great interest in the
federation and has been largely responsible for many
of the recent improvements in the rules. In 1973
he became patron of the British Driving Society,
and it is mainly due to his efforts that driving has
become so popular and that international competitions are now recognized.

Phillips, Capt. Mark, (born 1948) A member of
the Beaufort Pony Club, Mark Phillips competed in
the branch's horse trials team for five successive
years. Since 1967, when he was fourth at
Burghley, riding Rock On, he has met with considerable success in three-day events. He was a
reserve for the Olympic Games at Mexico in 1968,
and the following year competed as an individual
in the European Championships at Haras du Pin.
In 1970, riding Bertie Hill's Chicago, he was in the
British team which won the World Championship
in Punchestown, Ireland, and in 1971 he was a
member of the team which won the European
Championship at Burghley. On this occasion he
rode the 16.3 h.h. brown gelding GREAT OVATION
(by Three Cheers out of Cyprus Valence), foaled
in 1963 and jointly owned by Mark Phillips and
his aunt Flavia Phillips. With Great Ovation he won
the Badminton Horse Trials in 1971 and 1972, and
the pair were selected to compete in the Olympic
Games at Munich, where they were members of
the gold medal team. The following year he
accepted a last-minute offer to ride Bertie Hill's
Maid Marion at Burghley, and went on to win the
event.
  In November 1973 he married Princess Anne.
Riding the Queen's horse Columbus he won the
Badminton Horse Trials in 1974 and later that year
was selected for the British team which competed in the World Three Day Event Championships at Burghley. At the end of the cross-country
he was in the lead, but unfortunately he had to
withdraw from the final phase of the competition
because Columbus had gone lame.

photo-finish *racing* the result of a race photo-
graphed by a camera with a very narrow field of
vision situated at the winning post on a racecourse.
Now installed on many racecourses, it must be
used by the judge to determine the outcome of a
race if the horses are very close together as they
pass the post. A camera was first used for recording
a photo-finish in 1890 by John Hemment at
Sheepshead Bay in the United States.

phaeton a popular four-wheeled, open carriage
of light construction, which first appeared at the
end of the eighteenth century. There were many
variations. See also BEAUFORT PHAETON, EQUIROTAL
PHAETON, MAIL PHAETON, PARK PHAETON, PONY
PHAETON, SPIDER PHAETON, STANHOPE PHAETON,
T CART PHAETON.

piaffe a classical high-school air, closely resembling the passage, except that it is performed on the
spot and with less elevation. See also PASSAGE.

Piccadilly Hunt Club a club formed in 1949 by a group of hunting enthusiasts who rode down Piccadilly in London as a protest against a private member's bill which was being introduced into the House of Commons at that time and, had it been passed, would have abolished various forms of hunting and made provision for the abolition of foxhunting. The members still meet annually.

piebald a horse whose coat consists of large irregular and clearly defined patches of black and of white. Also called PAINT HORSE (US), PINTO (US). See also SKEWBALD.

Piggott, Lester Keith, (born 1935) Lester Piggott has retained the family interest in racing. Both his grandfather and his father were jockeys, and his father, Keith Piggott, still trains horses. During a five-year apprenticeship, which he served with his father, Lester Piggott rode his first winner, The Chase, at Haydock in 1948, and was the leading apprentice in 1950 and 1951, with fifty-two and fifty-one winners, respectively.

He has ridden all over the world, and has been champion jockey in England on nine occasions: in 1960, and from 1964 to 1971. His most successful season was 1966, when he rode 191 winners. He has won the Derby no less than six times: in 1954 riding Never Say Die, in 1957 riding Crepello, in 1960 riding St Paddy, in 1968 riding Sir Ivor, in 1970 riding Nijinsky and in 1972 riding Roberto; and the Oaks on three occasions: in 1957 riding Carrozza, in 1959 riding Petite Etoile and in 1966 riding Valoris. He has also won the 2000-Guineas on three occasions: in 1957 riding Crepello, in 1968 riding Sir Ivor and in 1970 riding Nijinsky; the St Leger on seven occasions: in 1960 riding St Paddy, in 1961 riding Aurelius, in 1967 riding Ribocco, in 1968 riding Ribero, in 1970 riding Nijinsky, in 1971 riding Athens Wood and in 1972 riding Boucher; and the King George VI and Queen Elizabeth Stakes five times: in 1965 riding Meadow Court, in 1966 riding Aunt Edith, in 1969 riding Park Top, in 1970 riding Nijinsky and in 1974 riding Dahlia. He won the Washington International at Laurel Park in 1968 and 1969, riding Sir Ivor and Karabas, respectively, and there is hardly a major race he has not won.

His wife Susan, daughter of the well-known trainer, Sam Armstrong, won the Newmarket Town Plate in 1961 on Fulminate and in 1963 riding Bingo.

pigsticking the hunting of the wild boar on horseback and with a spear which is used to kill the boar. Considered by many to be the toughest and most dangerous of all equestrian sports, it entails riding at full speed over rough country and close-quarter combat with a wild animal. The pursuit of the wild boar on horseback had been a traditional European sport for centuries but modern pigsticking originated among British Army officers in India early in the nineteenth century.

pillar 1. *show-jumping* a special solid type of wing placed at each side of a wall in order to mark the extremes of the obstacle. **2.** an upright post with a ring attachment to which a horse can be tied for training or exercise purposes. Pillars of some form were used in stalls nearly 2000 years ago, so that horses could be exercised in their stables. In the seventeenth century they were introduced into high-school training by Antoine de Pluvinel. During the early schooling of a horse it was tied to one pillar by means of a rope attached to the cavesson and was then made to go round the pillar carrying out the turns and circles of the high school. Later it would be tied between two pillars in order to learn the more advanced movements. Pillars are still used in the training of the Spanish Riding School horses in Vienna.

pillion a small saddle or pad attached behind the saddle for a passenger, usually a woman, who sat sideways. Pillions were used extensively before the introduction of the side-saddle, and can still be seen in certain parts of Spain.

pillion post See MOUNTING BLOCK.

pilot *hunting* **1.** a person who knows the country well and leads the field. **2.** a name sometimes given to the fox.

pin firing See under FIRING.

Pinto (US) a piebald or skewbald. It is not possible to breed Pintos, and there is no standard type. They may be found among Shetland ponies, and many other breeds which have coloured horses in their history. Also called PAINT HORSE.

pin toes toes which turn inwards; a less serious fault than dishing.

pipe opener *racing* a gallop designed to clear the horse's windpipe before a race.

pirouette *dressage* a turn within the horse's length; the shortest turn which it is possible to make. There are three different kinds of pirouette: the turn on the centre, the turn on the forehand, and the turn on the haunches. The turn on the centre is the easiest and the most natural for the horse to perform.

pistol (Western US) a young and inexperienced rider.

place betting backing a horse to finish first, second or third in a race, or, in the United States, first or second.

placed *racing* finishing second or third in a race; in the United States finishing second only.

placing judge one of the officials at a trotting track responsible for recording the order in which the horses finish.

plaited reins a type of riding rein in which the leather is split into five strips, which are plaited to provide a better grip for the rider. Reins of this type are also made in nylon but they tend to become slimy in wet weather and very hard in dry periods.

planchette a footrest for the rider, formerly attached to side-saddles for formal and state occasions.

planks a show-jumping obstacle made up of painted planks, which should be nine to twelve inches wide. As they are considerably heavier than poles, planks should always be put on flat fittings rather than in cups. They may be used in either straight or spread fences, but in a spread fence a pole should always be used at the back. Also called ROAD-CLOSED BARRIER.

Plantation Walking Horse See TENNESSEE WALKING HORSE.

plate See RACING PLATE.

'Pliohippus' the final important stage in the evolution of the horse. *Pliohippus*, which lived some five to ten million years ago, during the early Pliocene Epoch, included some species which had the proportions of a small horse. It eventually lost its side toes and its teeth closely resembled those of the modern horse, of which it was the direct ancestor. See also EOHIPPUS, EQUUS, MERYCHIPPUS, MESOHIPPUS.

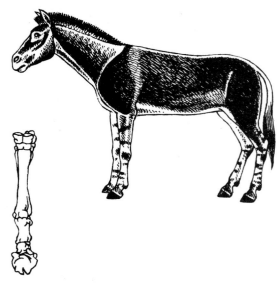

'Pliohippus'.

plough *hunting* any type of agricultural land except grassland; it may be ploughed, fallow, seeded or covered in stubble.

plug (Western US) a broken-down horse.

Plumb, Michael, *US* (born 1940) Michael Plumb has been the leading three-day event rider in the United States five times. He is a veteran of three silver medal teams at the Olympic Games; in 1964, riding Bold Minstrel, in 1968, riding Plain Sailing, and in 1972, riding Free and Easy. He was also in the teams which won the gold medal at the Pan American Games of 1963 and 1967, and in the latter, riding Plain Sailing, he also won the individual gold medal. In 1974, riding Good Mixture, he was the individual silver medallist in the World Championships at Burghley, as well as being a member of the gold medal team.

Podhajsky, Col. Alois, (1898–1973) Born in Austria-Hungary, Col. Podhajsky was one of the world's top riding instructors. He joined the army as an officer riding instructor and became a leading authority on dressage and an international rider. In 1939 he was appointed director of the Spanish Riding School in Vienna, a position he held until 1963.

poincon an instrument introduced by Antoine de Pluvinel in the seventeenth century, having a short wooden handle and an iron point which was applied to the croup in order to make a horse kick up its hind legs.

point *hunting* the distance covered by a hunt as measured in a straight line, or 'as the crow flies', as opposed to the actual distance as hounds ran.

point firing See under FIRING.

point rider (US; in cattle driving) one of usually two men who rode at the head of the cattle to pilot the herd. If it was necessary to change direction they rode abreast of the leading cattle, gradually turning them in the direction required.

point the leaders *driving* (of a coachman) to prepare the leader or leaders to change direction by applying pressure on the reins.

point-to-point originally, a race across country from one landmark to another. Between the wars point-to-points were held annually, normally on a circuit which had proper steeplechase fences, but which usually also included some hilly country and certainly included plough. Since the last war, however, they have become much more professionalized and are almost miniature steeplechase meetings.

Each hunt, together with certain special clubs, is allowed to hold a point-to-point. Races are generally over a distance of 3 to 3½ miles, and competitors, who must be amateurs, must also be members, subscribers and farmers of a particular hunt, their sons and daughters, or serving officers in the army, navy or air force. Every horse competing has to be issued with a certificate from the master of the hunt to which it belongs to say

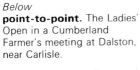

Below
point-to-point. The Ladies' Open in a Cumberland Farmer's meeting at Dalston, near Carlisle.

that it has been regularly and fairly hunted, and the certificate has to be lodged with Weatherby's, the governing body. The minimum weight carried by each horse is 12 st. 7 lb, or 11 st. in women's races.

The season for point-to-points lasts from February to May, and each meeting normally has five races as follows: a members', subscribers' and farmers' race; an adjacent hunt's race (for six adjoining hunts); an open race; a women's race; and a maiden race, restricted to horses that have never won a race under point-to-point rules.

poitrel See PEYTREL.

pole 1. a long, rounded shaft placed between a pair of harness horses or between the wheelers of a team, having at one end a metal socket for attaching the pole chains or pole pieces, which are secured to the horses' collars, and at the other end a bolt or pin for fastening the pole to the vehicle. **2.** a rounded shaft, which should be no less than 12 feet long with a diameter of $3\frac{1}{2}$ to $4\frac{1}{2}$ inches, used as part of a show-jumping obstacle.

pole chain a short burnished or black steel chain of oval links attached at one end to the pole and at the other end to one of the hames on the collar. In some vehicles leather straps called POLE PIECES are used in place of chains.

pole piece See under POLE CHAIN.

pole position See under HOLE.

poling See RAPPING.

poling up the act of attaching the pole chains or the pole pieces to the hames in harnessing a pair or team of horses.

poll evil See under FISTULA.

polo a game resembling hockey played between two teams of mounted players. Each team consists of four players, though in former times there were as many as nine in a team. The positions of the four players on the field are as follows: Nos. 1 and 2 are the forwards; No. 3 is the half-back; and No. 4 the back. Each member of the team marks his opposite number for any line-up or hit-in. All polo players are given a handicap ranging from minus 2 to plus 10 goals. The total handicap of the four players is added together to give the handicap for the team. In handicap matches the team with the higher handicap concedes to the other team the difference between the two handicaps if there are to be eight chukkas; if there are to be four this number is halved, and so on. There may be a referee and two mounted umpires, or, by agreement between the team captains, a referee and one umpire or simply one umpire alone.

In England the size of a polo ground is 300 yards by 200 yards, or if there are side boards the width is 160 yards. In the United States and Argentina the grounds are sometimes slightly larger. The goals, which must be at least 10 feet high and 8 yards wide, must be no less than 250 yards apart.

There are records showing that polo was played in Persia during the reign of Darius I (521–c. 486 B.C.). From there it is said to have spread west to Byzantium and eastwards into China and Japan, where it became the national game. It reached India from China in the north-east and with the Muslim invaders from the north-west.

From about 1850, with Manipur and Cachar under British administration, soldiers and tea planters started to play the game and the first British polo club was formed at Silchar in Cachar in 1859, followed three years later by the Calcutta Polo Club. The game became very popular with the army and within ten years most British and Indian regiments had teams. Small ponies were found to be ideal and were cheap and plentiful.

The first recorded match in England was played at Hounslow in 1869 between the 9th Lancers and the 10th Hussars, each team consisting of eight members. The match generated considerable interest, and as a result grounds were opened in many parts of London, one of the first being at Lillie Bridge, near Earl's Court. The first match at Hurlingham was played in 1874, and very soon this became the headquarters of polo in England. The first rules were produced here and even today the game in England is played according to the rules laid down by the Hurlingham Polo Club.

Development of the sport was somewhat hindered, as the height of the ponies was limited to 14 hands and it was not until 1895 that it was increased to 14.2 hands. The first country club was opened in Monmouthshire in 1872, and the game spread to the north, with clubs opening in Liverpool, Hull and Edinburgh. The Hurlingham Champion Cup was first played for in 1876 and was won by the Royal Horse Guards. Two years later the Inter-Regimental Tournament and Oxford and Cambridge Universities Match were introduced. The Roehampton Club was opened in 1901, and by the start of the First World War there were some sixty clubs all over the British Isles.

Polo was not played in England during the war, and when activities were subsequently resumed England and India agreed to come into line with Argentina and the United States by abolishing the height limit of ponies. Between the wars the game became immensely popular in the London area, although many of the country clubs had not reopened, and teams from Argentina, India, Australia and the United States were regular visitors. During the Second World War there was again no polo in England, and for a time it seemed doubtful whether it would start again. However, the Ham Club reopened, followed shortly afterwards by Cowdray. A new club was formed by the Household Brigade and they were allowed to play on Smith's Lawn in Windsor Great Park. Because of the enthusiasm of these clubs and also of Prince Philip, Duke of Edinburgh, the game soon regained its former popularity, not only with players, but also with spectators, but whereas the game between the wars had been played by cavalry regiments, it now became very much a game for civilians.

In the United States the game was introduced by James Gordon-Bennett, who founded the Westchester Polo Club at Newport in 1876, and in 1886 the first of the matches for the Anglo-American Westchester Cup was held. In 1890 the United States Polo Association was formed and introduced a system of handicapping players, hitherto unheard of in England and India. At the turn of the century there were some forty-four clubs affiliated. There were also five clubs in California, which played under Hurlingham Rules. The clubs are now divided into six circuits, the North-Eastern, Central, South-Eastern, South-Western, Pacific Coast and North-Western. There is an annual inter-circuit championship, the United States Championship, which was first competed for in 1904.

polo stick a long-handled mallet used in the game of polo. The shaft is usually made of either malacca cane, which is rigid, or whanger, which is springy; the length depends on the height of the rider and the pony he is to ride, but is normally forty-eight to fifty-four inches. The head is cylindrical in shape, though some are now tapered like a cigar,

Right
polo. Eddie Moore of Stowell Park and C. Garros of Cowdray Park going for the ball.

Below
polo. A match between Great Britain and the United States.

Above
polo. A dramatic race for the ball.

Right
polo. W. R. Linfoot and D. Gonzalez seen in action in the Cowdray Park Gold Cup.

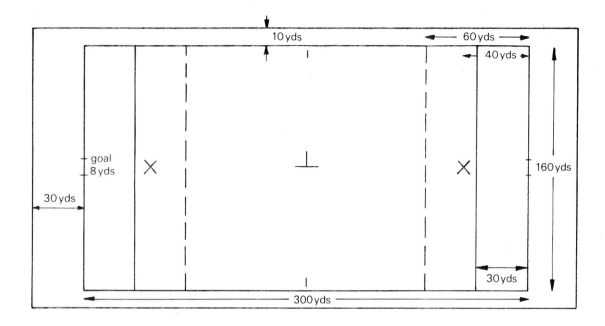

10 yds

60 yds

40 yds

goal 8 yds

160 yds

30 yds

30 yds

300 yds

and made of a light, tough wood, such as bamboo, ash or sycamore. Also called MALLET (US).

polo whip the type of whip used in polo; it is normally about forty-two inches long, so that the rider can use it without taking his hands off the reins.

pommel the protuberance at the front and top of a saddle.

Ponies of Britain Club a club founded in 1952 by Gladys Yule and Glenda Spooner to encourage the breeding of ponies and promote their welfare. The club's annual show, which was first held at Ascot racecourse in 1953, has now become a major event. In addition, a stallion show is held every year in the spring. It is largely due to the work of the club, especially of the chairman, Glenda Spooner, that there has been such a revival of interest — not only in Britain but also overseas — in the British native breeds of pony, and by the introduction of their approved certificates scheme for pony-trekking centres the standard of such centres has been considerably improved.

pony 1. a horse not exceeding 14.2 h.h. at maturity. **2.** (in gambling) the sum of £25.

Pony Club an organization founded in 1929 with the object of encouraging young people to ride and enjoy equestrian sports, and providing them with skilled instruction in riding and horsemanship. The Pony Club is affiliated to the British Horse Society, and there are now some 1200 branches. Many are connected with hunts; others are found in towns where there is no hunt, and there are also many overseas branches. Membership is open to all those under the age of seventeen interested in riding, and associate membership is open to those aged between seventeen and twenty-one.

Pony Express a rapid postal system formerly operated in the United States by using relays of ponies. The most famous was the one from St Joseph in Missouri to Sacramento in California, which operated between 1860 and 1862. The distance of approximately 2000 miles was covered in ten days.

Pony of the Americas a breed of pony developed in the United States since the Second World War by crossing Shetland pony stallions with Appaloosa mares. Although considerably smaller — between 11.2 h.h. and 13 h.h. — the breed carries all the markings and characteristics of the Appaloosa.

Pony of the Americas, a relatively new breed, which was developed in the United States by crossing a Shetland pony stallion with an Appaloosa mare.

pony trekking in Lancashire.

pony phaeton a type of phaeton, originally made of wickerwork and therefore very light and comparatively inexpensive. It was primarily a carriage for the family. As the years went by pony phaetons were built of a more durable material, which was easier to clean. They were produced in various shapes such as boat, clothes-basket or wagonette and were designed to be pulled by a cob, pony or donkey.

pony trekking cross-country riding on mountain or moorland ponies. In recent years pony trekking has become a very popular recreation in Britain, particularly with townspeople who want to see more of the countryside. There are numerous trekking centres, and most of them return their riders to a base at night, having covered a distance of not more than fifteen miles during one day. The riders go on a different trek each day. In POST TREKKING the riders set off one day and are accommodated at various places overnight before returning to their base.

Since they are expensive to maintain, trekking centres are only open seasonally, unlike most riding schools which are open all the year round. The best centres are in the New Forest, on the moors of Devon and Somerset, in the Highlands and Lowlands of Scotland, the Lake District, Northumberland, Cumbria and Yorkshire, and parts of Wales.

popular side *hunting* that part of the area of a hunt where conditions are most favourable, usually where there is more grass than plough, not a great deal of barbed wire and open country as opposed to woodland.

post *racing* either the starting or the winning post.

post and rails 1. a type of fencing consisting of a series of upright posts with one or more horizontal rails, used for enclosing fields, paddocks, etc., and often encountered in the hunting field. **2.** a similar construction used as an obstacle or forming part of an obstacle in a show-jumping or cross-country course. In show-jumping the horizontals are supported by but not fixed to the two uprights, while in a cross-country obstacle all the parts are firmly fixed, and the top rail may be secured to the top of the posts or to the sides.

post entry an entry made after the official closing date of a competition. Post entries are accepted by some horseshows, usually at a slightly increased fee. They are never accepted in racing, entries for all races closing very strictly on the advertised date.

post-horn See COACH-HORN.

postilion a person who rides the near horse of a pair used to draw a vehicle, or the near leader if four or more horses are used. Also POSTILLION.

posting the act of rising from the saddle at the trot.

post trekking See under PONY TREKKING.

poultice boot a large boot, usually made of rubber, used for holding a poultice against the injured foot of a horse. Poultice boots were formerly made of canvas with leather or wooden soles.

power jump test See PUISSANCE.

Far right
Pretty Polly, with W. Lane up. One of the outstanding fillies of this century, she won twenty-two races in four seasons and was beaten on only two occasions.

President's Cup. Made of silver, it portrays Queen Elizabeth II riding Winston at the Trooping the Colour ceremony.

Pratt and Company a company which, besides being responsible for the management of a number of racecourses, also acts as receivers of entries and stakeholders for National Hunt racing, and keeps accounts for owners, trainers and jockeys. Founded by John Pratt at New Barnet, the company moved to London in 1874, where the present headquarters was established in 1883.

Preakness Stakes a race over $1\frac{3}{16}$ miles for three-year-old horses, held since 1873 at Pimlico racecourse, Baltimore, Maryland, except in 1890, when it was held at Morris Park, New York, and from 1894 to 1908, when it was run at Gravesend, New York. In 1918 there were so many starters that the race was run in two divisions. Up to 1894 the distance of the race was $1\frac{1}{2}$ miles, except in 1889, when it was $1\frac{1}{4}$ miles. From 1894 to 1900 and in 1908 the distance was $1\frac{1}{16}$ miles; from 1901 to 1907 1 mile 70 yards; in 1909 and 1910 the distance was 1 mile, and from 1911 to 1924 $1\frac{1}{8}$ miles. (For results see pages 254–255.)

preliminary canter *racing* a canter given to the horse by a jockey on the racecourse on the way from the paddock to the starting post.

premium stallion a Thoroughbred stallion between four and twenty years old which is awarded a premium at the annual Stallion Show of the Hunters Improvement Society held in the spring. The stallion is allocated to a county district which it tours from 13th April to 31st July of that year, serving mares brought to it at prearranged centres for a set fee, part of which goes to the Hunters Improvement and National Light Horse Breeding Society.

President's Cup an international show-jumping team championship instituted in 1965 by Prince Philip, Duke of Edinburgh, as president of the F.E.I. The trophy, a silver model depicting Queen Elizabeth II at the ceremony of Trooping the Colour, is awarded annually to the national team gaining most points in Prix des Nations during the twelve-month period between 1st December and 30th November. When five teams or fewer take part in a competition, the winning team receives five points, the second four, and so on; when there are six teams the winning team is awarded six points; and when there are seven teams or more the maximum score is seven points. Teams placed seventh or below are awarded one point each.

The championship is open to any nation which is represented in Prix des Nations by a minimum of six different riders during the year. There is no restriction as to the number of Prix des Nations a team may compete in, but only the best six scores are counted.

Pretty Polly (by Gallinule out of Admiration. After his two-year-old season, Gallinule did not win a race, but as well as Pretty Polly he sired three classic winners and was champion sire on two occasions.) Foaled in 1901, Pretty Polly was bred by Major Loder and trained at Newmarket by Peter Gilpin. She was one of the most outstanding fillies this century; in four seasons she won twenty-two races, with total winnings amounting to over £37,000.

In her debut as a two-year-old she won the British Dominion Plate at Sandown, officially by ten lengths, though the unofficial verdict was nearer forty lengths. She went on to win all her other races that season; the National Breeders' Produce Stakes at Sandown, the Mersey Stakes at Liverpool, the Champagne Stakes at Doncaster, the Autumn Breeders Foal Plate at Manchester, and the Cheveley Park Stakes, the Middle Park Plate, the Criterion Stakes and the Moulton Stakes at Newmarket. As a three-year-old she continued her brilliant career, winning the 1000-Guineas at Newmarket, the Oaks at Epsom, the Coronation Stakes at Ascot, the Nassau Stakes at Goodwood, the St Leger and the Park Hill Stakes at Doncaster, and the Free Handicap at Newmarket. Her only defeat came in the Prix du Conseil Municipal at Longchamp, which she lost by two lengths to Presto II. She ran four times as a four-year-old and was unbeaten, winning the Coronation Cup at Epsom, the Champion Stakes, the Limekiln Stakes and the Jockey Club Cup, all at Newmarket. In 1906 she had three races; she won the March Stakes at Newmarket and the Coronation Cup at Epsom, but in the Ascot Gold Cup she was beaten, for only the second time in her career, by one length by Bachelor's Button.

At stud she was not a success — her most notable daughters were Molly Desmond and Polly Flinders — and in 1931 she was put down.

price the odds quoted by a bookmaker at a race meeting for a particular horse.

Price, Captain Henry Ryan, (born 1912) After his first steeplechase win in 1926, Captain Price went on to have many more successes as an amateur jockey, before turning professional in 1937, the year in which he began to train. Since the Second World War, he has been an important and most successful trainer.

Among his major successes are Kilmore, winner of the Grand National in 1962; Clair Soleil in the Champion Hurdle at Cheltenham in 1955, Fare Time in 1959 and Eborneezer in 1961; Done Up in the Whitbread Gold Cup at Sandown in 1959 and What a Myth in 1966; Rosyth in the Schweppes Gold Trophy Hurdle Race in 1963 and 1964, Le Vermontois in 1966 and Hill House in 1967.

Although he had always trained both National Hunt and flat-race horses, it was not until 1971 that he really turned his attention to the flat. In 1972 he trained over seventy winners, including Ginevra, the Oaks winner, and in 1973 he trained Giacometti, winner of the Gimcrack Stakes.

pricker boot a rectangular piece of leather studded with tacks, which is strapped over bandaged injuries on the leg to prevent the horse tearing the bandages off.

prick on a deer *hunting* to urge on a carted stag at a meet when it has been released and before the hounds are laid on.

Prince Philip Cup a perpetual challenge cup presented in 1957 by Prince Philip, Duke of Edinburgh, for the Pony Club mounted games. The competition is open to all branches of the Pony Club. Regional qualifying rounds are held annually at Easter and from there the six leading teams go forward to the finals held the following October at the Horse of the Year Show. Each team consists of a non-riding captain and five members who must be under the age of sixteen and whose pony may not exceed 14.2 h.h. Four members of the teams take part in each of the games, which include such events as sack races, relay bending races, etc., designed to promote a team spirit among the children and to encourage them to school their ponies.

private pack a pack of hounds owned and maintained entirely by the master.

Prix des Nations an international, team show-jumping competition held at a C.S.I.O. Also called NATIONS' CUP.

The competition, at which a minimum of three different countries must be represented, is decided over two rounds, which are jumped on the same day, and judged under Barème A rules of the F.E.I. The course consists of thirteen or fourteen obstacles and remains unchanged throughout the competition.

It is open to teams of three or four riders, each rider being permitted to use only one horse for the entire competition. Only the best three scores in each round count, so that teams of four clearly have an advantage in that their worst score in each round is discarded.

All members of each team must take part in the first round, but if in the second round a team is in an unbeatable position after the third rider has jumped, the fourth member of the team need not jump a second time. Should a competitor be eliminated in either of the rounds he is not eliminated from the competition, but is given the worst score of the round plus an additional twenty faults.

The winning team is the one with the lowest overall score. In the event of equality of points, all the members of the tying teams are required to take part in the jump-off. If there is still a tie, time becomes the deciding factor, and the team with the fastest total time for its best three rounds in the jump-off is the winner.

No prize money is given and there are no individual awards. In Prix des Nations teams are simply awarded points which count towards the President's Cup.

probable *racing* a likely runner in a particular race.

professional Under international rules a professional is defined as follows: any person who, having attained the age of eighteen years, accepts remuneration for riding competition horses in show-jumping, dressage or three-day event competitions; sells more than three international competition horses during the current year; hires out competition horses for the purposes of show-jumping, dressage or three-day event competitions; receives payment for training competition horses; allows or has allowed his name or photograph to promote or advertise any product; is considered for any other reason as a professional by the Fédération Equestre Internationale and/or his own national federation.

Professionals may take part in national, international and official international events as laid down by the conditions of the organizers. A professional who wishes to compete in international competitions must obtain an annual licence from his national federation.

progressive fault and out *show-jumping* a competition in which points are awarded instead of faults — 2 points for each obstacle jumped clear, 1 point for an obstacle knocked down and 1 point for going through the finish within the time allowed. As soon as a competitor knocks down an obstacle or makes some other mistake he ends his round. Competitors jumping clear go through to the next round, the full course being jumped each time. The competition is ended after the third round, and if there are competitors equal on points the prizes are divided.

prompter (US) a galloping horse which acts as the pacemaker for a trotter or is used to encourage a sluggish horse.

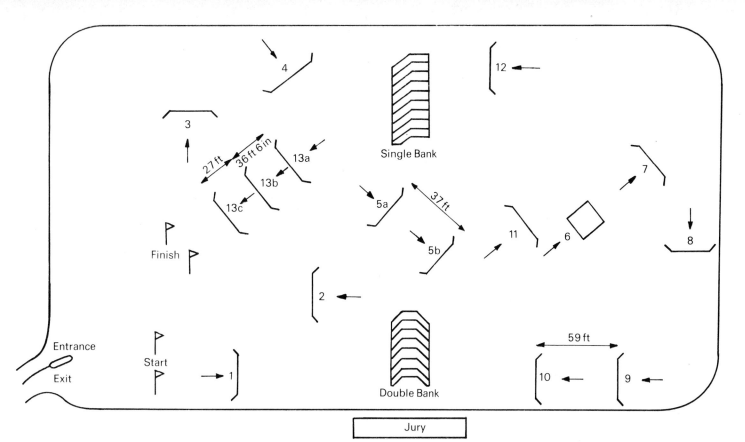

Provinces See under SHIRES.

p.u. pulled up.

public clock *show-jumping* a digital clock erected in the arena to show the time taken by each competitor to complete the course.

pugri standing martingale a type of standing martingale used only in polo, consisting of a cloth as opposed to a leather strap running from the noseband to the girth.

puissance *show-jumping* a competition designed to test the horse's ability to jump height. In the first round the course consists of no more than eight obstacles. These are reduced in number and increased in size (height and width) for the jump-off, though there may never be less than two — one spread and one straight fence, usually a wall. In 1974, in order not to overface horses, an experiment was tried whereby there should never be less than five fences for the jumps-off. Also called POWER JUMP TEST.

pull to remove superfluous hair from the mane or tail of a horse using a mane and tail comb; the hair should never be cut.

pulled up *racing* (of a horse) having been stopped and taking no further part in the race. This may be due to any number of reasons, such as injury, lameness or because it is so far back in the race it stands no chance of winning.

puller a horse which continually pulls at the reins.

pulse The pulse of a horse normally beats between 38 and 43 times per minute. It can be taken under the lower jaw, on the inside of the forearm at the elbow, or on the inside of the fetlock joint.

punter *racing* a person who bets regularly on horses.

puppy walker *hunting* a person living in the country, usually a farmer or landowner, who looks after a hound puppy (or puppies) from the time it is weaned until the following spring when it joins the pack. During this time the puppy should, ideally, be given as much freedom as possible, so that it becomes used to livestock, and be well fed. Some landlords used to make it a condition in the tenancy agreement when a farm was let that a tenant would actually look after hound puppies.

quad a horse.

quarters the area of the horse's body extending from the rear of the flank to the root of the tail and downwards on either side to the top of the gaskin; the hindquarters.

quarter sheet a rectangular sheet or blanket, generally about four feet long, used, especially on racehorses, to cover the loins when at exercise or in the paddock and kept in place either by means of the saddle (if the horse is being exercised) or by a light roller and breastplate.

Queen Elizabeth II The Queen is the patron of many horse societies. She is a founder member of the National Equestrian Centre, and is a regular visitor to the Badminton Horse Trials and the Royal International Horse Show, to which she presented a challenge cup (the Queen Elizabeth II Cup) in 1949.

As well as owning a number of successful three-day event horses, notably, Countryman (ridden by Bertie Hill), Columbus and Goodwill (the horse Princess Anne rode in the European Championships in 1973 and in the World Championships in 1974), she is also very successful as a racehorse owner. Among her winners are Aureole, winner of the King George VI and Queen Elizabeth Stakes and the Coronation Cup, Alexander, winner of the Royal Hunt Cup, Pall Mall, winner of the 2000-Guineas and the New Stakes, Agreement, winner in two consecutive years of the Doncaster Cup and winner of the Chester Cup, and Choir Boy, winner of the Royal Hunt Cup.

Queen Elizabeth II Cup an international show-jumping challenge trophy for women riders presented by Queen Elizabeth II, when Princess Elizabeth, in 1949 for perpetual competition at the Royal International Horse Show (For results see page 228.)

Above
Queen Elizabeth II Cup, presented by the Queen as Princess Elizabeth in 1949.

Queen Elizabeth, The Queen Mother An enthusiastic supporter of National Hunt racing, the Queen Mother has owned many very successful steeplechasers, including Devon Loch, probably the unluckiest horse not to win the Grand National, Manicou, winner of the King George VI Chase, Monaveen, winner of the Queen Elizabeth Chase, The Rip, winner of the Grand Sefton Trial Chase, and Chaou II, winner of the Worcester Royal Porcelain Chase. Until his death in 1973, the majority of her horses were trained by Captain Peter Cazalet at Tonbridge in Kent.

Queen's Vase a horserace over a distance of 2 miles, held annually at Ascot since 1838. Formerly called (until 1959) GOLD VASE. (For results see page 244.)

quittor a fistulous sore which forms at the coronet, towards the heel, as a result of a direct blow or injury, such as a tread, or, more seriously, as a result of pus working up from an infected injury in some other part of the foot, such as a corn, punctured sole or sand crack.

r. refused.

rabies a highly contagious incurable disease of the brain which occurs in all warm-blooded animals, including the horse. The symptoms are over-excitement, manger biting, excessive thirst combined with an inability to drink, depression and paralysis. The disease becomes fatal within three to four days. Rabies has been stamped out in Britain but is still common in eastern countries.

race 1. See HORSERACE. **2.** See STRIPE.

race card the printed programme of a race meeting, giving information including the time of each race, the name of each race and the names of all horses, their owners and trainers.

racecourse a race track properly constructed for flat and/or steeplechasing and hurdle racing, together with all the necessary facilities, such as grandstands, paddock, stables, office buildings, etc., and administered by appointed officials.

Racecourse Association an organization whose objects are to consider all questions affecting the welfare of racecourse owners, to watch over matters affecting their rights and liabilities, to protect their interests, to negotiate on their behalf, and to initiate and promote improvements in any laws or regulations directly or indirectly affecting racecourse owners.

Racecourse Technical Services a subsidiary of the Horse Race Betting Levy Board, which provides the following services and equipment for horseracing in Britain: photofinish and race timing; camera patrol by means of film or television; public address system, including racecourse commentaries; and starting stalls and barriers.

racegoer the name given to a person who attends race meetings regularly.

Racegoers' Club a club for racing enthusiasts founded in May 1968 with the object of promoting racing as a spectator sport. To this end a number of racecourses in Britain now offer concession days to club members, a move which has greatly increased the number of people passing through their turnstiles. As well as organizing trips to major international race meetings abroad, the club also arranges visits to training establishments and holds discussions at which members have the opportunity to meet and talk to owners, trainers and jockeys. It has some 20,000 members and has owned racehorses and sponsored some races.

racehorse a horse bred and trained for racing, either on the flat, or over hurdles or steeplechase obstacles.

Racehorse Owners Association an association which looks after the interests of the owners of horses which run under Jockey Club rules.

race meeting 1. a meeting at a given place for the purpose of holding a fixed number of horseraces. **2.** the period during which this meeting takes place.

race strip a racecourse where trotting meetings are held. Also called RACEWAY.

race track the area on a racecourse where the horses race.

raceway See RACE STRIP.

racing over fences a popular name for steeplechasing.

racing plate a thin, very lightweight horseshoe used on racehorses.

racing saddle a saddle designed for use on race-horses. The lightest racing saddles, which weigh only one to two pounds and are about fourteen inches long, are made of pigskin and have no external bars, the leathers being passed through a slot and attached to the tree itself. The panels are generally very full and are cut well forward. In the past the panels were covered with cloth, silk or nylon, but now a light leather is generally preferred as it is less absorbent to sweat. The heavier saddles, used in hurdle racing and steeplechasing as opposed to flat racing, have lead inlaid into the tree (with more at the front than the rear) to make them up to the required weight.

rack the most spectacular movement of the five-gaited American Saddle Horse; a very fast even gait in which each foot strikes the ground separately in quick succession. Over a straight course a mile may be covered in 2 minutes 19 seconds.

rags and tatters the condition of the horns of a stag when the velvet is torn and frayed after being rubbed against a tree.

rails the barrier marking the edges of a race track, usually consisting of a strongly built, white-painted wooden fence.

ralli car a light two-wheeled vehicle, introduced at the beginning of the twentieth century, resembling the dogcart, but lower and more comfortable, with shafts inside the body rather than under it, and with curved, panelled sides.

random three horses driven in single file.

range horse (Western US) a horse which is born and brought up on the range; such a horse is never handled until it is brought in to be broken.

rangy (of a horse) having great scope and potential.

rapping the act of raising a pole, either at one end or at both ends, as a horse is jumping, so that the horse hits the pole and is thus encouraged to jump higher in future. Under F.E.I. and B.S.J.A. rules rapping is not permitted, and there are severe penalties for practising it. However, under A.H.S.A. rules it is allowed, provided that only a bamboo pole is used and that the rapping takes place in a supervised area. Also called POLING (US).

ratcatcher informal hunting dress, consisting of a bowler hat, stock, tweed riding jacket, breeches and boots.

rat-tailed horse (Western US) a horse with very little hair in its tail.

rattle *hunting* (of hounds) to be in close pursuit of the fox and in full cry.

rawhide cowhide which has been subjected to a vegetable tannage, making it exceptionally strong, used mainly for stirrup leathers and girths.

rear (of a horse) to rise on the hind legs. If a horse rears, the reaction of the rider should be to sit well forward, dropping the reins low in order to exert a downward pressure on the horse's head. If he sits back, he may cause the horse to overbalance and come down on top of him.

receive weight *racing* (of a horse) to be set to carry less weight than another.

recognized horseshow (US) a horseshow which is affiliated to the American Horse Shows Association.

recognized meeting a race meeting held under the rules of a recognized turf authority.

red flag a marker used in equestrian sports to denote the right-hand extremity of any obstacle. It is also used to mark a set track, and must always be passed on the left-hand side.

red ribbon a piece of red ribbon tied round the tail of a horse, especially when hunting, to indicate that it is a known kicker.

red roan See under ROAN.

refusal 1. *racing* the failure of a horse to attempt to jump a hurdle or steeplechase fence. **2.** *show-jumping, combined training* the act of passing an obstacle which is to be jumped or stopping in front of it. Stopping without stepping back, followed immediately by a standing jump, is not penalized, but if the horse steps back this constitutes a refusal. If a horse which has already refused is then re-presented at the obstacle and halts or steps back a second time, this constitutes a second refusal, and so on. After a refusal a competitor may make one circle or more in order to retake the track without further penalty.

When a competitor has been eliminated for three refusals, he may make up to two attempts to jump any other obstacle before leaving the show-jumping ring.

In three-day events refusals on the cross-country course are penalized only if they occur inside the penalty zone.

rein back to make a horse step backwards while being ridden or driven. In dressage it is necessary for the horse to remain collected, with the head carried high, bent at the poll and with the face held in an almost vertical position. The actual paces should be equal and deliberate but slow, and the halt should be smooth.

reins a pair of long narrow straps attached to the bit or bridle and used by the rider or driver to guide or restrain his horse. For normal riding purposes reins are five feet long. It is important that they should be in a pair (as opposed to one continuous length) joined by a buckle in the centre, so that they can be undone in an emergency. However, if the reins are to be slipped to the full extent they should be knotted; otherwise, the pressure exerted on the buckle may cause it to break. See also DARTNALL REINS, PLAITED REINS, RUBBER-COVERED REINS, WEB REINS.

rejoneador a mounted bullfighter.

remain in training *racing* (of a horse) to be kept in a fit condition with a view to further racing.

remount any horse kept by an army or service unit.

Remuda (Western US) a herd of horses on a cattle ranch used as mounts by the cowboys in their daily work.

renvers *dressage* a movement executed like the travers, but with the hind legs on the outer track and the forelegs on the inner track. Also called TAIL TO THE WALL. See also TRAVERS.

rep a cowboy employed to search for and round up cattle which have strayed from the ranch of his employer. Such cattle would be recognizable by their brand.

re-ride (in a rodeo) a second ride in the same go-round for a bronco- or bull-rider, if, for some reason, the first mount has been judged as unsatisfactory.

resinback See ROSINBACK.

resistance the act of refusing to go forward,

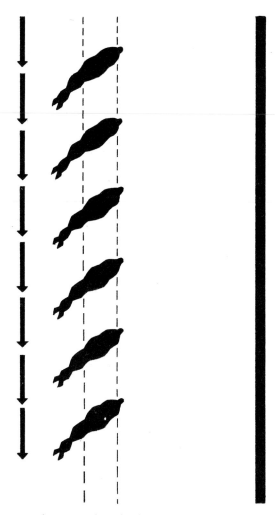

1930 on Singapore, in 1937 on Chulmleigh, in
1940 on Turkhan, in 1942 on Sun Chariot and in
1944 on Tehran, but it was not until 1953, riding
Pinza, that he had his first and only Derby win.

On retiring as a jockey, he took out a licence to
train and then, in 1970, he became a racing
manager. He was knighted in 1953 for his services
to racing.

ride a lane or road, approximately seventy feet
wide, made for riding on horseback, especially one
cut through a wood. Apart from being very useful
for both hunting and shooting, a ride makes a very
good firebreak.

ride, drive and jump class a competition held
at horseshows in the United States in which horses
have to compete in harness, under saddle and
over jumps.

ride into the ground to ride a horse to its
absolute limit.

ride off *polo* to push one's pony against that of
another player in order to prevent him from playing
the ball.

ride out *racing* to ride a horse hard to the end of a
race.

riding school an establishment where people are
taught to ride and horses hired for riding or taken
for livery, or both. In Great Britain, under the Riding
Establishment Act of 1965, these schools have to
be licensed by the local authority and are open for
inspection.

rig a male horse which has been unsuccessfully or
incompletely castrated, usually because one of the
testicles is retained in the abdomen. A rig behaves
like a stallion and is normally difficult to handle.

right-hand course a racecourse which is run in
a clockwise direction.

Rimell, Thomas Frederick, (born 1913) At the
age of twelve Fred Rimell rode his first winner in
an apprentice race at Chepstow. In all he had
thirty-four wins on the flat before being forced by
weight problems to turn instead to National Hunt
racing. He was champion National Hunt jockey in
the 1938/39 season, riding sixty-one winners, and
again the following season with twenty-four
winners. In the 1944/45 season he shared the title
with Frenchie Nicholson, each riding fifteen
winners, but the following season he again won
the title outright with fifty-four winners. In 1947,

stopping, running back or rearing. In show-
jumping, and also in horse trials if it occurs within
a penalty zone, a resistance is penalized in exactly
the same way as a refusal. If an unruly horse continues to resist and takes longer than one minute to
jump the obstacle it is eliminated.

restraint Among the simplest methods of restraint
are:
1. holding up one of the forefeet;
2. holding the tail firmly downwards, upwards, or
   to one side;
3. applying a twitch;
4. blindfolding.

return service the second service of a mare by the
same stallion, the mare having remained barren
after the first service.

reversed oxer *show-jumping* a spread fence consisting of a central pole with a brush fence in front
and behind. The pole should be the highest part of
the obstacle.

r.h. right-hand course.

ribbon a rosette.

ribbons *driving* reins.

Richards, Sir Gordon (born 1904) One of the
most famous flat race jockeys of all times, Sir
Gordon Richards' career spanned from 1920 to
1954. During that period he was champion
jockey no less than twenty-six times. He won the
2000-Guineas on three occasions; in 1938 on
Pasch, in 1942 on Big Game and in 1947 on
Tudor Minstrel; and the 1000-Guineas three
times; in 1942 on Sun Chariot, in 1948 on Queen-
pot and in 1951 on Belle of All. He won the Oaks
twice; in 1930 on Rose of England and in 1942
on Sun Chariot; and the St Leger five times; in

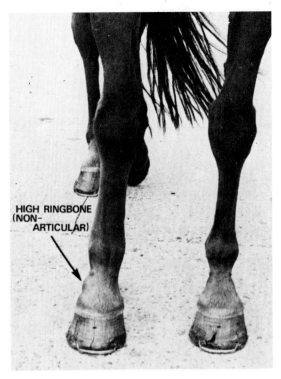

HIGH RINGBONE (NON-ARTICULAR)

Above
Capt. Fred Rimell, one of the leading trainers of National Hunt horses, pictured here with Ordnance at his stables in Severn Stoke, Worcestershire.

Above right
ringbone.

riding Coloured School Boy, he had a crashing fall in the Cheltenham Gold Cup, which brought his career as a jockey to an end.

He then devoted his time to training National Hunt horses at Kinnersley, near Worcester, having first taken out a licence to train in 1945. He very soon became a formidable force, and was the leading trainer in 1950/51 with sixty-four winners, a success he repeated in 1968/69 with sixty-two winners and again in 1969/70 with seventy-seven winners.

He has trained winners of nearly all the major steeplechase races, including E.S.B., winner of the Grand National in 1956; Nicolaus Silver, who won it in 1961; Woodland Venture, winner of the Cheltenham Gold Cup in 1967; Gay Trip, winner of the Heinz Chase in 1968, of the Mackeson Gold Cup in 1969 and 1971, and of the Grand National in 1970; Mackeson Gold Cup winners Jupiter Boy (1968) and Chatham (1970); and Comedy of Errors, winner of the Champion Hurdle at Cheltenham in 1973.

His daughter, a very accomplished horsewoman, won the Newmarket Town Plate at the age of fourteen and has also won many point-to-points.

rim firing (Western US) the act of placing a burr under the saddle blanket of a horse in order to make it buck.

rim rocker (Western US) a horse which is able to climb steep hills and travel over rocks and rough country.

ring bit a severe bit used by early cowboys. On the port it had a ring which encircled the lower jaw, pressing on a sensitive nerve, and it also had a curb under the jaw.

ringbone a bony outgrowth on the lower part of a horse's limb, in the region of the pastern. HIGH RINGBONE involves the long pastern bone or the pastern joint, while LOW RINGBONE affects the short pastern bone or the joint between the short pastern bone and the pedal bone. In both cases a painful swelling appears over the affected area and there is marked lameness, which, if the joint is affected, may be permanent. The condition may be caused by direct injury, by concussion, or there may be an hereditary weakness.

ringer a horse entered in a race under the name of another horse, the object being to win bets illegally on a good horse which the public and bookmakers believe is an inferior one.

ringing fox *hunting* a fox which, when hunted, tends to run in smallish circles without leaving the area where it lives.

ringman a bookmaker.

riot (of hounds) to hunt any animal other than the normal quarry, as, for example, foxhounds hunting a hare.

rising trot the practice of rising from the saddle at every alternate stride when the horse is trotting.

r.o. run out.

roach back a prominent malformed convex spinal column. Also called HOG BACK, SWAY BACK.

road-closed barrier See PLANKS.

road coach 1. a public stagecoach introduced at the time of the coaching revival between 1860 and 1890. **2.** a privately owned sports coach, usually painted in gay colours, having a mail coach body with leaded windows and carrying four passengers inside and eight on the roof seats.

roan a horse having a black, bay or chestnut coat with an admixture of white hairs, especially on the body and neck, which modifies the colour. A BLUE ROAN is basically black, the white hairs giving the coat a bluish cast. In a RED ROAN (also called BAY ROAN) the basically bay or brown-bay coat has a reddish cast, and in a STRAWBERRY ROAN (also called CHESTNUT ROAN) the coat is light chestnut with a pinkish cast. In both the blue roan and the red roan the lower part of the legs, below the knee or hock, is black.

roarer a horse which makes a loud noise as it breathes in when it exerts itself, owing to a malfunction of its respiratory system.

roaring the noise made by a roarer.

Robeson, Peter David, *GB* (born 1929) Peter Robeson is widely regarded as one of the most stylish riders in show-jumping today. During a career which has spanned over twenty years he has

competed in over sixty Prix des Nations, and with his three principal horses, Craven A, Firecrest and Grebe, has won many important national and international competitions. He was reserve for the British team at the Olympic Games in 1952 and, riding Scorchin', was a member of the team which won the bronze medal in Stockholm in 1956. At the 1964 Olympic Games in Tokyo he won the individual bronze medal, riding Firecrest, and with Grebe he was reserve for the Munich Olympics in 1972. In the same year he won the Prix des Vainqueurs in Barcelona and the Grand Prix in Palermo. He is a member of the executive committee of the British Show Jumping Association.

rocker shoe a type of horseshoe which is deeper at the quarter than at the heel and toe, thus producing a rocker effect as the horse moves. Like the bar shoe, which it resembles, the rocker shoe is useful for horses which have weak feet, or have had laminitis or any other complaint causing inflammation of the foot. Also called ROUND SHOE.

rocking chair gait (US) the canter.

Rodzianko, Col. Paul, (died 1965) Colonel Rodzianko probably did more than any other person to train English and Irish show-jumpers and to establish these two countries at the top in this sport. Born in Russia, he joined the cavalry and was sent to Italy to study Caprilli's methods. On returning to Russia he trained a show-jumping team, of which he was a regular member, and they competed at the International Horse Show in London, winning outright the King Edward VII

Cup for the Prix des Nations in 1912, 1913 and 1914. Following the First World War he travelled to England, and after serving in the British Army set up a training establishment near Windsor. Then, in the early 1930s, he was appointed director of the cavalry school in Dublin. It was during this time that the Irish Army team became one of the strongest teams in the world. After serving in the British Army during the Second World War, he returned to Ireland. Then in 1955 he moved to England, where he trained several British riders and teams.

roller 1. a girth-like device, usually about four to five inches wide and made of hemp and leather, fastened over a day or night rug to hold it in place. It is secured by means of one or two buckles and on the underside has two well-stuffed pads which fit one on each side of the horse's spine. Pressure on the spine can be further reduced by attaching a breast strap so that the roller need not be fastened so tightly to prevent it from slipping back. See also ARCH ROLLER. **2.** one of a series of small rings, usually of metal, placed round or within the mouthpiece of a bit. By encouraging the horse to mouth the bit, rollers are designed to prevent it from taking hold of the bit and tearing away.

roller bolt See under SPLINTER BAR.

Roman nose a face with a convex, as opposed to the more usual concave, profile.

Roman riding a form of stunt riding in which the rider stands on the horse's back with the reins in his hand; some riders are able to manage as many as five horses running abreast.

rope horse (US) any horse which is especially trained and used for roping cattle.

rope-shy (US; of a horse) tending to turn away from the rope when a cowboy is roping cattle.

rosette a rose-shaped arrangement of coloured ribbon, usually mounted on cardboard, awarded to each of the prize winners at a horseshow and customarily displayed on the horse's bridle. A different coloured rosette is awarded for each place; for example, red for first place, blue for second place and yellow for third place. Also called RIBBON.

rosinback a circus horse used bareback for acrobatic acts, etc., so called because resin is rubbed into its coat to prevent the performer from slipping. Also RESINBACK.

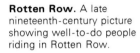

Rotten Row. A late nineteenth-century picture showing well-to-do people riding in Rotten Row.

its being torn when the hound is hunting:

round shoe See ROCKER SHOE.

rowel a small wheel forming the extremity of certain types of spur.

Royal International Horse Show an international horseshow which opened at Olympia, London, on 7th June 1907, under the presidency of the fifth Earl of Lonsdale. One half of the capital for the show was subscribed by American directors, who were Alfred Vanderbilt, Clarence McKay, E. T. Stotesbury and Lawrence Jones, and the other half by British directors.

The show ran annually until it closed its doors in June 1914, and because of the war it was not restarted until June 1920. After the Second World War the site of the show was changed from indoors

Rotten Row an area of Hyde Park, London, extending from Hyde Park Corner to Alexandra Gate, reserved for horse riding.

rough (of a horse) unclipped and ungroomed.

roughed out (Western US; of a horse) having been ridden a few times but still likely to buck.

roughing off the procedure followed before turning a stabled horse out to grass. This involves omitting heating foodstuffs, such as oats, from the animal's diet, ceasing to groom or exercise it and gradually reducing the number or weight of its rugs.

rough shoeing the insertion of extra nails into a horseshoe in order to prevent the horse slipping on a frozen or snowbound surface.

rough the curb to increase the severity of a curb chain by twisting the links.

round action the type of movement found in a high-stepping horse, such as the hackney, in which the legs, though raised high, are replaced close to the spot from which they were lifted, so that little ground is covered with each step.

rounded ear the ear of a hound which has been trimmed, usually at the puppy stage, to prevent

to outdoors, at the White City Stadium, London, where it was held under the chairmanship of Col. V. D. S. Williams, and with Col. Michael Ansell as the show director. It continued to be held there until 1967 and was then held for two years at the vast Wembley Stadium, before moving indoors again in 1970 to the Empire Pool Wembley.

In 1909 King Edward VII presented a cup for the Prix des Nations, and this was won outright by Russia in 1914. Edward, Prince of Wales, presented a cup, which was won outright by Great Britain in 1928 and was re-presented by the Army Council. Among the major individual show-jumping competitions held at the Royal International are the King George V Gold Cup, which was first presented in 1911, and the Queen Elizabeth II Cup, presented in 1949. There is also a wide variety of other classes, including show classes for hunters, hacks, children's ponies and hackneys, as well as driving championships and ride-and-drive competitions.

Royal Windsor Horse Show Club a society founded in 1943 to help charities and to promote the well-being of horses. An annual show is held in the Home Park at Windsor, usually in early May, and it provides some of the best early season competition for all types of horses.

Above
Royal Windsor. One of the most attractive show grounds in England is the Royal Windsor, which has as a natural backcloth the famous castle. This picture shows former international rider Johnny Kidd in action.

Below
running martingale.

Roycroft, James William, *Australia* (born 1915) Bill Roycroft is one of the world's leading three-day-event riders, as well as being a noted steeplechase rider. The winner of twenty-two three-day events in Australia, he competed in the Olympic Games of 1960, 1964, 1968 and 1972. On the first occasion he was a member of the team which won the gold medal, and in 1968 of the bronze medal team. Among his best horses have been Stoney Crossing, Eldorado, Avatar and Sabre.

In 1969 he was awarded the O.B.E. for his services to equestrian sport. At the end of 1972 he announced his retirement from competitive riding. Two of his three sons have also represented Australia in international three-day events.

rubber-covered reins a type of riding rein, having a central rubber-covered strip about thirty inches long, designed to give extra grip in wet weather and also useful on horses which sweat profusely.

rugby panel See under PANEL.

rugby Pelham a Pelham bit in which the cheek-pieces are fixed and the snaffle rings are set on independent links, thus making the bit stronger and producing greater curb and poll pressure. The mouthpiece may be either plain or with a port and rollers.

rumble seat See DICKY.

run-in *racing* the last part of a race track leading immediately to the finish. In steeplechasing or hurdling it is the distance from the last obstacle to the winning post.

run mute *hunting* (of hounds) to run very fast and thus not have time to speak.

runner *racing* any horse taking part in a particular race.

running martingale a martingale consisting of a strap which is attached to the girth by a loop and divides at the chest into two arms, each terminating in a ring, through which the respective rein is passed. Because the running martingale is fixed only at the girth end, it allows much more play than the standing martingale. It is therefore considered to be the more suitable if the horse is required to jump, and under F.E.I. rules it is the only type permitted in show-jumping competitions. See also BIB MARTINGALE, STANDING MARTINGALE.

run-off *combined training* a deviation which occurs when a horse leaves the defined course in an event and has to come back on to the course at the point where it left in order to continue.

run out 1. *show-jumping, combined training* to avoid an obstacle which is to be jumped by running to one side or the other of it. In show-jumping the

Orlov. A Russian breed
started in the 1770s, it was
developed for harness racing
and has also been used for
drawing carriages and
coaches.

Percheron. A breed of
heavy draught horse taking
its name from the La Perche
region of France, where it
originated.

**Peterborough Royal
Foxhound Show.** The
major foxhound show in the
British Isles.

Lester Piggott. Champion
apprentice in 1950 and 1951
and champion jockey in 1960
and from 1964 to 1971, he
has ridden winners all over
the world.

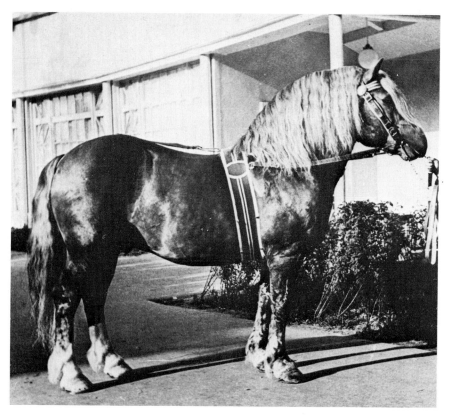

Above
Russian Heavy Draught Horse, a very powerful and hardy breed, originally from the Ukraine.

Far right
saddle-soap. Regular applications of saddle-soap help to keep leather pliable and in good condition.

penalty is always as for a refusal, and this also applies in combined training if the offence is committed inside a penalty zone. **2.** *racing* to avoid an obstacle which is to be jumped, or to pass on the wrong side of a marker flag.

Russian Heavy Draught Horse a breed of heavy draught horse developed mainly in the Ukraine by crossing local carthorse mares with Ardennes and Percheron stallions, and to a lesser extent with Orlov trotters, with the specific intention of producing an animal which was powerful and hardy but not too heavy. About 15 h.h. and usually chestnut or dark chestnut, it has a strong muscular body and relatively short legs, giving it great pulling power.

Russian trotter a breed of trotting horse developed in the Soviet Union by crossing Orlov mares with American trotter stallions. About 16 h.h., the Russian trotter is characterized by a well-proportioned, slightly convex head, a long well-shaped neck, powerful shoulders, a broad deep chest and stout legs. The most usual colours are bay, black and chestnut. Russian trotters are faster than Orlov trotters, but experience has shown that they do not crossbreed so well with agricultural horses.

saddle a seat for a rider on horseback. Different designs of saddles have been developed for different purposes, but all with the object of providing the rider with the maximum security, control and comfort and of placing him at the horse's centre of balance. Some of the greatest innovations in saddle design resulted from the crouch seat adopted by the American jockey, Tod Sloan, and the forward riding system subsequently produced by Federico Caprilli. See also DRESSAGE SADDLE, ENGLISH SHOW-SADDLE, FELT PAD, GENERAL-PURPOSE SADDLE, HUNTING SADDLE, MCCLELLAN SADDLE, SHOW-JUMPING SADDLE, WESTERN SADDLE.

saddle bronc riding one of the standard events in a rodeo. The rider has to use a regulation saddle; he is allowed to use only one rein attached to a simple halter, and is not allowed to touch the saddle, the horse or himself with his free hand. He must remain mounted for ten seconds and is judged according to how hard the horse bucks and how well he rides.

saddle cloth a cloth worn under the saddle which, in racing, clearly shows the number of the horse corresponding to the number on the race card. Saddle cloths were first used in National Hunt racing in 1910, but were not made compulsory on the flat until some years later. In combined training, show-jumping and dressage they are worn at an international event and carry the flag of the nation the horse is representing.

saddle flap the large leather flap extending below the skirt on either side of a saddle.

saddle furniture the metal parts of a saddle.

saddle-horse 1. any horse suited for or trained for riding. **2.** a wooden framework having a pitched top used for cleaning or storing saddles.

saddle mark 1. a saddle-shaped area of hair left unclipped on the back of a horse. **2.** a patch of white hair on the back of a horse, often resulting from sores or galls caused by a badly fitting saddle.

saddler a person who makes or deals in saddlery and/or harness for horses. See also BLACK SADDLER, BROWN SADDLER.

saddlery the bridle, saddle and other equipment used on a horse which is to be ridden as opposed to driven.

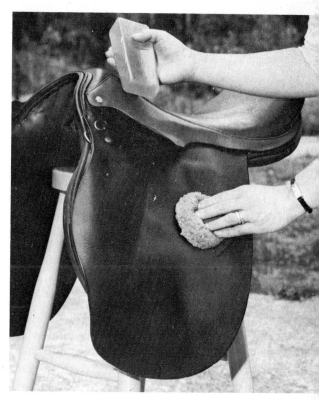

saddle-soap a soap consisting mainly of glycerine or castile, used for cleaning and preserving saddlery and harness. Regular applications, which should be made with a slightly damp cloth or sponge, help to keep the leather soft and pliable.

saddle sore an injury on a horse caused either by badly fitting saddlery or harness, or by bad riding. If a horse newly in from grass is made to carry a saddle for excessive periods before it has hardened off properly, saddle sores are likely to develop.

saddletree the frame of a saddle. It is traditionally

made of beechwood, treated and coated with a black gluelike mixture to make it waterproof. The shape of the tree commands the shape of the saddle. Also called TREE.

salivary glands In the horse there are three pairs of these, as follows: the parotid glands, just below each ear; the sublingual, underneath the tongue; and the submaxillary, below and within the angle of the lower jaw.

salt Salt helps to keep a horse in good health and a lump of rock salt should always be kept in the manger.

salty (Western US; of a horse) hard-bucking.

sand crack.

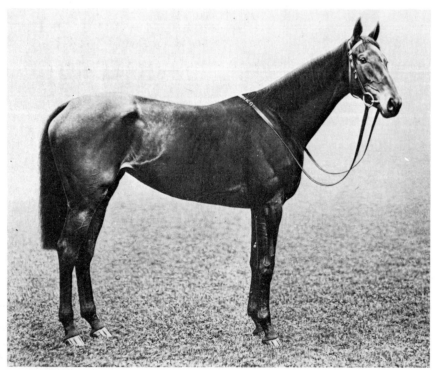

sand crack a split or fissure in the wall of the hoof, extending in a downward direction from the coronet and usually resulting from an injury to the coronary band, which, depending on the severity of the damage, causes a temporary or permanent arrest in the secretion of new horn. As the hoof grows, the sand crack gradually extends downwards. Under the horse's weight it tends to spread

Below
Sceptre. In 1902 she won both the 1000-Guineas and the 2000-Guineas.

at the base and, if left untreated, grit or dirt may penetrate the sensitive tissues in the depth of the crack, causing inflammation and acute lameness.

Saratoga a racecourse at Saratoga Springs, New York, first opened in 1863, the oldest surviving course in the United States. The Futurity Stakes was held there in 1910 and 1914.

Saumur panel See under PANEL.

sausage boot a stuffed leather ring strapped round the coronet in order to prevent a capped elbow, which is caused by pressure of the inner heel of the shoe on the elbow as the horse lies down or gets up.

Scamperdale a Pelham bit in which the mouthpiece is turned back slightly at each end so that the cheekpiece is behind the mouth to prevent any chafing.

Scawbrig bridle a bitless bridle consisting of a bridle head and cheeks, with a broad nosepiece, a backstrap, which holds the nosepiece in position, and a rein passed through the rings on either side of the nosepiece.

scent *hunting* the distinctive odour of the fox which is given off from the glands under the tail and from the pads. It varies considerably in strength and is at its best when the ground temperature is higher than the air temperature. Once the hounds have located the fox they seldom see it again before the kill and hunt it nearly all the time by its scent alone. The scent of a fox is said to be PATCHY when hounds are only able to hunt very sketchily, HOLDING when the hounds are able to hunt a line and SERVING where there is a good scent. BREAST HIGH is the very best scent, for then it is not necessary for the hounds to hunt by sniffing the ground.

Sceptre (by Persimmon out of Ornament. Persimmon won the Derby, the St Leger, the Eclipse Stakes and the Ascot Gold Cup.) Foaled in 1899 at the Duke of Westminster's Eaton Hall Stud at Chester, Sceptre was bought as a yearling by Robert Sievier, who sent her to be trained by Charles Morton. Her first race as a two-year-old was in the Woodcote Stakes at Epsom. She then won the July Stakes at Newmarket and was third in her only other race, the Champagne Stakes at Doncaster. At the end of the season Charles Morton became a private trainer for J. B. Joel, and Robert Sievier decided to train his horses himself at Shrewton.

Sceptre's first outing as a three-year-old was in the Lincoln, in which she finished a close second. She then went on to Newmarket and pulled off an incredible double, winning the 2000-Guineas and, only two days later, the 1000-Guineas. She started as favourite in the Derby but finished fourth. Two days later, however, she won the Oaks, and then went on to win the St James' Palace Stakes at Ascot and the Nassau Stakes at Goodwood, finishing the season with a win in the St Leger.

As a four-year-old she won the Hardwicke Stakes at Ascot, the Jockey Club Stakes at Newmarket, the Duke of York Stakes at Kempton, and the Champion Stakes and the Limekiln Stakes at Newmarket. She had three races as a five-year-old, but the best she could manage was second in the Coronation Cup.

She then went to stud and after changing hands several times was finally bought by Lord Glanely, who retired her in 1922. She died in 1927 at the age of twenty-eight. Her own offspring were disappointing, but among her descendants were a number who made their mark on the turf, including Tiberius, Flyon and Petition.

schedule a booklet or pamphlet giving details of the conditions of entry, classes, prize money and entry fees, and other relevant information on all the competitions to be held at a show or event. It also includes the general regulations of the meeting.

Schleswig a breed of medium-heavy horse from northern Germany. In the Middle Ages the breed was strongly influenced by the Danish Jutland Horse, as a horse heavy enough to carry a knight in armour during times of war. At about the end of the nineteenth century the breed society was formed to introduce standards, and two types of the breed were established: one for use in war and the other to be used for haulage, such as pulling buses. Since the Second World War the French Boulonnais breed has had a strong effect, as stallions of this breed have been used.

The predominant colour is chestnut, but bays and greys are also found. The breed society is the Society of Schleswig Horse Breeding Clubs, which has its headquarters in Kiel.

school 1. to train a horse for whatever purpose it may be required. **2.** an enclosed area, either covered or open, where a horse can be trained or exercised.

school canter one of the high-school airs, which is particularly hard to perform: a slow, very collected canter, requiring great impulsion, the horse keeping a balanced long stride and moving in true three-pace time.

school jump See AIR ABOVE THE GROUND.

school riding any work done with a horse in a school.

score a preliminary warm up on the track before a trotting race is actually called. Two, or sometimes three, scores are usually allowed.

Scorrier snaffle a type of twisted snaffle having four rings, as opposed to two (such a formation being known as WILSON RINGS); the two inner rings are fixed in slots in the mouthpiece itself and are attached to the cheekpieces of the bridle, while the outer rings, which are fixed to the ends of

the mouthpiece in the normal way, are attached to the reins only, thus giving greater effect to the reins. Also called CORNISH SNAFFLE.

scratch 1. to withdraw a horse from an equestrian event after the entry has been made. **2.** (US) to spur vigorously.

screen a frame made of hessian, usually about five feet high and supported by wooden uprights about eight feet apart, which is held round an injured horse in order to hide it from the public. It is an important piece of equipment for all equestrian events.

scut the tail of a hare.

seat 1. the position of the rider in the saddle. **2.** the part of the saddle between the pommel and the cantle.

second horse *hunting* a fresh horse made available for a huntsman or whip who wants to change horses during the day. The second horse will be ridden by a SECOND HORSEMAN who will try to find out in which direction the hounds are expected to run and then, by taking short cuts and not joining in the hunt, so that his horse does not become tired, will arrange to meet the rider of the first horse at an appointed time and effect the changeover.

second horseman See under SECOND HORSE.

second saddle a horse which is being ridden for only the second time.

second thigh See GASKIN.

Secretariat (by Bold Ruler out of Something Royal) Foaled in 1970, Secretariat is owned by the Meadow Stud. As a two-year-old he won seven races, including the Belmont Futurity, the Laurel Futurity, the Sanford Stakes, the Hopeful Stakes and the Garden State Stakes. The following year he ran in one race as a warm-up before making his attempt to become the first winner of the American Triple Crown since Citation in 1948. He won the first two legs, the Kentucky Derby and the Preakness Stakes, and then went to Belmont Park for the third leg, where, ridden by Ron Turcotte, he not only won the Belmont Stakes, but also broke the 1½-mile track record with a time of 2 minutes 24 seconds. Altogether Secretariat ran in twenty-one races before he was retired to stud at the end of the 1973 season. Of these he won sixteen and was second on three occasions and third once. His total winnings amounted to 1,316,808 dollars.

seedy toe a separation of the wall of the hoof from the sensitive laminae, usually affecting the forefeet at the toe, and caused by an injury, laminitis, faulty shoeing or general neglect of the feet. Within the cavity degenerate horn with a soft, crumbling, sawdust-like appearance is formed. If the affected area is large, the condition is usually accompanied by lameness.

Sefton racecourse See under NEWMARKET.

Selby, James, (1844–1888) A well-known coachman who drove many London coaches. James Selby was also the proprietor of the famous Old Times Coach, which ran from London to Brighton. In 1888 he accepted a challenge to drive the London–Brighton return journey in under eight hours; the stake was £1000. He started and finished in Northumberland Avenue in the centre of London and completed the journey in the record time of 7 hours 50 minutes. One change of horses was made in the incredible time of 47 seconds.

Below
Secretariat, with jockey Ron Turcotte up, being congratulated by trainer Lucien Lauren and owner Mrs Penny Tweedy after winning the first leg of the American Triple Crown in 1973.

Selby apron a driving apron which is fastened round the waist by means of a leather strap and buckle, so named after James Selby.

seller See SELLING RACE.

selling plate See SELLING RACE.

selling race a race immediately after which any runner, if a loser, may be claimed for a previously stated price, or, if the winner, must be offered for sale at auction. Also called SELLER, SELLING PLATE.

send on *hunting* to send horses which are to be used for hunting to the meet in advance of their riders. They may either be ridden by a groom or transported in a horsebox.

sensitive frog the part of the internal structure of the horse's foot which lies between the wings of the pedal bone, above the horny frog. Its function is to act as a cushion, supporting the weight of the horse as it moves. Also called FATTY FROG, FLESHY FROG.

sensitive lamina one of the sensitive structures in a horse's foot which form the link between the pedal bone and the wall of the hoof. The sensitive laminae on the surface of the pedal bone interleave with corresponding horny laminae on the inner surface of the wall of the hoof.

sensitive sole the part of a horse's foot lying between the base of the pedal bone and the horny sole. Attached to the pedal bone, it secretes horn through minute papillae. Also called FLESHY SOLE.

service the mating of a mare by a stallion.

service collar a padded leather collar fitted round the neck of a mare when she is being served to protect her from being bitten by the stallion.

serving See under SCENT.

sesamoiditis an inflammation of the joint at the rear of the fetlock, sometimes resulting from faulty conformation or from an injury, either to the small bones or the ligaments. The affected parts become swollen and tender to the touch, and the animal will take short steps, showing a reluctance to place the heel of the shoe on the ground.

set the pace *racing* (of a horse) to go out in front and lead the field.

sewn-in bit a bit which is not separable from the bridle because the cheekpieces are sewn rather than buckled round it.

Shapiro, Neal *US* (born 1945) Neal Shapiro started riding at the age of seven. His potential was noticed when he won the National High Points Championship with Jacks or Better. He became a member of the United States Equestrian Team in 1964, and the following year, on his first international tour, won the coveted Aachen Grand Prix, riding Jacks or Better. He has had numerous wins in the United States, including the Grand Prix at Harrisburg in 1971, when his mount was Sloopy. The following year, again with Sloopy, he won the individual bronze medal at the Olympic Games in Munich and was also a member of the silver medal team.

shark's teeth a show-jumping obstacle made up of planks painted in a zigzag pattern.

shave-tail (US) a horse with a short-haired tail. In the north-west of the United States it was a common practice to pull the tails of horses which had been broken before turning them out on the ranch, so that they could be distinguished from those which had not been broken.

sheepskin a numnah made of sheepskin.

Shetland pony an extremely hardy breed of pony native to the Shetland Isles, which lie to the north of Scotland. The present-day pony is thought to be a direct descendant of the original pony of Tundra origin which came to the area before the end of the Ice Age. The early ponies were probably about 13.2 h.h., but owing to the extreme climatic conditions and very sparse vegetation — often the only food available to them was seaweed — they now vary from twenty-six to forty-two inches in height.

The inhabitants of the Shetland Isles came to rely on the ponies not only as a means of transport, but also for haulage since, in spite of their lack of height, they are remarkably strong and capable of carrying heavy loads. When, in the middle of the last century, the demand came for ponies to work in the mines, the Shetland was found to be ideally suited, and many ponies were taken to the north-east of England.

The breed society, the Shetland Pony Stud Book Society, was formed in 1890. At the turn of the century and again in the 1950s large numbers of ponies were exported to North America.

The Shetland is still one of the most popular breeds in Britain, especially as a children's riding pony. The predominant colours are black, bay and brown, but there are also piebalds, skewbalds, etc., and no colour restrictions are imposed by the breed society. The head, with well-placed ears, is small, well shaped and broad between the eyes, which should be dark and intelligent. The strong, muscular neck should have a good crest — especially important in stallions — and rise off well-laid oblique shoulders. The body must be deep, with a broad chest, a short back with well-sprung ribs and strong quarters. The forelegs should be well placed on the shoulders, with muscular forearms, strong knees, and broad flat bone with springy pasterns. The hind legs should be strong with muscular thighs and broad clean hocks, and the feet should be open, round and tough. The mane and tail should be thick and flowing, and the tail should be set high.

shippon a stable.

Shire the largest and heaviest of the British native breeds. The Shire is said to have descended from the medieval Great Horse, a breed developed for use in war. It is the perfect example of a draught horse, having all the qualities of strength, constitution, stamina and adaptability, and for many years was used on farms and for transport and haulage. Indeed, many breweries in London still use Shires to pull their drays, since for short journeys they have proved more economical than lorries.

Traditionally the Shire is bred mainly in Cambridgeshire, Huntingdonshire and Lincolnshire.

Stallions stand between 16.2 h.h. and 17.2 h.h. and weigh about 20 to 22 cwt, while the mares are usually 16 h.h. to 16.2 h.h. The colours are black, brown, bay or grey, with usually a lot of white hair from the knees/hocks to the fetlocks. The neck should be long, slightly arched and well set on deep, oblique shoulders. The girth measurement should be six to eight feet, and the back should be short, strong and muscular.

The breed society, the Shire Horse Society, was formed in 1877. In recent years considerable interest in the breed has been shown abroad, and large numbers have been exported, mainly to the United States, Canada and South America.

Shires *hunting* the area hunted by the Belvoir, Cottesmore, Fernie, Pytchley and Quorn hunts,

Far right
show-jumping saddle
with a spring tree. Note how
much further forward the
panel is cut than in the
general-purpose saddle.

mainly in Leicestershire and Northamptonshire, acknowledged as being the best hunting country in the British Isles. The term PROVINCES is applied to hunting country elsewhere in Great Britain.

shoeing the act of putting horseshoes on the feet of a horse. Normally a horse requires shoeing every six to eight weeks, although this varies according to the type of work the animal is used for and whether it is worked mainly on roads or soft ground.

In most cases, before the shoe can be fitted a certain amount of trimming is necessary and this has to be done with care and judgement. The shoe must be made to fit level, and on the ground surface it should be slightly larger than the foot, continuing the angle of inclination of the wall of the hoof. The shoe should be applied just hot enough to char the horn, so that the farrier can see whether the surface is level.

In attaching the horseshoe to the hoof as few nails as possible should be used; generally four are put on the outside and three on the inside. As a rule the nail holes are made so that the nails have an inward bearing, particularly at the toe, in order to keep in line with the angle of the hoof. If the holes are made too oblique, the nails tend to break off at the neck. When the nail is driven in, care has to be taken not to go into or near the sensitive parts of the foot.

shoeing forge the work place of a farrier. Today many farriers have mobile forges and travel from one stable to another.

shoot the wheelers to send the wheelers forward into the collar in order to draw the load.

short-coupled (of a horse) having a short back, deep chest and well-sprung ribs.

short head *racing* one of the measurements of the distance by which a horse may be said to win a race: any distance less than a head.

short of a rib (of a horse) having a marked space between the last rib and the point of the hip, so that there is a slackness over the loins.

short panel See under PANEL.

short pastern bone See under PASTERN BONE.

short stirrup leathers *racing* stirrup leathers used when the stirrups are pulled up in order that the jockey may attain greater balance and control at speed with his knees up.

shotgun cavvy (Western US) a band of saddle-horses employed on a cattle round-up, consisting of mounts from several different ranches.

shotgun chaps (Western US) chaps whose outside seams are sewn together all the way down the leg, so that they look like the barrels of a shotgun.

shoulder-in *dressage* a schooling movement carried out on two tracks, in which the horse is required to bend inwards in an even curve from head to dock, while moving sideways and at the same time forwards, on a straight line in the direction of its convex side. The legs of the concave side (in the left shoulder-in, the nearside) cross in front of those on the convex side.

show 1. to compete in a horseshow. **2.** (US) to finish third in a horserace.

show class any of various competitions held at horseshows in which animals are judged for their conformation, condition, action, and/or suitability for whatever purpose they are used or intended to be used. Such competitions include classes for children's riding ponies, hacks, hunters and cobs,

as well as those for horses of specific breeds, which are normally further divided into separate classes for stallions, brood mares, young stock, etc. Depending on the type of competition, the animals may be shown in hand or under saddle.

show hack bit a curb bit closely resembling the globe cheek Pelham, except that the cheekpieces, as opposed to being straight, are curved in a forward direction.

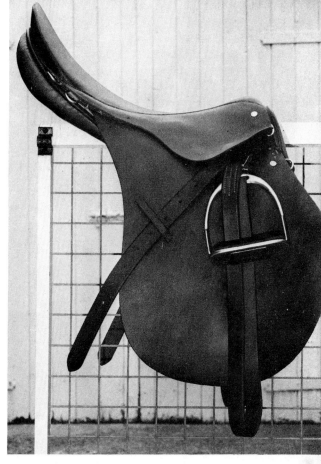

show-jumping saddle a modified form of the general-purpose saddle designed for use in show-jumping. It invariably has a spring tree and, since in show-jumping the rider's weight is generally forward over his knees, the seat only occasionally coming into contact with the saddle, the flap and panel lie further forward than in the general-purpose saddle. Because of its design, there is sometimes a tendency for the jumping saddle to rock when used for general riding, the shorter leathers pushing the rider's seat towards the back of the saddle.

shuttle bone See under NAVICULAR DISEASE.

shy to swerve away suddenly in fear from an obstacle or sound.

sickle hocks bent and weak-looking hocks which when viewed from the side have a sickle-like outline.

sidebone the ossification of one or both of the lateral cartilages of the foot. The condition, which may cause lameness, occurs mainly in heavy horses, often for no apparent reason. In light horses it usually results from an injury of some kind.

side jockey the leather side extension to the seat of a Western saddle.

side-lines See under CASTING.

side rein one of two fixed leather straps passing

from the bit to the roller (if the horse is being lunged) or to the saddle (if it is being ridden) used, especially in training, to obtain a good head carriage.

side-saddle a saddle designed for women on which the rider sits with both feet on the same side, normally the nearside. On that side the saddle has two padded projections (pommels), placed diagonally one above the other. The rider hooks her right leg over the upper one, and places the left leg under and against the lower pommel, resting her left foot in the single stirrup iron.

Side-saddle riding is said to have been introduced into the British Isles by Anne of Bohemia, who married Richard II in 1382, but contemporary pictures dépict riders sitting sideways on their horses, with their feet resting on a planchette, and it was probably several centuries later that the side-saddle as we know it today came into use.

Above
Signorinetta, one of the only four horses ever to win both the Derby and the Oaks.

Signorinetta (by Chaleureux out of Signorina. Chaleureux was a winner of the Manchester November Handicap and the Cesarewitch, while Signorina won over £20,000 and was unbeaten as a two-year-old in 1889.) Foaled in 1905, Signorinetta was bred, owned and trained at Newmarket by Chevalier Ginistrelli. Of her six races as a two-year-old, she won only the last, the Criterion Nursery Handicap at Newmarket. She made an unimpressive start to the following season. In two races at Newmarket — one of them was the 1000-Guineas — she was unplaced. However, as she was already entered for the Derby, it was decided to let her run, and she started at 100–1. Coming into the straight she took the lead and won the race, beating Primer by two lengths. Two days later she appeared at Epsom again and won the Oaks, thus completing the incredible double achieved by only three other horses: Eleanor, Blink Bonny and Fifinella.

Although she ran on three further occasions, she was unplaced each time, and at the end of the season she was bought by Lord Rosebery and retired to stud. As a dam she was not particularly successful, though she produced six winners.

silks the peaked cap and silk or woollen blouse, both carrying the colours of the owner, worn by a jockey in racing.

single gamblers' stakes *show-jumping* a competition held under similar rules to the multiple gamblers' stakes, except that no obstacle may be jumped more than once.

singular a boar aged four years or more which has left the rest of the herd and gone off accompanied by a young boar.

sire the male parent of a foal.

sired being the offspring of a particular stallion.

sit down in front of a horse (US; in a trotting race) to block the path of a horse deliberately so enabling another to win the race.

six bars *show-jumping* a competition which is a special test of power and skill, consisting of six obstacles of identical construction placed in a straight line and about 11 metres apart. The obstacles may all be at the same height or at progressive heights. Competitors jumping a clear round go into the next round, and so on, until the fourth or fifth round, the obstacles being raised after each round. If a horse has a refusal it makes a second attempt at the same obstacle and does not go back to the start. The competition is never jumped against the clock.

skate (Western US) a horse of poor quality.

skeleton break a four-wheeled vehicle consisting of a box seat for the driver and a low platform behind, which a groom could stand on. It was used for breaking horses to harness, and could be drawn by two horses, so that an inexperienced animal could be put alongside an experienced one.

skeleton panel See under ENGLISH SHOW-SADDLE.

skewbald a horse whose coat consists of large irregular and clearly defined patches of white and of any other colour except black. Also called PAINT HORSE (US), PINTO (US). See also PIEBALD.

skirt either of the two short leather flaps on either side of the pommel which cover the stirrup bars.

skirter *hunting* a hound which does not hunt with the rest of the pack following the true line of the fox, but tends to cut corners and take short cuts.

Slaski a breed of horse derived from the Oldenburg, found in south-west Poland. There are two distinct types: a heavier kind, which is an excellent hard-working animal used in towns for hauling wagons, and a lighter kind, which has a good fast action and is very suitable for driving.

sleeper (US) a horse which unexpectedly wins a race, having previously shown poor form.

slick-heeled (US) not wearing spurs.

slip (of a mare) to miscarry.

slipped up *racing* (of a horse) having slipped or stumbled, thus taking no further part in the race.

Sloan, James Todhunter, (1874–1933) the American jockey who first adopted the crouch seat for racing. He was frequently run away with, and leant forward to hold the horse round the neck. He soon found that with the rider in this position — a seat maintained by riding with short stirrup leathers — the horse ran very much better. He popularized the seat in America, and after he had ridden in France in 1897 European jockeys began to adopt his style. By the time he died it had come to be the accepted seat for flat race jockeys all over the world.

slot the foot or footprint of a deer.

slow gait one of the gaits of the five-gaited American Saddle Horse. It is a true prancing action, in which each foot in turn is raised and then held momentarily in mid-air before being brought down.

slowly away *racing* (of a horse) behind the other runners, having started badly.

small pastern bone See under PASTERN BONE.

Smith, Robert Harvey, *GB* (born 1938) Harvey Smith first came to the fore in 1958, when, riding Farmer's Boy, he was the highest placed British competitor in the King George V Gold Trophy at the Royal International Horse Show. Since then he has won nearly every British championship, as well as many abroad, and has become one of the best-known and most controversial figures in show-jumping. On five occasions he has ridden the horse with the highest money winnings in the season's national competitions. He is the only person to have won the British Jumping Derby at Hickstead two years in succession – 1970 and 1971, with Mattie Brown – and has won the John Player Trophy at the Royal International Horse Show no less than five times. In 1963 he became only the second British rider to win the Italian Grand Prix in Rome, riding Mr Hanson's Canadian-bred O'Malley. He was third in the European Championship in 1963 and second in 1967, in 1970 he was third in the World Championship. Riding his own horse, Summertime, he competed in the 1972 Olympic Games in Munich, and at the end of the same year was the first of several British riders to turn professional. In 1974, riding Salvador, he again won the British Jumping Derby.

smooth (Western US; of a horse) unshod.

smooth-mouthed (of a horse) aged.

S. M. Pelham a bit of American origin having cheekpieces which move independently in a restricted arc and a broad, flat-ported mouthpiece, which gives wide coverage over the bars of the mouth.

Smythe, Pat See KOECHLIN-SMYTHE, PATRICIA.

snaffle bit the oldest and simplest form of bit, consisting principally of a single bar with a ring at each end to which one pair of reins is attached. The main division in the snaffle family is between those which have a jointed mouthpiece and those which have a MULLEN MOUTH, a half-moon-shaped bar. In both types there is an upward motion against the corners of the mouth, although the jointed type produces more of a nutcracker effect on the mouth, making it the more severe of the two. The mullen has a slight bearing on the tongue; the mildest form is made of flexible indiarubber, with a chain passed through the centre, or of thick rolled leather. Also called BRADOON, BRIDOON. See also CHEEK SNAFFLE, D-CHEEK SNAFFLE, DICK CHRISTIAN, EGG-BUTT SNAFFLE, FULMER SNAFFLE, GERMAN SNAFFLE.

snaffle bridle the simplest form of bridle; the type used with a snaffle bit.

snaking team a team of horses used for dragging logs along the ground.

snip a white marking between or close to the nostrils.

snorter an excitable horse.

Snowbound *US* (brown gelding, 16.1 h.h.) Owned by the Princess de la Tour Auvergne, Californian-bred Snowbound was at one time a racehorse. He competed in his first horseshow in 1962 as a green hunter at the Channel City in Santa Barbara. He was then purchased by the Princess's father, Sir John Galvin, and sent to Ireland to be schooled by Colonel Dudgeon. On his return to America, he was loaned to the United States Equestrian Team and was ridden by Bill Steinkraus. In 1965 they won the International Grand Prix in New York. This was the first of a long series of major successes, both in the United States and Europe, which culminated in the individual gold medal at the 1968 Olympic Games in Mexico.

snub to tie a horse by the head to some fixed obstacle.

sock a white marking extending from the coronet as far as the fetlock joint.

soil (of a hunted stag) to take to water, either rolling in a stream or wallowing in mud, before going on.

sole the slightly concave under-portion of the hoof which fills the space between the bars and the ground surface of the crust or wall. It consists of thin layers of horny material, and the internal surface presents a very fine honeycombed appearance.

sound (of a horse) free from any illness, disease, blemish, physical defect or imperfection which might impair in any way its usefulness or ability to work.

sounder a herd of wild boar.

sound foot a good strong foot, preferably bluish-grey in colour, which has its front wall inclined at an angle of 45 to 50 degrees, the outer wall more rounded than the inner, and has a good concave sole.

soup-plate foot an abnormally large foot, out of proportion to the size of the animal. Horses with this type of foot are usually found to be low at heel.

Soviet Heavy Draught Horse an exceptionally strong and muscular draught horse originally bred in the Soviet Union from local agricultural breeds crossed with imported stallions, especially Percherons. On average about 16 h.h., the breed is characterized by a long body and stout legs.

spade bit a very severe bit formerly used by cowboys. On the port it had a plate which lay across the horse's tongue.

span 1. a pair of horses in harness. **2.** the distance between the bay and tray tine of an antler.

Spanish Riding School See IMPERIAL SPANISH RIDING SCHOOL.

Spanish walk a spectacular movement, used

Below
snaffle bridle with laced reins and an eggbutt snaffle bit.

Far right
Spanish walk, demonstrated by the great Portuguese rider, Nuno Oliveira on Euclides.

spring-mouth snaffle.

Far right
spur. The correct position and fitting of long-necked spurs.

mainly in circuses, in which the horse as it walks raises the forelegs very high and stretches them out in front.

speak (of a hound) to bark or bay on finding a scent.

spear a person taking part in pigsticking.

spear of honour See FIRST SPEAR.

speedy cut a cut or bruise on the inside of the hock, knee or cannon bone caused by a blow from the opposite hoof or shoe. Most likely to occur in horses with a high action, such as trotting horses, speedy cutting may result from faulty conformation, lack of condition or bad shoeing. See also BRUSHING.

spider phaeton a type of phaeton, introduced at the end of the nineteenth century, consisting of a Tilbury gig body with a small seat behind for a servant. It was mounted on four wheels, was very light and could be drawn by either one or two horses. It was used mainly as a town carriage.

spike team (US) a team of five coach-horses, harnessed with the lightest horse in front, the heaviest pair at the back as the wheelers and the lighter pair between.

spinner (Western US) a horse which bucks in small circles, spinning either to the right or to the left.

splashing leather See DASHING LEATHER.

splint a bony growth which gradually forms between the cannon bone and one of the splint bones as a result of excess strain or concussion. Splints usually occur in the forelegs and appear mainly in young animals. Once a splint is set it is unlikely to cause lameness unless it lies at the head of one of the splint bones, in which case it may interfere with the knee joint, or if it forms on the inside of the bone, where it can interfere with the flexor tendons which run down the back of the cannon bone between the splint bones.

splint bone either of two metacarpal bones which lie at the back of the cannon bone on each side.

splinter bar a movable horizontal bar attached to the front of the undercarriage of a coach or other vehicle, to which are fastened the traces of a pair of horses by passing the looped ends of the traces over the ROLLER BOLTS, which are strong bolts with flat heads. For a team of four horses three splinter bars are also attached to the end of

the shaft, using hooks instead of bolts for the traces.

spooky (of a horse) having a nervous temperament.

sporting tandem (US) a tandem in which one of the horses is a hunter. At horseshows in the United States there are often show classes for sporting tandems, during which the hunter has to be unharnessed, saddled up and ridden over show-jumps.

spread a plate *racing* (of a horse) to have a loose shoe.

spread fence *show-jumping* any of various obstacles which are wide, as opposed to simply high, such as a hogs back, parallel bars, triple bar, or water jump.

spring to encourage a team of coach-horses to gallop by use of the voice or a whip.

spring-mouth snaffle two clips jointed in the middle which are attached to the rings of a snaffle to strengthen the action of the bit. Also called BUTTERFLY SNAFFLE.

spring tree a type of saddletree in which two strips of light steel are laid along the underside from front to rear.

sprinter a horse which is able to produce great speed over a short distance, but which is not usually able to maintain it over a long distance.

sprung hock a sprain of the soft structures of the hock. In slight cases the ligaments only may be injured, but in more severe cases tendons and bones may also be affected. Great pain is shown, and the animal develops a high fever.

spur a pointed device attached to the heel of a rider's boot and used to urge the horse onwards, etc.

spurrier a person who makes spurs.

stable 1. a building in which one or more horses are kept. **2.** a collection of horses belonging to one person, such as a racehorse owner or riding-school proprietor, or kept at one establishment.

stableboy a person of any age who works in a stable looking after horses.

stable companion a horse which comes from the same stable as another; a term used particularly in racing when there are two such horses in the same race.

stable jockey a jockey retained by a particular stable to ride the horses of that stable.

stable rubber a piece of cloth, normally linen, used for producing a gloss on a horse's coat.

stables work performed in stables, especially in racing stables or in the army, at two recognized times of the day: MORNING STABLES when the first work of the day is done and EVENING STABLES when the final tasks are carried out.

Queen Elizabeth II,
accompanied by the Duke of
Edinburgh, at the Trooping
the Colour ceremony on
Horse Guards Parade.

Schleswig, an immensely
strong horse from northern
Germany.

Shetland pony, one of the
most popular breeds of
British pony.

Shire, a breed of heavy
draught horse, noted for its
sound constitution, stamina
and docility.

stag a male deer aged four years or more.

staghound a hound used primarily for hunting stags, resembling the foxhound, but larger.

staghunting the hunting of wold, red, fallow, roe or other deer with a pack of hounds. At the end of the hunt the deer is killed humanely by the huntsman. At the end of a hunt after a carted deer, the deer is recaptured and taken back to its home paddock.

stain See FOIL.

stale (of a horse) to urinate.

stale line *hunting* the line of a fox which has passed some time previously.

stall 1. a compartment, usually one of a number inside a stable, in which a horse is kept. Unlike a loosebox, a stall is open-ended, so that the horse has to be tied up all the time and is restricted in its movements. **2.** *racing* a standing, usually covered, on a racecourse where a horse may be saddled up before a race.

stallion an ungelded male horse aged four years or over.

stallion hound a male hound used for breeding purposes.

stamp a pointed chisel-like punch of iron used by farriers for making the nail holes in horseshoes.

stand a horse up to make a horse stand evenly on all four legs when it is being shown, so that its conformation may be seen to best advantage.

Standardbred a breed of trotters and pacers developed in the United States during the nineteenth century. Most Standardbred racers trace their history to the famous stallion Hambletonian 10, foaled in 1849. The breed was officially established in 1880, when a speed standard over one mile became a requirement for entry in the American Trotting Register. Today, with improved tracks and the development of the very special gait of the trotter, the standard time for the mile is 2 minutes 20 seconds.

The average height of the breed is about 15.2 h.h. The Standardbred has a long body with shortish legs, and is noted for its stamina.

standard event any of the five rodeo events recognized by the governing body, the Rodeo Cowboys Association, namely, (1) bareback riding, (2) bull riding, (3) calf-roping, (4) saddle bronc riding, or (5) steer wrestling.

stand back (of a horse) to take off some distance in front of an obstacle.

standing martingale a martingale consisting of a single undivided strap with adjustable loop

185

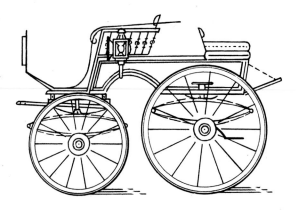

attachments, which passes from the girth to the noseband. Also called FAST MARTINGALE. See also CHESHIRE MARTINGALE, GRAINGER MARTIN-GALE, PUGRI STANDING MARTINGALE, RUNNING MARTINGALE.

Stanhope gig a type of gig mounted on four springs, making it a much more comfortable ride than other gigs mounted on two springs. It was invented about 1820 by Fitzroy Stanhope, and built by a coachbuilder called Tilbury. See also GIG, TILBURY GIG.

Stanhope phaeton a type of phaeton, made by placing the body of a Stanhope gig on four wheels and adding a seat behind for a servant. Invented by Fitzroy Stanhope, it was built for him by the coach-builder Tilbury. It was an attractive carriage for those who liked to drive themselves and could be drawn by a single horse or a pair of horses.

star a white mark of any shape or size on the fore-head of a horse.

stargazer a horse which holds its head un-naturally high; a dangerous animal to ride, as it does not look where it is going, and may be a particularly unpleasant ride when jumping.

staring coat a coat which does not lie flat, as when the horse is cold, out of condition, or suffering from some disease or illness, such as worms.

starter's orders *racing* When the starter of a race has satisfied himself that all runners are present and ready to race, a flag is raised to denote that the horses are under 'starter's orders'. For the purposes of betting all horses which come under starter's orders are deemed to have run, even if they are subsequently withdrawn.

starting gate the point at which a race starts. Also called BARRIER, STARTING POST. See also STARTING STALLS, STARTING TAPES.

starting post See STARTING GATE.

starting price *racing* the odds obtaining at the moment a race starts.

starting price betting *racing* the placing of bets, the settlement of which is to be made at the starting price, as opposed to ante-post betting.

starting stalls *racing* a piece of mobile equip-ment consisting of compartments into which horses are led at the start of a flat race. When the starter pulls a handle all the mechanically operated doors to the compartments are released in unison, giving a much more even start than an ordinary barrier. Starting stalls are now used in most flat races.

starting tapes *racing* vertical tapes behind which the runners are lined up at the start of a race, and which are released by being raised by the starter.

State Coach the coach used in the coronation processions of British sovereigns, it was built in 1762, too late for the coronation of King George III. The total cost of the coach, including the harness for the horses was £7562. Before the coronation of Queen Elizabeth II in 1953 the coach was slightly modernized, with the introduction of special cushions and modern lighting. The wheels, the rear ones measuring nearly six feet in diameter, were mounted on rubber tyres. Also called CORONATION COACH.

stayer a horse which has great strength and power of endurance and is therefore likely to be successful over a long distance.

Steenken, Hartwig, *Germany* (born 1941) Hartwig Steenken had the first of his many inter-national show-jumping successes in 1965. He competed only as an individual in the 1968 Olympic Games in Mexico. However, four years later, after winning the 1971 European Champion-ship at Aachen with Simona, he was selected to represent his country in the team competition at Munich, where West Germany won the gold medal. On this occasion, too, he was riding Simona, and with the same mare he won the Men's World Show Jumping Championship at Hickstead in 1974.

steeplechase a race over a certain course of a specified distance and on which there are a number of obstacles to be jumped. The first steeplechase is said to have taken place in Ireland in 1752, and later on in the eighteenth century the sport became popular in England. Racing over properly constructed fences and obstacles was first introduced at Bedford in 1810.

steeplechaser a horse which takes part in steeplechasing.

steer wrestling one of the standard events in a rodeo, in which the contestant rides alongside a running steer, and jumps from the saddle on to the head of the steer, the object being to stop the steer, twist it to the ground, and hold it there with the head and all four feet facing in the same direction. It is a timed event, the contestant completing in the shortest time being the winner. Also called BULLDOGGING.

Steinkraus, William Clark, *US* (born 1925) One of the first members of the American Pony Club, Bill Steinkraus started show-jumping in 1938. He joined the United States Equestrian Team in 1951, and was appointed captain in 1955. One of the most likeable and stylish riders, he was at the top of international show-jumping for over twenty years, and in national competitions he carried off almost every major prize. In 1952, riding

Democrat, he won no less than eight competitions at Harrisburg, New York and Toronto, and in the same year, riding Hollandia, was a member of the bronze medal team in the Helsinki Olympics. In 1956 he won the King George V Cup, on First Boy, a success he was to repeat with Sinjon in 1964. His greatest triumph came at the 1968 Olympic Games in Mexico when, riding Snowbound, he won the individual gold medal. Riding Main Spring, he was a member of the team which won the silver medal at the 1972 Olympic Games in Munich. At the end of the 1972 season he retired from the United States Equestrian Team and was appointed its president.

stern the tail of a hound.

steward *racing* an official at a race meeting appointed to see that the meeting is conducted according to the rules.

stifle cap the patella; the bone at the front of the stifle joint.

stifle joint the joint of the hind leg of a horse between the femur and the tibia. Also called STIFLE.

stifle joint disease a disease, akin to rheumatoid arthritis, affecting the stifle joint. The bone becomes worm-eaten, the cartilages are absorbed, and a porcellaneous deposit builds up between the end

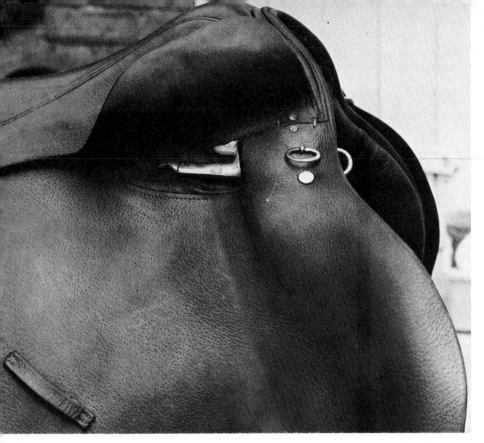

(For results see page 245.)

Above
stirrup bar, the part of the saddle to which the leathers are attached. The catch should always be down, so that in the event of a fall the whole leather is released if the rider's foot becomes caught in the iron.

Far right
strangles. Swelling of the lymphatic glands of the head.

of the tibia and the patella. The lameness which accompanies this complaint is gradual at first and then becomes progressive.

stirrup bar either of the two metal fittings on a saddle to which the stirrup leathers are attached. The bars are fitted on to the tree, behind the head and on the point of the tree. They have a catch or thumbpiece so that the leather can be slipped on and off. The catch should always be left down so that, should a rider fall and his foot become caught in the stirrup iron, the leather will be released from the saddle.

stirrup cup a drink offered to the hunt followers at a meet.

stirrup iron a loop, ring, or similar device made of metal, wood, leather, etc., suspended from a saddle to support the rider's foot. The commonest type of iron, used for general riding and hunting, is made of metal — the best being of stainless steel — and is completely symmetrical, with a centrally placed eye for the leather. Stirrup irons should always be sufficiently large for the rider to slip his feet in and out without difficulty. Otherwise, in the event of a fall, there is a danger that he may be dragged. See also AUSTRALIAN SIMPLEX PATTERN SAFETY IRON, BENT-TOP IRON, CRADLE PATTERN IRON, KOURNAKOFF IRON, PEACOCK SAFETY IRON.

stirrup leather the adjustable strap by which the stirrup iron is attached to the saddle. For ordinary riding the length of the leather should roughly correspond to the length of the rider's arm from armpit to fingertip. Stirrup leathers are made of cowhide, rawhide or buffalo hide, all of which stretch to a certain degree. As a rider naturally puts more weight on one leg than the other, it is advisable to alternate the leathers when they are new so that they both stretch the same amount. In racing it is necessary for everything to be as light as possible, and the leathers are made of web, with leather rings reinforcing the buckle holes. The HOOK-UP STIRRUP LEATHER has an extension on the nearside which can be unhooked to give an extra drop of six to eight inches for ease of mounting.

St Leger a horserace over 1 mile 6 furlongs

(1¾ miles) held annually at Doncaster since 1776, except from 1915 to 1918 when a wartime substitute race was run at Newmarket and from 1940 to 1945 when wartime substitute races were held at Thirsk (1940), Manchester (1941), Newmarket (1942–44) and York (1945). There was no race in 1939. The race, the first for three-year-olds at Doncaster, was a sweepstake sponsored by a group of sportsmen including Lord Rockingham and General St Leger, and was run on the Cantley Common Course at Doncaster over a distance of 2 miles. The first winner was Lord Rockingham's Allabaculia. It was not until 1778 that the race was given a name, that of the popular St Leger, and the distance was reduced to 1 mile 6 furlongs when it was run for the first time on the Turf Moor course. (For results see page 245.)

stock 1. a white neckcloth worn for hunting and formal occasions. Also called HUNTING TIE, HUNTING STOCK. **2.** the handle of a whip.

stock class a show class at American horse-shows for stock or ranch ponies.

stocking a white marking extending from the knee or hock to the coronet on the leg of a horse.

stomach staggers a disorder in which the stomach becomes distended with solid food. The condition may be brought on by bulky or indigestible foods, foods containing little moisture, such as ryegrass, barley, etc., or by large feeds after long periods without food. The animal becomes dull and lethargic, its gait unsteady, its breathing slow and laboured and its pulse full and slow.

straight fence *show-jumping* any obstacle which has all its parts in the same vertical plane, such as a gate, planks, or post and rails.

straight forecast pool See under FORECAST (def. 2).

straight-necked fox *hunting* a fox which sets a straight course, and consequently gives a good hunt.

straight ticket (US) a bet to win and not for a place.

strangles an infectious and highly contagious disease caused by the organism *Streptococcus equi*, and occurring most commonly in young

the stages in tying a hunting stock. Reading from left to right, 1 and 2 (*top*), 3 and 4 (*middle*), 5 and 6 (*bottom*).

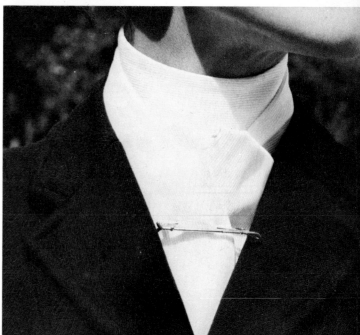

horses. It is marked by a rise in temperature, a thick nasal discharge and swelling of the sub-maxillary and other lymphatic glands of the head. Eventually abscesses form in these glands. In some cases glands in other parts of the body become affected, a condition known as BASTARD STRANGLES.

strawberry roan See under ROAN.

stretch to make a horse camp.

strike See under TENT PEGGING.

strike a fox (US) to find a fox.

string 1. *racing* a number of horses in training at one particular stable. **2.** a number of horses allocated to a cowboy as his mounts which he alone rides.

strip to remove the saddle from a horse in a show class so that it can be judged for conformation.

stripe a narrow white facial marking extending from the forehead to the muzzle. Also called RACE.

Stroller See under MOULD, MARION JANICE.

stud 1. an establishment at which horses are kept for breeding purposes. **2.** any large establishment of racehorses, hunters, etc., belonging to one owner. **3.** (US) a studhorse or stallion. **4.** a metallic head screwed into a horseshoe in order to give the horse a better grip on a slippery surface. Studs should not be used for riding on roads.

stud groom a senior groom, especially at a stud farm.

s.u. slipped up.

Suffolk Punch a breed of heavy horse which originated in Suffolk, in East Anglia. It is descended from the progeny of Norman stallions crossed with the old Suffolk mares, and it is claimed that every horse of the breed now in existence traces its descent in an unbroken chain in the male line to a horse foaled in 1768 and known as Crisp's Horse of Ufford.

Always chestnut in colour, often with a white star or other small white marking on the face, the Suffolk stands about 16 h.h. It has a fairly large head and is deep in rib from elbow to flank, with massive hindquarters, short clean legs, and hard feet. The action should be a good swinging walk, with well-balanced movement all round.

It is an extremely docile animal, noted for its longevity — at one early show a mare of thirty-seven was shown with her foal — and is still used for certain specialized work in agriculture and also for pulling brewers' drays. The breed has been exported to Australia, Africa, the Soviet Union and the United States.

The Suffolk Stud Book Association, which later became the Suffolk Horse Society, was founded in 1877.

sulkette a two-wheeled single-seater cart, somewhat heavier and sturdier than the sulky, used for training and exercising trotters and pacers.

sulky a very light two-wheeled single-seater cart with a skeleton body and rubber tyres, used in racing trotters and pacers. The sulky was first built at the beginning of the nineteenth century, when it had very large wheels and a high seat.

summing the antlers of a fully grown stag.

Sun Chariot (by Hyperion out of Clarence) Foaled in 1939, Sun Chariot was owned by King George VI and trained for him in Wiltshire at the Beckhampton stables of Fred Darling. Her first outing as a two-year-old was at Newbury, where she won the Acorn Plate. At Newmarket she won the Queen Mary Stakes and, at the end of the season, the Middle Park Stakes. She was ridden in all three races by Harry Wragg.

Ridden by Gordon Richards, she was third at Salisbury in her first attempt as a three-year-old. Soon afterwards, however, she made amends for this by winning the Sarum Stakes on the same course. A short while later she easily beat Perfect Peace to win the 1000-Guineas and, in spite of a very erratic race, she won the Oaks (also run at Newmarket that year), beating Afterthought by a length. She then completed a hat-trick of classic wins with a three-length victory in the St Leger over Watling Street, the Derby winner.

At the end of the season she was retired to stud, where she produced some useful foals. Among them were Landau, winner of the Rous Memorial Stakes and the Sussex Stakes, and Pudari, winner of the King Edward VII Stakes and the Great Voltigeur Stakes. Sun Chariot died at the National Stud in 1963.

Sunsalve *GB* (chestnut gelding, 16.2 h.h.) Bred and owned by Oliver Anderson, Sunsalve is the only horse to have won both the King George V Gold Trophy and the Queen Elizabeth II Cup at the Royal International Horse Show. Ridden by the owner's daughter, Elizabeth, he won the Queen's Cup in 1957, and with David Broome, the King's Trophy in 1960. He was again ridden by David Broome to win the individual bronze medal at the Rome Olympics in 1960 and the European Championship at Aachen the following year.

Sunstar (by Sundridge out of Doris) Foaled in 1908, Sunstar was owned by J. B. Joel, a great patron of racing, and trained at Wantage, Berkshire, by Charles Morton. As a two-year-old the horse was impressive, winning the International Stakes at Kempton, the Exeter Stakes at Newmarket and dead-heating in the Hopeful Stakes there in the autumn.

The following year it was decided to engage the leading French jockey, Georges Stern, to ride him in the 2000-Guineas, which he won by two lengths. The pair then won the Newmarket Stakes, and as a result the horse was very heavily backed for the Derby. In training, however, he went lame and was found to have strained a suspensory ligament. After consultations between the owner and trainer, it was agreed every effort be made to have him

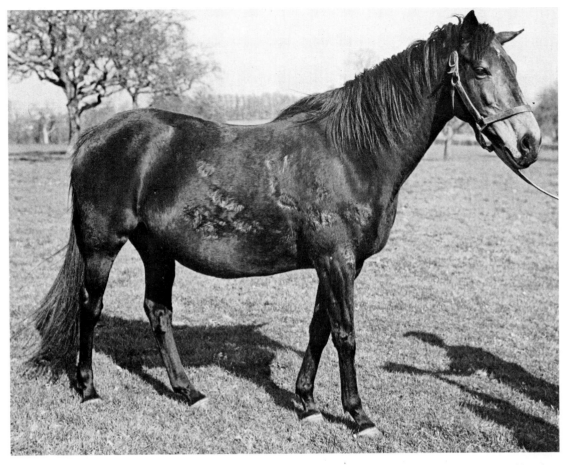

Sun Chariot, winner of the 1000-Guineas, the Oaks and the St Leger, seen here at the National Stud. At the time of this picture she was in foal to Big Game.

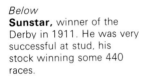

Below
Sunstar, winner of the Derby in 1911. He was very successful at stud, his stock winning some 440 races.

sound for the Derby, and in spite of the severe setback he started favourite for the race, which he won by two lengths, although he again went lame. It was then decided to retire him to stud, where he proved very successful, his stock winning some 440 races.

surcingle a webbing belt, usually $2\frac{1}{2}$ to 3 inches wide, which passes over a racing or jumping saddle and girth and is used to hold the saddle in position, or which can be used in place of a roller to secure a day or night rug.

Sussex Stakes a one-mile race held at Goodwood since 1841, originally for three-year-olds, but since 1969 also open to four-year-olds. (For results see pages 245–246.)

Swales a Pelham having a fixed mouthpiece and rings attached, inside the cheekpieces, to the mouthpiece, thus producing a very severe, squeezing action.

Swaps (by Khaled out of Iron Reward. By Hyperion, Khaled was a winner of the Coventry Stakes, the Middle Park Stakes and the St James' Palace Stakes and was second in the 2000-Guineas; he was exported in 1948 to a stud in California. Iron Reward had eight races, finishing second in four of them.) Foaled in 1952, Swaps had particularly good conformation. He was raced only lightly as a two-year-old and won two of his four races at Hollywood Park. His first major race as a three-year-old was in the San Vicenti Stakes at Santa Anita, which he won. A month later he won the Santa Anita Derby and then went to Churchill Downs, where he won the Kentucky Derby by one and a half lengths. He won the Californian Stakes at Hollywood Park and the American Derby at Washington Park, Chicago. Shortly after this, on the same course, he took part in a $100,000 match with Nashua, and was beaten by six lengths.

As a four-year-old, Swaps was brilliant, winning the American Handicap, the Hollywood Gold Cup and the Sunset Handicap, all at Hollywood Park, and the Washington Park Handicap at Illinois. In his ten races that season he was beaten only once — in the Californian Stakes — and he was elected Horse of the Year. In the September he injured his heel, and then fractured his fetlock. The veterinary surgeons were able to save him, but his racing days were over, and he was retired to stud at the Spendthrift Farm in Kentucky. He was the sire of Chateaugay, winner of the 1963 Kentucky Derby.

sway back See HOG BACK.

Swaps, winner of the Kentucky Derby in 1955. The following year he ran ten times and was beaten only once.

sweat scraper a curved metal blade with a wooden handle used to scrape sweat from a horse.

Swedish Warm Blood a Swedish breed of horse, originally developed from native mares crossed with Spanish and Oriental stallions, with later additions of Hanoverian and other imported blood. Usually chestnut in colour, the Swedish Warm Blood horse is an excellent utility animal, suitable both for riding or driving.

sweet itch a dermatitis usually found in horses that are allergic to a particular pasture plant, and therefore more likely to occur during the spring and summer months. It affects particularly the crest, croup and withers, causing intense irritation and producing patches of thick scaly, sometimes ulcerated skin, which the horse often rubs bare. If an animal is prone to sweet itch, it is advisable to keep it in a stable in spring and summer.

swing horse the middle horse in a random, or either of the middle pair in a six-horse team.

swing team the pair of horses in a six-horse team between the wheelers and the leaders.

switch See CABERLACH.

switch tail a horse's tail which has been pulled at the bottom so that it ends in a point.

table any of five sets of conditions set by the British Show Jumping Association under which national show-jumping competitions are held in Great Britain:
Table A1 If, after the second jump-off, there are still competitors equal for first place, the prize money is divided equally between them.

Table A2 If, after the second jump-off, there are still competitors equal for first place, time is the deciding factor.
Table A3 If, after the first jump-off, competitors are equal for first place, time is the deciding factor.
Table A4 Time is the deciding factor in the first round and all competitors are placed according to the number of faults incurred and the time to complete the round.
Table S For each obstacle knocked down six seconds are added to the time taken to complete the round.
See also BARÈME.

tack saddlery.

tack up to put tack on a horse; to saddle up.

tail The tail of a horse includes the dock together with all the hair, which is usually allowed to grow about four inches below the point of the hock.

tail guard a rectangular piece of soft leather or canvas fastened round the dock by means of tapes or buckles, over a tail bandage, in order to protect the tail when a horse is travelling.

tail hound *hunting* one of the hounds running at the rear of the pack.

tail set a device applied to a horse's tail after a setting operation in order to make the tail grow in an exaggerated arch, used principally in the United States on the Tennessee Walking Horse.

tail to the wall See RENVERS.

take-off side the side of an obstacle from which a horse takes off.

Right
tail guard.

Far right
teeth. The process of ageing as shown by the teeth. From top to bottom.

Three years.

Four years.

Five years. Corner incisors coming together only in front.

Six years. Corner teeth now level. Cup marks visible on all incisors.

Seven years. Hook. Cup marks beginning to fade.

Ten years. Central incisors become more triangular in shape; cup marks less distinct.

Fifteen years. All teeth are more triangular in shape; cup marks have disappeared.

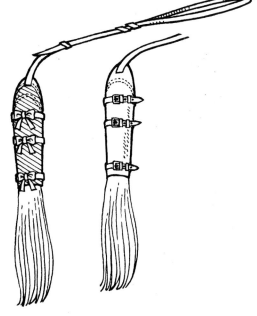

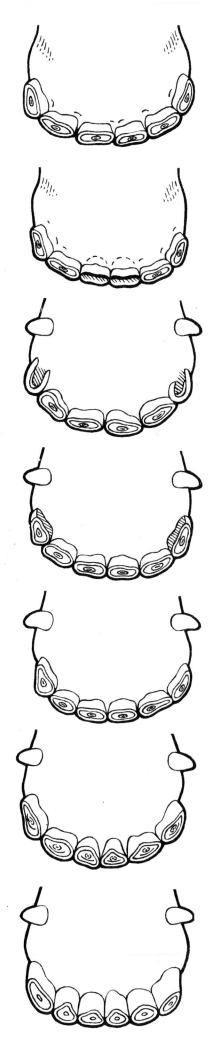

Talbot-Ponsonby, Lt Col. Jack, *GB* (1908–1969) Jack Talbot-Ponsonby became the first person to win the King George V Gold Trophy three times — in 1930 and 1932, riding Chelsea, and in 1934, riding Best Girl. From 1949 to 1960 he was the part-time trainer of the British show-jumping team. He then became the course designer for the Royal International Horse Show and the Horse of the Year Show, a position he held until his sudden death in December 1969.

tandem a team of two horses driven one behind the other.

tapadero the stiff leather casing of the stirrups on a Western saddle, used to protect the rider's feet.

Right
t cart phaeton.

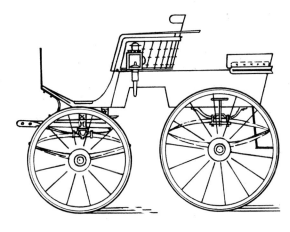

t cart phaeton a type of phaeton, deriving its name from its shape; it was a variation of the Stanhope phaeton, cut down in size and with the rear seat narrowed down so as to carry only one person. See also STANHOPE PHAETON.

team At any C.S.I.O. an official team consists of a maximum of a captain, six riders and twelve horses. In addition, two individual competitors from the same nation may be invited to compete.

teaser a secondary stallion kept at studs to determine whether or not a mare is actually in season before she is presented to the stallion with which she is to be mated.

technical delegate the person at an international horseshow or three-day event who is responsible for seeing that the competition is carried out according to international rules and that the course is correct. He may or may not be a judge, and is usually from a country other than the host nation.

teeth When fully mouthed, the horse has forty teeth consisting of: twelve incisors (six in each jaw); four canines (one on each side of the upper and lower jaw); and twenty-four molars (six above and six below on each side).

The marks on the tables of the lower incisors are an indication of the age of the horse up to eight years. The marks in the central incisors are nearly worn away at six years, in the lateral at seven years, and in the corner incisors at eight years. From the age of nine to ten the teeth begin to grow longer and become triangular in shape. It is at this stage that the Galvayne's groove begins to appear, and this serves as a further indication of the horse's age. See also GALVAYNE'S GROOVE.

temperature The normal temperature of a horse is 100·5 °F. It is taken by inserting the bulb of the thermometer into the horse's anus for one to two minutes.

tenet See under HAME.

Tennessee Walking Horse a breed of saddle-horse originally bred in the south of the United States for carrying planters and farmers at a smooth comfortable walk through their plantations, and now widely used as a show and pleasure horse. The breed traces back to one prepotent stallion called Black Allan, foaled in 1886. He was trained as a trotter, but preferred the walking gait, at which he was capable of travelling very quickly.

Usually reaching 15.2 h.h. to 16 h.h., the Tennessee Walking Horse is plainer in appearance, heavier and more robust than the American Saddle-Horse, having a large plain head, rather a short neck, and a large solid body supported by stout legs. The most usual colours are black and chestnut, and white markings are not uncommon.

The characteristic gait is a running walk with a great overreach in stride, for which careful training is required. Also called PLANTATION WALKING HORSE.

tent club (formerly) any body of persons, especially in India, associated for the purpose of pigsticking.

tent pegging a fast and spectacular equestrian sport which originated in India and was formerly very popular with the British Army. A white soft-wood peg about 4 inches wide is driven into the ground, leaving approximately 9 inches showing. In order to make a CARRY, the rider, at the gallop, has to impale the peg on the end of his sword or lance and carry it to the finish. If he marks the peg but fails to carry it, he makes a STRIKE. Points are awarded for a carry, a strike and also for the style of the rider. The game is played either between teams or between individuals.

terre à terre a movement in which the horse turns on his haunches or circles, with the hind legs following in the track of the forelegs.

Tersk a breed of saddle-horse established in the northern Caucasus region of the Soviet Union after the First World War in order to preserve the famous Strelets strain, which had been almost wiped out during the war. The only two remaining Strelets stallions were crossed with pure-bred and cross-bred Arabs, and the Tersk was gradually established by very careful selective breeding from their produce. The Tersk very closely resembles the pure-bred Arab, although it is larger — the average height is about 15.2 hands. It has a good disposition and temperament, and has proved very successful in the fields of dressage and racing. Because of its colouring — usually grey or white — and the natural sheen of its coat, the Tersk has also become a popular circus animal.

tetanus an infectious, often fatal disease caused by the micro-organism *Tetanus bacillus*, which inhabits the soil and enters the body through wounds, especially of the foot. One of the first visible symptoms is that the horse will stand with its head pointed forwards, its front legs wide apart, its hind legs straddled with the hocks turned outwards, and its tail raised. If made to move, the animal will walk stiffly. As the disease advances, the horse may become nervous and excited, and

tetanus.

the facial muscles become so rigid that the animal is unable to open its mouth. Also called LOCKJAW.

The Daisies the Preakness Stakes; so called because a garland of daisies is placed round the neck of the winner.

the flat 1. flat racing. **2.** the season during which flat racing is held.

The Guineas either of two classic races held annually at Newmarket for three-year-old horses: the 1000-GUINEAS, a one-mile race for fillies carrying 9 st., first run in 1814; or the 2000-GUINEAS, a one-mile race for colts carrying 9 st. and fillies carrying 8 st. 9 lb., first run in 1809. (For results see pages 246–247.)

the hunt a collective name given to all the people taking part in a day's hunting.

the kill *hunting* the killing by the hounds of their quarry.

the Military See THREE-DAY EVENT.

The National See GRAND NATIONAL HANDICAP STEEPLECHASE.

the ring 1. an enclosure on a racecourse frequented by bookmakers. **2.** bookmakers collectively.

The Rock *Italy* (grey gelding) Foaled in Ireland in 1948. The Rock was purchased by the Italian Equestrian Federation in the early 1950s and started his first season of international show-jumping in 1957. Ridden until the end of 1963 by Captain Piero d'Inzeo, and then until the end of his career by Graziano Mancinelli, The Rock won a total of 172 competitions and a silver medal at the 1960 Olympic Games in Rome. He died in September 1966.

The Roses the Kentucky Derby; so called because a garland of roses is put round the neck of the winner.

the take the end of a stag hunt, when the deer has been either killed or captured.

The Tetrarch (by Roi Herode out of Vahren) Foaled in 1911 in County Kildare, Ireland, The Tetrarch, owned by Edward Kennedy, was sold at the Doncaster sales as a yearling to Hampshire trainer Atty Persse, who in turn sold him to his cousin, Major Dermont McCalmont. As a two-year-old The Tetrarch ran seven times. Ridden on each occasion by Steve Donoghue, he was unbeaten; he won the Maiden Two Year Old Plate at Newmarket, the Woodcote Stakes at Epsom, the Coventry Stakes at Ascot, the National Breeders' Produce Stakes at Sandown, the Rous Memorial Stakes at Goodwood, the Champion Breeders' Foal Stakes at Derby and the Champagne Stakes at Doncaster.

Because of injury to his legs he was unable to race as a three-year-old and was retired to Major McCalmont's stud at Kilkenny in Ireland, where he died in 1935. Between 1918 and 1930 his stock won 257 races, worth almost £180,000, and he was the leading sire in 1919. Among his progeny were the outstanding filly, Mumtaz Mahal, and Tetratema, who won the 2000-Guineas and was unbeaten both as a two-year-old and as a four-year-old, as well as three St Leger winners: Polemarch, Caligula and Salmon Trout.

Thoroughbred a breed of racehorse developed in Britain and Ireland during the seventeenth and eighteenth centuries from imported eastern stock (Arabs, Barbs and Turks) crossed with home-bred mares, possibly of rather mixed origins. All Thoroughbreds trace their descent in the male line to one of three stallions, the Byerley Turk, the Darley Arabian or the Godolphin Arabian.

In order for a horse to be eligible for entry in the General Stud Book, it must be able either to be traced at all points of its pedigree to strains which already appear in earlier volumes, or to satisfactorily prove some eight or nine generations of pure blood which trace back for at least a century, and to show such performance of its immediate family on the turf as to warrant belief in the purity of its blood. There are now over 10,000 Thoroughbred mares entered in the General Stud Book.

Thoroughbred Breeders Association an association whose main object is to encourage by means of educational and research facilities the science of producing and improving the Thoroughbred horse.

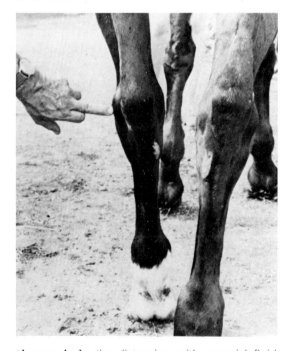

thoroughpin the distension with synovial fluid of the tendon sheaths just above and on either side of the point of the hock. Thoroughpins seldom cause lameness, but can be very unsightly.

three-day event a combined training competition completed over three consecutive days. The most advanced form of horse trials, the three-day event differs from two- and one-day events in that, in addition to the cross-country, competitors are also required to complete a steeplechase course and two circuits of roads and tracks. Depending on the degree of difficulty of the cross-country course and the conditions of the competition, three-day events are classed as championship or standard events.

Far right
thoroughpin.

The Tetrarch, by Roi Herode out of Vahren, winner of seven races as a two-year-old.

Before the dressage test on the first day each horse has to undergo a veterinary examination.

The second day is the most important, consisting of the speed and endurance test, which is made up in championship events as follows:

Phases A and C, roads and tracks (normally carried out at a slow canter or trot) — in C.C.I.s a distance of 10 to 16 kilometres at a speed of 240 metres per minute; or, in C.C.I.O.s, a distance of 16 to 20 kilometres at a speed of 240 metres per minute.

Phase B, steeplechase (normally carried out at the gallop) — in C.C.I.s a distance of 3000 to 3600 metres at a speed of 550 to 600 metres per minute; or, in C.C.I.O.s, a distance of 3600 to 4200 metres at a speed of 600 metres per minute.

Obstacles are normally similar to those used in regulation steeplechase courses. In both C.C.I.s and C.C.I.O.s the fixed and solid part of the obstacles does not exceed 1 metre in height, and bush fences do not exceed an overall height of 1·4 metres; spread obstacles do not exceed 3·5 metres in width, and water jumps 4 metres. In C.C.I.s obstacles with spread and height must be no more than 1·8 metres wide at the highest point and 2·8 metres at the lowest point; in C.C.I.O.s these obstacles do not exceed a spread of 2 metres at the highest point and 3 metres at the lowest point.

Phase D, cross-country (normally carried out at the gallop) — in C.C.I.s a distance of 5400 to 7200 metres at a speed of 400 to 450 metres per minute; in C.C.I.O.s a distance of 7200, 7650 or 8100 metres at a speed of 450 metres per minute.

There should be an average of four obstacles per 1000 metres. The fixed and solid part of any obstacle must not exceed 1·2 metres in height. In C.C.I.s water jumps are no more than 4 metres, and spread obstacles are no more than 3·5 metres wide. Obstacles with both height and spread are no more than 1·8 metres wide at the highest point and 2·8 metres at the lowest point. In C.C.I.O.s the same applies to spread obstacles, but in obstacles with both height and spread the spread does not exceed 2 metres at the highest point and 3 metres at the lowest point.

There is a compulsory halt between Phases C and D, and each horse has to undergo a second veterinary examination.

Riders are free to choose their pace for each phase. In Phases A and C they may walk beside their horses, but they must pass the finishing post mounted. In Phases B and D riders must be mounted. They are free, however, to dismount outside a penalty zone, but must remount and continue the course from the same point. Dismounting in a penalty zone is penalized. Penalties are also given for falls and disobediences at obstacles (see PENALTY ZONE), but a bonus is awarded for completing the test within the prescribed time, so that it is possible for competitors to finish on the third day with plus scores, as opposed to penalties.

Before beginning the show-jumping, each horse is again examined by a veterinary surgeon. The object of the show-jumping is to test whether in spite of the demands of the previous day the horse is still fit and supple enough to continue in service.

In championship events the course is winding and involves changes of direction, designed to test the horse's handiness. It consists of ten to twelve obstacles, including a double and, where possible, a water jump. The spread of the water jump does not exceed 3 metres in C.C.I.s (3·5 metres in C.C.I.O.s), and in C.C.I.s obstacles with both height and spread must be not more than 1·8 metres (2 metres in C.C.I.O.s) wide at the

highest point or more than 2·8 metres (3 metres in C.C.I.O.s) at the lowest point.

In Britain standard events are held under the rules of the F.E.I., modified as follows:
dressage, the elementary or novice test is used, unless special permission is obtained from the British Horse Society for an alternative test;
speed and endurance, the speeds and distances are as for a C.C.I., and the dimensions of obstacles as for an intermediate horse trial;
show-jumping, the speed and distance are as for an advanced horse trial, and the dimensions of obstacles as for an intermediate horse trial.

Also called THE MILITARY. See also COMBINED TRAINING COMPETITION.

three-fold girth a girth consisting of a piece of baghide folded in three along its width. In order to prevent chafing, it should always be used with the rounded edge at the front.

three-gaited saddler See under AMERICAN SADDLE-HORSE.

throat lash a strap, incorporated in the headpiece of a bridle, which fastens under the horse's throat in order to prevent the bridle from slipping over the head. When properly fastened the throat lash should allow for the insertion of two fingers between the strap and the throat. Also called THROAT LATCH.

thrush inflammation of the frog of a horse's foot, characterized by a foul-smelling discharge. The condition is found chiefly in animals that have been standing in a filthy wet box. If left untreated it may spread and affect the sensitive parts of the foot, destroying the healthy growth of the horn, and eventually lead to canker.

tick-tack a system of signalling with the arms and hands which is used by bookmakers at race meetings to relay the betting odds on horses.

tied in below the knee having legs which are considerably narrower immediately below the knee than they are lower down towards the fetlock joint. This means that the horse is light of bone, and it is a bad fault.

tiger a small groom dressed in livery who, on coaches, rode on the seat beside the coachman or, on other vehicles, sat behind on his own, always with his arms folded. If there was no seat at the back, he stood on a small platform, supporting himself by gripping a pair of hand straps.

tiger trap a cross-country obstacle consisting of a knife-rest construction with additional rails attached to the sides. It may be built either on a level site, or over a ditch, channel, wire fence or permanent upright fence.

Tilbury gig a comparatively heavy kind of gig, supported by seven springs. It was invented, like the Stanhope gig, by Fitzroy Stanhope, and built by the coachbuilder, Tilbury, who insisted that it be named after him. See also GIG, STANHOPE GIG.

time allowed *show-jumping* the prescribed period of time in which a competitor must complete the course if he is not to incur penalty points. Every competition has its time allowed, which is calculated according to the distance of the course and the speed at which it is to be covered; for example, 300, 350, 382 or 436 yards per minute. For each second or part of a second over the time allowed the competitor is penalized a quarter of a fault. See also MINIMUM TIME.

Above
Janou Tissot, French women's show-jumping champion and winner of the Ladies' World Championships in 1970 and 1974, seen here riding Rocket.

Far right
Toric. Khango, a Toric stallion.

timed fault-and-out competition *show-jumping* an against-the-clock competition over a course of medium-sized obstacles. Since it is not only a test of jumping ability but also of handiness and obedience, the course involves a number of changes of direction.

As in a progressive fault-and-out competition, points are awarded instead of faults, and each competitor's round finishes with the first knock-down, refusal or fall, etc. When an obstacle is knocked down the judge rings the bell and the competitor goes to the next obstacle, which becomes the timing obstacle, and the time is taken as the horse's forefeet touch the ground. If a competitor completes the course without fault he must go through the finish so that the time can be taken as he crosses the line. The winner is the competitor scoring the greatest number of points in the shortest time.

time judge See TIMEKEEPER.

timekeeper the person on a cross-country course or in a show-jumping competition responsible for operating the stopwatches or automatic timing apparatus, and for recording the time of each competitor. Also called TIME JUDGE.

time limit the prescribed period of time in which a competitor must complete the course if he is not to be eliminated. The time limit is double the time allowed (show-jumping) or double the minimum time (combined training).

time of entry the date fixed for the closing of the entries for a race.

tine one of the branches of a stag's antler. In the red deer the lowest tine on each antler is called the BROW TINE, the second the BAY (also BEZ) TINE, and the third the TRAY (also TREZ) TINE. At the top of the antler is a CUP (also called CROWN) which forks into a number of TOPS.

tip a shortened horseshoe put on horses out at grass to protect their toes.

tipster *racing* one who makes a business of providing information or tips about the chances of a particular horse winning a race. In 1840 when the public in Britain started to bet on horses they had little or no information about their previous form, and the tipsters became immensely popular, since they could provide details of this kind. One of the first to appear in public was LIVERPOOL CHARLIE who sold envelopes with tips in them outside Aintree Racecourse.

Tissot, Janou, *France* (born 1945) Janou Tissot first made her mark in show-jumping when she was a member of the French team at the Junior European Championships in 1961, the same year in which she won the French National Championship. In 1964 she became the youngest rider to compete in the Olympic Games at Tokyo, where she was a member of the team which won the silver medal, a feat she was to repeat in Mexico four years later. In 1970, in Copenhagen, she became the Ladies' World Show Jumping Champion.

toe-riding the act of riding with only the toes in the stirrups.

tongue grid a metal port suspended in the mouth above the bit to prevent the tongue from coming over the bit.

tongue port a rubber device fitted to a mullen mouthpiece to prevent the horse putting its tongue over the bit.

tooling the act of driving a team or a tandem, especially in traffic.

tooth to determine the age of a horse by examining its teeth. Also termed MOUTH.

top rein See OVERCHECK.

tops See under TINE.

top weight 1. the horse in a handicap race carrying the most weight. **2.** one of the brass or lead weights attached by clips to the front shoes of a trotter in order to improve its stride. To compensate for the top weights the horse develops a powerful high action which is retained once the weights are removed.

Toric a breed of strong draught horse originally developed in Estonia at the beginning of the twelfth century. The Toric stands about 15.3 h.h.; it has a long muscular body and short powerful legs, and, for its size, it has a good free action.

totalizator 1. a form of betting in which the total amount wagered, after deduction of a percentage for costs, etc., is divided among the holders of winning and place tickets. Betting by this method, which is under the control of the Horserace Totalizator Board, first began on British racecourses in 1930. **2.** The electromechanical apparatus for recording the number and amount of bets staked by this method. Also called TOTE.

tote See TOTALIZATOR.

touched-up fox See DOPED FOX.

to you *hunting* the expression used to warn people that there is a ditch or similar hazard on the take-off side of an obstacle. See also AWAY FROM YOU.

trace one of a pair of long heavy leather straps, ropes or chains by which a horse or other draught animal is harnessed to a coach, cart, harrow or the like. Normally one end of the trace is attached to the horse's collar and the other end is attached to the vehicle. In order to level up two horses which are working unevenly, the traces are sometimes crossed, that is, passed from the inside of one horse to the outside hook on the bar behind the partner horse.

track 1. the prescribed path which must be followed by the riders in various types of equestrian competition, such as show-jumping. The distance of a course is measured along the track and must be correct to within a few yards. **2.** the footprint of a wild boar.

trail horse (US) a horse trained, bred or used for cross-country rides. It is essential for such a horse to be sure-footed, obedient and trustworthy.

trainer a person qualified to superintend the training of a horse for a particular sport. In racing it is necessary to obtain a licence from the Jockey Club before being permitted to train.

Below
Tudor Minstrel, with Gordon Richards up, winning the Somerset Stakes at Bath in 1947. In all he ran ten times and was beaten on only two occasions.

training gallops a stretch of grassland or downland where a racehorse trainer exercises and trains his horses.

trakener a cross-country obstacle consisting of a knife-rest construction, built in a ditch, with a second rail attached to the crosspieces. When built at the bottom of a wide ditch it has the appearance of a very large obstacle.

travelling lad a stable lad who travels with horses, especially racehorses, to look after them when they are away from home.

travers *dressage* a movement on two tracks in which the horse moves obliquely, at an angle of not more than thirty degrees, along the long side of the arena, with the forelegs on the outer and the hind legs on the inner track. The horse looks in the direction in which it is going, but is bent slightly round the inside leg of the rider. Also called HEAD TO THE WALL. See also RENVERS.

tray tine Also TREZ TINE. See under TINE.

tree See SADDLETREE.

trencher-fed (of a hound) not kept in hunt kennels, but looked after by a farmer, subscriber or supporter of the hunt, and collected and taken to the meet on hunting days.

triple bar *show-jumping* a spread fence consisting of three sets of poles built in staircase fashion, with the highest at the back. This obstacle can be made more solid by putting two poles at the front, or by adding brush fences of varying heights between the second and third parts. If brush fences are introduced, however, they should always be lower than the poles.

Triple Crown 1. (GB) the name given to three races: the 2000-Guineas, the Derby and the St Leger. **2.** (US) the name given to three races: the Kentucky Derby, the Preakness Stakes and the Belmont Stakes.

trot one of the gaits of the horse; a pace of two-time in which the legs move in diagonal pairs (near fore and off hind; off fore and near hind), but not quite simultaneously. See also COLLECTED TROT, EXTENDED TROT.

trotter a horse used in harness racing which moves its left front leg and right rear leg almost simultaneously, and then the right front and left rear.

trotting colours the coloured silk cap and jacket worn by the drivers in trotting races to distinguish one horse from another. They may be the colours of the owner, but usually are those of the trainer or driver.

trotting race a contest of speed, generally over a track of 1 mile or $1\frac{1}{2}$ miles, for trotters and pacers in harness and drawing a sulky.

tubing a surgical operation carried out on a horse, such as a roarer, that has difficulty in breathing. An incision is made into the trachea or windpipe and a metal-plated tube inserted. The tube has to be removed regularly for cleaning.

tucked up (of a horse) having the loins drawn up tightly behind the ribs.

Tudor Minstrel (by Owen Tudor out of Lady Juror. Owen Tudor won the Derby and the Ascot Gold Cup during the war, and Lady Juror won the Jockey Club Stakes.) Foaled in 1944, Tudor Minstrel was bred and owned by J. A. Dewar, and trained by Fred Darling. He was a brilliant horse in

Above
Tulyar, with a smiling Charlie Smirke up, heading for victory in the 1952 King George VI and Queen Elizabeth Stakes at Ascot.

Far right
Turkoman. The colt Sushnyak.

was unimpressive, winning only the Nursery Stakes at Haydock Park and Birmingham. The following season he won the Henry VIII Stakes at Hurst Park, following this with a win in the Ormonde Stakes at Chester and a very convincing win in the Derby Trial Stakes at Lingfield. Then came the Derby itself, in which he started favourite; ridden by Charlie Smirke, he won by half a length from Gay Time. In the Eclipse Stakes at Sandown and the King George VI and Queen Elizabeth Stakes at Ascot he was again victorious. He crowned his racing career by winning the St Leger by three lengths from Kingsfold. With total winnings amounting to £76,417, he broke the record set by Isinglass in 1895.

He was sold by the Aga Khan to the Irish National Stud. His career there was not very successful, and in 1955 he was sold to an American syndicate.

tumbril an English two-wheeled farm cart pulled by one or two horses.

turf 1. any course over which horseracing is conducted. **2.** the world of racing in general.

turf accountant See BOOKMAKER.

turf authority any body whose jurisdiction is recognized by the Jockey Club, and which in turn recognizes and upholds decisions made by the Jockey Club.

distances up to one mile. During his career he ran ten times and was defeated only twice — in the Derby, in which he came fourth, and in the Eclipse Stakes, in which he was second. These were the only two races he ran in which were over a distance of more than one mile.

As a two-year-old he won all of his four races; the Lansdown Stakes at Bath, the Salisbury Foal Stakes, the Coventry Stakes at Ascot and the National Breeders' Produce Stakes at Sandown. The following year he won the Somerset Stakes at Bath, the 2000-Guineas at Newmarket, the St James' Palace Stakes at Ascot and the Knights' Royal Stakes, also at Ascot.

He was then retired to stud at East Grinstead in Sussex. Among his progeny were King of the Tudors, winner of the Eclipse Stakes, the Sussex Stakes and the Knights' Royal Stakes, Toro, winner of the French 1000-Guineas and Tomy Lee, winner of the Kentucky Derby. In 1959 Tudor Minstrel was exported to the United States.

Tufnell, Meriel, (born 1949) In 1972 Meriel Tufnell made English racing history, when, riding the outsider, Scorched Earth, owned by her mother and trained by Peter Bailey, she became the winner of the first ladies' flat race to be run under the rules of racing, the Goya Stakes at Kempton Park. She finished the season as the first champion woman jockey of Britain. She has also raced in Sweden, Norway and Denmark.

tufter *staghunting* one of a group of experienced hounds which is taken from the pack at the meet and, while the remainder of the pack is kennelled, is taken to find the stag and push him into the open before the other hounds are released.

Tulyar (by Tehran out of Neocracy) Foaled in 1949, Tulyar was owned by the Aga Khan and trained by Marcus Marsh. As a two-year-old he

Turkoman an ancient breed of light horse found in Iran. The Turkoman continues to grow until it is about seven years old, usually reaching a height of about 15.2 hands. Noted for its beauty, speed and stamina, the breed is extremely popular on the racecourse in the USSR and Iran, showing exceptional ability over long distances.

turned out (of a horse) out to grass, as opposed to being in a stable.

turn on the forehand a movement in which the horse pivots on the forehand, while describing concentric circles with the hind legs.

turn on the quarters a movement in which the horse pivots on the hind legs, while describing concentric circles with the forelegs.

turnout 1. any two- or four-wheeled vehicle, complete with horse or horses. Competitions are now held at many horse and agricultural shows for turnouts, usually for trade vehicles. Apart from the conformation and performance of the horse or horses, the cleanliness and state of the harness and vehicle are also taken into consideration in the judging. **2.** the general appearance, presentation and cleanliness, etc., of a horse, its saddlery and the rider. In certain ridden classes, such as army, police and riding club competitions, a proportion of the marks are awarded for turnout.

tusker a fully grown wild boar.

twisted snaffle a more severe type of snaffle in which the jointed mouthpiece is twisted. It may be fixed with loose rings, D or eggbutt fittings.

twisting fox *hunting* a fox which sets a twisting or tortuous course.

twitch a device consisting of a long wooden handle with a loop of cord or string which is tightened round a horse's upper lip and the tip of its nose as a means of restraint so that minor operations can be performed on the animal.

A twitch is easily made by drilling a hole through the end of a piece of wood about $1\frac{1}{2}$ inches in diameter and 18 to 24 inches long and passing a piece of cord through the hole; the two ends are then knotted together to form the loop.

two hole position the position directly behind the leader in a trotting or pacing race.

u. unseated.

undershot (of a horse) having a deformity of the mouth so that the lower jaw protrudes beyond the upper jaw.

unentered (of a hound) not having completed a cub-hunting season.

unicorn a team of three horses driven in a triangular formation with one leader and two wheelers.

United States Trotting Association the governing body of harness racing in the United States, founded in 1939. Every breeder, owner, trainer, driver and race track must be a member of the U.S.T.A. in order to be licensed. The organization maintains pedigrees, performance records, racing eligibility papers, and full statistical information on the harness-racing sport. It also maintains a security division for the sport, and publishes record books, brochures, information booklets, and the official journals of harness racing, including the monthly magazine *Hoof Beats*. Although each separate state racing commission has autonomous power, virtually all adopt rules in close conformity with those of the U.S.T.A.

unraced (of a horse) not yet having taken part in a race.

unseated (of a rider) having in some way been put out of the saddle, for example, the horse may have jumped an obstacle in such a way that the rider may have been unable to stay in the saddle.

unsoundness any defect which renders a horse unable to function properly.

Untouchable *US* (chestnut gelding, 16.1 h.h.) Foaled in 1952, Untouchable was originally a race-horse, and was first noticed in the Middle West by the leading professional show-jumping rider, Benny O'Meara, who sold him to Mr and Mrs Patrick Butler. He was very successfully ridden for them by Kathy Kusner, who was second with him in the Ladies' World Championship in 1965 and first in the 1967 European Championship at Fontainebleau. Untouchable was the first horse to win the Irish Grand Prix two years running — 1964 and 1965 — and, in addition to many victories in

the United States, the pair won the Canadian Championship at Toronto in 1967.

unwind (Western US; of a horse) to start to buck.

upright a type of simple wooden-based support for holding the poles in position in a show-jump. Uprights are sometimes used in preference to wings because they are more compact and easier to handle.

vanner a harness horse used by a tradesman.

vegetable poisons Among the most common of the plants which are poisonous to horses are autumn crocus or meadow saffron, *Colchicum autumnale*, deadly nightshade or belladonna, *Atropa belladonna*, fool's parsley, *Aethusa cynapium*, hemlock, *Conium maculatum*; various species of aconite, such as monkshood, *Aconitum napellus*, ragwort (*Senecio*), and vetch (*Vicia*); bracken, *Pteridium aquilinum*, ivy, *Hedera helix*, privet, *Ligustrum vulgare*, rhododendron, *Rhododendron* spp., and yew, *Taxus* spp. Acorns, especially when unripe, are poisonous if eaten in large quantities.

velvet the soft protective covering of a growing antler. When growth is complete and the antler is hard, the velvet peels off.

victoria an expensive low four-wheeled carriage with a folding hood, a seat for two passengers, and a box seat in front for the driver and a footman. As the hood covered only the rear half, and the sides were open with no doors, the victoria was not suitable for use in bad weather or at night. Nevertheless, it was a very popular and fashionable conveyance in the latter part of the nineteenth century.

vixen a female fox. Also called BITCH FOX (US).

Vladimir a breed of heavy horse found in the area around Vladimir in the central Soviet Union. It was developed by crossing local mares with Shire and Percheron stallions, which were imported towards the end of the nineteenth century. Standing over 16 h.h., it is a massive horse with a long body and stout legs. In spite of its size and pulling power, the Vladimir has a remarkable turn of speed.

volte *dressage* a full turn on the haunches; the smallest circle a horse is able to execute on either one or two tracks, the radius being equal to the length of the horse. Also VOLT.

wagonette a four-wheeled, usually open vehicle, ideal for use in the country, with a box seat for the driver and a servant at the front, and outside the door at the back two spoonlike seats for the grooms. Inside there were usually three seats (one in front running crosswise and two behind running lengthwise and facing each other), which could accommodate six passengers or could be let down on hinges to make room for luggage or hay. The first wagonette, built in 1846 under the personal direction of the Prince Consort, was designed to combine the best features of various other vehicles, and could be constructed to suit one pony or horse, a pair or a four-in-hand.

Waler 1. a breed of saddle-horse founded in New South Wales, Australia, in the mid-nineteenth century by crossing local mares, largely of Dutch or Spanish origin, with imported Arab and Thorough-bred stallions. During the First World War vast numbers of Australian horses were exported for the Allied armies, and the Waler became virtually extinct. Up to 16 h.h., the Waler could be any

Harvey Smith, riding the
German-bred Salvador, on
which he has had many
successes, including in 1974
the Hickstead Jumping
Derby and the Sunday
Times Cup.

**Soviet Heavy Draught
Horse,** the most popular
breed of agricultural horse in
the Soviet Union, it was
developed by crossing
locally bred horses with
imported stallions, especially
Percherons.

Swedish Warm Blood. A breed equally suitable for riding or driving, it was developed from native mares crossed with imported Spanish and Oriental stallions.

Tersk, a breed which has
been developed in the
northern Caucasus during
the past fifty years and has
proved particularly successful
in the circus.

Above
Waler, an Australian breed with a reputation for soundness and endurance.

Far right
War Admiral, by Man O'War out of Brush Up. He won the American Triple Crown and was also unbeaten in his other five races as a three-year-old.

narrow topped bank. Hard edges should be protected by a securely fixed rail.

wall eye an eye in which the iris totally or partially lacks pigment so that it has a pinkish-white or bluish-white appearance. Also called BLUE EYE, CHINA EYE, GLASS EYE.

wall of the hoof the part of the hoof which is visible when the foot is placed flat on the ground. It is divided into toe, quarters (sides) and heels. At the heels the wall turns inwards to form the bars, which lie on each side of the frog. The wall is thickest at the toe, gradually tapering towards the heels, and is said to contain about twenty-five per cent moisture.

colour, though grey was not favoured. **2.** any Australian horse of unknown or uncertain breeding.

walk one of the gaits of the horse; a pace of four-time in which the hoofs strike the ground in the following sequence: near hind, near fore, off hind, off fore. See also COLLECTED WALK, EXTENDED WALK.

walking boot a canvas or rubber boot with a wooden or leather sole, used to cover an injured foot so that the horse can be given light exercise.

walking horse class any of various competitions for walking horses, held at horseshows in the United States.

Particular emphasis is laid on the walk, and under the rules laid down by the A.H.S.A. classes are judged as follows: 20 per cent for conformation, 20 per cent for flat-footed walk, 20 per cent for canter and 40 per cent for running walk. It is therefore essential for the horse to have a good overstride and speed at the running walk; the average stride is 36 inches.

There are usually separate classes for stallions, geldings, and mares, as well as open, stake, amateur to ride, novice and junior classes.

walkover a race in which only one horse has been declared. In order to qualify for the prize money the horse has to be saddled, paraded in front of the stand and then has to walk past the winning post. It is not necessary for it to complete the whole course.

walk-trot horse (US) a normal three-gaited horse, as opposed to the five-gaited American Saddle-Horse.

wall 1. an upright show-jumping obstacle made of hollow wooden blocks, which are painted and stacked to look like a brick wall. Each successive row above the base is usually three inches deep. The top should always be a layer of white bricks or coping stones. As it has such a solid appearance, a wall is always used in puissance competitions, where great height is required. **2.** a cross-country obstacle built of brick, concrete blocks, sleepers or stone. Such obstacles are normally built as upright fences, but dry stone walls may be as wide as a

War Admiral (by Man O'War out of Brush Up) Foaled in 1934, War Admiral was owned by Samuel D. Riddle and trained by George Conway. He made his first appearance on the racecourse in 1936, when he won at Havre de Grace, following this with a win at Belmont Park. He then won the Eastern Shore Handicap at Havre de Grace, and in his final race as a two-year-old was second in the Richard Johnson Handicap at Laurel Park.

He was unbeaten in all eight of his races as a three-year-old. These included the Chesapeake Stakes at Havre de Grace, and as a result of this win it was decided he should run in the Kentucky Derby at Churchill Downs, a race he won by one and three-quarter lengths from Pompoon. The following week the two met again in the Preakness Stakes at Pimlico; the result was the same, but the distance was only a head. At Belmont Park three weeks later he ran in the Belmont Stakes and won by three lengths, thus clinching the much-coveted Triple Crown. He went on to win the Washington Handicap and the first running of the Pimlico Special, an invitation race, before the end of the season.

His first major victory the following year was in the Queen's County Handicap. The racing scene then moved to Saratoga, where he won the Wilson Mile, the Saratoga Handicap, the Whitney Stakes and the Saratoga Cup, before going on to Belmont Park to win the Jockey Club Gold Cup. His final win of the season was the Rhode Island Handicap. In this, as in all his major races, he was ridden by Charlie Kurtsinger. The following year it was intended to keep him in training, but he went lame and was retired to stud.

warble fly The warble fly lays its eggs at the base of the hairs on the lower part of the legs of a horse. When the larvae hatch out they penetrate the skin and migrate throughout the body, eventually reaching the back, where they appear as small, hard, painful lumps under the skin, especially in the region of the saddle. As soon as a lump appears fomentations should be applied until a small hole forms in the centre and the mature larvae can be eased out with the thumbs. Quite frequently in horses the larvae are under the skin, producing an abscess or fistula. When this happens they have to be removed by surgery.

'ware wire *hunting* a shout by a rider who has seen barbed wire, warning other people not to jump at that particular place.

warrantable stag a stag aged five years, the minimum age at which stags are normally hunted, unless they are weak or deformed.

Warwick a dark-brown shade of leather made from cowhide.

washerwoman's day *hunting* a bad day for scenting, when the sun from a cloudless sky dries up all trace of scent, conditions being more suitable for washing than for hunting.

water to provide a horse with water to drink.

water brush 1. a brush used to wash the feet and to dampen the mane and tail as, for example, to lay the mane before plaiting it or bandaging the tail.

2. *show-jumping* a small sloping brush fence placed in front of a water jump in order to help a horse take off. There is no penalty for knocking it down.

water jump a show-jumping obstacle consisting of a sunken trough of water with minimum recommended frontage (face) of fourteen feet; the wider the face, the better horses will jump it. The length should at least equal the face, but the width should not exceed it. The deepest point of the water — about twelve inches — should be in the middle, and the base should slope upwards on both sides so that the obstacle can be jumped from either direction. A pole may be placed over the jump and/or a small brush fence in front of it, on the take-off side. The landing side must always have a white lath or tape on the ground at the edge of the water, and if there is no brush in front of the water jump there must be a lath or tape on the take-off side as well.

water out to cool a trotter or pacer after a race by walking it about and allowing it occasional drinks of water.

weaning Foals are normally weaned at four to five months but this may vary depending on the condition of the mare and foal and also on the amount and quality of grass available.

Weatherby and Sons the agents for the Jockey Club, with headquarters at Wellingborough, Northamptonshire. Weatherbys are responsible for

Below
water jump. Clearing the jump at Hickstead.

the production of the racing calendar and for accepting all racing entries. The names of all owners, racehorses and racing colours have to be registered with them.

web reins a type of riding rein made of web, usually with leather finger-slots. The material is very hard wearing and gives a good grip.

Weedon a famous English cavalry school in Northamptonshire. Until 1940, when it was closed because of the war, it was the centre of British military equitation and was the first such school to adopt the Italian style of riding in England.

weigh in (of a rider) to be weighed after a race. In certain equestrian sports, such as combined training and racing, where it is necessary for the horse to carry a certain weight, the rider must be weighed immediately after the race or competition, in order to ensure that the weight carried was in fact the correct one.

weighing room the place on a racecourse where the jockeys are weighed, admission to which is strictly controlled. Apart from the jockeys themselves, only qualified persons, such as owners and trainers, are allowed to enter.

weigh out (of a rider) to be weighed before a race. In certain equestrian sports such as combined training and racing, where it is necessary for the horse to carry a certain weight, the rider is weighed before the event in which he is due to compete to ensure that his weight is the correct one.

weight allowance *racing* an allowance which may be claimed by an apprentice or jockey who has not ridden a certain number of winners, i.e. the weight the horse is required to carry is reduced. In Great Britain these allowances are as follows:
flat racing

7 lb until he has won ten races;
5 lb until he has won fifty races;
3 lb until he has won seventy-five races.
These allowances may be claimed only in handicaps, selling races and races where the prize money is not more than £1500.
steeplechasing or hurdle racing
7 lb until he has won ten races;
5 lb until he has won fifteen races;
3 lb until he has won twenty-five races.
Except in opportunity races, these allowances may be claimed only when the prize money does not exceed £2000.

weight cloth a cloth carried under the saddle on a horse. It is equipped with pockets in which lead weights are inserted. See also WEIGHTS.

weight for age a method of handicapping horses in a race by their age.

weights If a rider is not heavy enough to make the specified weight for an event he is required to carry weights, usually lead, which are placed in a weight cloth.

well let down (of hocks) long and low and dropping in a straight line to the ground.

well ribbed up having ribs which are flat at the front and well sprung at the back, providing plenty of room for the heart and lungs.

well topped (of a horse) having good conformation above the legs.

Wels cavesson a breaking cavesson which closely resembles the Orssich cavesson, but is very much lighter in design, and has projecting driving rings attached to the plate itself, thus reducing the amount of pressure exerted on the nose.

Welsh Cob a sturdy breed of small horse which originated in Wales. For many centuries it was the

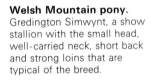

Welsh Mountain pony.
Gredington Simwynt, a show stallion with the small head, well-carried neck, short back and strong loins that are typical of the breed.

mainstay of life in rural Wales until the introduction of the motor car, and the breed can certainly be traced back as far as the twelfth century. It was a general utility animal, used not only for farm work but also driven and raced at trotting meetings. During the two world wars many Welsh Cobs were bought by the War Department for use as pack-horses and remounts. The usual height is 14 h.h. to 15 h.h. The Welsh Cob should have quality with strength, and in its action there should be freedom in all movements. It makes a very good riding horse, having plenty of stamina, and is a bold jumper. It is also used in harness.

The WELSH PONY (COB-TYPE) is a stronger type of Welsh Pony with some Cob blood in it. It makes an ideal pony for trekking and for hunting, suitable both for adults and children, and it also makes a

very good harness pony. The average height is 13.2 h.h.

welsher a person, especially a bookmaker, who leaves a racecourse without paying his debts.

Welsh Mountain pony an ancient breed of small strong hardy pony found in Wales. Generally acknowledged as one of the most beautiful of the native British breeds, the Welsh Mountain pony is also renowned for its intelligence, courage, soundness and endurance. It stands about 12 h.h., and has a small, clean-cut head, with a fine muzzle, large bold eyes and small pricked ears, a well-carried neck, short back with strong loins, and a well-set tail. The limbs should have strong forearms, clean flat bone, and short cannon bones. The hocks should be strong and well let down and

Welsh Pony, with its youthful rider.

the feet should be round and hard. A reasonable amount of silky feather is accepted. The action must be true and straight, with great freedom from the shoulders and the hocks well flexed.

Under the regulations of the Welsh Pony and Cob Society, which was formed in 1901, all colours except piebald and skewbald are permitted.

Welsh Pony a breed of pony, originally produced by crossing Welsh Cobs with Welsh Mountain ponies, and formerly used in Wales mainly for shepherding and hunting in the hills.

It stands between 12.2 h.h. and 13.2 h.h., and should possess the strength, toughness and hard flinty bone of the true native pony. It has an

Western saddle.

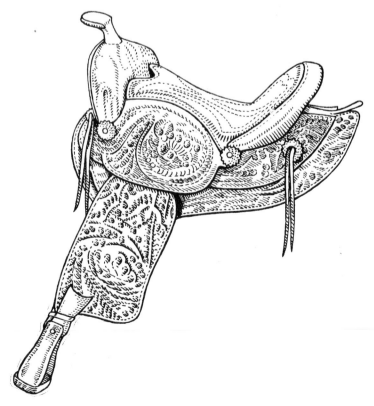

excellent temperament, making it a very suitable mount for a child.

The breed society is the Welsh Pony and Cob Society, which was formed in 1901.

See also under WELSH COB.

Wembley Stadium a sports stadium situated in Middlesex, on the west side of London. It was the venue of the Prix des Nations in the 1948 Olympics, and of the Royal International Horse Show in 1968 and 1969, but because of the damage caused to the turf by the horses it was not possible for the show to continue there.

Western horse any horse which is ridden under a Western saddle, and is trained to perform one or more of the activities associated with the Western range, such as cutting or roping.

Western saddle an American saddle having a deep seat and high cantle. It is heavy in appearance, but is made in such a way as to spread the weight evenly. At the head of the high pommel it has a horn, which is used for carrying a rope for cattle roping.

Weymouth bit a curb bit having either loose or fixed cheeks. With fixed cheekpieces the action is more direct and there is less leverage than with slide cheekpieces.

Weymouth bridle See DOUBLE BRIDLE.

Weymouth dressage bit a curb bit having a very broad mouthpiece with the port sometimes offset slightly forward. The bradoon it is used with similarly has a broad flattish mouthpiece.

wheeler one of the pair of horses in a team which are nearest to the vehicle. See also LEADER.

whip an amateur or professional driver of a sporting or pleasure vehicle.

whip off *hunting* to stop the hounds hunting a certain line, usually if they are pursuing a fox in a direction in which it is not desired to hunt.

whipper-in 1. the huntsman's assistant with a pack of hounds. **2.** the second of the huntsman's assistants, if there is more than one. See also FIRST WHIPPER-IN.

whiskey a fast light giglike vehicle with a cane body joined directly to the shafts and undercarriage. It was introduced towards the end of the eighteenth century, and was drawn by one horse. Also WHISKY.

whistling a high-pitched form of roaring. It often develops into roaring, and, similarly, is caused usually by paralysis of the muscles of the larynx, or more rarely by an obstruction in the nose or pharynx.

Whitechapel dogcart See under DOGCART.

White City Stadium a greyhound racetrack and former sports stadium on the west side of London. From 1947 until 1967 it was the home of the Royal International Horse Show, but in 1968 the venue had to be changed because of major alterations in the surrounding road system.

white flag a marker used in equestrian sports to denote the left-hand extremity of an obstacle. It is also used to mark a set track and must always be passed on the right-hand side.

white line a structure of soft horn containing approximately fifty per cent of moisture, which forms the connection between the sole and the wall of the hoof. It indicates the thickness of the wall, and so can be used as a guide by the farrier as to where he can safely nail the shoe. The nails may penetrate the white line but they must not go beyond it.

whittler (US) any horse which excels at cutting.

wid a horse which is gone in the wind.

Wielkopolska a breed of horse found in central and western Poland. The breed is noted for its good temperament and, since it is a large strong animal, it is equally suitable for riding and for use in harness.

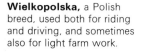

Wielkopolska, a Polish breed, used both for riding and driving, and sometimes also for light farm work.

Above
Sheila Willcox on High and Mighty splashes through the lake on the way to the first of her three consecutive wins at Badminton Horse Trials.

Far right
windgall.

wiggler See PACER.

Willcox, Sheila, *GB* (born 1936) Between 1956 and 1971 Sheila Willcox was one of the greatest women riders in three-day events, but a heavy fall in 1971 brought her riding career to a premature end. She is the only person to have won the Badminton Horse Trials three years in succession — in 1957 and 1958, with High and Mighty, and in 1959 with Airs and Graces. In 1957 she also won the European Championship at Copenhagen, and in 1968, riding Fair and Square, she was the winner of the Burghley Horse Trials.

Wilson rings See under SCORRIER SNAFFLE.

wind a fox (of hounds) to smell the scent of a fox.

windgall a puffy, elastic swelling of the knee or fetlock joints caused by an over-secretion of synovia, a fluid similar to joint oil. Windgalls are very common in all types of horses and are caused by overwork. They rarely produce lameness and are not considered an unsoundness.

windsucking a harmful habit in which a horse draws in and swallows air. The animal usually stands with its head elevated and its neck strangely arched, making a peculiar, characteristic noise; or the tongue may be curled and protrude in front of the lips, while the animal sucks as hard as possible.

wing one of a pair of upright stands with cups or similar fittings used to support the poles or other suspended parts of a show-jumping obstacle. Wings are seldom used in cross-country obstacles, but when they are they should not be set at an angle to the obstacle, but should form a natural extension of it.

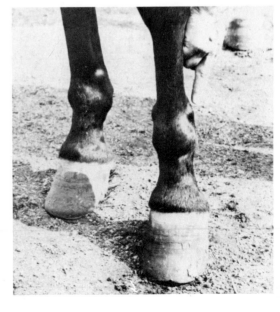

win in a canter *racing* (of a horse) to pass the winning post at an easy pace because it is so far in front of all the other competitors.

Winkler, Hans Günter, *Germany* (born 1926) Hans Winkler made his debut in international show-jumping in 1952. He won the Men's World Championship in 1954 and 1955, riding Halla, and the European Championship in 1957 with Sonnenglaz. In 1965, riding Fortun, he won the King George V Gold Cup and again in 1968 with Enigk. In the course of his outstanding career he has competed in over seventy Prix des Nations competitions and five Olympic Games, winning both a team and the individual gold medal in Stockholm (1956), riding Halla, a team gold medal in Rome (1960), again with Halla, a team gold medal in Tokyo (1964) with Fidelitas, a team bronze medal in Mexico (1968), riding Enigk, and a team gold medal in Munich (1972) with Torphy.

winner's enclosure the place on a racecourse reserved for the first three horses in a race and to which their riders have to return mounted at the end of the race.

Winter, Frederick T., (born 1926). The son of a jockey — in 1911, by the age of sixteen, his father had won seventy-six races, including the Oaks — Fred Winter rode 929 winners under National Hunt rules and four on the flat. He was the champion National Hunt jockey in 1952/53 with 121 winners — a record which was unbeaten until the 1966/67 season — and again in 1955/56, 1956/57 and 1957/58.

During his racing career he won most of the major National Hunt races, and was associated with such famous horses as Mandarin, Saffron Tartan, Clair Soleil, Beaver II and Halloween. One of his most memorable victories was in the 1962 Grand Steeplechase de Paris, when he rode Mandarin. The bridle broke three fences from home, but he still managed to bring in Mandarin to win by a short head.

At the end of the 1963/64 season, after a total of 4298 rides and 319 falls, which included a broken back, leg, collar bones and a fractured skull, he hung up his boots and took out a licence to train. His success was immediate, for in 1965 he trained the American horse Jay Trump, ridden for his owner, Mrs M. Stephenson, by Tommy Crompton-Smith, to win the Grand National, following this with a repeat success in 1966, when he sent out Anglo, ridden by Tim Norman. Since then he has been the leading trainer under National Hunt Rules in 1970/71, 1972/73 and 1973/74, training such horses as Into View, Bula, Crisp, Killiney, Pendil and Lanzarote.

winter horse a horse which is kept at a home ranch for use during the winter.

winter out (of a horse) to be left out in a field during the winter, rather than being brought into a stable.

with a stain (of a horse) well bred but having some common blood.

withers the highest part of a horse's back; the area at the base of the neck, between the shoulder blades.

Below
Fred Winter. For many years the top steeplechase jockey and now a leading National Hunt trainer, Fred Winter has a word with What Next at his Lambourn stables. On the right is the ex-Australian horse Crisp.

Vladimir Heavy Draught Horse, a breed developed in the Vladimir region of the Soviet Union by crossing local mares with imported Shire and Percheron stallions.

Mary Gordon-Watson.
With Cornishman (pictured
here), she was the individual
winner of the 1970 World
Three-Day Event
Championship and in 1972
she was a member of the
gold medal team in the
Munich Olympics.

Welsh Cob. A sturdy breed
of small horse.

Hans Günter Winkler, one
of the stars of the West
German show-jumping team
which won the gold medal at
the 1972 Olympics, seen here
riding Torphy at Hickstead.

withney panel See under PANEL.

W-mouth snaffle a severe snaffle having two jointed mouthpieces, which are so arranged that the joints are one on either side of the mouth. When applied this type of bit does pinch the lips and possibly also the tongue. Also called Y-MOUTH SNAFFLE.

wolf tooth either of a pair of rudimentary teeth which are found in the upper jaw immediately in front of the first molars and are generally lost when the horse casts the crowns of the two first molars on rising three. They normally cause no harm unless they do not grow straight, in which case they have to be extracted.

work horse (US) a horse which is worked in harness, as opposed to one which is ridden.

World Three-Day Event Championships a three-day event comprising concurrent individual and team competitions, held every second year after an Olympic Games since 1966. The championship is open to teams of four riders from each country and to a limited number of individual competitors. The scores of the three best riders of each team count in the team championship. The winner of the individual championship is the rider with the best overall score. The country of the winning team has the right to hold the next championship, but it may not be held in the same country on two consecutive occasions. (For results see page 227.)

wrangle to round up, herd and care for horses.

Far right
W. S. bitless Pelham.

Right
W-mouth snaffle.

Below
Anneli Wucherpfennig,
with Merely-a-Monarch.

W. S. bitless Pelham a bitless bridle having relatively short movable metal cheeks. It is for use with two reins, the lower pair operating the curb chain, so that pressure can be applied to either the nose or the curb groove. Also called DISTAS BRIDLE.

Wucherpfennig, Elizabeth Ann, *GB* (born 1937) Anneli Wucherpfennig is one of the few people to have competed internationally both in three-day events and show-jumping with the same horse – the 16.3 h.h. black gelding, MERELY-A-MONARCH. Before turning their attention to show-jumping, the pair won the Burghley Horse Trials in 1961 and the Badminton Horse Trials in 1962.
  Their first international show was the 1962 Royal International Horse Show, where they won the Imperial Cup. With Merely-a-Monarch, Anneli won championships and grand prix competitions all over the world including the Grand Prix in Toronto in 1966, the Swiss Grand Prix in Geneva in 1967 and the Grand Prix in Madrid in 1970. Winner of the Ladies' European Championship in Rome in 1968, the following year, riding Xanthos, she won the inaugural Italian Derby, a victory which she repeated in 1970. In the same year, with Merely-a-Monarch, she won the Queen Elizabeth II Cup, a championship which had eluded her for so many years, and was third in the Ladies' World Championship in Copenhagen. In 1971, riding Sporting Ford, she won the first High Jump Championship to be held in Great Britain since the war.

Württemberg a medium-sized coblike breed of horse developed for use on smallholdings in the former German state of Württemberg by crossing native mares with Anglo-Norman stallions.

Yakut.

Yakut a hardy versatile breed of pony found in the north-east of the Soviet Union, in areas of extreme cold extending into the Arctic Circle. Up to 14 h.h. and usually light grey in colour, it has a deep chest and long body. The Yakut serves many purposes; it is used for riding, in harness and for carrying packs.

yearling head collar See ADJUSTABLE HEAD COLLAR.

yellow dun a black-skinned horse having a diffuse yellow pigment in the hair. The mane and tail are black, and there may be a black dorsal stripe and bars on the legs. See also BLUE DUN.

Y-mouth snaffle See W-MOUTH SNAFFLE.

York Racecourse a racecourse at Knavesmire, a short distance from the centre of York and some 190 miles from London. Racing was first held there in 1709, during the reign of Queen Anne, and because of the popularity of the city itself was an immediate success, attracting large crowds. Two of the major races held on the course are the Ebor Handicap and the Gimcrack Stakes.

Yorkshire halter a type of halter made of hemp rope. It differs from an ordinary halter in that it has a throat latch, which keeps it in place, preventing it from being pulled over the ears, and so is especially useful for a horse that does not easily lead.

young entry *hunting* the name applied to young hounds before the beginning of the cub-hunting season when they are 'unentered'. During cubbing they are trained to hunt the quarry, so that by the time the hunting season starts they are 'entered', usually when they are about eighteen months old.

Foxhounds, Harriers and Staghounds

FOXHOUNDS
Packs of foxhounds in the British Isles, with the country they hunt.

Afonwy Radnorshire. (Hunting is on foot.)
Albrighton Staffordshire and Shropshire.
Albrighton Woodland Between Halesowen, Bromsgrove, Bewdley, Bridgnorth and Wolverhampton.
Ashford Valley The Weald of Kent.
Atherstone Mainly in west Leicestershire and north Warwickshire.
Avondhu East of County Cork, with centres at Fermoy, Mallow and Motchelstown.
Avon Vale Wiltshire.
Badsworth Adjoining the Grove, the Bramham Moor, the Holderness and the York and Ainsty hunts in Yorkshire.
Ballymacad North of Kells and on the borders of Cavan and Westmeath, with centres at Castlepollard, Kells, Oldcastle and Virginia.
Banwen Miners' West Glamorgan.
Barlow North-east Derbyshire.
Bedale The North Riding of Yorkshire.
Belvoir Leicestershire and Lincolnshire.
Berkeley Adjoining the Cotswold Vale Farmers, Cotswold and Ledbury in the north, and the Duke of Beaufort's in the east; bounded by the River Severn in the west and Bristol in the south.
Bermingham and North Galway North County Galway and the south of County Mayo, with centres at Headford and Tuam.
Berwickshire Berwickshire, with centres at Coldstream, Duns and Greenlaw.
Bewcastle The borders of Scotland, Northumberland and Cumberland.
Bicester and Warden Hill Buckinghamshire, Oxfordshire, Northamptonshire and Warwickshire. In the north it joins the Pytchley, in the west the Warwickshire and the Heythrop, in the south the Vale of Aylesbury and in the east the Whaddon Chase and the Grafton.
Bilsdale Yorkshire.
Bisley and Sandhurst North-west Surrey and the adjacent corners of Hampshire and Berkshire.
Blackmore and Sparkford Vale Dorset and Somerset.
Blankney Lincolnshire and Nottinghamshire.
Blencathra The Lake District. (Hunting is on foot.)
Border The valleys of the Tyne, Rede and Coquet in the north-west of Northumberland, and the Kale district of Roxburghshire.
Braes of Derwent South Northumberland and north-west Durham.
Bramham Moor The West Riding of Yorkshire.
Brecon Between the Brecon Beacons in the south and the River Wye in the north.
Brocklesby North Lincolnshire.
Burton A rectangle with Lincoln at the centre of the south side, and the Brocklesby to the north, the Grove to the west, the Southwold to the east and the Blankney to the south.
Cambridgeshire Cambridgeshire, Huntingdonshire, Bedfordshire and Hertfordshire. To the north is the Fitzwilliam, to the south the Vale of Aylesbury and the Puckeridge, to the east the Newmarket and Thurlow and to the west the Oakley.
Carbery County Cork, with the centre at Ballineen.
Carlow County Carlow, with parts in Kildare, Leix and Wicklow, with centres at Bagenalstown, Carlow and Tullow.
Carmarthenshire An area of about fifteen miles around Carmarthen.

Cattistock Dorset and a small part of south Somerset, from Yeovil in the north to Plymouth in the south, and from Dorchester in the east to Bridport in the west.
Cheshire The country area of Cheshire, except for the Wirral.
Cheshire Forest The whole of the Wirral.
Chiddingfold and Leconfield Surrey and Sussex.
Cleveland The whole Cleveland area in the North Riding of Yorkshire.
Clifton-on-Teme Loaned by the Worcestershire, North Hereford and the Ludlow, and since the war country previously hunted by the North Ledbury and loaned by the Ledbury.
College Valley Both sides of the Scottish border in north Northumberland and Roxburghshire.
Coniston Partly in Westmorland and Lancashire.
Cotswold Gloucestershire, with centres at Cheltenham, Andoversford and Cirencester.
Cotswold Vale Farmers The Cotswold Vale and the Newent area.
Cottesmore Rutland, Leicestershire and Lincolnshire, with centres at Oakham and Melton Mowbray.
County Galway (The Blazers) County Galway, with centres at Athenry, Gort and Loughrea.
County Limerick County Limerick, with centres at Croom and Adare.
Cowdray West Sussex, with centres at Midhurst and Chichester.
Crawley and Horsham Sussex, from Horsham in the north to the coast in the south.
Croome About twenty square miles covering parts of Worcestershire, Warwickshire and Gloucestershire.
Cumberland Cumberland, with centres at Wigton and Aspatria.
Cumberland Farmers' Between Penrith, Carlisle and Wigton.
Cury Cornwall; south to the sea from Penryn, Helston and Porthleven.
Dartmoor Devon and the southern part of Dartmoor, with centres at Ivybridge and South Brent.
David Davies The upper reaches of the Severn Valley and the surrounding hills in central Montgomeryshire.
Derwent The North Riding of Yorkshire, with centres at Scarborough and at Thornton-le-Dale.
Duhallow The north of County Cork, extending thirty miles from north to south, and thirty-six miles from east to west, with centres at Cork, Doneraile, Liscarroll and Mallow.
Duke of Beaufort's Gloucestershire, Somerset and Wiltshire.
Duke of Buccleuch's Roxburghshire, Selkirk and Berwickshire, covering an area of twenty miles from north to south and thirty miles from east to west, with centres at Kelso and St Boswells.
Dumfriesshire Dumfriesshire, with the centre at Lockerbie.
Dungannon Between the rivers Blackwater and Ballinderry, with the centre at Dungannon.
East Cornwall East Cornwall.
East Devon Twenty square miles in south-east Devon, with centres at Exeter, Budleigh Salterton, Sidmouth and Honiton.
East Down Within a fifteen-mile radius of Seaforde in County Down.
East Dulverton The south-eastern part of Exmoor and surrounding country on the borders of Devon and Somerset.
East Essex North and east Essex, with centres at Braintree and Halstead.
East Galway Bounded by County Clare in the south, by the River Shannon in the east and by the County Galway Hunt in the west.
East Kent About twenty miles east to west and

fifteen miles north to south, with centres at Canterbury, Folkestone and Dover.
East Sussex and Romney Marsh Mainly in Sussex, but extending into Kent, with centres at Battle, Bexhill, Eastbourne, Hastings and Rye.
Eggesford Between Okehampton, Hatherleigh, South Molton and Copplestone.
Eglinton Ayrshire, with centres at Ayr, Kilmarnock and Troon.
Enfield Chase Hertfordshire and Middlesex, with centres at Hatfield and Hertford.
Eridge To the south of Tunbridge Wells.
Eskdale and Ennerdale Cumberland, Westmorland and Lancashire, with centres at Eskdale and Whitehaven.
Essex Essex, with centres at Harlow, Ongar, Chelmsford and Dunmow.
Essex and Suffolk Both sides of the River Stour, partly in Essex and partly in Suffolk.
Essex Farmers' Between the East Essex and the Essex Union, with centres at Maldon and Southminster.
Essex Union South-east Essex, with centres at Brentwood, Billericay and Chelmsford.
Exmoor North Devon and west Somerset, with centres at Exford, Simonsbath and Porlock.
Farndale Between Farndale and Castleton in north Yorkshire.
Fernie South Leicestershire, with the centre at Kibworth.
Fife Fife; an area seventeen miles from north to south and forty miles from east to west, with centres at Cupar and Kirkcaldy.
Fitzwilliam Northamptonshire and Huntingdonshire, with centres at Peterborough, Oundle, Huntingdon and Stamford.
Flint and Denbigh The western part of Flintshire and Denbighshire.
Four Burrow Cornwall, with centres at Redruth and Truro.
Garth and South Berks South and east Berkshire, south Oxfordshire and part of north Hampshire, with centres at Reading, Windsor, Maidenhead and Basingstoke.
Gellygaer Farmers' North-east Glamorgan and parts of Monmouthshire.
Glaisdale The North Riding of Yorkshire between the Goathland, the Cleveland and the Farndale.
Glamorgan The Vale of Glamorgan, with centres at Cardiff and Cowbridge.
Goathland Both sides of the River Esk, with centres at Goathland and Whitby.
Gogerddan The whole of north Cardiganshire, with centres at Aberystwyth and Talybont.
Golden Valley Within Hertfordshire, Radnorshire and Breconshire, with the centre at Hay, via Hereford.
Grafton Mainly in south Northamptonshire and a part of north Buckinghamshire, with centres at Towcester, Brackley and Weedon.
Grove and Rufford Nottinghamshire, Yorkshire and Derbyshire, with centres at Retford, Worksop and Newark.
Hambledon Hampshire, with centres at Winchester, Portsmouth, Petersfield and Bishop's Waltham.
Hampshire (H.H.) From Aldershot to Winchester, and Basingstoke to West Meon.
Haydon South-west Northumberland.
Heythrop Oxfordshire and Gloucestershire with centres at Chipping Norton, Stow-on-the-Wold, Moreton-in-Marsh and Kingham.
Holderness East Riding of Yorkshire, with the centre at Beverley.
Hursley Between the Winchester–Southampton road and the Salisbury–Andover–Stockbridge road, in Hampshire.
Hurworth North Yorkshire and south Durham, with the centre at Northallerton.
Irfon and Towy North Breconshire, with the centre at Llanwrtyd Wells.
Island Between Gorey, Enniscorthy, Bunclody

and Kilmuckridge, with centres at Gorey, Enniscorthy and Ferns.

Isle of Wight The whole of the Isle of Wight.

Jed Forest Roxburghshire, with the centre at Jedburgh.

Kildare Counties Kildare and West Wicklow, and also in County Meath and the south of County Dublin, with centres at Dublin and Naas.

Kilkenny County Kilkenny, with centres at Kilkenny and Waterford.

Lamerton West Devon and north-east Cornwall, with centres at Launceston and Lewdon.

Lanarkshire and Renfrewshire Almost entirely in Renfrewshire, with centres at Bridge of Weir, Glasgow, Kilmalcolm and Paisley.

Laois (Queen's County) County Leix, with centres at Abbeyleix and Portlaois.

Lauderdale North of the railway from Greenlaw to Galashiels, with centres at Galashiels and Lauder.

Ledbury Part of Gloucestershire, Hereford and Worcester, with centres at Ledbury, Malvern, Gloucester and Tewkesbury.

Liddesdale Roxburghshire, with centres at Hawick and Langholm.

Linlithgow and Stirlingshire Midlothian, West Midlothian and Stirlingshire, with centres at Edinburgh and Linlithgow.

Llandilo Farmers Carmarthenshire and Glamorgan, with centres at Llandilo and Swansea.

Llangeinor Glamorgan, with centres at Blackmill, Maesteg, Pontycymmer and Margam.

Llangeitho Mid-Cardiganshire and includes some of the Cambrian Mountains, with centres at Tregaron, Lampeter and Aberaeron.

Llangibby Monmouthshire; about fourteen miles from north to south and the same from east to west, with the centre at Usk.

Lochaber and Sunart Farmers Bounded by Loch Quoich in the north, the Sound of Mull in the south, the Atlantic in the west and Loch Treig in the east, with centres at Fort William and Strontian.

Louth An area of fifteen miles by thirty-five miles in Counties Louth, Neath and Monaghan, with centres at Ardee, Drogheda and Dundalk.

Ludlow Shropshire, Herefordshire and Worcestershire, with centres at Ludlow and Tenbury Wells.

Lunesdale The fells in Westmorland, the West Riding of Yorkshire and north Lancashire, with centres at Kendal and Sedbergh. (Hunting is on foot.)

Macroom Mid County Cork, with centres at Bawnmore, Clondrohid, Inchigeela and Toames.

Meath Throughout County Meath, with centres at Dublin, Dunshauglin and Navan.

Melbreak West Cumberland, with centres at Buttermere, Cockermouth and Loweswater.

Mendip Farmers Adjoining the Duke of Beaufort's and the Avon Vale in the north, the Blackmore Vale in the south, and the Avon Vale in the east, with centres at Bristol, Bath, Shepton Mallet and Wells.

Meynell and South Staffordshire South Staffordshire and Derbyshire, together with parts of Warwickshire, with centres at Derby, Ashbourne, Uttoxeter and Lichfield.

Mid Devon Dartmoor, with centres at Chagford and Okehampton.

Middleton The North and East Ridings of Yorkshire, from York and Malton in the west to Filey and Flamborough Head in the east.

Milvain (Percy) Northumberland; embraces the north part of the Percy Hunt country, with centres at Chatton, Eglingham and Belford.

Monmouthshire The northern half of Monmouthshire, from Abergavenny in the west to Monmouth in the east and Pontrilas in the north.

Morpeth South-east Northumberland, with centres at Whalton and Longhorsley.

Mr Goschen's From the Odiham to the Farnham road in Surrey in the north to the Midhurst–Haslemere road bounded by the River Rother, in the south.

Muskerry North and south of the River Lee, from Carrigrohane Bridge to Macroom, with centres at Cork and Macroom.

New Forest The New Forest; Hampshire, extending into Wiltshire and Dorset, with centres at Brockenhurst, Burley and Lyndhurst.

North Cornwall From Boscastle and Padstow Bay in the north to Fowey in the south.

North Cotswold Gloucestershire and Worcestershire, with centres at Broadway and Chipping Camden.

North Herefordshire Herefordshire, with centres at Hereford, Leominster and Bromyard.

North Kilkenny The north of Kilkenny, with centres at Ballyragget and Freshford.

North Ledbury The area not hunted by the Clifton-on-Teme, and a part loaned by the Ledbury, with centres at Bosbury and Cradley Acton.

North Lonsdale North Lonsdale, not including Low Furness and the Duddon Valley. (Hunting is on foot.)

North Northumberland Extending about twenty miles from east to west and fifteen miles from north to south, with centres at Berwick, Cornhill-on-Tweed and Wooler.

North Shropshire Shropshire; about twenty-seven miles from north to south and eighteen miles from east to west, with centres at Shrewsbury, Wellington and Wem.

North Staffordshire North of the town of Stafford, bordering Cheshire, Derbyshire and Shropshire, with centres at Eccleshall, Market Drayton and Woore.

North Tipperary The North Riding of County Tipperary, with the centre at Nenagh.

North Tyne North-west Northumberland, with centres at Wark and Falstone.

North Warwickshire North Warwickshire, with the centre at Leamington Spa.

North York and Ainsty Mainly between the rivers Ure and Nidd in the West Riding of Yorkshire, and between Easingwold and Thirsk.

Oakley Bedfordshire, Buckinghamshire, Huntingdonshire and Northamptonshire, with centres at Bedford, Wellingborough, Higham Ferrers, St Neots and Newport Pagnell.

Old Berkshire Berkshire and Oxfordshire.

Old Surrey and Burstow Surrey, Sussex and Kent, with centres at Edenbridge, East Grinstead and Oxted.

Ormond North Tipperary and south Offaly, with centres at Rathcabbin and Dunkerrin.

Pembrokeshire Pembrokeshire north of Milford Haven, with centres at Haverfordwest and Fishguard.

Pennine The part of the Pennine Range not hunted by any other hounds, extending from Malhamdale and Wharfedale in the north to Edale and Derwentdale in the south.

Pentyrch Between Cardiff and Pontypridd, with centres at Pentyrch, Pontypridd and Caerphilly.

Percy Northumberland, approximately twenty miles from north to south and twelve miles east to west, with centres at Alnwick, Bamburgh and Warkworth.

Plas Machynlleth Within a six-mile radius of Machynlleth. (Hunting is on foot.)

Portman Dorset, with the centre at Blandford.

Puckeridge and Thurlow North-east Hertfordshire, north-west Essex, south-east Cambridgeshire and south-west Suffolk, with centres at Buntingford, Bishops Stortford, Haverhill and Saffron Walden.

Pytchley Northamptonshire and Leicestershire, with centres at Brixworth, East and West Haddon and Guilsborough.

Quorn Mainly in Leicestershire, with centres at Loughborough, and Melton Mowbray.

Radnorshire and West Herefordshire North-west Hereford and part of Radnorshire, with centres at Eardisley, Kington and Pembridge.

Royal Artillery Between Salisbury, Wylye, West Lavington and the northern extremity of Salisbury Plain, with centres at Amesbury, Salisbury and Tidworth.

Rufford Forest From the south Nottinghamshire border in the south to the Worksop–Retford railway in the north.

Saltersgate Farmers' Between Whitby and Pickering in Yorkshire, with centres at Lockton and Newton on Rawcliffe.

Scarteen (Black and Tans) Counties Tipperary and Limerick, with centres at Killmallock, Knocklong and Tipperary.

Seavington Dorset and Somerset, with centres at Bridport, Crewkerne, Matlock and Langport.

Sennybridge and District Farmers' Within a five-mile radius of Sennybridge.

Silverton Devonshire, with centres at Exeter, Crediton, Tiverton and Cullompton.

Sinnington The North Riding of Yorkshire, with centres at Helmsley, Kirbymoorside and Malton.

Sir Watkin Williams-Wynn's Denbighshire, Flintshire, Cheshire and Shropshire, with centres at Ellesmere, Malpas, Whitchurch and Wrexham.

South and West Wiltshire Bounded by Shaftesbury, Shepton Mallet, Frome, Westbury, Stapleford, Wylye and Fovant.

South Devon South Devon.

South Dorset Dorset, with centres at Dorchester and Blandford.

Southdown The Sussex coast, with centres at Lewes and Hurstpierpoint.

South Durham County Durham, with centres at Darlington and Stockton.

South Herefordshire Herefordshire, between Hereford, Ross-on-Wye, Peterchurch and Whitchurch.

South Nottinghamshire Nottinghamshire and Derbyshire, with centres at Nottingham, Newark and Bingham.

South Pembrokeshire Mainly in south Pembrokeshire and a small part of Carmarthenshire, with centres at Pembroke and Tenby.

South Shropshire Within a radius ten miles south of Shrewsbury.

South Tetcott Borders of Devon and Cornwall, with centres at Holsworthy and Launceston.

South Union County Cork, with centres at Cork and Kinsale.

South Wold From Louth to Boston and from the Burton Hunt to the sea.

South York and Ainsty North, west and south of York, which is the centre.

Spooner's and West Dartmoor Within a twelve-mile radius of Tavistock, plus the old West Dartmoor country covering a line from Hexworthy–Cadover Bridge–Plymouth, with centres at Yelverton and Tavistock.

Staintondale Yorkshire, between Scarborough and Whitby.

Stevenstone North Devon, with centres at Bideford and Torrington.

Strabane Counties Tyrone and Donegal, with centres at Donegal, Londonderry and Strabane.

Suffolk Mainly west Suffolk, extending from Shadwell in the north to Long Melford in the south, and from Redgrave in the east to Denston in the west.

Surrey Union From Reigate to Guildford in the north, from Three Bridges to Horsham in the south, and from the Brighton–Redhill railway line in the east to the Horsham–Guildford road in the west, with centres at Dorking and Horsham.

Talybont Joining the Brecon Hunt in the west and the Monmouthshire in the east, with centres at Crickhowell, Talybont and Gilwern.

Tanat-Side Eastern Montgomeryshire and the

Shropshire border, with centres at Guilsfield and Welshpool.

Taunton Vale Somerset, extending fourteen miles from north to south and twenty-five miles from east to west, with centres at Ilminster and Taunton.

Tedworth Wiltshire and Hampshire, extending twenty-five miles from north to south and twenty-two miles from east to west, with centres at Andover, Marlborough and Pewsey.

Teme Valley About 300 square miles in Herefordshire, Radnorshire and Shropshire, with centres at Knighton, Llandrindod Wells and Penybont.

Tetcott Borders of Devon and Cornwall, with centres at Bradworthy, Bude and Holsworthy.

The Curre Between Usk and Chepstow.

Tickham North Kent, with centres at Lenham, Bredgar and Throwley.

Tipperary County Tipperary, with centres at Cahin, Cashal, Clonmel and Fethard.

Tiverton Devon and a small area of Somerset, extending fourteen miles from north to south and thirty miles from east to west, with centres at Bampton, Tiverton and Witheridge.

Tivyside North Pembrokeshire and south Cardiganshire, with centres at Cardigan, Newcastle-Emlyn and Newport.

Torrington Farmers' East of the River Torridge, with centres at Horwood, Roborough and Torrington.

Towy and Cothi North Carmarthenshire, from Rhandirmyn in the north to Llangadog in the south, with centres at Llandovery, Cilycwm and Llangadog.

Tredegar Farmers' From Gellygaer in the north to the Bristol Channel in the south, and from Newport and Cardiff in the east to Pentyrch in the west.

Tynedale Northumberland, with centres at Corbridge, Hexham and Stamfordham.

Ullswater Westmorland and Cumberland, with centres at Patterdale and Penrith.

United Hunt Club North and east County Cork, with centres at Cork, Fermoy and Midleton.

United Pack Montgomeryshire and Shropshire, with the centre at Bishop's Castle.

Vale of Aylesbury Bedfordshire, Buckinghamshire, Hertfordshire and Oxfordshire, with centres at Aylesbury and Thame.

Vale of Clettr North and west Carmarthenshire and south Cardiganshire, with centres at Llanbyther, Pentrecourt and Talgarreg.

Vine and Craven Mainly in north Hampshire and a part of Berkshire, with centres at Hungerford, Kingsclere and Newbury.

V.W.H. Gloucestershire, Oxfordshire and Wiltshire, with centres at Cirencester, Cricklade, Fairford, Lechlade and Malmesbury.

Warwickshire Warwickshire, Gloucestershire, Oxfordshire and Worcestershire, with centres at Banbury, Kineton and Shipston-on-Stour.

Waterford Between the coast in the south, the River Suir in the north and the Comeragh Mountains in the west.

West Dulverton North Devon and west Somerset, with centres at Dulverton, Exmoor, Barnstaple and Ilfracombe.

Western West Cornwall, with centres at Penzance and St Ives.

West Kent About seventeen square miles, with centres at Sevenoaks and Tonbridge.

Westmeath Westmeath County, with the centre at Mullingar.

West Norfolk Norfolk, with centres at Dereham, Fakenham and Swaffham.

West of Yore From west of the River Yore to Coverdale in the north and to the River Nidd in the south, with centres at Masham and Ripon.

West Percy Northumberland; mainly hilly, but includes the Whittingham Vale, with centres at Alnwick, Rothbury and Whittingham.

West Shropshire West Shropshire, stretching from Chirk in the north to the River Wyrnwy in the south and from the A5 road in the east to the Shropshire county boundary in the west.

West Somerset Somerset from the Quantock Hills to the Dunster-Wheddon crossroad and from Wiveliscombe to Bridgetown, with centres at Williton, Dunster and Wiveliscombe.

West Somerset Vale The vale between Perry Goyle and Bridgwater, with centres at Cannington, Halford and Nether Stowey.

West Street Kent, with centres at Dover and Sandwich.

West Warwickshire Farmers' From Norton Lindsay westward to the Worcestershire border near Alcester, and then north to the Beoley Vale and east to Earlswood and Shirley, with centres at Stratford-on-Avon and Alcester.

West Waterford The west of County Waterford, with centres at Cappoquin, Lismore and Youghal.

Wexford County Wexford: an area about thirty square miles, bounded by the sea to the south and east, the Island Hunt to the north and the Kilkenny Hunt to the west.

Whaddon Chase Buckinghamshire, with centres at Aylesbury, Bletchley, Leighton Buzzard and Winslow.

Wheatland South Shropshire, with centres at Bridgnorth, Morville and Much Wenlock.

Wicklow The south of County Wicklow and north of County Wexford, with centres at Arklow and Gorey.

Wilton From south of Salisbury to the north Dorset border, with centres at Fordingbridge, Nunton, Salisbury and Verwood.

Woodland Pytchley Northamptonshire, with centres at Kettering, Oundle and Thrapston.

Worcestershire The central part of Worcestershire, from Hereford to the Warwickshire border, with centres at Bromsgrove, Droitwich and Worcester.

Ynysfor South Caernarvonshire and north Merionethshire, with centres at Maentwrog and Portmadoc. (Hunting is on foot.)

Ystrad Both sides of the Aberdare and Rhonnda Valleys.

Zetland South Durham and north Yorkshire, with centres at Barnard Castle, Darlington and Richmond.

HARRIERS

Packs of harriers in the British Isles, with the country they hunt.

Aldenham Hertfordshire, Buckinghamshire and Bedfordshire; mainly in the Vale of Aylesbury Hunt country.

Axe Vale Within an area bounded by Sidmouth, Honiton, Axminster and Lyme Regis, with centres at Axminster, Colyton and Seaton.

Bolventor Within a radius of seven miles of Bolventor in Cornwall.

Bray The north of County Wicklow and the south of County Dublin, with centres at Ashford and Rathnew.

Cambridgeshire Around Cambridge, which is the centre.

Cotley South of the Crewkerne—Honiton road, running north of the Honiton—Axminster railway line to the sea at Charmouth, with centres at Chard and Axminster.

County Clare Around Newmarket-on-Fergus, Quin and Tulla.

County Dublin South South Dublin, Kildare and Wicklow, with centres at Blackchurch, Brittas, Blessington, Kildare and Newcastle.

County Longford An area about twenty miles by eighteen miles, bounded by Counties Cavan, Westmeath and Roscommon.

County Sligo The whole of County Sligo and part of County Roscommon, near Boyle, with centres at Ballisedare, Ballymore and Sligo.

Dart Vale and Haldon The greater part of south Devon from the Dart Valley to the River Exe, with centres at Bishopsteignton, Newton Abbot, Torquay and Totnes.

Derrygallon West Duhallow and north Cork, with centres at Banteer, Kanturk and Newmarket.

Dungarvan From east of Cappoquin Bridge to Youghal Bridge, and in the Waterford Hunt country as far as Clonea Castle and the Pike, with centres at Colligan and Mill Street.

Dunston South Norfolk, with centres at Attleborough, Long Stratton and Wymondham.

East Antrim Between Belfast, Antrim and Larne, with centres at Belfast and Ballyclare.

Easton East Suffolk (about twenty-five square miles), with centres at Framlingham, Wickham Market and Woodbridge.

Edmonstone South of Edinburgh, Dalkeith and East Lothian, with centres at Edinburgh and Dalkeith. (The only pack of harriers in Scotland.)

Eryri Caernarvonshire and Anglesey, with centres at Beddgelert and Betws-y-Coed.

Fermanagh The whole of County Fermanagh and adjoining parts of Counties Monaghan, Tyrone and Donegal, with centres at Enniskillen, Clones and Irvinestown.

Fingal North County Dublin and east County Meath, with centres at Dublin and Malahide.

High Peak Around Bakewell and Buxton in Derbyshire.

Holcombe Central Lancashire, south of the River Ribble and north of a line through Rochdale, Bury, Bolton, Wigan and Ormskirk, with centres at Bury, Bolton and Chorley.

Iveagh Mainly in Counties Down and Armagh, with centres at Banbridge, Dromore and Lurgan.

Killinick The south-east of County Wexford, with centres at Ballycogley, Bridgetown and Killinick.

Kilmoganny North of Carrick-on-Suir, extending to Fiddown and Waterford City. The boundary in the east runs from Fiddown to Ballyhale, and in the west from Kilshellan to Mullinahone, with centres at Carrick-on-Suir, Clonmel, Kilkenny and Waterford.

Limerick Within a twenty-mile radius of Limerick City, with centres at Crecora, Croom and Fedamore.

Mid-Antrim In mid-Antrim, with centres at Antrim, Ballymena and Randalstown.

Minehead West Somerset, with centres at Dunster, Minehead, Porlock and Wootton Courtenay.

Modbury South Devon, with centres at Modbury and Ivybridge.

Naas County Kildare and part of West Wicklow and, by arrangement, part of County Carlow, with centres at Clare, Kilcullen, Kildare and Naas.

Newry South County Down and the south of County Armagh, with centres at Banbridge and Newry.

North Down The northern part of County Down, with centres at Ballygowan, Comber, Greyabbey, Newtownards and Saintfield.

North Mayo County Mayo, in a square bounded by Crossmolina, Ballinrobe, Clavemorris and Enniscrone, with centres at Ballina and Enniscrone.

North Norfolk North of a line from Bawdeswell in the west to Ludham in the east to the coast.

Old Rock, Killutagh and Chichester Lisburn and Antrim, east of Lough Neagh, with centres at Antrim, Crumlin and Dundrod.

Pendle Forest and Craven East Lancashire and the West Riding of Yorkshire, with centres at Gargrave, Gisburn and Skipton.

Rockwood The West Riding of Yorkshire, with centres at Huddersfield, Penistone and Wakefield.

Ross South Herefordshire, with centres at Harewood End and Ross-on-Wye.

Route The north of Counties Antrim and Londonderry, with the centre at Coleraine.

Sennowe Park Sennowe Park, consisting of some 7000 acres in Norfolk.

South Pool South Devon, with the centre at Kingsbridge.

South Tyrone East County Tyrone, north Monaghan and south Derry, with centres at Cookstown and Dungannon.

Tara Central and northern County Meath, with centres at Enfield, Kells, Kilmessan, Navan and Trim.

Taunton Vale Devon and Somerset, with the centre at Wellington.

Tynan and Armagh Within an eight-mile radius of Tynan, with the centre at Killylea.

Vale of Lune On the borders of Lancashire, Westmorland and Yorkshire, with centres at Hornby, Kirkby Lonsdale and Lancaster.

Waveney Norfolk and Suffolk, covering an area of thirty miles by sixteen miles, with centres at Halesworth and Bungay.

Welbeck To the west of the A614 road, from the border of the South Nottinghamshire Foxhounds in the south to the Worksop–Retford railway line in the north.

Wensleydale The watershed of the River Ure above Aysgarth, with centres at Askrigg, Aysgarth, Bainbridge and Hawes.

Weston and Banwell Somerset, with centres at Brent Knoll, Kewstoke and Loxton.

Windermere Most of Westmorland and parts of Cumberland, with centres at Ambleside, Kendal, Keswick and Windermere.

STAGHOUNDS

Packs of staghounds in England and Ireland, with the country they hunt.

County Down County Down, with centres at Ballynahinch, Dromore and Banbridge.

Devon and Somerset West Somerset and north Devon, with centres at Dulverton, Exford, North Molton, Porlock and Withypool.

New Forest Buckhounds The New Forest in Hampshire, with centres at Brockenhurst, Burley, Lyndhurst and Stoney Cross.

Quantock The Quantock Hills in Somerset, with centres at Bridgwater, Taunton and Williton.

Tiverton The Chumleigh and Stoodleigh districts of Somerset.

Ward Union The north of County Dublin and the south of County Meath, with the centre at Dublin.

Packs of Foxhounds in the United States

Alabama
Mooreland Hunt

Arizona
Grass Ridge Hounds

California
Los Altos Hunt
Santa Fe Hunt
West Hills Hunt

Colorado
Arapahoe Hunt
Roaring Fork Hounds

Connecticut
Fairfield County Hounds
Mr Haight, Jnr's Litchfield County
Middlebury Hunt

Delaware
Foxcatcher Hounds
Vicmead Hunt

Florida
Two Rivers Hunt

Georgia
Belle Meade Hunt
Midland Fox Hounds
Shakerag Hounds
Tri-County Hounds

Illinois
Fox River Valley Hunt
Mill Creek Hunt
Oak Brook Hounds
Old Stonington Hounds
Southern Illinois Open Hunt
Wayne DuPage Hunt
Wolf Creek Hounds

Indiana
Hound and Horn Hunt
New Britton Hunt
Traders Point Hunt
Romwell Fox Hounds

Kansas
Fort Leavenworth Hunt
Mission Valley Hunt

Kentucky
Iroquois Hunt
Licking River Hounds
Long Run Hounds

Maryland
Antietam Hunt
De La Brooke Foxhounds W
Elkridge-Harford Hunt
New Market Hounds
Goshen Hunt
Green Spring Valley Hounds
Howard County Hunt
Mr Hubbard's Kent County Hounds
Marlborough Hunt
Middletown Valley Hunt
Potomac Hunt
Wicomico Hunt
Wye River Hounds

Massachusetts
Myopia Hunt
Nashoba Valley Hunt
Norfolk Hunt
Old North Bridge Hounds

Michigan
Battle Creek Hunt
Metamora Hunt
Waterloo Hunt

Minnesota
Long Lake Hounds

Mississippi
Austin Hunt

Missouri
Bridlespur Hunt

Nebraska
North Hills Hunt

New Jersey
Amwell Valley Hounds
Essex Fox Hounds
Monmouth County Hunt
Spring Valley Hounds

New Mexico
Juan Tomás Hounds

New York
Genesee Valley Hunt
Golden's Bridge Hounds
Hopper Hills Hunt
Limestone Creek Hunt
Millbrook Hunt
Old Chatham Hunt
Rombout Hunt
Smithtown Hunt
Windy Hollow Hunt

North Carolina
Mecklenburg Hounds
Moore County Hounds
Sedgefield Hunt
Triangle Hunt
Tryon Hounds

Ohio
Camargo Hunt
Chagrin Valley Hunt
Lauray Hunt
Miami Valley Hunt
Rocky Fork-Headley Hunt

Oklahoma
Lost Hound Hunt

Pennsylvania
Beaufort Hunt
Brandywine Hounds
Chestnut Ridge Hunt
Dutch Fork Hunt
Harts Run Hunt
Huntingdon Valley Hunt
Mr Jeffords' Andrews Bridge Hounds
Limekiln Hunt
Pickering Hunt
Radnor Hunt
Rolling Rock-Westmoreland Hunt
Rose Tree Fox Hunting Club
Sewickley Hunt
Mr Stewart's Cheshire Foxhounds

Rhode Island
Bradbury Fox Hounds

South Carolina
Aiken Hounds
Camden Hunt
Greenville County Hounds
Woodside Hounds

Tennessee
Cedar Knob Foxhounds
Hillsboro Hounds
Longreen Fox Hounds
Mells Fox Hounds
Oak Grove Hunt

Texas
Hickory Creek Hunt

Vermont
Green Mountain Hounds
Windsor County Hounds

Virginia
Bedford County Hunt
Blue Ridge Hunt
Bull Run Hunt
Casanova Hunt
Deep Run Hunt
Fairfax Hunt
Farmington Hunt
Glenmore Hunt
Keswick Hunt
Loudon Hunt
Middleburg Hunt
Montpelier Hunt
Old Dominion Hounds
Orange County Hunt
Piedmont Fox Hounds
Princess Anne Hunt
Rapidan Hunt (inactive)
Rappahannock Hunt
Rockbridge Hunt
Warrenton Hunt

Washington
Woodbrook Hunt

Show-Jumping and Three-Day Event Results

European Championships

European Junior Show Jumping Championships

1952 Ostend	1. Italy 2. Belgium	
1953 Rome	1. France 2. Italy 3. Belgium	
1954 Rotterdam	1. Italy 2. West Germany 3. Netherlands	
1955 Bilbao	1. West Germany 2. Netherlands 3. Spain	
1956 Spa	1. Great Britain 2. France 3. West Germany	
1957 London	1. Great Britain 2. Italy 3. France	
1958 Hanover	1. Great Britain 2. South Africa 3. Italy	
1959 London	1. Great Britain 2. West Germany 3. France	
1960 Venice	1. Great Britain 2. Poland 3. Italy	**Jane Kidd** Manka **Douglas Coakes** Catriona **Michael Cresswell** Mackeson **Elizabeth Broome** Gay Monty
1961 Hickstead	1. West Germany 2. Netherlands 3. Great Britain	**H. von Zychlinski** Drossel **R. Bucholz** Chica **H. von Opel** Cari **B. Bagusat** Listo
1962 Berlin	1. Great Britain 2. West Germany 3. France	**John Kidd** Copper Castle **Vivien Oliver** Red Mint **Marion Coakes** Stroller **Michael Kane** Lough Foyle
1963 Rotterdam	1. Great Britain 2. West Germany 3. France	**Jackie Doney** Glenshelane **Andrew Fielder** Vibart **William Barker** North Flight **Marion Coakes** Spring Shandy
1964 Budapest	1. Italy 2. Great Britain 3. Belgium	**R. Castagua** It's a Pleasure **G. Ulrich** Shillelagh **G. Binetti** Quaso di Ghilarza **P. Baccaglini** Vallombrosa
1965 Salice Terme (Milan)	1. Great Britain	**Lynne Raper** Keewis **Sarah Roger-Smith** Foxtrot **Ann Moore** Kangaroo **John Baillie** Dominic IV
	2. Italy 3. West Germany	
1966 Copenhagen	1. Italy 2. Belgium 3. Switzerland	**F. Ricciotti** Snowflake **M. Fillippucci** Carabella **A. Bacigalupe** Magical Boy **G. Castellini** Kings Coin
1967 Jessolo	1. Great Britain 2. France 3. West Germany	**John Reid** Dunbell **Mallowry Spens** Meridian **Gay Traherne** Black Fury **Ann Moore** Hop-a-Long Cassidy

1968
Stoneleigh
	1. Great Britain
	
	2. France
	3. Denmark,
	   Ireland,
	   West Germany
		Ann Moore Psalm
		Michael Docherty
		  Government Grant
		Michael Hall-Hall Pablo
		Gay Traherne Black Fury

1969 Dinard	1. Switzerland 2. France 3. West Germany	**B. Nater** Lanceur **Jurg Notz** Sherrif **R. Beat** Donauschwalbe **C. Grandjean** Grandios
1970 St Moritz	1. Great Britain 2. Switzerland 3. West Germany	**John Francome** Red Paul **Ann Coleman** Havana Royal **Fiona Wilson-Kay** Lonely Boy II **Michael Hall-Hall** Washington
1971 Hickstead	1. Ireland 2. West Germany 3. Switzerland	**Kevin Barry** Costo **Charlie Curtis** Feltrim **Paul Darragh** Woodpecker **Marilyn Dawson** Clare Cottage
1972 Cork	1. Belgium 2. Netherlands 3. Ireland	**Eva van Paesschen** Hunt- master **Ferdi Tyteca** Mitsouko **Patrick Ronge** White City **Alain Storme** Condylus
1973 Hoogboom	1. Switzerland 2. France 3. West Germany	**Dieter Frauenfelder** Saltarin **Dieter Hauser** Iron Flock **Marcus Fuchs** Lady Seven **Thomas Fuchs** Royal Can

European Junior Three-Day Event Championships

	Individual Competition			Team Competition
1967 Eridge	1. Alain Sonchon	Roi d'Asturie	France	(no team finished)
	2. Richard Walker	Pasha	Great Britain	
	3. Philippe Girand	Saphir d'Eau	France	
1968 Craon	1. Richard Walker	Pasha	Great Britain	1. France
	2. Philippe Girand	Gallax	France	2. Great Britain
	3. A. Sarrant	Palestro	France	3. Poland
1969 Euskirchen	1. Hans Otto Bolten	Lausbub XIII	West Germany	1. USSR
	2. Vladimir Tichkin	Elion	USSR	2. France
	3. Aly Pattinson	Sharon	Great Britain	3. West Germany
1970 Holstebro	1. Nils-Olav Barkander	Pegasus	Sweden	1. West Germany
	2. Albrecht Fenner	Anemone V	West Germany	2. France
	3. Burkhard Wahler	Marcus IV	West Germany	3. Great Britain
1971 Wesel	1. Christopher Brooke	Olive Oyl	Great Britain	1. Great Britain
	2. François Lault	Un de la Cote	France	2. France
	3. Fabio Giulani	Harvest Moon	Italy	3. Italy
1972 Eridge	1. Bernard Clément	Quel Pich	France	1. Great Britain
	2. Anthony Hill	Maid Marion	Great Britain	2. France
	3. G. Heyligers	Fullspeed	Netherlands	3. Netherlands
1973 Pompadour	1. Virginia Holgate	Dubonnet	Great Britain	1. Great Britain
	2. Sarah Bailey	Red Amber	Great Britain	2. Italy
	3. Alessandro Miserocchi	Friday	Italy	3. Ireland

European Three-Day Event Championships

	Individual Competition			Team Competition
1953 Badminton	1. Maj. A. Lawrence Rook	Starlight	Great Britain	1. Great Britain
	2. Maj. Frank W. C. Weldon	Kilbarry	Great Britain	2. —
	3. Capt. Hans Schwarzenbach	Vae Victis	Switzerland	3. —
1954 Basle	1. Albert E. Hill	Crispin	Great Britain	1. Great Britain
	2. Maj. Frank W. C. Weldon	Kilbarry	Great Britain	2. West Germany
	3. Maj. A. Lawrence Rook	Starlight	Great Britain	3. —
1955 Windsor	1. Maj. Frank W. C. Weldon	Kilbarry	Great Britain	1. Great Britain
	2. Lt Cmdr John Oram	Radar	Great Britain	2. Switzerland
	3. Albert E. Hill	Countryman III	Great Britain	3. —
1957 Copenhagen	1. Sheila Willcox	High and Mighty	Great Britain	1. Great Britain
	2. August Lütke-Westhues	Franko II	West Germany	2. West Germany
	3. J. Lindgren	Eldorado	Sweden	3. Sweden
1959 Harewood	1. Maj. Hans Schwarzenbach	Burn Trout	Switzerland	1. West Germany
	2. Lt Col. Frank W. C. Weldon	Samuel Johnson	Great Britain	2. Great Britain
	3. Maj. Derek Allhusen	Laurien	Great Britain	3. France
1962 Burghley	1. Capt. James R. Templar	M'Lord Connolly	Great Britain	1. USSR
	2. G. Gazumov	Granj	USSR	2. Ireland
	3. Jane Wykeham-Musgrave	Ryebrooks	Great Britain	3. Great Britain
1965 Moscow	1. M. Babirecki	Volt	Poland	1. USSR
	2. Lev Baklyshkin	Ruon	USSR	2. Ireland
	3. Horst Karsten	Condora	West Germany	3. Great Britain
1967 Punchestown	1. Maj. Eddie Boylan	Durlas Eile	Ireland	1. Great Britain
	2. Martin Whiteley	The Poacher	Great Britain	2. Ireland
	3. Maj. Derek Allhusen	Lochinvar	Great Britain	3. France
1969 Haras du Pin	1. Mary Gordon-Watson	Cornishman V	Great Britain	1. Great Britain
	2. Richard Walker	Pasha	Great Britain	2. USSR
	3. Bernd Messman	Windspiel	West Germany	3. West Germany
1971 Burghley	1. Princess Anne	Doublet	Great Britain	1. Great Britain
	2. Deborah West	Baccarat	Great Britain	2. USSR
	3. Stewart Stevens	Classic Chips	Great Britain	3. Ireland
1973 Kiev	1. Alex Evdokimov	Jeger	USSR	1. West Germany
	2. Herbert Blöcker	Albrandt	West Germany	2. USSR
	3. Horst Karsten	Sioux	West Germany	3. Great Britain

Ladies' European Show Jumping Championship

Year / Place		Rider	Horse	Country
1957 Spa	1.	Pat Smythe	Flanagan	Great Britain
	2.	Giulia Serventi	Doly	Italy
	3.	M. d'Orgeix	Ocean	France
1958 Palermo	1.	Giulia Serventi	Doly	Italy
	2.	Anna Clement	Nico	West Germany
	3.	Irene Jansen	Adelbloom	Netherlands
1959 Rotterdam	1.	Ann Townsend	Bandit IV	Great Britain
	2.	Pat Smythe	Flanagan	Great Britain
	3. {	Anna Clement	Nico	West Germany
		Giulia Serventi	Doly	Italy
1960 Copenhagen	1.	Susan Cohen	Clare Castle	Great Britain
	2.	Dawn Wofford	Hollandia	Great Britain
	3.	Anna Clement	Nico	West Germany
1961 Deauville	1.	Pat Smythe	Flanagan	Great Britain
	2.	Irene Jansen	Icare	Netherlands
	3.	Michèle Cancre	Ocean	France
1962 Madrid	1.	Pat Smythe	Flanagan	Great Britain
	2.	Helga Kohler	Fremond	West Germany
	3.	Paula de Goyoaga	Kif Kif	Spain
1963 Hickstead	1.	Pat Smythe	Flanagan	Great Britain
	2.	Arline Givaudan	Huipil	Brazil
	3.	Anneli Drummond-Hay	Merely-a-Monarch	Great Britain
1964	(no championship held)			
1965	(Ladies' World Championship)			
1966 Gijon	1.	Janou Lefèbvre	Kenavo	France
	2.	Monica Bachmann	Sandro	Switzerland
	3.	Lalla Novo	Oxo Bob	Italy
1967 Fontainebleau	1.	Kathy Kusner	Untouchable	USA
	2.	Lalla Novo	Predestine	Italy
	3.	Monica Bachmann	Erbach	Switzerland
1968 Rome	1.	Anneli Drummond-Hay	Merely-a-Monarch	Great Britain
	2.	Giulia Serventi	Gay Monarch	Italy
	3. {	Marion Coakes	Stroller	Great Britain
		Janou Lefèbvre	Rocket	France
1969 Dublin	1.	Iris Kellett	Morning Light	Ireland
	2.	Anneli Drummond-Hay	Xanthos	Great Britain
	3.	Alison Westwood	The Maverick	Great Britain
1970	(Ladies' World Championship)			
1971 St Gallen	1.	Ann Moore	Psalm	Great Britain
	2.	Alison Dawes	The Maverick	Great Britain
	3.	Monika Leitenberger	Umbarra de Porto Conte	Austria
1972	(no championship held)			
1973 Vienna	1.	Ann Moore	Psalm	Great Britain
	2.	Caroline Bradley		Great Britain
	3.	Monica Weier		Switzerland

Men's European Show Jumping Championship

Year / Place		Rider	Horse	Country
1957 Rotterdam	1.	Hans G. Winkler	Sonnenglanz	West Germany
	2.	Capt. Bernard de Fombelle	Bucéphale	France
	3.	Salvatore Oppes	Pagoro	Italy
1958 Aachen	1.	Fritz Thiedemann	Meteor	West Germany
	2.	Capt. Piero d'Inzeo	The Rock	Italy
	3.	Hans G. Winkler	Halla	West Germany
1959 Paris	1.	Capt. Piero d'Inzeo	Uruguay	Italy
	2.	Pierre Jonquères d'Oriola	Virtuoso	France
	3.	Fritz Thiedemann	Godewind	West Germany
1960	(no championship held)			
1961 Aachen	1.	David Broome	Sunsalve	Great Britain
	2.	Capt. Piero d'Inzeo	Pioneer	Italy
	3.	Hans G. Winkler	Romanus	West Germany
1962 London	1.	C. David Barker	Mister Softee	Great Britain
	2. {	Hans G. Winkler	Romanus	West Germany
		Capt. Piero d'Inzeo	The Rock	Italy
1963 Rome	1.	Graziano Mancinelli	Rockette	Italy
	2.	Alwin Schockemöhle	Freiherr	West Germany
	3.	Harvey Smith	O'Malley	Great Britain
1964	(no championship held)			
1965 Aachen	1.	Hermann Schridde	Dozent	West Germany
	2.	Alfonso Queipo de Llano	Infernal	Spain
	3.	Alwin Schockemöhle	Exakt	West Germany
1966 Lucerne	1.	Nelson Pessoa	Gran Geste	Brazil
	2.	Frank Chapot	San Lucas	USA
	3.	Dr Hugo M. Arrambide	Chimbote	Argentina
1967 Rotterdam	1.	David Broome	Mister Softee	Great Britain
	2.	Harvey Smith	Harvester	Great Britain
	3.	Alwin Schockemöhle	Donald Rex	West Germany
1968	(no championship held)			
1969 Hickstead	1.	David Broome	Mister Softee	Great Britain
	2.	Alwin Schockemöhle	Donald Rex	West Germany
	3.	Hans G. Winkler	Enigk	West Germany
1970	(no championship held)			
1971 Aachen	1.	Hartwig Steenken	Simona	West Germany
	2.	Harvey Smith	Evan Jones	Great Britain
	3.	Capt. Paul Weier	Wulf	Switzerland
1972	(no championship held)			
1973 Hickstead	1.	Paddy McMahon	Pennwood Forge Mill	Great Britain
	2.	Alwin Schockemöhle	The Robber	West Germany
	3.	Hugo Parot	Tic	France

World Championships

Ladies' World Show Jumping Championship

1965 Hickstead	1. Marion Coakes	Stroller	Great Britain
	2. Kathy Kusner	Untouch- able	USA
	3. Alison Westwood	The Maverick	Great Britain
1970 Copenhagen	1. Janou Lefèbvre	Rocket	France
	2. Marion Mould	Stroller	Great Britain
	3. Anneli Drummond-Hay	Merely-a- Monarch	Great Britain
1974 La Baule	1. Janou Tissot	Rocket	France
	2. Michèle McEvoy	Mr Muskie	USA
	3. Barbara Kerr	Magnor	Canada

Men's World Show Jumping Championship

1953 Paris	1. Francisco Goyoaga	Quorum	Spain
	2. Fritz Thiedemann	Diamant	West Germany
	3. Pierre Jonquères d'Oriola	Ali Baba	France
1954 Madrid	1. Hans G. Winkler	Halla	West Germany
	2. Pierre Jonquères d'Oriola	Arlequin	France
	3. Francisco Goyoaga	Quorum	Spain
1955 Aachen	1. Hans G. Winkler	Halla	West Germany
	2. Capt. Raimondo d'Inzeo	Nadir	Italy
	3. Maj. Ronald Dallas	Bones	Great Britain
1956 Aachen	1. Hans G. Winkler	Halla	West Germany
	2. Francisco Goyoaga	Fahnen- könig	Spain
	3. Fritz Thiedemann	Meteor	West Germany
1960 Venice	1. Capt. Raimondo d'Inzeo	Gowran Girl	Italy
	2. Carlos Delia	Huipil	Argentina
	3. David Broome	Sunsalve	Great Britain
1966 Buenos Aires	1. Pierre Jonquères d'Oriola	Pomone B	France
	2. Alvarez de Bohorques	Quizas	Spain
	3. Capt. Raimondo d'Inzeo	Bowjak	Italy
1970 La Baule	1. David Broome	Beethoven	Great Britain
	2. Graziano Mancinelli	Fidux	Italy
	3. Harvey Smith	Mattie Brown	Great Britain
1974 Hickstead	1. Hartwig Steenken	Simona	West Germany
	2. Eddie Macken	Pele	Ireland
	⌠Frank Chapot	Main Spring	USA
	⌡Hugo Simon	Lavendel	Austria

World Three-Day Event Championships

	Individual Competition			Team Competition	
1966 Burghley	1. Capt. Carlos Moratorio 2. Richard Meade 3. Virginia Freeman-Jackson	Chalan Barberry Sam Weller	Argentina Great Britain Ireland	1. Ireland 　Maj. Eddie A. Boylan 　Penny Moreton 　Virginia Freeman-Jackson 　Tommy Brennan 2. Argentina (all other teams 　eliminated)	Durlas Eile Loughlin Sam Weller Kilkenny
1970 Punchestown	1. Mary Gordon-Watson 2. Richard Meade 3. James Wofford	Cornishman V The Poacher Kilkenny	Great Britain Great Britain United States	1. Great Britain 　Mary Gordon-Watson 　Richard Meade 　Lt Mark Phillips 　Stewart Stevens 2. France (all other teams 　eliminated)	Cornishman V The Poacher Chicago III Benson
1974 Burghley	1. Bruce Davidson 2. Michael Plumb 3. Hugh Thomas	Irish Cap Good Mixture Playamar	United States United States Great Britain	1. United States 　Don Sachery 　Edward Emerson 　Bruce Davidson 　Michael Plumb 2. Great Britain 3. West Germany	Plain Sailing Victor Dakin Irish Cap Good Mixture

Major Show-Jumping Competitions in Great Britain

British Jumping Derby

1961	Seamus Hayes	Goodbye III	Ireland
1962	Pat Smythe	Flanagan	Great Britain
1963	Nelson Pessoa	Gran Geste	Brazil
1964	Seamus Hayes	Goodbye III	Ireland
1965	Nelson Pessoa	Gran Geste	Brazil
1966	David Broome	Mister Softee	Great Britain
1967	Marion Coakes	Stroller	Great Britain
1968	Alison Westwood	The Maverick VII	Great Britain
1969	Anneli Drummond-Hay	Xanthos	Great Britain
1970	Harvey Smith	Mattie Brown	Great Britain
1971	Harvey Smith	Mattie Brown	Great Britain
1972	Hendrik Snoek	Shirokko	West Germany
1973	Alison Dawes	Mr Banbury	Great Britain
1974	Harvey Smith	Salvador	Great Britain

John Player Trophy

1961	Pat Smythe	Scorchin	Great Britain
1962	Harvey Smith	O'Malley	Great Britain
1963	Capt. Raimondo d'Inzeo	Posillipo	Italy
1964	Mary Mairs	Tomboy	United States
1965	Harvey Smith	Harvester VI	Great Britain
1966	Harvey Smith	Harvester VI	Great Britain
1967	Harvey Smith	Harvester VI	Great Britain
1968	Marion Coakes	Stroller	Great Britain
1969	Alwin Schockemöhle	Donald Rex	West Germany
1970	Marion Mould	Stroller	Great Britain
1971	William C. Steinkraus	Fleet Apple	United States
1972	Harvey Smith	Summertime	Great Britain
1973	Harvey Smith	Salvador	Great Britain
1974	Rodney Jenkins	Number One Spy	United States

King George V Gold Cup

1935	Capt. J. J. Lewis	Tramore Bay	Ireland
1936	Cmdt J. G. O'Dwyer	Limerick Lace	Ireland
1937	Capt. X. Bizard	Honduras	France
1938	Maj. J. C. Friedberger	Derek	Great Britain
1939	Lt A. Beltoni	Adigrat	Italy
1940–6 (no show)			
1947	P. Jonquères d'Oriola	Marquis III	France
1948	Lt Col. H. M. Llewellyn	Foxhunter	Great Britain
1949	B. Butler	Tankard	Great Britain
1950	Lt Col. H. M. Llewellyn	Foxhunter	Great Britain
1951	Capt. K. Barry	Ballyneety	Ireland
1952	Don Carlos Figueroa	Gracieux	Spain
1953	Lt Col. H. M. Llewellyn	Foxhunter	Great Britain
1954	Fritz Thiedemann	Meteor	West Germany
1955	Lt Col. Cartesegna	Brando	Italy
1956	William C. Steinkraus	First Boy	United States
1957	Capt. Piero d'Inzeo	Uruguay	Italy
1958	H. Wiley	Master William	United States
1959	H. Wiley	Nautical	United States
1960	David Broome	Sunsalve	Great Britain
1961	Capt. Piero d'Inzeo	The Rock	Italy
1962	Capt. Piero d'Inzeo	The Rock	Italy
1963	Tommy Wade	Dundrum	Ireland
1964	William C. Steinkraus	Sinjon	United States
1965	Hans G. Winkler	Fortun	West Germany
1966	David Broome	Mister Softee	Great Britain
1967	Peter Robeson	Firecrest	Great Britain
1968	Hans G. Winkler	Enigk	West Germany
1969	Ted Edgar	Uncle Max	Great Britain
1970	Harvey Smith	Mattie Brown	Great Britain
1971	Gert Wiltfang	Askan	West Germany
1972	David Broome	Sportsman	Great Britain
1973	Paddy McMahon	Pennwood Forge Mill	Great Britain
1974	Frank Chapot	Main Spring	United States

Queen Elizabeth II Cup

1949	Iris Kellett	Rusty	Ireland
1950	Jill Palethorpe	Silver Cloud	Great Britain
1951	Iris Kellett	Rusty	Ireland
1952	Gill Rich	Quicksilver III	Great Britain
1953	Marie Delfosse	Fanny Rosa	Great Britain
1954	Josie Bonnaud	Charleston	France
1955	Dawn Palethorpe	Earlsrath Rambler	Great Britain
1956	Dawn Palethorpe	Earlsrath Rambler	Great Britain
1957	Elizabeth Anderson	Sunsalve	Great Britain
1958	Pat Smythe	Mr Pollard	Great Britain
1959	Anna Clement	Nico	West Germany
1960	Susan Cohen	Clare Castle	Great Britain
1961	Lady Sarah Fitzalan Howard	Oorskiet	Great Britain
1962	Judy Crago	Spring Fever	Great Britain
1963	Julie Nash	Trigger Hill	Great Britain
1964	Gillian Makin	Jubilant	Great Britain
1965	Marion Coakes	Stroller	Great Britain
1966	Althea Roger-Smith	Havana Royal	Great Britain
1967	Betty Jennaway	Grey Leg	Great Britain
1968	Mary Chapot	White Lightning	United States
1969	Alison Westwood	The Maverick VII	Great Britain
1970	Anneli Drummond-Hay	Merely-a-Monarch	Great Britain
1971	Marion Mould	Stroller	Great Britain
1972	Ann Moore	Psalm	Great Britain
1973	Alison Dawes	Mr Banbury	Great Britain
1973	Ann Moore	Psalm	Great Britain
1974	Jean Davenport	All Trumps	Great Britain

Major Three-Day Events in Great Britain

Badminton Horse Trials

1949	John Shedden	Golden Willow	Great Britain
1950	Capt. J. A. Collings	Remus	Great Britain
1951	Capt. H. Schwarzenbach	Vae Victis	Switzerland
1952	Capt. M. A. Q. Darley	Emily Little	Great Britain
1953	Maj. A. Lawrence Rook	Starlight	Great Britain
	European Championship		
1954	Margaret Hough	Bambi	Great Britain
1955	(European Championships held at Windsor)		
1956	Lt Col. Frank W. C. Weldon	Kilbarry	Great Britain
1957	Sheila Willcox	High and Mighty	Great Britain
1958	Sheila Willcox	High and Mighty	Great Britain
1959	Sheila Waddington (Willcox)	Airs and Graces	Great Britain
1960	William Roycroft	Our Solo	Australia
1961	Lawrence Morgan	Salad Days	Australia
1962	Anneli Drummond-Hay	Merely-a-Monarch	Great Britain
1963	(cancelled)		
1964	Capt. James R. Templar	M'Lord Connolly	Great Britain
1965	Maj. Eddie A. Boylan	Durlas Eile	Ireland
1966	(cancelled)		
1967	Celia Ross-Taylor	Jonathan	Great Britain
1968	Jane Bullen	Our Nobby	Great Britain
1969	Richard Walker	Pasha	Great Britain
1970	Richard Meade	The Poacher	Great Britain
1971	Lt Mark Phillips	Great Ovation	Great Britain
1972	Lt Mark Phillips	Great Ovation	Great Britain
1973	Lucinda Prior-Palmer	Be Fair	Great Britain
1974	Capt. Mark Phillips	Columbus	Great Britain

Burghley Horse Trials

1961	Anneli Drummond-Hay	Merely-a-Monarch	Great Britain
1962	Capt. James R. Templar	M'Lord Connolly	Great Britain
	European Championship		
1963	Capt. Harry Freeman-Jackson	St Finbarr	Ireland
1964	Richard Meade	Barberry	Great Britain
1965	Capt. Jeremy Beale	Victoria Bridge	Great Britain
1966	Capt. Carlos Moratorio	Chalan	Argentina
	World Championship		
1967	Lorna Sutherland	Popadom	Great Britain
1968	Sheila Willcox	Fair and Square	Great Britain
1969	Gillian Watson	Shaitan	Great Britain
1970	Judy Bradwell	Don Camillo	Great Britain
1971	Princess Anne	Doublet	Great Britain
	European Championship		
1972	Janet Hodgson	Larkspur	Great Britain
1973	Capt. Mark Phillips	Maid Marion	Great Britain
1974	Bruce Davidson	Irish Cap	United States
	World Championship		

Harewood Horse Trials

1953	Vivien Machin-Goodall	Neptune	Great Britain
1954	Penelope Molteno	Carmena	Great Britain
1955	Lt Col. Frank W. C. Weldon	Kilbarry	Great Britain
1956	Sheila Willcox	High and Mighty	Great Britain
1957	Ian Hume-Dudgeon	Charleville	Ireland
1958	Ottokar Pohlmann	Polarfuchs	West Germany
1959	Maj. Hans Schwarzenbach	Burn Trout	Switzerland
	European Championship		

Olympic Games

Dressage – Team

1912 Stockholm
Twenty-one riders took part representing eight nations: Belgium, Denmark, France, Germany, Norway, Russia, Sweden and the United States.
1. Sweden
2. Germany
3. France

1916
(no Olympic Games)

1920 Antwerp
Seventeen riders took part representing five nations: Belgium, France, Norway, Sweden and the United States.
1. Sweden
2. France
3. USA

1924 Paris
Twenty-four riders took part representing nine nations: Austria, Belgium, Bulgaria, Czechoslovakia, France, Netherlands, Sweden, Switzerland and Yugoslavia.
1. Sweden
2. France
3. Czechoslovakia

1928 Amsterdam
Thirty riders took part representing twelve nations: Austria, Belgium, Bulgaria, Czechoslovakia, Denmark, France, Germany, Japan, Netherlands, Norway, Sweden and Switzerland.
1. Germany
2. Sweden
3. Netherlands

1932 Los Angeles
Ten riders took part representing four nations: France, Mexico, Sweden and the United States.
1. France
2. Sweden
3. USA

1936 Berlin
Twenty-nine riders took part representing eleven nations: Austria, Czechoslovakia, Denmark, France, Germany, Hungary, Netherlands, Norway, Sweden, Switzerland and the United States.
1. Germany
2. France
3. Sweden

1940 and 1944
(no Olympic Games)

1948 London
Nineteen riders took part representing nine nations: Argentina, Austria, France, Mexico, Portugal, Spain, Sweden, Switzerland and the United States.
1. France
2. USA
3. Portugal

1952 Helsinki
Twenty-six riders took part representing ten nations: Chile, Denmark, France, Germany, Norway, Portugal, Sweden, Switzerland, the United States and the USSR.
1. Sweden
2. Switzerland
3. Germany

1956 Stockholm
Thirty-seven riders took part representing eighteen nations: Argentina, Austria, Bulgaria, Canada, Denmark, Finland, France, Germany, Great Britain, Netherlands, Norway, Portugal, Romania, Spain, Sweden, Switzerland, the United States and the USSR.

1. Sweden
2. Germany
3. Switzerland

1960
Rome

(no team event)

1964
Tokyo

Twenty-two riders took part representing nine nations: Argentina, Canada, Germany, Great Britain, Japan, Sweden, Switzerland, the United States and the USSR.
1. Germany
2. Switzerland
3. USSR

1968
Mexico

Twenty-six riders took part representing nine nations: Canada, Chile, East Germany, Great Britain, Mexico, Switzerland, the United States, the USSR and West Germany.
1. West Germany
2. USSR
3. Switzerland

1972
Munich

Thirty-three riders took part representing twelve nations: Brazil, Canada, Denmark, France, Great Britain, Japan, Netherlands, Sweden, Switzerland, the United States, the USSR and West Germany.
1. USSR
2. West Germany
3. Sweden

Show-Jumping — Team

1912
Stockholm

Thirty-four riders took part representing nine nations: Belgium, Chile, France, Germany, Great Britain, Norway, Russia, Sweden and the United States.

1. Sweden — **Count Casimir Lewenhaupt** Medusa
Count Hans von Rosen Lord Iron
Gustaf Kilman Gatan
F. Rosencrantz Drabant

2. France — **Lt d'Astafort** Amazone
Capt. Jean Cariou Mignon
F. Meyer Allons
Lt Seigneur Cocotte

3. Germany — **Sigismund Freyer** Ultimus
Count von Hohenau Pretty Girl
Lt Ernst Deloch Hubertus
Prinz Karl von Preussen Gibson Boy

1916
(no Olympic Games)

1920
Antwerp

Twenty-seven riders took part representing six nations: Belgium, France, Italy, Norway, Sweden and the United States.

1. Sweden — **Count Hans von Rosen** Poor Boy
Claes König Tresor
Daniel Norling Eros

2. Belgium — **Count d'Oultremont** Lord Kitchener
Lt Coumans Lisette
Baron de Gaiffier Miss

3. Italy — **Maj. Ettore Caffaratti** Trebecco
Giulio Cacciandra Cento
Maj. Alessandro Alvisi Neruccio

1924
Paris

Thirty-four riders took part representing eleven nations: Belgium, Czechoslovakia, France, Great

Britain, Italy, Poland, Portugal, Spain, Sweden, Switzerland and the United States.

1. Sweden — **Ake Thelming** Loke
Axel Stähle Cecil
Age Lindström Anvers

2. Switzerland — **Alphons Gemuseus** Lucette
Werner Stüber Girandole
Hans Bühler Boy

3. Portugal — **Borges d'Almeida** Reginald
Martins Souza Avro
Mouzinho d'Albuquerque Hetrago

1928
Amsterdam

Forty-six riders took part representing sixteen nations: Argentina, Belgium, Czechoslovakia, France, Germany, Hungary, Italy, Japan, Netherlands, Norway, Poland, Portugal, Spain, Sweden, Switzerland and the United States.

1. Spain — **Marqués de los Trujillos** Zalamero
J. N. Morenes Zapatoso
J. Garcia Fernandez Revistado

2. Poland — **G. Gzowski** My Lord
Kazimierz Szosland Alli
Michael Antoniewicz Readglet

3. Sweden — **Karl Hansen** Gerold
Carl Björnstjerna Kornett
Capt. Ernst Hallberg Loke

1932
Los Angeles

Eleven riders took part representing four nations: Japan, Mexico, Sweden, and the United States. Since no team finished the course, there were no team awards.

1936
Berlin

Fifty-four riders took part representing eighteen nations: Austria, Belgium, Czechoslovakia, France, Germany, Great Britain, Hungary, Italy, Japan, Netherlands, Norway, Poland, Portugal, Romania, Sweden, Switzerland, Turkey and the United States.

1. Germany — **Lt Kurt Hasse** Tora
Marten von Barnekow Nordland
Heinz Brandt Alchimist

2. Netherlands — **Johan Greter** Ernica
Jan de Bruine Trixie
Henri van Schaik Santa Bell

3. Portugal — **José Beltrano** Biscuit
Marqués de Funchal Merle Blanc
Luis Mena De Silva Fossette II

1940 and 1944   (no Olympic Games)

1948
London

Forty-four riders took part representing fifteen nations: Argentina, Brazil, Denmark, Finland, France, Great Britain, Ireland, Italy, Mexico, Netherlands, Portugal, Spain, Sweden, Turkey and the United States.

1. Mexico — **Col. Humberto Mariles Cortes** Arete
A. Valdes Chihucho
Lt Ruben Uriza Hatvey

2. Spain — **J. Garcia Cruz** Bizarro
J. N. Morenes Quorum
G. J. Ponce de Leon Farajido

3. Great Britain — **Lt Col. Harry M. Llewellyn** Foxhunter
Maj. Henry M. V. Nicoll Kilgeddin
Maj. Arthur Carr Monty

1952 Helsinki	Fifty-two riders took part representing twenty nations: Argentina, Brazil, Chile, Egypt, Finland, France, Germany, Great Britain, Italy, Japan, South Korea, Mexico, Norway, Portugal, Romania, Spain, Sweden, Switzerland, the United States and the USSR.	
	1. Great Britain	Wilfred H. White Nizefela Lt Col. Harry M. Llewellyn Foxhunter Lt Col. Douglas N. Stewart Atherlow
	2. Chile	Ricardo Echeverria Lindo Pearl Oscar Cristi Bambi Cesar Mendoza Pillan
	3. USA	Arthur McCashin Miss Budweiser John Russell Democrat William C. Steinkraus Hollandia

1956 Stockholm	Seventy riders took part representing twenty-five nations: Argentina, Austria, Australia, Belgium, Brazil, Cambodia, Finland, France, Germany, Great Britain, Hungary, Ireland, Italy, Japan, Norway, Portugal, Romania, Spain, Switzerland, Turkey, the United Arab Republic, the United States, the USSR and Venezuela.	
	1. Germany	Hans G. Winkler Halla Fritz Thiedemann Meteor August Lütke-Westhues Ala
	2. Italy	Lt Raimondo d'Inzeo Merano Capt. Piero d'Inzeo Uruguay Salvatore Oppes Pagoro
	3. Great Britain	Wilfred H. White Nizefela Patricia Smythe Flanagan Peter Robeson Scorchin

1960 Rome	Fifty-four riders took part representing eighteen nations: Argentina, Brazil, France, Germany, Great Britain, Hungary, Ireland, Italy, Japan, Portugal, Romania, Spain, Sweden, Turkey, the United Arab Republic, the United States, Uruguay and the USSR.	
	1. Germany	Alwin Schockemöhle Ferdl Fritz Thiedemann Meteor Hans G. Winkler Halla
	2. USA	George Morris Sinjon Frank Chapot Trail Guide William C. Steinkraus Ksar d'Esprit
	3. Italy	Antonio Oppes The Scholar Capt. Piero d'Inzeo The Rock Capt. Raimondo d'Inzeo Merano

1964 Tokyo	Forty-six riders took part representing seventeen nations: Argentina, Australia, Brazil, Chile, France, Germany, Great Britain, Italy, Japan, Mexico, New Zealand, Portugal, South Korea, Spain, Switzerland, the United States and the USSR.	
	1. Germany	Hermann Schridde Dozent Hans G. Winkler Fidelitas Kurt Jarasinski Torro
	2. France	Pierre Jonquères d'Oriola Lutteur B Janou Lefèbvre Kenavo B Capt. Guy Lefrant Monsieur de Littry
	3. Italy	Capt. Piero d'Inzeo Sunbeam Capt. Raimondo d'Inzeo

Posillipo
Graziano Mancinelli Rockette

1968 Mexico	Forty-two riders took part representing fifteen nations: Argentina, Australia, Bolivia, Brazil, Canada, France, Great Britain, Italy, Japan, Mexico, Poland, Switzerland, the United States, the USSR and West Germany.	
	1. Canada	Thomas Gayford Big Dee James Day Canadian Club James Elder The Immigrant
	2. France	Marcel Rozier Quo Vadis Janou Lefèbvre Rocket Pierre Jonquères d'Oriola Nagir
	3. West Germany	Hermann Schridde Dozent Alwin Schockemöhle Donald Rex Hans G. Winkler Enigk

1972 Munich	Sixty-eight riders took part representing seventeen nations: Argentina, Belgium, Canada, Chile, France, Great Britain, Hungary, Italy, Japan, Mexico, Poland, Portugal, Spain, Switzerland, the United States, the USSR and West Germany.	
	1. West Germany	Fritz Ligges Robin Gerd Wiltfang Askan Hartwig Steenken Simona Hans G. Winkler Torphy
	2. USA	William C. Steinkraus Main Spring Neal Shapiro Sloopy Kathryn Kusner Fleet Apple Frank Chapot White Lightning
	3. Italy	Vittorio Orlandi Fulmer Feather Duster Capt. Raimondo d'Inzeo Fiorello II Graziano Mancinelli Ambassador Col. Piero d'Inzeo Easter Light

Three-Day Event – Team

1912 Stockholm	Twenty-seven riders from Belgium, Denmark, France, Germany, Great Britain, Sweden and the United States competed.	
	1. Sweden	Capt. Nils Aldercreutsz Atout Lt Axel Nordlander Lady Artist Lt E. G. Casparsson Irmelin Count Horn of Ammine Omen
	2. Germany	Lt von Rochow Idealist Lt von Lütcken Blue Boy Count Rudolf von Schaesberg-Thannheim Grundsee Lt von Moers May Queen
	3. USA	Lt Benjamin Lear Poppy Lt John C. Montgomery Deceive II Capt. Guy V. Henry Chiswell Lt Ephraim F. Graham Connie

1916	(no Olympic Games)

1920 Antwerp	Twenty-five riders from Belgium, Finland, France, Italy, the Netherlands, Norway, Sweden and the United States competed. The competition was entirely different from any other Olympic Games, in that the Dressage Test was eliminated and there were two long-distance rides – one of

15 kilometres with eighteen obstacles and the second of 20 kilometres — followed by a 4000-metre steeplechase and a show-jumping test.

1. Sweden — **Count Helmer Mörner** Germania
Lt Age Lundström Yrsa
Georg von Braun Diana

2. Italy — **Maj. Ettore Caffaratti** Traditore
Garibaldi Spighi Othello
Giuseppe Cacciandra Faceto

3. Belgium — **Roger Moeremans d'Emans** Sweet Girl
Lt Lints Martha
J. Bonvalet Wippelgem

1924 Paris
Forty-four riders from Belgium, Bulgaria, Czechoslovakia, Denmark, Finland, France, Great Britain, Italy, the Netherlands, Poland, Sweden, Switzerland and the United States competed.

1. Netherlands — **Lt Adolph van der Voort van Zijp** Silver Piece
Lt Ferdinand Pahud de Mortanges Johnnie Walker
Gerard P. de Kruyff Addis

2. Sweden — **G. von König** Bojan
L. Sylvan Anita
O. W. Hagelin Varius

3. Italy — **Alberto Lombardi** Pimplo
Alessandro Alvisi Capiligo
Emanuele di Pralormo Mount Felix

1928 Amsterdam
Forty-six riders from Belgium, Bulgaria, Czechoslovakia, Denmark, Finland, France, Germany, Hungary, Italy, Japan, the Netherlands, Norway, Poland, Spain, Sweden, Switzerland and the United States competed.

1. Netherlands — **Lt Ferdinand Pahud de Mortanges** Marcroix
Gerard P. de Kruyff Va-t'En
Lt Adolph van der Voort van Zijp Silver Piece

2. Norway — **Arthur Qurst** Hidalgo
Bjart Ording Andover
Eugen Johansen Baby

3. Poland — **Josef Trenkwald** Lwi Pazur
Michael Antoniewicz Moja Mila
Baron C. von Rómmel Donzef

1932 Los Angeles
Thirteen riders from Japan, Mexico, the Netherlands, Sweden and the United States competed.

1. USA — **Lt Earl F. Thomson** Jenny Camp
Harry D. Chamberlin Pleasant Smiles
Edwin Y. Argo Honolulu Tomboy

2. Netherlands — **Lt Ferdinand Pahud de Mortanges** Marcroix
Karel J. Schummelketel Duneltje
Aernout van Lennep Henk

(no other team finished)

1936 Berlin
Fifty riders from Austria, Bulgaria, Czechoslovakia, Denmark, Finland, France, Germany, Great Britain, Hungary, Italy, Japan, the Netherlands, Norway, Poland, Romania, Sweden, Switzerland, Turkey and the United States competed.

1. Germany — **Capt. Ludwig Stubbendorff** Nurmi
Rudolf Lippert Fasan
Konrad F. von Wangenheim Kurfurst

2. Poland — **Henryk Rojcewicz** Arlekin III
Zdislaw Kawecki Bambino
Severyn Kulesza Toska

3. Great Britain — **Capt. A. Scott** Bob Clive
Lt. E. Howard-Vyse Blue Steel
Capt. R. Fanshawe Bowie Knife

1940 and 1944 (no Olympic Games)

1948 London
Forty-six riders from Argentina, Austria, Brazil, Denmark, Finland, France, Great Britain, Italy, Mexico, the Netherlands, Portugal, Spain, Sweden, Switzerland, Turkey and the United States competed.

1. USA — **Lt Col. Frank S. Henry** Swing Low
Charles H. Anderson Reno Palisade
Lt Earl F. Thomson Reno Rhythm

2. Sweden — **Capt. J. Robert Selfelt** Claque
Sigurd Svensson Dust
Nils O. Stahre Komet

3. Mexico — **Humberto Mariles Cortes** Parral
Raul Campero Tatahumara
Joaquín Solano Malinche

1952 Helsinki
Fifty-nine riders from Argentina, Brazil, Bulgaria, Canada, Chile, Denmark, Finland, France, Germany, Great Britain, Ireland, Italy, Mexico, the Netherlands, Portugal, Romania, Spain, Sweden, Switzerland, the United States and the USSR competed.

1. Sweden — **Capt. Hans G. von Blixen-Finecke** Jubal
Nils O. Stahre Komet
Karl Frölen Fair

2. Germany — **Wilhelm Büsing** Hubertus
Klaus Wagner Dachs
Otto Rothe Trux von Kamax

3. USA — **Charles Hough** Cassivellaunus
Walter Staley Graigwood Park
John Wofford Benny Grimes

1956 Stockholm
Fifty-seven riders from Argentina, Australia, Bulgaria, Canada, Denmark, Finland, France, Germany, Great Britain, Ireland, Italy, Portugal, Romania, Spain, Sweden, Switzerland, Turkey, the United States and the USSR competed.

1. Great Britain — **Lt Col. Frank W. C. Weldon** Kilbarry
Maj. A. Lawrence Rook Wild Venture
Albert E. Hill Countryman III

2. Germany — **August Lütke-Westhues** Trux von Kamax
Klaus Wagner Prinzess
Otto Rothe Sissi

3. Canada — **John Rumble** Cilroy
James Elder Colleen
Brian Herbinson Tara

1960 Rome	Seventy-three riders from Argentina, Australia, Bulgaria, Canada, Czechoslovakia, Denmark, France, Germany, Great Britain, Ireland, Italy, Poland, Portugal, Romania, Spain, Sweden, Switzerland, the United States and the USSR competed.		
	1. Australia	**Lawrence Morgan** Salad Days **Neale Lavis** Mirrabooka **William Roycroft** Our Solo	
	2. Switzerland	**Anton S. Bühler** Gay Spark **Capt. Hans Schwarzenbach** Burn Trout **Rudolf Gunthardt** Atbara	
	3. France	**Jack le Goff** Image **Capt. Guy Lefrant** Nicias **Jean le Roy** Garden	

1964 Tokyo	Forty-eight riders from Argentina, Australia, France, Germany, Great Britain, Ireland, Italy, Japan, Korea, Mexico, the United States and the USSR competed.		
	1. Italy	**Mauro Checcoli** Surbean **Paolo Angioni** King **Giuseppe Ravano** Royal Love	
	2. USA	**Michael Page** Grasshopper **Kevin Freeman** Gallopade **Michael Plumb** Bold Minstrel	
	3. Germany	**Fritz Ligges** Donkosak **Horst Karsten** Condora **Lt Gerhard Schultz** Balza X	

1968 Mexico	Forty-nine riders from Argentina, Australia, Canada, East Germany, France, Great Britain, Ireland, Italy, Mexico, the United States, the USSR and West Germany competed.		
	1. Great Britain	**Maj. Derek Allhusen** Lochinvar **Richard Meade** Cornishman V **Sgt Ben Jones** The Poacher **Jane Bullen** Our Nobby	
	2. USA	**James Wofford** Kilkenny **Michael Page** Foster **Michael Plumb** Plain Sailing **Kevin Freeman** Chalan	
	3. Australia	**Brian Cobcroft** Depeche **Wayne Roycroft** Zhivago **William Roycroft** Warrathoola **James Scanlon** The Furtive	

1972 Munich	Seventy-three riders from Argentina, Australia, Austria, Bulgaria, Canada, East Germany, France, Great Britain, Hungary, Ireland, Italy, Mexico, the Netherlands, Poland, Sweden, Switzerland, the United States, the USSR and West Germany competed.		
	1. Great Britain	**Richard Meade** Laurieston **Mary Gordon-Watson** Cornishman V **Bridget Parker** Cornish Gold **Lt Mark Phillips** Great Ovation	
	2. USA	**Kevin Freeman** Good Mixture **Bruce Davidson** Plain Sailing **James Wofford** Kilkenny **Michael Plumb** Free and Easy	
	3. West Germany	**Harry Klugmann** Christopher Robert **Ludwig Goessing** Chicago **Kurt Schultz** Pisco **Horst Karsten** Sioux	

Dressage — Individual

1912 Stockholm	1. Sweden	**Count Carl Bonde** Emperor
	2. Sweden	**Maj. Gustav A. Boltenstern** Neptune
	3. Sweden	**Lt Hans von Blixen-Finecke** Maggie
1916	(no Olympic Games)	
1920 Antwerp	1. Sweden	**Capt. Janne Lundblad** Uno
	2. Sweden	**Lt Bertil Sandström** Sabel
	3. Sweden	**Count Hans von Rosen** Running Sister
1924 Paris	1. Sweden	**Gen. Ernst Linder** Piccolomini
	2. Sweden	**Lt Bertil Sandström** Sabel
	3. France	**Capt. François Lesage** Plunard
1928 Amsterdam	1. Germany	**Baron Carl F. von Langen** Draufgänger
	2. France	**Cmdt Charles L. P. Marion** Linon
	3. Sweden	**Ragnar Olson** Günstling
1932 Los Angeles	1. France	**Capt. François Lesage** Taine
	2. France	**Cmdt Charles L. P. Marion** Linon
	3. USA	**Hiram Tuttle** Olympic
1936 Berlin	1. Germany	**Lt Heinrich Pollay** Kronos
	2. Germany	**Maj. Friedrich Gerhard** Absinth
	3. Austria	**Maj. Alois Podhajsky** Nero
1940 and 1944	(no Olympic Games)	
1948 London	1. Switzerland	**Capt. Hans Moser** Hummer
	2. France	**Col. André Jousseaume** Harpagon
	3. Sweden	**Capt. Gustav A. Boltenstern** Trumf
1952 Helsinki	1. Switzerland	**Maj. Henri St Cyr** Master Rufus
	2. Denmark	**Lis Hartel** Jubilee
	3. France	**Col. André Jousseaume** Harpagon
1956 Stockholm	1. Switzerland	**Maj. Henri St Cyr** Juli XXX
	2. Denmark	**Lis Hartel** Jubilee
	3. Germany	**Liselott Linsenhoff** Adular
1960 Rome	1. USSR	**Sergei Filatov** Absent
	2. Switzerland	**Gustav Fischer** Wald
	3. West Germany	**Josef Neckermann** Asbach
1964 Tokyo	1. Switzerland	**Henri Chammartin** Wörmann
	2. West Germany	**Harry Boldt** Remus
	3. USSR	**Sergei Filatov** Absent
1968 Mexico	1. USSR	**Ivan Kizimov** Ikhor
	2. West Germany	**Josef Neckermann** Mariano
	3. West Germany	**Dr Reiner Klimke** Dux
1972 Munich	1. West Germany	**Liselott Linsenhoff** Piaff
	2. USSR	**Elena Petushkova** Pepel
	3. West Germany	**Josef Neckermann** Venezia

Show-Jumping – Individual

1912 Stockholm	1. France	Capt. Jean Cariou Mignon
	2. Germany	Lt von Kröcher Dohna
	3. Belgium	Baron Emanuel Blommaert de Soye Clonmore
1916	(no Olympic Games)	
1920 Antwerp	1. Italy	Lt Tommaso Lequio Trebecco
	2. Italy	Maj. Alessandro Valerio Cento
	3. Sweden	Capt. Gustaf Lewenhaupt Mon Coeur
1924 Paris	1. Switzerland	Lt Alphons Gemuseus Lucette
	2. Italy	Lt Tommaso Lequio Trebecco
	3. Poland	Lt Adam Królikiewicz Picador
1928 Amsterdam	1. Czechoslovakia	Capt. Frantisek Ventura Eliot
	2. France	Capt. M. L. M. Bertram de Balanda Papillon
	3. Switzerland	Maj. Chasimir Kuhn Pepita
1932 Los Angeles	1. Japan	Lt Takeichi Nishi Uranus
	2. USA	Maj. Harry Chamberlin Show Girl
	3. Sweden	Lt Clarence von Rosen Empire
1936 Berlin	1. Germany	Lt Kurt Hasse Tora
	2. Romania	Lt Henri Rang Delphis
	3. Hungary	Capt. József Platthy Selloe
1940 and 1944	(no Olympic Games)	
1948 London	1. Mexico	Col. Humberto Mariles Cortez Arete
	2. Mexico	Lt Ruben Uriza Hatvey
	3. France	Jean F. M. d'Orgeix Sucre de Pomme
1952 Helsinki	1. France	Pierre Jonquères d'Oriola Ali Baba
	2. Chile	Oscar Cristi Bambi
	3. Germany	Fritz Thiedemann Meteor
1956 Stockholm	1. Germany	Hans G. Winkler Halla
	2. Italy	Lt Raimondo d'Inzeo Merano
	3. Italy	Capt. Piero d'Inzeo Uruguay
1960 Rome	1. Italy	Capt. Raimondo d'Inzeo Posillipo
	2. Italy	Capt. Piero d'Inzeo The Rock
	3. Great Britain	David Broome Sunsalve
1964 Tokyo	1. France	Pierre Jonquères d'Oriola Lutteur B
	2. Germany	Hermann Schridde Dozent
	3. Great Britain	Peter Robeson Firecrest
1968 Mexico	1. USA	William C. Steinkraus Snowbound
	2. Great Britain	Marion Coakes Stroller
	3. Great Britain	David Broome Mister Softee
1972 Munich	1. Italy	Graziano Mancinelli Ambassador
	2. Great Britain	Ann Moore Psalm
	3. USA	Neal Shapiro Sloopy

Three-Day Event – Individual

1912 Stockholm	1. Sweden	Lt Axel Nordlander Lady Artist
	2. Germany	Lt von Rochow Idealist
	3. France	Capt. Jean Cariou Cocotte
1916	(no Olympic Games)	
1920 Antwerp	1. Sweden	Count Helmer Mörner Germania
	2. Sweden	Lt Age Lundström Yrsa
	3. Italy	Maj. Ettore Caffaratti Traditore
1924 Paris	1. Netherlands	Lt Adolph van der Voort van Zijp Silver Piece
	2. Denmark	Lt Fröde Kirkebjerg Metoo
	3. USA	Maj. Sloan Doak Pathfinder
1928 Amsterdam	1. Netherlands	C. Ferdinand Pahud de Mortanges Marcroix
	2. Netherlands	Capt. Gerard P. de Kruyff Va-t'En
	3. Germany	Maj. Bruno Neumann Ilja
1932 Los Angeles	1. Netherlands	C. Ferdinand Pahud de Mortanges Marcroix
	2. USA	Lt Earl F. Thomson Jenny Camp
	3. Sweden	Lt Clarence von Rosen Sunnyside Maid
1936 Berlin	1. Germany	Capt. Ludwig Stubbendorf Nurmi
	2. USA	Capt. Earl F. Thomson Jenny Camp
	3. Denmark	Capt. Hans Lunding Jason
1940 and 1944	(no Olympic Games)	
1948 London	1. France	Capt. Bernard Chevallier Aiglonne
	2. USA	Lt Col. Frank S. Henry Swing Low
	3. Sweden	Capt. J. Robert Selfelt Claque
1952 Helsinki	1. Sweden	Capt. Hans G. von Blixen-Finecke Jubal
	2. France	Lt Guy Lefrant Verdun
	3. Germany	Wilhelm Büsing Hubertus
1956 Stockholm	1. Sweden	Petrus Kastenman Illuster
	2. Germany	August Lütke-Westhues Trux von Kamax
	3. Great Britain	Lt Col. Frank W. C. Weldon Kilbarry
1960 Rome	1. Australia	Lawrence Morgan Salad Days
	2. Australia	Neale Lavis Mirrabooka
	3. Switzerland	Anton S. Bühler Gay Spark
1964 Tokyo	1. Italy	Mauro Checcoli Surbean
	2. Argentina	Carlos Moratorio Chalan
	3. West Germany	Fritz Ligges Donkosak
1968 Mexico	1. France	Jean-Jacques Guyon Pitou
	2. Great Britain	Maj. Derek Allhusen Lochinvar
	3. USA	Michael Page Foster
1972 Munich	1. Great Britain	Richard Meade Laurieston
	2. Italy	Alessandro Argenton Woodland
	3. Sweden	Jan Jonsson Sarajevo

Racing Results

Results of Major Races in Great Britain

Ascot Gold Cup

Year	Horse	Owner	Trainer	Jockey
1930	Bosworth	Lord Derby	Frank Butters	T. Weston
1931	Trimdon	Brig. Gen. C. Lambton	J. Lawson	J. Childs
1932	Trimdon	Brig. Gen. C. Lambton	J. Lawson	J. Childs
1933	Foxhunter	E. Esmond	J. Jarvis	H. Wragg
1934	Felicitation	Aga Khan	Frank Butters	G. Richards
1935	Tiberius	Sir A. Bailey	J. Lawson	T. Weston
1936	Quashed	Lord Stanley	C. Leader	R. Perryman
1937	Precipitation	Lady Z. Wernher	C. Boyd-Rochfort	P. Beasley
1938	Flares	W. Woodward	C. Boyd-Rochfort	R. Jones
1939	Flyon	Lord Milford	J. Jarvis	E. Smith
1940		(no race)		
1941	Finis	Sir H. Cunliffe-Owen	O. Bell	H. Wragg
1942	Owen Tudor	Mrs R. Macdonald-Buchanan	F. Darling	G. Richards
1943	Ujiji	A. Allnatt	J. Lawson	G. Richards
1944	Umiddad	Aga Khan	Frank Butters	G. Richards
1945	Ocean Swell	Lord Rosebery	J. Jarvis	E. Smith
1946	Caracalla II	M. Boussac	C. Semblat	C. Elliott
1947	Souverain	F. Schmitt	H. Delevaud	M. Lollierou
1948	Arbar	M. Boussac	C. Semblat	C. Elliott
1949	Alycidon	Lord Derby	W. Earl	D. Smith
1950	Supertello	W. Harvey	J. C. Waugh	D. Smith
1951	Pan II	E. Constant	E. Pollet	R. Poincelet
1952	Aquino II	Maharanee of Baroda	F. Armstrong	G. Richards
1953	Souepi	G. Digby	G. Digby	C. Elliott
1954	Elpenor	M. Boussac	C. Elliott	J. Doyasbere
1955	Botticelli	Marchese della Rocchetta	Marchese della Rocchetta	E. Camici
1956	Macip	M. Boussac	C. Elliott	S. Boullenger
1957	Zarathustra	T. Gray	C. Boyd-Rochfort	L. Piggott
1958	Gladness	J. McShain	V. O'Brien	L. Piggott
1959	Wallaby II	Baron de Waldner	P. Carter	F. Palmer
1960	Sheshoon	Aly Khan	A. Head	G. Moore
1961	Pandofell	H. W. Daw	F. Maxwell	L. Piggott
1962	Balto	A. Reuff	M. Bonaventure	F. Palmer
1963	Twilight Alley	Lady Sassoon	N. Murless	L. Piggott
1964		(no race)		
1965	Fighting Charlie	Lady M. Bury	F. Maxwell	L. Piggott
1966	Fighting Charlie	Lady M. Bury	F. Maxwell	G. Starkey
1967	Parbury	Maj. H. P. Holt	D. Candy	J. Mercer
1968	Pardallo II	Mme L. Volterra	C. Bartholomew	W. Pyers
1969	Levmoss	S. McGrath	S. McGrath	W. Williamson
1970	Precipice Wood	R. J. McAlpine	Mrs R. Lomax	J. Lindley
1971	Rock Roi	F. R. Hue-Williams	P. Walwyn	D. Keith
1972	Erimo Hawk	Y. Yammamoto	G. Barling	P. Eddery
1973	Lassalle	Z. Yoshida	R. Carver	J. Lindley
1974	Ragstone	Duke of Norfolk	J. Dunlop	R. Hutchinson

Cambridgeshire Stakes

Year	Horse	Owner	Trainer	Jockey
1930	The Pen	Mrs M. Hartigan	M. Hartigan	G. Richards
1931	Disarmament	H. Clayton	C. Elsey	W. Nevett
1932	Pullover	Mrs C. Robinson	M. Peacock	A. Richardson
1933	Raymond	Sir A. Bailey	J. Lawson	G. Nicoll'
1934	Wychwood Abbot	O. Watney	T. Leader	R. Perryman
1935	Commander III	G. Foster	A. B. Briscoe	T. Hawcroft
1936	Dan Bulger	Sir A. Bailey	H. Cottrill	T. Weston
1937	Artist's Prince	Maj. R. Glover	J. Dines	A. Richardsor
1938	Helleniqua	J. Meller	W. Webb	B. Guimard
1939	Class I: Gyroscope	Mrs H. Leader	H. Leader	R. Lacey
	Class II: Orichalque	Lord Dufferin	W. Beatty	J. Simpson
1940	Caxton	Maj. T. Rigg	F. Armstrong	P. Evans
1941	Rue de la Paix	L. Abelson	G. Beeby	T. Carey
1942–4		(no race)		
1945	Esquire	J. Bueno	R. Colling	G. Packer
1946	Sayani	Mme J. Lieux	J. Lieux	W. Johnstone
1947	Fairey Fulmar	G. Tachmindji	O. Bell	T. Gosling
1948	Sterope	J. Townley	P. Beasley	D. Schofield
1949	Sterope	J. Townley	P. Beasley	C. Elliott
1950	Kelling	C. Jarvis	A. Waugh	D. Smith
1951	Fleeting Moment	Mrs M. Johnson	T. Barlam	A. Breasley
1952	Richer	G. Baylis	S. Ingham	K. Gethin
1953	Jupiter	Lord Lambton	P. Beasley	G. Richards
1954	Minstrel	Lord Rosebery	J. Jarvis	C. Gaston
1955	Retrial	Lady Z. Wernher	C. Boyd-Rochfort	P. Robinson
1956	Loppylugs	J. Beary	J. Beary	E. Smith
1957	Stephanotis	A. Plesch	J. Rogers	W. Carr
1958	London Cry	M. Sobell	G. Richards	A. Breasley
1959	Rexequus	J. Adam	G. Boyd	N. Stirk
1960	Midsummer Night II	P. Mellon	P. Hastings-Bass	D. Keith
1961	Violetta III	R. Moller	H. Wragg	C. Parkes
1961	Henry the Seventh	H. Joel	W. Elsey	E. Hide
1962	Hidden Meaning	Cmdr K. Grant	H. Leader	A. Breasley
1963	Commander-in-Chief	H. Whitehouse	E. Cousins	F. Durr
1964	Hasty Cloud	G. Walters	H. Wallington	J. Wilson
1965	Tarqogan	J. McGrath	S. McGrath	W. Williamson
1966	Dites	R. Midwood	H. Leader	D. Maitland
1967	Lacquer	R. Moller	H. Wragg	R. Hutchinson
1968	Emerilo	D. Green	P. Allden	M. Thomas
1969	Prince de Galles	A. Swift	P. Robinson	F. Durr
1970	Prince de Galles	A. Swift	P. Robinson	F. Durr
1971	King Midas	Maj. H. P. Holt	D. Candy	D. Cullen
1972	Negus	R. Watson	D. Candy	P. Waldron
1973	Siciliana	D. Back	I. Balding	G. Lewis
1974	Flying Nelly	S. Digby	W. Wightman	D. Maitland

Cesarewitch

Year	Horse	Owner	Trainer	Jockey
1930	Ut Majeur	Aga Khan	R. Dawson	M. Beary
1931	Noble Star	F. Cundell	L. Cundell	F. Fox
1932	Nitsichin	D. Kennedy	P. Thrale	M. Beary
1933	Seminole	J. Widener	C. Boyd-Rochfort	F. Fox
1934	Enfield	M. Field	C. Boyd-Rochfort	J. Sirett
1935	Near Relation	Sir A. Butt	Frank Butters	E. Smith
1936	Fet	S. Freeman	H. Hedges	A. Richardson
1937	Punch	T. Westhead	C. Tabor	S. Wragg
1938	Contrevent	Princess de F. Lucinge	H. Count	A. Tucker
1939	Cantatrice II	Sir A. Butt	Frank Butters	D. Smith
1940	Hunter's Moon IV	E. Esmond	F. Darling	G. Richards
1941	Filator	Lady Cun-liffe-Owen	O. Bell	S. Wragg
1942–4		(no race)		
1945	Kerry Piper	Sir H. Bruce	F. Armstrong	E. Britt
1946	Monsieur l'Amiral	H. Barnard-Hankey	E. Charlier	H. Wragg
1947	Whiteway	Capt. D. FitzGerald	W. Pratt	W. Evans
1948	Woodburn	Lord Allen-dale	C. Elsey	E. Britt
1949	Strathspey	J. Rank	N. Cannon	E. Smith
1950	Above Board	King George VI	C. Boyd-Rochfort	E. Smith
1951	Three Cheers	C. Crofts	P. Thrale	E. Mercer
1952	Flush Royal	G. MacLean	J. Fawcus	W. Nevett
1953	Chantry	S. Ingham	S. Ingham	K. Gethin
1954	French Design	S. Banks	G. Todd	D. Smith
1955	Curry	F. Honour	F. Armstrong	P. Tulk
1956	Prelone	A. Allen	W. Hide	E. Hide
1957	Sandiacre	T. Farr	W. Dutton	D. Smith
1958	Morecambe	J. Bullock	S. Hall	J. Sime
1959	Come to Daddy	T. Farr	W. Lyde	D. Smith
1960	Alcove	Lord Derby	J. Watts	D. Smith
1961	Avon's Pride	Maj. L. Holliday	W. Hern	E. Smith
1962	Golden Fire	G. Ridley	D. Marks	D. Yates
1963	Utrillo	J. Gerber	H. Price	J. Sime
1964	Grey of Falloden	Lord Astor	W. Hern	J. Mercer
1965	Mintmaster	E. Collington	A. Cooper	J. Sime
1966	Persian Lancer	Lord Belper	H. Price	D. Smith
1967	Boismoss	J. G. Spriggs	M. W. Easterby	E. Johnson
1968	Major Rose	R. L. Heaton	H. Price	L. Piggott
1969	Floridian	A. Patchett	L. Shedden	D. McKay
1970	Scoria	J. Lang	C. Crossley	D. McKay
1971	Orosio	C. St George	H. Cecil	G. Lewis
1972	Cider with Rosie	A. Mullings	S. Ingham	M. Thomas
1973	Flash Imp	Mrs O. Negus-Fancy	R. Smyth	T. Cain
1974	Ocean King	V. Lawson	A. Pitt	T. Carter

Champion Stakes

Year	Horse	Owner	Trainer	Jockey
1930	Rustom Pasha	Aga Khan	R. Dawson	H. Wragg
1931	Goyescas	M. Boussac	B. Jarvis	C. Elliott
1932	Cameronian	J. Dewar	F. Darling	G. Richards
1933	Dastur	Aga Khan	Frank Butters	M. Beary
1933	Chatelaine	E. Thornton-Smith	F. Templeman	G. Richards
1934	Umidwar	Aga Khan	Frank Butters	F. Fox
1935	Wychwood Abbot	O. Watney	T. Leader	R. Perryman
1936	Wychwood Abbot	O. Watney	T. Leader	R. Perryman
1937	Flares	W. Woodward	C. Boyd-Rochfort	P. Beasley
1938	Rockfel	Sir H. Cunliffe-Owen	O. Bell	H. Wragg
1939		(no race)		
1940	Hippius	Lord Rosebery	J. Jarvis	E. Smith
1941	Hippius	Lord Rosebery	J. Jarvis	E. Smith
1942	Big Game	King George VI	F. Darling	G. Richards
1943	Nasrullah	Aga Khan	Frank Butters	G. Richards
1944	Hycilla	W. Woodward	C. Boyd-Rochfort	W. Nevett
1945	Court Martial	Lord Astor	J. Lawson	C. Richards
1946	Honeyway	Lord Milford	J. Jarvis	E. Smith
1947	Migoli	Aga Khan	Frank Butters	G. Richards
1948	Solar Slipper	J. McGrath	H. Smyth	E. Smith
1949	Djeddah	M. Boussac	C. Semblat	C. Elliott
1950	Peter Flower	Lord Rosebery	J. Jarvis	W. Rickaby
1951	Dynamiter	M. Boussac	C. Semblat	C. Elliott
1952	Dynamiter	M. Boussac	J. Glynn	C. Elliott
1953	Nearula	W. Humble	C. Elsey	E. Britt
1954	Narrator	Maj. L. Holliday	H. Cottrill	F. Barlow
1955	Hafiz II	Aga Khan	A. Head	R. Poincelet
1956	Hugh Lupus	Lady U. Vernon	N. Murless	W. Johnstone
1957	Rose Royale II	Aly Khan	A. Head	J. Massard
1958	Bella Paola	F. Dupré	F. Mathet	G. Lequeux
1959	Petite Etoile	Aly Khan	N. Murless	L. Piggott
1960	Marguerite Vernaut	Marchese della Rocchetta	U. Penco	E. Camici
1961	Bobar II	Mme G. Courtois	R. Corme	M. Garcia
1962	Arctic Storm	Mrs E. Carroll	J. Oxx	W. Williamson
1963	Hula Dancer	Mrs P. Widener	E. Pollet	J. Deforge
1964	Baldric II	Mrs H. Jackson	E. Fellows	W. Pyers
1965	Silly Season	P. Mellon	I. Balding	G. Lewis
1966	Pieces of Eight	Comtesse de la Valdène	V. O'Brien	L. Piggott
1967	Reform	M. Sobell	Sir Gordon Richards	A. Breasley
1968	Sir Ivor	R. Guest	V. O'Brien	L. Piggott
1969	Flossy	H. Berlin	F. Boutin	J. Deforge
1970	Lorenzaccio	C. St George	N. Murless	G. Lewis
1971	Brigadier Gerard	Mrs J. Hislop	W. Hern	J. Mercer
1972	Brigadier Gerard	Mrs J. Hislop	W. Hern	J. Mercer
1973	Hurry Harriet	M. Thorp	P. Mullins	J. Cruguet
1974	Giacometti	C. St George	H. Price	L. Piggott

Chester Cup

Year	Horse	Owner	Trainer	Jockey
1930	Mountain Lad	H. Sutton	R. Gooch	F. Lane
1931	Brown Jack	Sir H. Wernher	I. Anthony	M. Beary
1932	Bonny Brighteyes	Mrs C. Robinson	M. Peacock	J. Dines
1933	Dick Turpin	R. Watson	M. Hartigan	G. Richards
1934	Blue Vision	M. Evans	I. Anthony	F. Fox
1935	Damascus	G. Lambton	G. Lambton	H. Foster
1936	Cho-Sen	Mrs W. Ahern	W. Higgs	J. Dines
1937	Faites Vos Jeux	Lady Nuttall	H. Cottrill	P. Maher
1938	Mr Grundy	Sir A. Bailey	J. Lawson	C. Richards
1939	Winnebar	Sir F. Eley	F. Templeman	G. Richards
1940–5		(no race)		
1946	Retsel	H. Lester	G. Todd	C. Richards
1947	Asmodee II	P. Duboscq	W. Halsey	T. Burns
1948	Billet	B. Hilliard	H. Wragg	W. Nevett
1949	John Moore	W. Chapman	H. Weatherill	A. Carson
1950	Heron Bridge	J. Davies	D. Rogers	T. Burns
1951	Wood Leopard	Lord Durham	J. Colling	J. Egan
1952	Le Tellier	J. Westoll	G. Barling	G. Littlewood
1953	Eastern Emperor	Lord Milford	J. Jarvis	W. Rickaby
1954	Peperium	Capt. C. Elsey	C. Elsey	E. Britt
1955	Prescription	Lord Rosebery	J. Jarvis	W. Rickaby
1956	Golovine	Begum Aga Khan	H. Wragg	P. Robinson
1957	Curry	F. Honour	F. Armstrong	J. Gifford
1958	Sandiacre	M. Cowley	W. Dutton	L. Piggott
1959	Agreement	Queen Elizabeth II	C. Boyd-Rochfort	W. Carr
1960	Trelawny	Mrs L. Carver	S. Mercer	F. Durr
1961	Hoy	C. Spencer	L. Dale	G. Lewis
1962	Golden Fire	Mrs G. Ridley	D. Marks	D. Yates
1963	Narratus	D. Symonds	D. Thom	D. Yates
1964	Credo	L. M. Gelb	P. Prendergast	P. Cook
1965	Harvest Gold	T. Marshall	T. Robson	F. Durr
1966	Aegean Blue	Lt Cmdr P. Emmet	R. Houghton	L. Piggott
1967	Mahbub Aly	Lord Rotherwick	W. Hern	P. Cook
1968	Major Rose	R. Heaton	H. R. Price	L. Piggott
1969		(no race)		
1970	Altogether	W. B. Bolton	W. Murray	W. Bentley
1971	Random Shot	Mrs J. Benskin	A. Budgett	F. Durr
1972	Eric	J. Ismay	V. Cross	A. Cressy
1973	Crisalgo	J. Hanson	J. Turner	W. Bentley
1974	Attivo	P. O'Sullivan	C. Mitchell	R. Wernham

Chester Vase

Year	Horse	Owner	Trainer	Jockey
1930	Pinxit	Sir C. Hyde	N. Scobie	A. Burns
1931	Sandwich	Lord Rosebery	J. Jarvis	W. Nevett
1932	Bulandshar	Aga Khan	Frank Butters	F. Fox
1933	Hyperion	Lord Derby	G. Lambton	T. Weston
1934	Windsor Lad	Maharajah of Rajpipla	M. Marsh	F. Fox
1935	Valerius	Sir A. Bailey	J. Lawson	T. Weston
1936	Taj Akbar	Aga Khan	Frank Butters	G. Richards
1937	Merry Mathew	R. Bownass	M. Peacock	W. Nevett
1938	Cave Man	Lord Astor	J. Lawson	C. Richards
1939	Heliopolis	Lord Derby	W. Earl	T. Weston
1940–5	(no race)			
1946	Sky High	Lord Derby	W. Earl	T. Weston
1947	Edward Tudor	Mrs R. McDonald-Buchanan	F. Darling	G. Richards
1948	Valognes	Lt Col. R. McDonald-Buchanan	M. Marsh	E. Britt
1949	Swallow Tail	Lord Derby	W. Earl	D. Smith
1950	Castle Rock	Lord Rosebery	J. Jarvis	D. Smith
1951	Supreme Court	Mrs T. Lilley	E. Williams	W. Johnstone
1952	Summer Rain	Lord Milford	J. Jarvis	E. Mercer
1953	Summer Rain	Lord Milford	J. Jarvis	E. Mercer
1954	Blue Rod	D. de Rougemont	H. Leader	D. Greening
1955	Daemon	B. Mavroleon	P. Prendergast	J. Wilson
1956	Articulate	J. McGrath	W. Stephenson	D. Ryan
1957	King Babar	E. M. O'Ferrall	P. Prendergast	P. Robinson
1958	Alcide	Sir H. de Trafford	C. Boyd-Rochfort	W. Snaith
1959	Fidalgo	G. Oldham	H. Wragg	S. Clayton
1960	Mr Higgins	P. Winstone	H. Cottrill	W. Carr
1961	Sovrango	G. Oldham	H. Wragg	J. Mercer
1962	Silver Cloud	T. Blackwell	J. Jarvis	R. Hutchinson
1963	Christmas Island	Lord Ennisdale	P. Prendergast	L. Piggott
1964	Indiana	C. Engelhard	J. Watts	J. Mercer
1965	Gulf Pearl	J. Whitney	J. Tree	J. Lindley
1966	General Gordon	Lord Rosebery	J. Jarvis	P. Cook
1967	Great Host	L. M. Gelb	P. Prendergast	D. Lake
1968	Remand	J. Astor	W. Hern	J. Mercer
1969		(no race)		
1970	Politico	Mrs O. Phipps	N. Murless	A. Barclay
1971	Linden Tree	Mrs D. McCalmont	P. Walwyn	D. Keith
1972	Ormindo	G. Oldham	H. Wragg	B. Taylor
1973	Proverb	Lt Col. J. Chandos-Pole	B. Hills	E. Johnson
1974	Jupiter Pluvius	T. Blackwell	B. Hobbs	J. Gorton

Coronation Cup

Year	Horse	Owner	Trainer	Jockey
1930	Plantago	W. Singer	J. Lawson	C. Ray
1931	Parenthesis	Lord Wool-avington	F. Darling	F. Fox
1932	Salmon Leap	Mrs A. James	G. Lambton	T. Weston
1933	Dastur	Aga Khan	Frank Butters	C. Elliott
1934	King Salmon	Sir A. Brooke	O. Bell	H. Wragg
1935	Windsor Lad	M. Benson	M. Marsh	C. Smirke
1936	Plassy	Lord Derby	C. Leader	R. Perryman
1937	Cecil	Sir A. Bailey	J. Lawson	T. Weston
1937	His Grace	J. Rank	R. Dawson	G. Richards
1938	Monument	Duke of Marlborough	C. Boyd-Rochfort	P. Beasley
1939	Scottish Union	J. Rank	N. Cannon	G. Richards
1940		(no race)		
1941	Winterhalter	Aga Khan	Frank Butters	D. Smith
1942		(no race)		
1943	Hyperides	Lord Rosebery	J. Jarvis	E. Smith
1944	Persian Gulf	Lady Z. Wernher	C. Boyd-Rochfort	R. Jones
1945	Borealis	Lord Derby	W. Earl	H. Wragg
1946	Ardan	M. Boussac	C. Semblat	C. Elliott
1947	Chanteur II	P. Magot	H. Count	R. Brethes
1948	Goyama	M. Boussac	C. Semblat	C. Elliott
1949	Beau Sabreur			W. Cook
1950	Amour Drake	Mme L. Volterra	R. Carver	R. Poincelet
1951	Tantieme	F. Dupré	F. Mathet	J. Doyasbere
1952	Nuccio	Aga Khan	A. Head	R. Poincelet
1953	Zucchero	G. Rolls	W. Payne	L. Piggott
1954	Aureole	Queen Elizabeth II	C. Boyd-Rochfort	E. Smith
1955	Narrator	Maj. L. Holliday	H. Cottrill	F. Barlow
1956	Tropique	Baron de Rothschild	G. Watson	P. Blanc
1957	Fric	M. Calmann	P. Lallie	J. Deforge
1958	Ballymoss	J. McShain	V. O'Brien	A. Breasley
1959	Nagami	Mrs A. Plesch	H. Wragg	L. Piggott
1960	Petite Etoile	Aly Khan	N. Murless	L. Piggott
1961	Petite Etoile	Aga Khan	N. Murless	L. Piggott
1962	Dicta Drake	Mme L. Volterra	F. Mathet	Y. Saint-Martin
1963	Exbury	Baron de Rothschild	G. Watson	J. Deforge
1964	Relko	F. Dupré	F. Mathet	Y. Saint-Martin
1965	Oncidium	Lord H. de Walden	G. Todd	A. Breasley
1966	I Say	L. Freedman	W. Nightingall	D. Keith
1967	Charlottown	Lady Z. Wernher	G. Smyth	J. Lindley
1968	Royal Palace	H. Joel	N. Murless	A. Barclay
1969	Park Top	Duke of Devonshire	B. van Cutsem	L. Piggott
1970	Caliban	S. Joel	N. Murless	A. Barclay
1971	Lupe	Mrs S. Joel	N. Murless	G. Lewis
1972	Mill Reef	P. Mellon	I. Balding	G. Lewis
1973	Roberto	J. Galbraith	V. O'Brien	L. Piggott
1974	Buoy	R. D. Hollingsworth	W. Hern	J. Mercer

Derby

Year	Horse	Owner	Trainer	Jockey
1900	Diamond Jubilee	The Prince of Wales	R. Marsh	H. Jones
1901	Volodyovski	W. Whitney	J. Huggins	L. Reiff
1902	Ard Patrick	J. Gubbins	S. Darling	J. Martin
1903	Rock Sand	Sir J. Miller	G. Blackwell	D. Maher
1904	St Amant	L. de Rothschild	A. Hayhoe	K. Cannon
1905	Cicero	Lord Rosebery	P. Peck	D. Maher
1906	Spearmint	Maj. E. Loder	P. Gilpin	D. Maher
1907	Orby	R. Crocker	J. Allen	J. Reiff
1908	Signorinetta	E. Ginistrelli	E. Ginistrelli	W. Bullock
1909	Minoru	King Edward VII	R. Marsh	H. Jones
1910	Lemberg	Mr Fairie	A. Taylor	B. Dillon
1911	Sunstar	J. Joel	C. Morton	G. Stern
1912	Tagalie	W. Raphael	D. Waugh	J. Reiff
1913	Aboyeur	A. Cunliffe	T. Lewis	E. Piper
1914	Durbar II	H. Duryea	T. Murphy	M. MacGee
1915	Pommern	S. Joel	C. Peck	S. Donoghue
1916	Fifinella	E. Hulton	R. Dawson	J. Childs
1917	Gay Crusader	Mr Fairie	A. Taylor	S. Donoghue
1918	Gainsborough	Lady J. Douglas	A. Taylor	J. Childs
1919	Grand Parade	Lord Glanely	F. Barling	F. Templeman
1920	Spion Kop	Maj. G. Loder	P. Gilpin	F. O'Neill
1921	Humorist	J. Joel	C. Morton	S. Donoghue
1922	Captain Cuttle	Lord Woolavington	F. Darling	S. Donoghue
1923	Papyrus	B. Irish	B. Jarvis	S. Donoghue
1924	Sansovino	Lord Derby	G. Lambton	T. Weston
1925	Manna	H. Morriss	F. Darling	S. Donoghue
1926	Coronach	Lord Woolavington	F. Darling	J. Childs
1927	Call Boy	F. Curzon	J. Watts	C. Elliott
1928	Felstead	Sir H. Cunliffe-Owen	O. Bell	H. Wragg
1929	Trigo	W. Barnett	R. Dawson	J. Marshall
1930	Blenheim	Aga Khan	R. Dawson	H. Wragg
1931	Cameronian	J. A. Dewar	F. Darling	F. Fox
1932	April the Fifth	T. Walls	T. Walls	F. Lane
1933	Hyperion	Lord Derby	G. Lambton	T. Weston
1934	Windsor Lad	Maharaja of Rajpipla	M. Marsh	C. Smirke
1935	Bahram	Aga Khan	Frank Butters	F. Fox
1936	Mahmoud	Aga Khan	Frank Butters	C. Smirke
1937	Mid-day Sun	Mrs G. Miller	Fred Butters	M. Beary
1938	Bois Roussel	P. Beatty	F. Darling	C. Elliott
1939	Blue Peter	Lord Rosebery	J. Jarvis	E. Smith
1940	Pont l'Eveque	F. Darling	F. Darling	S. Wragg
1941	Owen Tudor	Mrs R. Macdonald-Buchanan	F. Darling	W. Nevett
1942	Watling Street	Lord Derby	W. Earl	H. Wragg
1943	Straight Deal	Hon. D. Paget	W. Nightingall	T. Carey
1944	Ocean Swell	Lord Rosebery	J. Jarvis	W. Nevett
1945	Dante	Sir E. Ohlson	M. Peacock	W. Nevett
1946	Airborne	J. Ferguson	R. Perryman	T. Lowrey
1947	Pearl Diver	Baron de Waldner	C. Halsey	G. Bridgland
1948	My Love	Aga Khan	R. Carver	W. Johnstone
1949	Nimbus	Mrs M. Glenister	G. Colling	C. Elliott
1950	Galcador	M. Boussac	C. Semblat	W. Johnstone
1951	Arctic Prince	J. McGrath	W. Stephenson	C. Spares
1952	Tulyar	Aga Khan	M. Marsh	C. Smirke
1953	Pinza	Sir V. Sassoon	N. Bertie	G. Richards
1954	Never Say Die	R. Clark	J. Lawson	L. Piggott
1955	Phil Drake	Mme L. Volterra	F. Mathet	F. Palmer
1956	Lavandin	P. Wertheimer	A. Head	W. Johnstone
1957	Crepello	Sir V. Sassoon	N. Murless	L. Piggott
1958	Hard Ridden	Sir V. Sassoon	J. Rogers	C. Smirke
1959	Parthia	Sir H. de Trafford	C. Boyd-Rochfort	W. Carr
1960	St Paddy	Sir V. Sassoon	N. Murless	L. Piggott
1961	Psidium	Mrs A. Plesch	H. Wragg	R. Poincelet
1962	Larkspur	R. Guest	V. O'Brien	N. Sellwood
1963	Relko	F. Dupré	F. Mathet	Y. Saint-Martin
1964	Santa Claus	J. Ismay	J. Rogers	A. Breasley
1965	Sea Bird II	J. Ternynck	E. Pollet	T. Glennon
1966	Charlottown	Lady Z. Wernher	G. Smyth	A. Breasley
1967	Royal Palace	H. Joel	N. Murless	G. Moore
1968	Sir Ivor	R. Guest	V. O'Brien	L. Piggott
1969	Blakeney	A. Budgett	A. Budgett	E. Johnson
1970	Nijinsky	C. W. Engelhard	V. O'Brien	L. Piggott
1971	Mill Reef	P. Mellon	I. Balding	G. Lewis
1972	Roberto	J. Galbraith	V. O'Brien	L. Piggott
1973	Morston	A. Budgett	A. Budgett	E. Hide
1974	Snow Knight	Mrs N. Phillips	P. Nelson	B. Taylor

Ebor Handicap

Year	Horse	Owner	Trainer	Jockey
1930	Gentleman's Relish	J. Arkwright	H. Persse	J. Dines
1930	Coaster	Sir H. Hurst	F. Templeman	F. Fox
1931	Brown Jack	Sir H. Wernher	I. Anthony	S. Donoghue
1932	Cat O'Nine Tails	Mrs J. Carruthers	J. Colling	G. Richards
1933	Dictum	Lady B. Smith	T. Rimell	J. Dines
1934	Alcazar	W. Woodward	C. Boyd-Rochfort	J. Childs
1935	Museum	Sir V. Sassoon	J. Rogers	S. Donoghue
1936	Penny Royal	E. Thornton-Smith	F. Templeman	G. Richards
1937	Weathervane	Sir A. Bailey	J. Lawson	T. Weston
1938	Foxglove II	P. Beatty	F. Darling	G. Richards
1939	Owenstown	Sir T. Dixon	M. Peacock	J. Taylor
1940–2	(no race)			
1943	Yorkshire Hussar	J. Hetherton	C. Elsey	G. Littlewood
1944	The Kernel	G. Oxtoby	G. Oxtoby	P. Evans
1945	Wayside Inn	Lord Derby	W. Earl	H. Wragg
1946	Foxtrot	H. Morriss	E. Lambton	E. Britt
1947	Procne	H. Joel	C. Elsey	J. Sime
1948	Donino	W. Cockerline	A. Cooper	J. Sime
1949	Miraculous Atom	H. Halmshaw	S. Hall	W. Nevett
1950	Cadzow Oak	Maj. G. Renwick	J. Thwaites	J. Thompson
1951	Bob	J. Hetherton	C. Elsey	E. Carter
1952	Signification	A. Bird	J. Pearce	H. Jones
1953	Norooz	Aga Khan	M. Marsh	R. Fawdon
1954	By Thunder!	J. Gerber	F. Armstrong	W. Swinburn
1955	Hyperion Kid	Miss R. Olivier	H. Wragg	P. Robinson

Year	Horse	Owner	Trainer	Jockey
1956	Donald	Lord Rosebery	J. Jarvis	D. Smith
1957	Morecambe	J. Bullock	S. Hall	J. Sime
1958	Gladness	J. McShain	V. O'Brien	L. Piggott
1959	Primera	S. Joel	N. Murless	L. Piggott
1960	Persian Road	J. Whitney	J. Tree	G. Moore
1961	Die Hard	Maj. L. Gardner	V. O'Brien	L. Piggott
1962	Sostenuto	P. Bull	W. Elsey	D. Morris
1963	Partholon	Mrs A. Biddle	T. Shaw	J. Sime
1964	Proper Pride	Maj. L. Holliday	W. Wharton	D. Smith
1965	Twelfth Man	R. Moller	H. Wragg	P. Cook
1966	Lomond	W. Ruane	R. Jarvis	E. Eldin
1967	Ovaltine	G. Cooper	J. Watts	E. Johnson
1968	Alignment	Lord Allendale	W. Elsey	E. Johnson
1969	Big Hat	Mrs M. Tennant	D. Hanley	R. Still
1970	Tintagel II	Mrs R. C. Sturdy	R. C. Sturdy	L. Piggott
1971	Knotty Pine	D. Robinson	M. Jarvis	F. Durr
1972	Crazy Rhythm	K. Dodson	S. Ingham	F. Durr
1973	Bonne Noel	Mrs Parker-Poe	P. Prendergast	C. Roche
1974	Anji	G. Coleman	J. Sutcliffe	T. McKeown

Eclipse Stakes

Year	Horse	Owner	Trainer	Jockey
1930	Rustom Pasha	Aga Khan	R. Dawson	H. Wragg
1931	Caerleon	Lord Derby	G. Lambton	T. Weston
1932	Miracle	Lord Rosebery	J. Jarvis	H. Wragg
1933	Loaningdale	Col. G. Wilson	C. Boyd-Rochfort	J. Childs
1934	King Salmon	Sir R. Brooke	O. Bell	H. Wragg
1935	Windsor Lad	M. Benson	M. Marsh	C. Smirke
1936	Rhodes Scholar	Lord Astor	J. Lawson	R. Dick
1937	Boswell	W. Woodward	C. Boyd-Rochfort	P. Beasley
1938	Pasch	H. Morriss	F. Darling	G. Richards
1939	Blue Peter	Lord Rosebery	J. Jarvis	E. Smith
1940–5	(no race)			
1946	Gulf Stream	Lord Derby	W. Earl	H. Wragg
1947	Migoli	Aga Khan	Frank Butters	C. Smirke
1948	Petition	Sir A. Butt	Frank Butters	K. Gethin
1949	Djeddah	M. Boussac	C. Semblat	C. Elliott
1950	Flocon	Baron de Waldner	P. Carter	F. Palmer
1951	Mystery IX	Mrs E. Esmond	P. Carter	L. Piggott
1952	Tulyar	Aga Khan	M. Marsh	C. Smirke
1953	Argur	M. Boussac	J. Glynn	C. Elliott
1954	King of the Tudors	F. Dennis	W. Stephenson	K. Gethin
1955	Darius	Sir P. Loraine	H. Wragg	L. Piggott
1956	Tropique	Baron de Rothschild	G. Watson	P. Blanc
1957	Arctic Explorer	Lt Col. G. Loder	N. Murless	L. Piggott
1958	Ballymoss	J. McShain	V. O'Brien	A. Breasley
1959	Saint Crespin III	Aly Khan	A. Head	G. Moore
1960	Javelot	Baron de Waldner	P. Carter	F. Palmer
1961	St Paddy	Sir V. Sassoon	N. Murless	L. Piggott
1962	Henry the Seventh	H. Joel	W. Elsey	E. Hide

Year	Horse	Owner	Trainer	Jockey
1963	Khalkis	Lord Elvedon	P. Prendergast	G. Bougoure
1964	Ragusa	J. Mullion	P. Prendergast	G. Bougoure
1965	Canisbay	Queen Elizabeth II	C. Boyd-Rochfort	S. Clayton
1966	Pieces of Eight	Comtesse de la Valdène	V. O'Brien	L. Piggott
1967	Busted	S. Joel	N. Murless	W. Rickaby
1968	Royal Palace	H. Joel	N. Murless	A. Barclay
1969	Wolver Hollow	Mrs C. Iselin	H. Cecil	L. Piggott
1970	Connaught	H. Joel	N. Murless	A. Barclay
1971	Mill Reef	P. Mellon	I. Balding	G. Lewis
1972	Brigadier Gerard	Mrs J. Hislop	W. Hern	J. Mercer
1973	Scottish Rifle	A. Struthers	J. Dunlop	R. Hutchinson
1974	Coup de Feu	F. Sasse	D. Sasse	P. Eddery

Gimcrack Stakes

Year	Horse	Owner	Trainer	Jockey
1930	Four Course	Lord Ellesmere	F. Darling	F. Fox
1931	Miracle	Lord Rosebery	J. Jarvis	H. Wragg
1932	Young Lover	Sir A. Butt	Frank Butters	R. Perryman
1933	Mrs Rustom	Aga Khan	Frank Butters	M. Beary
1934	Bahram	Aga Khan	Frank Butters	R. Perryman
1935	Paul Beg	Lord Milton	W. Easterby	H. Gunn
1936	Goya II	M. Boussac	G. Lambton	C. Elliott
1937	Golden Sovereign	Sir A. Bailey	H. Cottrill	T. Weston
1938	Cockpit	Lord Derby	C. Leader	R. Perryman
1939	Tant Mieux	Aly Khan	F. Darling	G. Richards
1941–4	(no race)			
1945	Gulf Stream	Lord Derby	W. Earl	H. Wragg
1946	Petition	Sir A. Butt	Frank Butters	H. Wragg
1947	Black Tarquin	W. Woodward	C. Boyd-Rochfort	W. Carr
1948	Star King	W. Harvey	J. C. Waugh	S. Wragg
1949	Palestine	Aga Khan	Frank Butters	G. Richards
1950	Cortil	M. Boussac	C. Semblat	W. Johnstone
1951	Windy City	R. Bell	P. Prendergast	G. Richards
1952	Bebe Grande	J. Gerber	F. Armstrong	W. Snaith
1953	The Pie King	R. Bell	P. Prendergast	G. Richards
1954	Precast	F. Ellison	R. Peacock	W. Nevett
1955	Idle Rocks	D. Robinson	G. Brooke	D. Smith
1956	Eudaemon	Mrs E. Foster	C. Elsey	E. Britt
1957	Pheidippides	P. Bull	C. Elsey	D. Smith
1958	Be Careful	W. Hill	C. Elsey	E. Hide
1959	Paddy's Sister	Mrs J. Mullion	P. Prendergast	G. Moore
1960	Test Case	Sir A. Jarvis	J. Jarvis	E. Larkin
1961	Sovereign Lord	Duke of Norfolk	G. Smyth	A. Breasley
1962	Crocket	D. van Clief	G. Brooke	D. Smith
1963	Talahasse	H. Loebstein	T. Corbett	L. Piggott
1964	Double Jump	C. Engelhard	J. Tree	J. Lindley
1965	Young Emperor	Mrs Parker-Poe	P. Prendergast	L. Piggott
1966	Golden Horus	Mrs D. M. Solomon	W. O'Gorman	J. Mercer
1967	Petingo	Capt. M. Lemos	F. Armstrong	L. Piggott
1968	Tudor Music	D. Robinson	M. Jarvis	F. Durr
1969	Yellow God	D. Robinson	P. Davey	F. Durr
1970	Mill Reef	P. Mellon	I. Balding	G. Lewis
1971	Wishing Star	D. Robinson	P. Davey	F. Durr
1972	Rapid River	Mrs W. Richardson	W. Stephenson	T. Kelsey
1973	Giacometti	C. St George	H. Price	A. Murray
1974	Steel Heart	R. Tikkoo	D. Weld	L. Piggott

Goodwood Cup

Year	Horse	Owner	Trainer	Jockey
1930	Brown Jack	Sir H. Wernher	I. Anthony	S. Donoghue
1931	Salmon Leap	Mrs A. James	G. Lambton	T. Weston
1932	Brulette	Lord Woolavington	F. Darling	G. Richards
1933	Sans Peine	E. Esmond	J. Jarvis	E. Smith
1934	Loosestrife	P. Johnson	E. Richards	G. Richards
1935	Tiberius	Sir A. Bailey	J. Lawson	T. Weston
1936	Cecil	Sir A. Bailey	J. Lawson	T. Weston
1937	Fearless Fox	A. Smith	J. Jarvis	E. Smith
1938	Epigram	J. Rank	N. Cannon	B. Carslake
1939	Dubonnet	J. Hornung	B. Jarvis	T. Lowrey
1940–5	(no race)			
1946	Marsyas II	M. Boussac	C. Semblat	C. Elliott
1947	Monsieur l'Amiral	Mrs I. Henderson	E. Charlier	C. Smirke
1948	Tenerani	F. Tesio	N. Bertie	E. Camici
1949	Alycidon	Lord Derby	W. Earl	D. Smith
1950	Val Drake	Mme L. Volterra	R. Carver	R. Poincelet
1951	Pan II	E. Constant	E. Pollet	R. Poincelet
1952	Medway	P. Bartholomew	F. Winter	D. Smith
1953	Souepi	G. Digby	G. Digby	C. Elliott
1954	Blarney Stone	M. McAlpine	V. Smyth	W. Rickaby
1955	Double Bore	J. Tree	J. Tree	T. Gosling
1956	Zarathustra	T. Gray	C. Boyd-Rochfort	W. Carr
1957	Tenterhooks	Lord Allendale	C. Elsey	E. Britt
1958	Gladness	J. McShain	V. O'Brien	L. Piggott
1959	Dickens	Lady Z. Wernher	C. Boyd-Rochfort	D. Smith
1960	Exar	Dr C. Vittadini	N. Murless	L. Piggott
1961	Predominate	H. Joel	T. Leader	E. Smith
1962	Sagacity	Lady Cholmondeley	C. Boyd-Rochfort	W. Carr
1963	Trelawny	Mrs L. Carver	G. Todd	A. Breasley
1964	Raise You Ten	P. Widener	C. Boyd-Rochfort	S. Clayton
1965	Apprentice	Queen Elizabeth II	C. Boyd-Rochfort	S. Clayton
1966	Gaulois	Queen Elizabeth II	C. Boyd-Rochfort	R. Hutchinson
1967	Wrekin Rambler	G. Murphy	Sir Gordon Richards	A. Breasley
1968	Ovaltine	G. Cooper	J. Watts	B. Taylor
1969	Richmond Fair	T. Blackwell	B. Hobbs	J. Gorton
1970	Parthenon	Sir R. MacDonald-Buchanan	H. Cecil	G. Starkey
1971	Rock Roi	F. R. Hue-Williams	P. Walwyn	D. Keith
1972	Erimo Hawk	Y. Yammamoto	G. Barling	P. Eddery
1973	Proverb	Lt Col. J. Chandos-Pole	B. Hills	E. Johnson
1974	Proverb	Lt Col. J. Chandos-Pole	B. Hills	L. Piggott

Great Metropolitan Handicap

Year	Horse	Owner	Trainer	Jockey
1930	Servus	Lord Derby	Frank Butters	T. Weston
1931	Summer Princess	C. Gulliver	R. Barclay	F. Sharpe
1932	Roi de Paris	J. Cooper	A. Douglas-Pennant	E. Smith
1933	Joyous Greeting	Maj. H. Lyons	F. Sneyd	S. Wragg
1934	Annihilation	J. Rank	H. Cottrill	J. Caldwell
1935	Crawley Wood	J. Cottrell	J. Waugh	F. Lane
1936	Quashed	Lord Stanley	C. Leader	R. Perryman
1936	Jack Tar	Lady Nuttall	H. Cottrill	E. Smith
1937	Corofin	M. McDonough	J. Parkinson	W. Wing
1938	Irish Stew	Miss B. Jameson	G. Beeby	P. Maher
1939	Lillibullero	J. de Rothschild	F. Pratt	B. Lynch
1940–5	(no race)			
1946	Golden Horus	W. Little	G. Duller	G. Richards
1947	Star Song	Mrs D. C. Marsh	V. Smyth	D. Smith
1948	Now or Never	F. Harris	V. Smyth	C. Elliott
1949	Yoyo	Lord Rosebery	J. Jarvis	W. Cook
1950	Blue Fox II	Aly Khan	H. Delavaud	P. Blanc
1951	Barnacle	A. Aman	A. Budgett	L. Piggott
1952	French Squadron	Miss Z. Daniels	M. Beary	W. Johnstone
1953	Father Thames	R. Deakin	M. Feakes	R. Fawdon
1954	Luxury Hotel	E. McAlpine	M. Pope	G. Richards
1955	Babylonian	G. Dowty	T. F. Rimell	J. Mercer
1956	Curry	F. Honour	F. Armstrong	P. Tulk
1957	Gay Ballad	J. Pearce	G. Brooke	J. Lynch
1958	Hollyhock	D. Hely-Hutchinson	A. Budgett	S. Millbanks
1959	Miss McTaffy	T. Holland-Martin	P. Walwyn	L. Piggott
1960	Kaffirboom	H. Oppenheimer	F. Armstrong	W. Snaith
1961	Little Buskins	T. Gray	C. Boyd-Rochfort	W. Snaith
1962	Narratus	R. Stone	D. Thom	E. Smith
1963	Byng	D. Griffiths	D. Griffiths	D. Cullen
1964	Gold Aura	Queen Elizabeth II	C. Boyd-Rochfort	J. Sime
1965	Romp Home	W. Hill	W. Elsey	D. Morris
1966	Cullen	M. Tate	M. Tate	F. Messer
1967	Moon Storm	Mrs S. J. Robinson	K. Cundell	A. Murray
1968	Pick Me Up	B. Jenks	T. F. Rimell	L. Piggott
1969	Clever Scot	H. S. Alper	C. Davies	R. Dicey
1970	Hickleton	R. Dawson	B. Hills	E. Johnson
1971	Tartar Prince	J. D. Parker	T. Waugh	G. Duffield
1972	Lyford Cay	Mrs E. Swainson	W. Swainson	W. Carson
1973	Quarrymaster	Mrs B. Cropp	A. Pitt	F. Durr
1974	Tim Ding	Mrs G. Lugg	T. Forster	G. Starkey

King George VI and Queen Elizabeth Stakes

Year	Horse	Owner	Trainer	Jockey
1951	Supreme Court	Mrs T. Lilley	E. Williams	C. Elliott
1952	Tulyar	Aga Khan	M. Marsh	C. Smirke
1953	Pinza	Sir V. Sassoon	N. Bertie	G. Richards
1954	Aureole	Queen Elizabeth II	C. Boyd-Rochfort	E. Smith
1955	Vimy	P. Wertheimer	A. Head	R. Poincelet
1956	Ribot	Marchese della Rocchetta	U. Penco	E. Camici
1957	Montaval	R. Strassburger	G. Bridgland	F. Palmer
1958	Ballymoss	J. McShain	V. O'Brien	A. Breasley
1959	Alcide	Sir H. de Trafford	C. Boyd-Rochfort	W. Carr
1960	Aggressor	Sir H. Wernher	J. Gosden	J. Lindley
1961	Right Royal V	Mme J. Couturié	E. Pollet	R. Poincelet
1962	Match III	F. Dupré	F. Mathet	Y. Saint-Martin
1963	Ragusa	J. Mullion	P. Prendergast	G. Bougoure
1964	Nasram II	Mrs H. Jackson	E. Fellows	W. Pyers
1965	Meadow Court	G. Bell	P. Prendergast	L. Piggott
1966	Aunt Edith	Lt Col. J. Hornung	N. Murless	L. Piggott
1967	Busted	S. Joel	N. Murless	G. Moore
1968	Royal Palace	H. Joel	N. Murless	A. Barclay
1969	Park Top	Duke of Devonshire	B. van Cutsem	L. Piggott
1970	Nijinsky	C. W. Engelhard	V. O'Brien	L. Piggott
1971	Mill Reef	P. Mellon	I. Balding	G. Lewis
1972	Brigadier Gerard	Mrs J. Hislop	W. Hern	J. Mercer
1973	Dahlia	N. Bunker-Hunt	M. Zilber	W. Pyers
1974	Dahlia	N. Bunker-Hunt	M. Zilber	L. Piggott

Lincoln Handicap

Year	Horse	Owner	Trainer	Jockey
1930	Leonidas II	M. Boussac	S. Darling	H. Southey
1931	Knight Error	Capt. A. Wilson	P. Whitaker	F. Fox
1932	Jerome Fandor	A. McKinlay	H. Peacock	W. Christie
1933	Dorigen	G. Lambton	G. Lambton	T. Weston
1934	Play On	M. Simon	J. Russell	J. Dines
1935	Flamenco	Lord Rosebery	J. Jarvis	E. Smith
1936	Over Coat	H. Selby	J. Russell	T. Weston
1937	Marmaduke Jinks	Mrs C. Robinson	H. Peacock	D. Smith
1938	Phakos	E. Esmond	J. Jarvis	E. Smith
1939	Squadron Castle	S. Oxenham	H. Smallwood	V. Mitchell
1940	Quartier Maitre	Mrs A. Bendir	I. Anthony	G. Richards
1941	Gloaming	S. Raphael	G. Lambton	D. Dick
1942	Cuerdley	E. Pilcher	R. Renton	J. Taylor
1943	Lady Electra	W. Richardson	C. Ray	R. Colven
1944	Backbite	A. Tully	A. Boyd	M. Pearson
1945	Double Harness	J. Hetherton	C. Elsey	D. Stansfield
1946	Langton Abbot	T. Best	E. Lambton	T. Weston
1947	Jockey Treble	S. Oxenham	W. Smallwood	E. Mercer
1948	Commissar	R. Budgett	A. Budgett	W. Rickaby
1949	Fair Judgement	C. Gordon	J. Jarvis	E. Smith
1950	Dramatic	A. Saunders	G. Todd	G. Richards
1951	Barnes Park	H. Lane	G. Boyd	J. Sime
1952	Phariza	C. O.-Lee	J. Powell	D. Forte
1953	Sailing Light	Mrs M. Farr	G. Armstrong	A. Roberts
1954	Nahar	Aly Khan	A. Head	J. Massard
1955	Military Court	Begum Aga Khan	H. Wragg	E. Mercer
1956	Three Star II	G. Graham	H. Davison	D. W. Morris
1957	Babur	Capt. S. Lord	C. Elsey	E. Hide
1958	Babur	Capt. S. Lord	C. Elsey	E. Britt
1959	Marshal Pil	Dr S. Lip	S. Hall	P. Robinson
1960	Mustavon	Mrs L. McVey	S. Hall	N. McIntosh
1961	Johns Court	K. Wheldon	E. Cousins	B. Lee
1962	Hill Royal	D. Murray	E. Cousins	J. Sime
1963	Monawin	R. Mason	R. Mason	J. Sime
1964	Mighty Gurkha	Mrs G. Lambton	E. Lambton	P. Robinson
1965	Old Tom	J. Ellis	M. H. Easterby	A. Breasley
1966	Riot Act	Mrs J. Bryce	F. Armstrong	A. Breasley
1967	Ben Novus	J. Peatt	W. Hide	P. Robinson
1968	Frankincense	Lady Halifax	J. Oxley	G. Starkey
1969	Foggy Bell	J. Forrester	D. Smith	A. Barclay
1970	New Chapter	C. P. Goulandris	F. Armstrong	A. Barclay
1971	Double Cream	R. F. Dennis	W. Elsey	E. Hide
1972	Sovereign Bill	W. Barr	P. Robinson	E. Hide
1973	Bronze Hill	Mrs E. Smith	M. H. Easterby	M. Birch
1974	Quizair	G. Macdonald	R. Jarvis	M. Thomas

Middle Park Stakes

Year	Horse	Owner	Trainer	Jockey
1930	Portlaw	Sir A. Bailey	H. Persse	H. Beasley
1931	Orwell	W. Singer	J. Lawson	R. Jones
1932	Felicitation	Aga Khan	Frank Butters	M. Beary
1933	Medieval Knight	J. Dewar	F. Darling	G. Richards
1934	Bahram	Aga Khan	Frank Butters	F. Fox
1935	Abjer	M. Boussac	G. Lambton	C. Elliott
1936	Fair Copy	Lord Derby	C. Leader	R. Perryman
1937	Scottish Union	J. Rank	N. Cannon	G. Richards
1938	Foxbrough II	W. Woodward	C. Boyd-Rochfort	P. Beasley
1939	Djebel	M. Boussac	C. Semblat	C. Elliott
1940	Hyacinthus	A. Bassett	H. Persse	P. Beasley
1941	Sun Chariot	King George VI	F. Darling	H. Wragg
1942	Ribbon	Lord Rosebery	J. Jarvis	E. Smith
1943	Orestes	Hon. D. Paget	W. Nightingall	T. Carey
1944	Dante	Sir E. Ohlson	M. Peacock	W. Nevett
1945	Khaled	Aga Khan	Frank Butters	G. Richards
1946	Saravan	Princess Aly Khan	Frank Butters	C. Elliott
1947	The Cobbler	Lt Col. G. Loder	F. Darling	G. Richards
1948	Abernant	Maj. R. MacDonald-Buchanan	N. Murless	G. Richards
1949	Masked Light	E. Wanless	N. Scobie	D. Smith
1950	Big Dipper	Mrs J. Bryce	C. Boyd-Rochfort	W. Carr
1951	King's Bench	A. Tompsett	M. Feakes	C. Elliott
1952	Nearula	W. Humble	C. Elsey	E. Britt
1953	Royal Challenger	A. Gordon	P. Beasley	G. Richards
1954	Our Babu	D. Robinson	G. Brooke	D. Smith
1955	Buisson Ardent	Aga Khan	A. Head	D. Smith
1956	Pipe of Peace	S. Niarchos	G. Richards	A. Breasley
1957	Major Portion	H. Joel	T. Leader	E. Smith

Year	Horse	Owner	Trainer	Jockey
1958	Masham	A. Ellis	G. Brooke	D. Smith
1959	Venture VII	Aly Khan	A. Head	G. Moore
1960	Skymaster	Duke of Norfolk	W. Smyth	A. Breasley
1961	Gustav	J. Whitney	J. Tree	J. Lindley
1962	Crocket	D. van Clief	G. Brooke	E. Smith
1963	Showdown	Mrs D. Prenn	F. Winter	D. Smith
1964	Spanish Express	Mrs G. Marcow	L. Hall	J. Mercer
1965	Track Spare	R. Mason	R. Mason	J. Lindley
1966	Bold Lad	Lady Granard	P. Prendergast	D. Lake
1967	Petingo	Capt. M. Lemos	F. Armstrong	L. Piggott
1968	Right Tack	J. R. Brown	J. Sutcliffe	G. Lewis
1969	Huntercombe	H. Renshaw	A. Budgett	E. Johnson
1970	Brigadier Gerard	Mrs J. Hislop	W. Hern	J. Mercer
1971	Sharpen Up	Mrs B. van Cutsem	B. van Cutsem	W. Carson
1972	Tudenham	L. B. Holliday	D. Smith	J. Lindley
1973	Habat	Dr C. Vittadini	P. Walwyn	P. Eddery
1974	Steel Heart	R. Tikkoo	D. Weld	L. Piggott

Oaks

Year	Horse	Owner	Trainer	Jockey
1900	La Roche	Duke of Portland	J. Porter	M. Cannon
1901	Cap and Bells II	F. Keen	S. Darling	M. Henry
1902	Sceptre	R. Sievier	R. Sievier	H. Randall
1903	Our Lassie	J. Joel	C. Morton	M. Cannon
1904	Pretty Polly	Maj. E. Loder	P. Gilpin	W. Lane
1905	Cherry Lass	W. H. Walker	W. Robinson	H. Jones
1906	Keystone II	Lord Derby	G. Lambton	D. Maker
1907	Glass Doll	J. Joel	C. Morton	H. Randall
1908	Signorinetta	E. Ginistrelli	E. Ginistrelli	W. Bullock
1909	Perola	W. Cooper	G. Davies	F. Wootton
1910	Rosedrop	Sir W. Bass	A. Taylor	C. Trigg
1911	Cherimoya	W. B. Cloete	C. Marsh	F. Winter
1912	Mirska	J. Prat	T. Jennings	J. Childs
1913	Jest	J. Joel	C. Morton	F. Rickaby
1914	Princess Dorrie	J. Joel	C. Morton	W. Huxley
1915	Snow Marten	L. Neumann	P. Gilpin	W. Griggs
1916	Fifinella	E. Hulton	R. Dawson	J. Childs
1917	Sunny Jane	Maj. W. Astor	A. Taylor	O. Madden
1918	My Dear	A. Cox	A. Taylor	S. Donoghue
1919	Bayuda	Lady J. Douglas	A. Taylor	J. Childs
1920	Charlebelle	A. Cunliffe	H. Braime	A. Whalley
1921	Love in Idleness	J. Watson	A. Taylor	J. Childs
1922	Pogrom	Lord Astor	A. Taylor	E. Gardner
1923	Brownhylda	Vicomte de Fontarce	R. Dawson	V. Smyth
1924	Straitlace	Sir E. Hulton	D. Waugh	F. O'Neill
1925	Saucy Sue	Lord Astor	A. Taylor	F. Bullock
1926	Short Story	Lord Astor	A. Taylor	R. Jones
1927	Beam	Lord Durham	Frank Butters	T. Weston
1928	Toboggan	Lord Derby	Frank Butters	T. Weston
1929	Pennycomequick	Lord Astor	J. Lawson	H. Jelliss
1930	Rose of England	Lord Glanely	T. Hogg	G. Richards
1931	Brulette	Lt Col. C. Birkin	F. Carter	C. Elliott
1932	Udaipur	Aga Khan	Frank Butters	M. Beary
1933	Chatelaine	E. Thornton-Smith	F. Templeman	S. Wragg
1934	Light Brocade	Lord Durham	Frank Butters	B. Carslake
1935	Quashed	Lord Stanley	C. Leader	H. Jelliss
1936	Lovely Rosa	Sir A. Bailey	H. Cottrill	T. Weston
1937	Exhibitionist	Sir V. Sassoon	J. Lawson	S. Donoghue
1938	Rockfel	Sir H. Cunliffe-Owen	O. Bell	H. Wragg
1939	Galatea II	R. Clark	J. Lawson	R. Jones
1940	Godiva	Lord Rothermere	W. Jarvis	D. Marks
1941	Commotion	J. Dewar	F. Darling	H. Wragg
1942	Sun Chariot	King George VI	F. Darling	G. Richards
1943	Why Hurry	J. Rank	N. Cannon	C. Elliott
1944	Hycilla	W. Woodward	C. Boyd-Rochfort	G. Bridgland
1945	Sun Stream	Lord Derby	W. Earl	H. Wragg
1946	Steady Aim	Sir A. Butt	Frank Butters	H. Wragg
1947	Imprudence	Mme P. Corbière	J. Lieux	W. Johnstone
1948	Masaka	Aga Khan	Frank Butters	W. Nevett
1949	Musidora	N. Donaldson	C. Elsey	E. Britt
1950	Asmena	M. Boussac	C. Semblat	W. Johnstone
1951	Neasham Belle	Maj. L. Holliday	G. Brooke	S. Clayton
1952	Frieze	A. Keith	C. Elsey	E. Britt
1953	Ambiguity	Lord Astor	J. Colling	J. Mercer
1954	Sun Cap	Mme R. Forget	R. Carver	W. Johnstone
1955	Meld	Lady Z. Wernher	C. Boyd-Rochfort	W. Carr
1956	Sicarelle	Mme L. Volterra	F. Mathet	F. Palmer
1957	Carrozza	Queen Elizabeth II	N. Murless	L. Piggott
1958	Bella Paola	F. Dupré	F. Mathet	M. Garcia
1959	Petite Etoile	Aly Khan	N. Murless	L. Piggott
1960	Never Too Late II	Mrs H. Jackson	E. Pollet	R. Poincelet
1961	Sweet Solera	Mrs S. Castello	R. Day	W. Rickaby
1962	Monade	G. Goulandris	J. Lieux	Y. Saint-Martin
1963	Noblesse	Mrs J. Olin	P. Prendergast	G. Bougoure
1964	Homeward Bound	Sir F. Robinson	J. Oxley	G. Starkey
1965	Long Look	J. C. Brady	V. O'Brien	J. Purtell
1966	Valoris	C. Clore	V. O'Brien	L. Piggott
1967	Pia	Countess M. Batthyany	W. Elsey	E. Hide
1968	La Lagune	H. Berlin	F. Boutin	G. Thiboeuf
1969	Sleeping Partner	Lord Rosebery	D. Smith	J. Gorton
1970	Lupe	Mrs S. Joel	N. Murless	A. Barclay
1971	Altesse Royale	F. R. Hue-Williams	N. Murless	G. Lewis
1972	Ginevra	R. Woods	H. R. Price	A. Murray
1973	Mysterious	G. A. Pope	N. Murless	G. Lewis
1974	Polygamy	L. Freedman	P. Walwyn	P. Eddery

Queen's Vase

Year	Horse	Owner	Trainer	Jockey
1930	Trimdon	Brig. Gen. C. Lambton	J. Lawson	R. Jones
1931	Pomme d'Api	Aga Khan	Frank Butters	M. Beary
1932	Silvermere	Mrs C. Rich	W. Nightingall	F. Lane
1933	Gainslaw	H. Simms	F. Leader	T. Weston
1934	Duplicate	Sir C. Hyde	N. Scobie	F. Sharpe
1935	Flash Bye	Lord Astor	J. Lawson	J. Sirett
1936	Rondo	J. de Rothschild	F. Pratt	P. Maher
1937	Fearless Fox	A. Smith	J. Jarvis	E. Smith
1938	Foxglove II	P. Beatty	F. Darling	G. Richards
1939	Atout Maitre	H. Blagrave	H. Blagrave	W. Sibbritt
1940–5	(no race)			
1946	Look Ahead	Sir H. de Trafford	C. Boyd-Rochfort	D. Smith
1947	Auralia	Mrs A. Johnston	R. Day	D. Smith
1948	Estoc	M. Boussac	C. Semblat	R. Bertiglia
1949	Lone Eagle	W. Woodward	C. Boyd-Rochfort	D. Smith
1950	Fastlad	Baron de Waldner	P. Carter	F. Palmer
1951	Faux Pas	Mrs R. Foster	J. Lawson	E. Smith
1952	Souepi	G. Digby	G. Digby	C. Elliott
1953	Absolve	Sir M. McAlpine	V. Smyth	L. Piggott
1954	Prescription	Lord Rosebery	J. Jarvis	E. Smith
1955	Prince Barle	J. Barker	J. Lawson	E. Mercer
1956	French Beige	R. Dennis	H. Peacock	G. Littlewood
1957	Tenterhooks	Lord Allendale	C. Elsey	E. Britt
1958	Even Money	C. Palmer	V. O'Brien	A. Breasley
1959	Vivi Tarquin	J. McGrath	S. McGrath	D. Greening
1960	Prolific	Mrs C. Evans	W. Nightingall	D. Keith
1961	Black King	H. Joel	W. Elsey	E. Hide
1962	Pavot	E. M. O'Ferrall	P. Prendergast	J. Sime
1963	Hereford	Mrs W. Macauley	H. Murless	J. Hunter
1964	I Titan	Mrs V. Hue-Williams	N. Murless	M. Giovannelli
1965	Beddard	R. Reynolds	H. Murless	J. Sime
1966	Bally Russe	F. R. Hue-Williams	N. Murless	A. Breasley
1967	The Accuser	Lord Rotherwick	W. Hern	F. Durr
1968	Zorba II	C. Clore	P. Prendergast	R. Hutchinson
1969	Tantivy	N. Hetherton	W. Elsey	A. Barclay
1970	Yellow River	D. Sung	A. Breasley	T. Carter
1971	Parnell	R. M. O'Ferrall	S. Quirke	R. Hutchinson
1972	Falkland	Lord Howard de Walden	H. Cecil	G. Starkey
1973	Tara Brooch	J. McGrath	S. McGrath	P. Eddery
1974	Royal Aura	Mrs J. Silcock	P. Walwyn	P. Eddery

Royal Hunt Cup

Year	Horse	Owner	Trainer	Jockey
1930	The McNab	J. Dewar	F. Darling	F. Fox
1931	Grand Salute	Lord Glanely	T. Hogg	G. Richards
1932	Totaig	V. Emanuel	G. Duller	B. Rosen
1933	Colorado Kid	Lt Col. G. Loder	V. Gilpin	C. Buckham
1934	Caymanas	C. Ewing	C. Easterbee	C. Ray
1935	Priok	H. Barnard-Hankey	P. Whitaker	S. Middleton
1936	Guinea Gap	Lady Nuttall	H. Cottrill	R. Jones
1937	Fairplay	R. Middlemas	P. Allden	P. Maher
1938	Couvert	H. Blagrave	H. Blagrave	C. Richards
1939	Caerloptic	Sir A. Bailey	H. Cottrill	M. Beary
1940–4	(no race)			
1945	Battle Hymn	J. Whitney	C. Boyd-Rochfort	P. Maher
1946	Friar's Fancy	O. Watney	T. Leader	E. Smith
1947	Master Vote	H. Blagrave	H. Blagrave	T. Sidebotham
1948	Master Vote	H. Blagrave	H. Blagrave	W. Johnstone
1949	Sterope	J. Townley	P. Beasley	J. Caldwell
1950	Hyperbole	J. Rank	N. Cannon	A. Breasley
1951	Val d'Assa	Maj. D. McCalmont	H. Persse	N. Sellwood
1952	Queen of Sheba	Maj. D. McCalmont	H. Persse	F. Barlow
1953	Choir Boy	Queen Elizabeth II	C. Boyd-Rochfort	D. Smith
1954	Chivalry	P. Hatvany	T. F. Rimell	D. Forte
1955	Nicholas Nickleby	J. Gerber	F. Armstrong	W. Snaith
1956	Alexander	Queen Elizabeth II	C. Boyd-Rochfort	W. Carr
1957	Retrial	Lady Z. Wernher	C. Boyd-Rochfort	P. Robinson
1958	Amos	L. Carver	S. Mercer	P. Boothman
1959	Faultless Speech	H. Wallington	H. Wallington	G. Lewis
1960	Small Slam	P. King	G. Barling	R. Elliott
1961	King's Troop	Mrs P. Hastings	P. Hastings-Bass	G. Lewis
1962	Smartie	R. Mason	R. Mason	J. Sime
1963	Spaniard's Close	Mrs B. Davis	F. Winter	L. Piggott
1964	Zaleucus	Maj. D. McCalmont	G. Brooke	D. Smith
1965	Casabianca	Lt Col. J. Hornung	N. Murless	L. Piggott
1966	Continuation	S. McGrath	S. McGrath	J. Roe
1967	Regal Light	Mrs L. Lazarus	S. Hall	G. Sexton
1968	Golden Mean	S. H. Lee	D. Smith	F. Durr
1969	Kamundu	J. Banks	F. Carr	L. Piggott
1970	Calpurnius	C. W. Engelhard	J. W. Watts	G. Duffield
1971	Picture Boy	K. MacKenzie	G. Todd	J. Wilson
1972	Tempest Boy	Lt Col. P. Hesse	J. Sutcliffe	R. Hutchinson
1973	Camouflage	J. Edwards	J. Dunlop	D. Cullen
1974	Old Lucky	N. Bunker-Hunt	B. van Cutsem	W. Carson

St Leger

Year	Horse	Owner	Trainer	Jockey
1900	Diamond Jubilee	Prince of Wales	R. Marsh	H. Jones
1901	Doricles	L. de Rothschild	A. Hayhoe	K. Cannon
1902	Sceptre	R. Sievier	R. Sievier	F. Hardy
1903	Rock Sand	Sir J. Miller	G. Blackwell	D. Maher
1904	Pretty Polly	Maj. E. Loder	P. Gilpin	W. Lane
1905	Challacombe	W. Singer	A. Taylor	O. Madden
1906	Trout Beck	Duke of Westminster	W. Waugh	G. Stern
1907	Wool Winder	Col. E. Baird	H. Enoch	W. Halsey
1908	Your Majesty	J. Joel	C. Morton	W. Griggs
1909	Bayardo	Mr Fairie	A. Taylor	D. Maher
1910	Swynford	Lord Derby	G. Lambton	F. Wootton
1911	Prince Palatine	T. Pilkington	H. Beardsley	F. O'Neill
1912	Tracery	A. Belmont	J. Watson	G. Bellhouse
1913	Night Hawk	Col. W. Hall-Walker	W. Robinson	E. Wheatley
1914	Black Jester	J. Joel	C. Morton	W. Griggs
1915	Pommern	S. Joel	C. Peck	S. Donoghue
1916	Hurry On	J. Buchanan	F. Darling	C. Childs
1917	Gay Crusader	Mr Fairie	A. Taylor	S. Donoghue
1918	Gainsborough	Lady J. Douglas	A. Taylor	J. Childs
1919	Keysoe	Lord Derby	G. Lambton	B. Carslake
1920	Caligula	M. Goculdas	H. Leader	A. Smith
1921	Polemarch	Lord Londonderry	T. Green	J. Childs
1922	Royal Lancer	Lord Lonsdale	A. Sadler	R. Jones
1923	Tranquil	Lord Derby	C. Morton	T. Weston
1924	Salmon-Trout	Aga Khan	R. Dawson	B. Carslake
1925	Solario	Sir J. Rutherford	R. Day	J. Childs
1926	Coronach	Lord Woolavington	F. Darling	J. Childs
1927	Book Law	Lord Astor	A. Taylor	H. Jelliss
1928	Fairway	Lord Derby	Frank Butters	T. Weston
1929	Trigo	W. Barnett	R. Dawson	M. Beary
1930	Singapore	Lord Glanely	T. Hogg	G. Richards
1931	Sandwich	Lord Rosebery	J. Jarvis	H. Wragg
1932	Firdaussi	Aga Khan	Frank Butters	F. Fox
1933	Hyperion	Lord Derby	G. Lambton	T. Weston
1934	Windsor Lad	M. Benson	M. Marsh	C. Smirke
1935	Bahram	Aga Khan	Frank Butters	C. Smirke
1936	Boswell	W. Woodward	C. Boyd-Rochfort	P. Beasley
1937	Chulmleigh	Lord Glanely	T. Hogg	G. Richards
1938	Scottish Union	J. Rank	N. Cannon	B. Carslake
1939		(no race)		
1940	Turkhan	Aga Khan	F. Butters	G. Richards
1941	Sun Castle	Lord Portal	C. Boyd-Rochfort	G. Bridgland
1942	Sun Chariot	King George VI	F. Darling	G. Richards
1943	Herringbone	Lord Derby	W. Earl	H. Wragg
1944	Tehran	Aga Khan	Frank Butters	G. Richards
1945	Chamossaire	S. Joel	R. Perryman	T. Lowrey
1946	Airborne	J. Ferguson	R. Perryman	T. Lowrey
1947	Sayajirao	Maharaja of Baroda	F. Armstrong	E. Britt
1948	Black Tarquin	W. Woodward	C. Boyd-Rochfort	E. Britt
1949	Ridge Wood	G. Smith	N. Murless	M. Beary
1950	Scratch II	M. Boussac	C. Semblat	W. Johnstone
1951	Talma II	M. Boussac	C. Semblat	W. Johnstone
1952	Tulyar	Aga Khan	M. Marsh	C. Smirke
1953	Premonition	Brig. W. Wyatt	C. Boyd-Rochfort	E. Smith
1954	Never Say Die	R. Clark	J. Lawson	C. Smirke

Year	Horse	Owner	Trainer	Jockey
1955	Meld	Lady Z. Wernher	C. Boyd-Rochfort	W. Carr
1956	Cambremer	R. Strassburger	G. Bridgland	F. Palmer
1957	Ballymoss	J. McShain	V. O'Brien	T. P. Burns
1958	Alcide	Sir H. de Trafford	C. Boyd-Rochfort	W. Carr
1959	Cantelo	W. Hill	C. Elsey	E. Hide
1960	St Paddy	Sir V. Sassoon	N. Murless	L. Piggott
1961	Aurelius	Mrs V. Lilley	N. Murless	L. Piggott
1962	Hethersett	Maj. L. Holliday	W. Hern	W. Carr
1963	Ragusa	J. Mullion	P. Prendergast	G. Bougoure
1964	Indiana	C. W. Engelhard	J. Watts	J. Lindley
1965	Provoke	J. Astor	W. Hern	J. Mercer
1966	Sodium	R. J. Sigtia	G. Todd	F. Durr
1967	Ribocco	C. W. Engelhard	R. Houghton	L. Piggott
1968	Ribero	C. W. Engelhard	R. Houghton	L. Piggott
1969	Intermezzo	G. Oldham	H. Wragg	R. Hutchinson
1970	Nijinsky	C. W. Engelhard	V. O'Brien	L. Piggott
1971	Athens Wood	Mrs J. Rogerson	H. Thomson-Jones	L. Piggott
1972	Boucher	O. Phipps	V. O'Brien	L. Piggott
1973	Peleid	Col. W. E. Behrens	B. Elsey	F. Durr
1974	Bustino	Lady Beaverbrook	W. Hern	J. Mercer

Sussex Stakes

Year	Horse	Owner	Trainer	Jockey
1930	Paradine	W. Cazalet	J. Lawson	R. Jones
1931	Inglesant	S. Tattersall	J. Lawson	R. Jones
1932	Dastur	Aga Khan	Frank Butters	M. Beary
1933	The Abbot	King George V	W. Jarvis	J. Childs
1934	Badruddin	Aga Khan	Frank Butters	F. Fox
1935	Hairan	Aga Khan	Frank Butters	R. Perryman
1936	Corpach	Lord Astor	J. Lawson	G. Richards
1937	Pascal	H. Morriss	F. Darling	G. Richards
1938	Faroe	Lord Derby	C. Leader	R. Perryman
1939	Olein	Lord Glanely	B. Jarvis	T. Lowrey
1940–5		(no race)		
1946	Radiotherapy	T. Lilley	F. Templeman	G. Richards
1947	Combat	J. Dewar	F. Darling	G. Richards
1948	My Babu	Maharaja of Baroda	F. Armstrong	C. Smirke
1949	Krakatoa	Lord Feversham	N. Murless	G. Richards
1950	Palestine	Aga Khan	M. Marsh	C. Smirke
1951	Le Sage	S. Sanger	T. Carey	G. Richards
1952	Agitator	J. Dewar	N. Murless	G. Richards
1953	King of the Tudors	F. Dennis	W. Stephenson	C. Spares
1954	Landau	Queen Elizabeth II	N. Murless	W. Snaith
1955	My Kingdom	J. Armstrong	W. Nightingall	D. Smith
1956	Lucero	G. Oldham	H. Wragg	E. Mercer
1957	Quorum	T. Farr	W. Lyde	A. Russell
1958	Major Portion	H. Joel	T. Leader	E. Smith
1959	Petite Etoile	Aly Khan	N. Murless	L. Piggott
1960	Venture VII	Aga Khan	A. Head	G. Moore
1961	Le Levanstell	J. McGrath	S. McGrath	W. Williamson

Year	Horse	Owner	Trainer	Jockey
1962	Romulus	C. W. Engelhard	F. Houghton	W. Swinburn
1963	Queen's Hussar	Lord Carnarvon	T. Corbett	R. Hutchinson
1964	Roan Rocket	T. Frost	G. Todd	L. Piggott
1965	Carlemont	L. Gelb	P. Prendergast	R. Hutchinson
1966	Paveh	P. A. B. Widener	T. Ainsworth	R. Hutchinson
1967	Reform	M. Sobell	Sir G. Richards	A. Breasley
1968	Petingo	Capt. M. Lemos	F. Armstrong	L. Piggott
1969	Jimmy Reppin	Mrs S. Bates	J. Sutcliffe	G. Lewis
1970	Humble Duty	Jean, Lady Ashcombe	P. Walwyn	D. Keith
1971	Brigadier Gerard	Mrs J. Hislop	W. Hern	J. Mercer
1972	Sallust	Sir M. Sobell	W. Hern	J. Mercer
1973	Thatch	J. Mulcahy	V. O'Brien	L. Piggott
1974	Ace of Aces	N. Bunker-Hunt	M. Zilber	J. Lindley

1000-Guineas

Year	Horse	Owner	Trainer	Jockey
1900	Winifreda	L. Brassey	T. Jennings	S. Loates
1901	Aida	Sir J. Miller	G. Blackwell	D. Maher
1902	Sceptre	R. Sievier	R. Sievier	H. Randall
1903	Quintessence	Lord Falmouth	J. Chandler	H. Randall
1904	Pretty Polly	Maj. E. Loder	P. Gilpin	W. Lane
1905	Cherry Lass	W. H. Walker	W. Robinson	G. McCall
1906	Flair	Sir D. Cooper	P. Gilpin	B. Dillon
1907	Witch Elm	W. H. Walker	W. Robinson	B. Lynham
1908	Rhodora	R. Crocker	G. Allen	L. Lyne
1909	Electra	L. Neumann	P. Gilpin	B. Dillon
1910	Winkipop	W. Astor	W. Waugh	B. Lynham
1911	Atmah	J. de Rothschild	F. Pratt	F. Fox
1912	Tagalie	W. Raphael	D. Waugh	L. Hewitt
1913	Jest	J. Joel	C. Morton	F. Rickaby
1914	Princess Dorrie	J. Joel	C. Morton	W. Huxley
1915	Vaucluse	Lord Rosebery	F. Hartigan	F. Rickaby
1916	Canyon	Lord Derby	G. Lambton	F. Rickaby
1917	Diadem	Lord d'Abernon	G. Lambton	F. Rickaby
1918	Ferry	Lord Derby	G. Lambton	B. Carslake
1919	Roseway	Sir E. Hulton	F. Hartigan	A. Whalley
1920	Cinna	Sir R. Jardine	T. Waugh	W. Griggs
1921	Bettina	W. Raphael	P. Linton	G. Bellhouse
1922	Silver Urn	B. W. Parr	H. Persse	B. Carslake
1923	Tranquil	Lord Derby	G. Lambton	E. Gardner
1924	Plack	Lord Rosebery	J. Jarvis	C. Elliott
1925	Saucy Sue	Lord Astor	A. Taylor	F. Bullock
1926	Pillion	A. de Rothschild	J. Watson	R. Perryman
1927	Cresta Run	Lt Col. G. Loder	P. Gilpin	A. Balding
1928	Scuttle	King George V	W. Jarvis	J. Childs
1929	Taj Mah	M. S. Guthmann	J. Torterolo	W. Sibbritt
1930	Fair Isle	Lord Derby	Frank Butters	T. Weston
1931	Four Course	Lord Ellesmere	F. Darling	C. Elliott
1932	Kandy	M. de St. Alary	F. Carter	C. Elliott
1933	Brown Betty	W. Woodward	C. Boyd-Rochfort	J. Childs
1934	Campanula	Sir G. Bullough	J. Jarvis	H. Wragg
1935	Mesa	P. Wertheimer	P. Corbière	W. Johnstone
1936	Tide-way	Lord Derby	C. Leader	R. Perryman
1937	Exhibitionist	Sir V. Sassoon	J. Lawson	S. Donoghue
1938	Rockfel	Sir H. Cunliffe-Owen	O. Bell	S. Wragg
1939	Galatea II	R. Clark	J. Lawson	R. Jones
1940	Godiva	Lord Rothermere	W. Jarvis	D. Marks
1941	Dancing Time	Lord Glanely	J. Lawson	R. Perryman
1942	Sun Chariot	King George VI	F. Darling	G. Richards
1943	Herringbone	Lord Derby	W. Earl	H. Wragg
1944	Picture Play	J. Joel	J. Watts	C. Elliott
1945	Sun Stream	Lord Derby	W. Earl	H. Wragg
1946	Hypericum	King George VI	C. Boyd-Rochfort	D. Smith
1947	Imprudence	Mme P. Corbière	J. Lieux	W. Johnstone
1948	Queenpot	Sir P. Lorraine	N. Murless	G. Richards
1949	Musidora	N. Donaldson	C. Elsey	E. Britt
1950	Camaree	J. Ternynck	A. Lieux	W. Johnstone
1951	Belle of All	H. Tufton	N. Bertie	G. Richards
1952	Zabara	Sir M. McAlpine	V. Smyth	K. Gethin
1953	Happy Laughter	H. Wills	J. Jarvis	E. Mercer
1954	Festoon	J. Dewar	N. Cannon	A. Breasley
1955	Meld	Lady Z. Wernher	C. Boyd-Rochfort	W. Carr
1956	Honeylight	Sir V. Sassoon	C. Elsey	E. Britt
1957	Rose Royale II	Aga Khan	A. Head	C. Smirke
1958	Bella Paola	F. Dupré	F. Mathet	S. Boullenger
1959	Petite Etoile	Aly Khan	N. Murless	D. Smith
1960	Never Too Late II	Mrs H. Jackson	E. Pollet	R. Poincelet
1961	Sweet Solera	Mrs S. Castello	R. Day	W. Rickaby
1962	Abermaid	R. M. O'Ferrall	H. Wragg	W. Williamson
1963	Hula Dancer	Mrs P. Widener	E. Pollet	R. Poincelet
1964	Pourparler	Lady Granard	P. Prendergast	G. Bougoure
1965	Night Off	Maj. L. Holliday	W. Wharton	W. Williamson
1966	Glad Rags	Mrs J. Mills	V. O'Brien	P. Cook
1967	Fleet	R. C. Boucher	N. Murless	G. Moore
1968	Caergwrle	Mrs N. Murless	N. Murless	A. Barclay
1969	Full Dress II	R. B. Moller	H. Wragg	R. Hutchinson
1970	Humble Duty	Jean, Lady Ashcombe	P. Walwyn	L. Piggott
1971	Altesse Royale	F. R. Hue-Williams	N. Murless	Y. Saint-Martin
1972	Waterloo	Mrs R. Stanley	J. Watts	E. Hide
1973	Mysterious	G. A. Pope	N. Murless	G. Lewis
1974	Highclere	Queen Elizabeth II	W. Hern	J. Mercer

2000-Guineas

Year	Horse	Owner	Trainer	Jockey
1900	Diamond Jubilee	Prince of Wales	R. Marsh	H. Jones
1901	Handicapper	Sir E. Cassel	F. Day	W. Halsey
1902	Sceptre	R. Sievier	R. Sievier	H. Randall
1903	Rock Sand	Sir J. Miller	G. Blackwell	J. Martin
1904	St Amant	L. de Rothschild	A. Hayhoe	K. Cannon
1905	Vedas	W. de Wend-Fenton	W. Robinson	H. Jones
1906	Gorgos	A. James	R. Marsh	H. Jones
1907	Slieve Gallion	Capt. J. Greer	S. Darling	W. Higgs
1908	Norman III	A. Belmont	J. Watson	O. Madden
1909	Minoru	King Edward VII	R. Marsh	H. Jones
1910	Neil Gow	Lord Rosebery	P. Peck	D. Maher
1911	Sunstar	J. Joel	C. Morton	G. Stern
1912	Sweeper II	H. Duryea	H. Persse	D. Maher
1913	Louvois	W. Raphael	D. Waugh	J. Reiff
1914	Kennymore	Sir J. Thursby	A. Taylor	G. Stern
1915	Pommern	S. Joel	C. Peck	S. Donoghue
1916	Clarissimus	Lord Falmouth	W. Waugh	J. Clark
1917	Gay Crusader	Mr Fairie	A. Taylor	S. Donoghue
1918	Gainsborough	Lady J. Douglas	A. Taylor	J. Childs
1919	The Panther	Sir A. Black	G. Manser	R. Cooper
1920	Tetratema	Maj. D. McCalmont	H. Persse	B. Carslake
1921	Craig An Eran	Lord Astor	A. Taylor	J. Brennan
1922	St Louis	Lord Queensborough	P. Gilpin	G. Archibald
1923	Ellangowan	Lord Rosebery	J. Jarvis	C. Elliott
1924	Diophon	Aga Khan	R. Dawson	G. Hulme
1925	Manna	H. Morriss	F. Darling	S. Donoghue
1926	Colorado	Lord Derby	G. Lambton	T. Weston
1927	Adam's Apple	C. Whitburn	H. Cottrill	J. Leach
1928	Flamingo	Sir L. Philipps	J. Jarvis	C. Elliott
1929	Mr Jinks	Maj. D. McCalmont	H. Persse	H. Beasley
1930	Diolite	Sir H. Hirst	F. Templeman	F. Fox
1931	Cameronian	J. Dewer	F. Darling	J. Childs
1932	Orwell	W. Singer	J. Lawson	R. Jones
1933	Rodosto	Princesse de Faucigny-Lucinge	H. Count	R. Brethes
1934	Colombo	Lord Glanely	T. Hogg	W. Johnstone
1935	Bahram	Aga Khan	Frank Butters	F. Fox
1936	Pay Up	Lord Astor	J. Lawson	R. Dick
1937	Le Ksar	M. de St Alary	F. Carter	C. Semblat
1938	Pasch	H. Morriss	F. Darling	G. Richards
1939	Blue Peter	Lord Rosebery	J. Jarvis	E. Smith
1940	Djebel	M. Boussac	A. Swann	C. Elliott
1941	Lambert Simnel	Duke of Westminster	F. Templeman	C. Elliott
1942	Big Game	King George VI	F. Darling	G. Richards
1943	Kingsway	A. Saunders	J. Lawson	S. Wragg
1944	Garden Path	Lord Derby	W. Earl	H. Wragg
1945	Court Martial	Lord Astor	J. Lawson	C. Richards
1946	Happy Knight	Sir W. Cooke	H. Jelliss	T. Weston
1947	Tudor Minstrel	J. A. Dewar	F. Darling	G. Richards
1948	My Babu	Maharaja of Baroda	F. Armstrong	C. Smirke
1949	Nimbus	Mrs M. Glenister	G. Colling	C. Elliott
1950	Palestine	Aga Khan	M. Marsh	C. Smirke
1951	Ki Ming	Ley On	M. Beary	A. Breasley
1952	Thunderhead II	E. Constant	E. Pollet	R. Poincelet
1953	Nearula	W. Humble	C. Elsey	E. Britt
1954	Darius	Sir P. Loraine	H. Wragg	E. Mercer
1955	Our Babu	D. Robinson	G. Brooke	D. Smith
1956	Gilles de Retz	A. Samuel	C. Jerdein	F. Barlow
1957	Crepello	Sir V. Sassoon	N. Murless	L. Piggott
1958	Pall Mall	Queen Elizabeth II	C. Boyd-Rochfort	D. Smith
1959	Taboun	Aly Khan	A. Head	G. Moore
1960	Martial	R. Webster	P. Prendergast	R. Hutchinson
1961	Rockavon	T. Yuill	G. Boyd	N. Stirk
1962	Privy Councillor	Maj. G. Glover	T. Waugh	W. Rickaby
1963	Only For Life	Miss M. Sheriffe	J. Tree	J. Lindley
1964	Baldric II	Mrs H. Jackson	E. Fellows	W. Pyers
1965	Niksar	W. Harvey	W. Nightingall	D. Keith
1966	Kashmir II	P. Butler	C. Bartholomew	J. Lindley
1967	Royal Palace	H. Joel	N. Murless	G. Moore
1968	Sir Ivor	R. Guest	V. O'Brien	L. Piggott
1969	Right Tack	J. R. Brown	J. Sutcliffe	G. Lewis
1970	Nijinsky	C. W. Engelhard	V. O'Brien	L. Piggott
1971	Brigadier Gerard	J. Hislop	W. Hern	J. Mercer
1972	High Top	Sir J. Thorn	B. van Cutsem	W. Carson
1973	Mon Fils	Mrs B. M. L. Davis	R. Hannon	F. Durr
1974	Nonoalco	Mme M. Berger	F. Boutin	Y. Saint-Martin

Triple Crown Winners (Great Britain)

1853	West Australian
1865	Gladiateur
1866	Lord Lyon
1886	Ormonde
1891	Common
1893	Isinglass
1897	Galtee More
1899	Flying Fox
1900	Diamond Jubilee
1903	Rock Sand
1915	Pommern
1917	Gay Crusader
1918	Gainsborough
1935	Bahram
1970	Nijinsky

Flat Race Champion Jockeys (Great Britain)

Year	Jockey	No. races won
1900	L. Reiff	143
1901	O. Madden	130
1902	W. Lane	170
1903	O. Madden	154
1904	O. Madden	161
1905	E. Wheatley	124
1906	W. Higgs	149
1907	W. Higgs	146
1908	D. Maher	139
1909	F. Wootton	165
1910	F. Wootton	137
1911	F. Wootton	187
1912	F. Wootton	118
1913	D. Maher	115
1914	S. Donoghue	129
1915	S. Donoghue	62
1916	S. Donoghue	43
1917	S. Donoghue	42
1918	S. Donoghue	66
1919	S. Donoghue	129
1920	S. Donoghue	143
1921	S. Donoghue	141
1922	S. Donoghue	102
1923	S. Donoghue	89
	C. Elliott	89
1924	C. Elliott	106
1925	G. Richards	118
1926	T. Weston	95
1927	G. Richards	164
1928	G. Richards	148
1929	G. Richards	135
1930	F. Fox	129
1931	G. Richards	145
1932	G. Richards	190
1933	G. Richards	259
1934	G. Richards	212
1935	G. Richards	217
1936	G. Richards	174
1937	G. Richards	216
1938	G. Richards	200
1939	G. Richards	155
1940	G. Richards	68
1941	H. Wragg	71
1942	G. Richards	67
1943	G. Richards	65
1944	G. Richards	88
1945	G. Richards	104
1946	G. Richards	212
1947	G. Richards	269
1948	G. Richards	224
1949	G. Richards	261
1950	G. Richards	201
1951	G. Richards	227
1952	G. Richards	231
1953	G. Richards	191
1954	D. Smith	129
1955	D. Smith	168
1956	D. Smith	155
1957	A. Breasley	173
1958	D. Smith	165
1959	D. Smith	157
1960	L. Piggott	170
1961	A. Breasley	171
1962	A. Breasley	179
1963	A. Breasley	176
1964	L. Piggott	140
1965	L. Piggott	166
1966	L. Piggott	191
1967	L. Piggott	117
1968	L. Piggott	139
1969	L. Piggott	163
1970	L. Piggott	162
1971	L. Piggott	162
1972	W. Carson	132
1973	W. Carson	163
1974	P. Eddery	148

Champion Hurdle Challenge Cup

Year	Horse	Owner	Trainer	Jockey
1930	Brown Tony	Mrs J. de Selincourt	J. Anthony	T. Cullinan
1931		(no race)		
1932	Insurance	Hon. D. Paget	A. B. Briscoe	T. Leader
1933	Insurance	Hon D. Pagett	A. B. Briscoe	W. Stott
1934	Chenango	G. Bostwick	I. Anthony	D. Morgan
1935	Lion Courage	R. F.-Clayton	F. Brown	G. Wilson
1936	Victor Norman	Mrs M. Stephens	M. Blair	H. Nicholson
1937	Free Fare	B. Warner	E. Gwilt	G. Pellerin
1938	Our Hope	R. Gubbins	R. Gubbins	Capt. R. Harding
1939	African Sister	H. Brueton	C. Piggott	K. Piggott
1940	Solford	Hon. D. Paget	O. Anthony	S. Magee
1941	Seneca	Sir M. M. McAlpine	V. Smyth	R. Smyth
1942	Forestation	V. Smyth	V. Smyth	R. Smyth
1943–4		(no race)		
1945	Brains Trust	F. Blakeway	G. Wilson	T. F. Rimell
1946	Distel	Hon. D. Paget	C. Rogers	R. O'Ryan
1947	National Spirit	L. Abelson	V. Smyth	D. Morgan
1948	National Spirit	L. Abelson	V. Smyth	R. Smyth
1949	Hatton's Grace	Mrs M. Keogh	V. O'Brien	A. Brabazon
1950	Hatton's Grace	Mrs M. Keogh	V. O'Brien	A. Brabazon
1951	Hatton's Grace	Mrs M. Keogh	V. O'Brien	T. Molony
1952	Sir Ken	M. Kingsley	W. Stephenson	T. Molony
1953	Sir Ken	M. Kingsley	W. Stephenson	T. Molony
1954	Sir Ken	M. Kingsley	W. Stephenson	T. Molony
1955	Clair Soleil	G. Judd	H. Price	F. Winter
1956	Doorknocker	C. Nicholson	W. Hall	H. Sprague
1957	Merry Deal	A. Jones	A. Jones	G. Underwood
1958	Bandalore	Mrs D. Wright	J. Wright	G. Slack
1959	Fare Time	G. Judd	H. Price	F. Winter
1960	Another Flash	J. Byrne	P. Sleator	H. Beasley
1961	Eborneezer	Dr B. Pajgar	H. Price	F. Winter
1962	Anzio	Sir T. Ainsworth	F. Walwyn	G. W. Robinson
1963	Winning Fair	G. Spencer	G. Spencer	Mr A. Lillingstone
1964	Magic Court	J. McGhie	T. Robson	P. McCarron
1965	Kirriemuir	Mrs D. Beddington	F. Walwyn	G. W. Robinson
1966	Salmon Spray	Mrs J. Rogerson	R. Turnell	J. Haine
1967	Saucy Kit	K. Adler	M. H. Easterby	R. Edwards
1968	Persian War	H. Alper	C. Davies	J. Uttley
1969	Persian War	H. Alper	C. Davies	J. Uttley
1970	Persian War	H. Alper	C. Davies	J. Uttley
1971	Bula	Capt. E. Edwards-Heathcote	F. Winter	P. Kelleway
1972	Bula	Capt. E. Edwards-Heathcote	F. Winter	P. Kelleway
1973	Comedy of Errors	E. Wheatley	T. F. Rimell	W. Smith
1974	Lanzarote	Lord Howard de Walden	F. Winter	R. Pitman

Cheltenham Gold Cup

Year	Horse	Owner	Trainer	Jockey
1930	Easter Hero	J. Whitney	J. Anthony	T. Cullinan
1931		(no race)		
1932	Golden Miller	Hon. D. Paget	A. B. Briscoe	T. Leader
1933	Golden Miller	Hon. D. Paget	A. B. Briscoe	W. Stott
1934	Golden Miller	Hon. D. Paget	A. B. Briscoe	G. Wilson
1935	Golden Miller	Hon. D. Paget	A. B. Briscoe	G. Wilson
1936	Golden Miller	Hon. D. Paget	O. Anthony	E. Williams
1937		(no race)		
1938	Morse Code	Lt Col. D. Part	I. Anthony	D. Morgan
1939	Brendan's Cottage	Mrs A. S. Bingham	G. Beeby	G. Owen
1940	Roman Hackle	Hon. D. Paget	O. Anthony	E. Williams
1941	Poet Prince	D. Sherbrooke	I. Anthony	R. Burford
1942	Medoc II	Lord Sefton	R. Hobbs	H. Nicholson
1943–4		(no race)		
1945	Red Rower	Lord Stalbridge	Lord Stalbridge	D. Jones
1946	Prince Regent	J. Rank	T. Dreaper	T. Hyde
1947	Fortina	Lord Grimthorpe	H. Christie	Mr R. Black
1948	Cottage Rake	F. Vickerman	V. O'Brien	A. Brabazon
1949	Cottage Rake	F. Vickerman	V. O'Brien	A. Brabazon
1950	Cottage Rake	F. Vickerman	V. O'Brien	A. Brabazon
1951	Silver Fame	Lord Bicester	G. Beeby	M. Molony
1952	Mont Tremblant	Hon. D. Paget	F. Walwyn	D. Dick
1953	Knock Hard	Mrs M. Keogh	V. O'Brien	T. Molony
1954	Four Ten	A. Strange	J. Roberts	T. Cusack
1955	Gay Donald	P. Burt	J. Ford	A. Grantham
1956	Limber Hill	J. Davey	W. Dutton	J. Power
1957	Linwell	D. Brown	C. Mallon	M. Scudamore
1958	Kerstin	G. Moore	C. Bewicke	S. Hayhurst
1959	Roddy Owen	Lord Fingall	D. Morgan	H. Beasley
1960	Pas Seul	J. Rogerson	R. Turnell	W. Rees
1961	Saffron Tartan	Col. G. Westmacott	D. Butchers	F. Winter
1962	Mandarin	Mme K. Hennessy	F. Walwyn	F. Winter
1963	Mill House	W. Gollings	F. Walwyn	G. W. Robinson
1964	Arkle	Duchess of Westminster	T. Dreaper	P. Taaffe
1965	Arkle	Duchess of Westminster	T. Dreaper	P. Taaffe
1966	Arkle	Duchess of Westminster	T. Dreaper	P. Taaffe
1967	Woodland Venture	H. H. Collins	T. F. Rimell	T. Biddlecombe
1968	Fort Leney	Col. J. Thomson	T. Dreaper	P. Taaffe
1969	What A Myth	Lady Weir	H. Price	P. Kelleway
1970	L'Escargot	R. Guest	D. L. Moore	T. Carberry
1971	L'Escargot	R. Guest	D. L. Moore	T. Carberry
1972	Glencaraig Lady	P. Doyle	F. Flood	F. Berry
1973	The Dikler	Mrs D. August	F. Walwyn	R. Barry
1974	Captain Christy	Mrs J. Samuel	P. Taaffe	H. Beasley

Grand National Handicap Steeplechase

Year	Horse	Owner	Trainer	Jockey
1900	Ambush II	The Prince of Wales	A. Anthony	A. Anthony
1901	Grudon	B. Bletsoe	J. Holland	A. Nightingall
1902	Shannon Lass	A. Gorham	Hackett	D. Read
1903	Drumcree	J. Morrison	Sir C. Nugent	P. Woodland
1904	Moifaa	S. Gollans	O. Hickey	A. Birch
1905	Kirkland	F. Bibby	Thomas	F. Mason
1906	Ascetic's Silver	Prince Hatzfeldt	Hon. A. Hastings	Hon. A. Hastings
1907	Eremon	S. Howard	T. Coulthwaite	A. Newey
1908	Rubio	Maj. F. Douglas-Pennant	W. Costello	H. Bletsoe
1909	Lutteur III	J. Hennessy	H. Escott	G. Parfrement
1910	Jenkinstown	S. Howard	T. Coulthwaite	R. Chadwick
1911	Glenside	F. Bibby	Capt. Collis	Mr J. Anthony
1912	Jerry M	Sir C. Assheton-Smith	R. Gore	E. Piggott
1913	Covertcoat	Sir C. Assheton-Smith	R. Gore	P. Woodland
1914	Sunloch	T. Tyler	T. Tyler	W. Smith
1915	Ally Sloper	Lady Nelson	A. Hastings	Mr J. Anthony
1916	Vermouth	P. Heybourn	J. Bell	J. Reardon
1917	Ballymacad	Sir G. Bullough	A. Hastings	E. Driscoll
1918	Poethlyn	Mrs H. Peel	A. Escott	E. Piggott
1919	Poethlyn	Mrs H. Peel	A. Escott	E. Piggott
1920	Troytown	Maj. T. Gerrard	A. Anthony	Mr J. Anthony
1921	Shaun Spadah	M. McAlpine	G. Poole	F. Rees
1922	Music Hall	H. Kershaw	O. Anthony	L. Rees
1923	Sergeant Murphy	S. Sanford	G. Blackwell	Capt. G. Bennett
1924	Master Robert	Lord Airlie	A. Hastings	R. Trudgill
1925	Double Chance	D. Goold	F. Archer	Maj. J. Wilson
1926	Jack Horner	A. Schwartz	H. Leader	W. Watkinson
1927	Sprig	Mrs M. Partridge	T. R. Leader	T. E. Leader
1928	Tipperary Tim	H. Kenyon	J. Dodd	Mr W. Dutton
1929	Gregalach	Mrs M Gemmell	T. R. Leader	R. Everett
1930	Shaun Goilin	W. Midwood	F. Hartigan	T. Cullinan
1931	Grakle	C. Taylor	T. Coulthwaite	R. Lyall
1932	Forbra	W. Parsonage	T. R. Rimell	J. Hamey
1933	Kellsboro' Jack	Mrs F. Clark	I. Anthony	D. Williams
1934	Golden Miller	Hon. D. Paget	A. B. Briscoe	G. Wilson
1935	Reynoldstown	Maj. N. Furlong	N. Furlong	Mr F. Furlong
1936	Reynoldstown	Maj. N. Furlong	N. Furlong	Mr F. Walwyn
1937	Royal Mail	H. Thomas	I. Anthony	E. Williams
1938	Battleship	Mrs M. Scott	R. Hobbs	B. Hobbs
1939	Workman	Sir A. Maguire	J. Ruttle	T. Hyde
1940	Bogskar	Lord Stalbridge	Lord Stalbridge	M. Jones
1941–5		(no race)		
1946	Lovely Cottage	J. Morant	T. Rayson	Capt. R. Petre
1947	Caughoo	J. McDowell	H. McDowell	E. Dempsey
1948	Sheila's Cottage	J. Proctor	N. Crump	A. Thompson
1949	Russian Hero	W. Williamson	G. Owen	L. McMorrow
1950	Freebooter	Mrs L. Brotherton	R. Renton	J. Power
1951	Nickel Coin	J. Royle	J. O'Donoghue	J. Bullock
1952	Teal	H. Lane	N. Crump	A. Thompson

249

Year	Horse	Owner	Trainer	Jockey
1953	Early Mist	J. Griffin	V. O'Brien	B. Marshall
1954	Royal Tan	J. Griffin	V. O'Brien	B. Marshall
1955	Quare Times	Mrs W. Welman	V. O'Brien	P. Taaffe
1956	E.S.B.	Mrs L. Carver	T. F. Rimell	D. Dick
1957	Sundew	Mrs G. Kohn	F. Hudson	F. Winter
1958	Mr What	D. Coughlan	T. Taaffe	A. Freeman
1959	Oxo	J. Bigg	W. Stephenson	M. Scudamore
1960	Merryman II	Miss W. Wallace	N. Crump	G. Scott
1961	Nicolaus Silver	C. Vaughan	T. F. Rimell	H. Beasley
1962	Kilmore	N. Cohen	H. Price	F. Winter
1963	Ayala	P. Raymond	K. Piggott	P. Buckley
1964	Team Spirit	J. Goodman	F. Walwyn	G. W. Robinson
1965	Jay Trump	Mrs M. Stephenson	F. Winter	Mr C. Smith
1966	Anglo	S. Levy	F. Winter	T. Norman
1967	Foinavon	C. Watkins	J. Kempton	J. Buckingham
1968	Red Alligator	J. Manners	D. Smith	B. Fletcher
1969	Highland Wedding	T. H. McKoy	G. Balding	E. Harty
1970	Gay Trip	A. Chambers	T. F. Rimell	P. Taaffe
1971	Specify	F. Pontin	J. Sutcliffe	J. Cook
1972	Well To Do	Capt. T. Forster	T. Forster	G. Thorner
1973	Red Rum	N. le Mare	D. McCain	B. Fletcher
1974	Red Rum	N. le Mare	D. McCain	B. Fletcher

Year	Horse	Owner	Trainer	Jockey
1959	Sabaria	R. Turnell	R. Turnell	Hon. J. Lawrence
1960	Proud Socks	V. Bishop	V. Bishop	Mr H. Thompson
1961	Superfine	I. Kerwood	F. Cundell	Sir W. Pigott-Brown
1962	Go Slow	Mrs I. Millar	A. Piper	Mr G. Small
1963	Time	J. Cheatle	W. Stephenson	Mr I. Balding
1964	Dorimont	M. Walshe	T. Taaffe	Mr C. Vaughan
1965	Red Vale	Mrs C. Smith	A. Piper	Mr G. Small
1966	Polaris Missile	M. J. Thorne	M. J. Thorne	Mr M. J. Thorne
1967	Master Tammy	G. Guilding	G. Guilding	Capt. B. Fanshawe
1968	Fascinating Forties	Lord Leverhulme	G. Owen	Mr M. Dickenson
1969	Lizzy the Lizard	A. R. Hartnoll	A. Hartnoll	Mr G. Cann
1970	Domason	H. W. Dufosee	H. W. Dufosee	Mr R. Alner
1971	Deblins Green	G. Yardley	G. Yardley	Mr J. Edmunds
1972	Charley Winking	L. Scott	L. Scott	Mr D. Scott
1973	Foreman	R. W. Dean	H. Thomson-Jones	Mr W. Shand-Kydd
1974	Mr Midland	B. Naughton	E. O'Grady	Mr M. F. Morris

National Hunt Steeplechase

Year	Horse	Owner	Trainer	Jockey
1930	Sir Lindsay	J. Whitney	J. Anthony	Lord Fingall
1931	Merriment IV	Lord Haddington	J. Wight	Lord Haddington
1932	Robin-a-Tiptoe	Maj. N. Furlong	W. Gale	Mr F. Furlong
1933	Ego	Lt Col. M. Lindsay	M. Lindsay	Mr R. Harding
1934	Crown Prince	Lord Rosebery	C. Beechener	Mr R. Stuitt
1935	Rod and Gun	J. Whitney	J. Anthony	Mr H. Jones
1936	Pucka Belle	E. Bailey	E. Bailey	Mr E. Bailey
1937	Hopeful Hero	H. Silley	H. Silley	Mr W. Dawes
1938	St George II	A. L. Gower	A. L. Gower	Mr R. Petre
1939	Litigant	Maj. N. Furlong	F. Furlong	Mr R. Black
1940–5	(no race)			
1946	Prattler	E. Manners	J. Hall	Maj. D. Daly
1947	Maltese Wanderer	G. Wells	T. Yates	Maj. D. Daly
1948	Bruno II	Maj. W. A.-Gray	W. A.-Gray	Maj. G. Cunard
1949	Castledermot	Mrs M. Keogh	V. O'Brien	Lord Mildmay
1950	Ellesmere	Lord Bicester	K. Cundell	Mr A. Corbett
1951	Cushendun	Mrs L. Brotherton	R. Renton	Mr P. Chisman
1952	Frosty Knight	Maj. I. Straker	I. Straker	Mr C. Straker
1953	Pontage	Lady H. Svejdar	D. Moore	Mr J. Cox
1954	Quare Times	Mrs R. Smyth	V. O'Brien	Mr J. Cox
1955	Reverend Prince	P. Dufosee	P. Dufosee	Mr C. Pocock
1956	Rosana III	J. Everitt	J. Everitt	Mr J. Everitt
1957	Kari Sou	A. Thomlinson	A. Thomlinson	Mr A. Lillingston
1958	Spud Tamson	Mrs T. Dun	T. Dun	Mr G. Dun

National Hunt Champion Jockeys (Great Britain)

Year	Jockey	No. races won	Year	Jockey	No. races won
1900	Mr H. S. Sidney	53	1938–9	T. F. Rimell	61
1901	F. Mason	58	1939–40	T. F. Rimell	24
1902	F. Mason	67	1940–1	G. Wilson	22
1903	P. Woodland	54	1941–2	R. Smyth	12
1904	F. Mason	59	1942–3	(no racing)	
1905	F. Mason	73	1943–4	(no racing)	
1906	F. Mason	58	1944–5	H. Nicholson	15
1907	F. Mason	59		T. F. Rimell	15
1908	P. Cowley	65	1945–6	T. F. Rimell	54
1909	R. Gordon	45	1946–7	J. Dodeswell	58
1910	E. Piggott	67	1947–8	B. Marshall	66
1911	W. Payne	76	1948–9	T. Molony	60
1912	I. Anthony	78	1949–50	T. Molony	95
1913	E. Piggott	60	1950–1	T. Molony	83
1914	Mr J. R. Anthony	60	1951–2	T. Molony	99
1915	E. Piggott	44	1952–3	F. Winter	121
1916	C. Hawkins	17	1953–4	R. Francis	76
1917	W. Smith	15	1954–5	T. Molony	67
1918	G. Duller	17	1955–6	F. Winter	74
1919	Mr H. Brown	48	1956–7	F. Winter	80
1920	F. B. Rees	64	1957–8	F. Winter	82
1921	F. B. Rees	65	1958–9	T. Brookshaw	83
1922	J. Anthony	78	1959–60	S. Mellor	68
1923	F. B. Rees	64	1960–1	S. Mellor	118
1924	F. B. Rees	108	1961–2	S. Mellor	80
1925	E. Foster	76	1962–3	J. Gifford	70
1925–6	T. Leader	61	1963–4	J. Gifford	94
1926–7	F. B. Rees	59	1964–5	T. Biddlecombe	114
1927–8	W. Stott	88	1965–6	T. Biddlecombe	102
1928–9	W. Stott	76	1966–7	J. Gifford	122
1929–30	W. Stott	77	1967–8	J. Gifford	82
1930–1	W. Stott	81	1968–9	B. R. Davies	77
1931–2	W. Stott	77		T. Biddlecombe	77
1932–3	G. Wilson	61	1969–70	B. R. Davies	91
1933–4	G. Wilson	56	1970–1	G. Thorner	74
1934–5	G. Wilson	73	1971–2	B. R. Davies	89
1935–6	G. Wilson	57	1972–3	R. Barry	125
1936–7	G. Wilson	45	1973–4	R. Barry	94
1937–8	G. Wilson	59			

Major Races in the United States

Belmont Stakes

Year	Horse	Owner	Trainer	Jockey
1867	Ruthless	F. Morris	A. J. Minor	J. Gilpatrick
1868	General Duke	McConnell & Harness	A. Thompson	R. Swim
1869	Fenian	A. Belmont	J. Pincus	C. Miller
1870	Kingfisher	D. Swigert	R. Colston	E. Brown
1871	Harry Bassett	D. McDaniel	D. McDaniel	W. Miller
1872	Joe Daniels	D. McDaniel	D. McDaniel	J. Rowe
1873	Springbok	D. McDaniel	D. McDaniel	J. Rowe
1874	Saxon	P. Lorillard	W. Prior	G. Barbee
1875	Calvin	H. P. McGrath	A. Williams	R. Swim
1876	Algerine	Doswell & Cammacks	T. W. Doswell	W. Donohue
1877	Cloverbrook	E. A. Clabaugh	J. Walden	C. Holloway
1878	Duke of Magenta	G. L. Lorillard	R. W. Walden	W. Hughes
1879	Spendthrift	J. R. Keene	T. Puryear	G. Evans
1880	Grenada	G. L. Lorillard	R. W. Walden	W. Hughes
1881	Saunterer	G. L. Lorillard	R. W. Walden	T. Costello
1882	Forester	Appleby & Johnson	L. Stuart	J. McLaughlin
1883	George Kinney	Dwyer Brothers	J. Rowe	J. McLaughlin
1884	Panique	Dwyer Brothers	J. Rowe	J. McLaughlin
1885	Tyrant	B. A. Haggin	W. Claypool	P. Duffy
1886	Inspector B	Dwyer Brothers	F. McCabe	J. McLaughlin
1887	Hanover	Dwyer Brothers	F. McCabe	J. McLaughlin
1888	Sir Dixon	Dwyer Brothers	F. McCabe	J. McLaughlin
1889	Eric	A. J. Cassatt	J. Huggins	W. Hayward
1890	Burlington	Hough Brothers	A. Cooper	S. Barnes
1891	Foxford	C. E. Rand	M. Donovan	E. Garrison
1892	Patron	L. Stuart	L. Stuart	W. Hayward
1893	Comanche	Empire Stable	G. Hannon	W. Simms
1894	Henry of Navarre	B. McClelland	B. McClelland	W. Simms
1895	Belmar	Preakness Stable	E. Feakes	F. Taral
1896	Hastings	Blemton Stable	J. J. Hyland	H. Griffin
1897	Scottish Chieftain	M. Daly	M. Byrnes	J. Scherrer
1898	Bowling Brook	J. A. & A. H. Morris	R. W. Walden	F. Littlefield
1899	Jean Bereaud	S. Paget	S. C. Hildreth	R. Clawson
1900	Ildrim	H. E. Leigh	H. E. Leigh	N. Turner
1901	Commando	J. R. Keene	J. Rowe	H. Spencer
1902	Masterman	A. Belmont	J. J. Hyland	J. Bullman
1903	Africander	Hampton Stable	R. Miller	J. Bullman
1904	Delhi	J. R. Keene	J. Rowe	G. Odom
1905	Tanya	H. P. Whitney	J. W. Rogers	E. Hildebrand
1906	Burgomaster	H. P. Whitney	J. W. Rogers	L. Lyne
1907	Peter Pan	J. R. Keene	J. Rowe	G. Mountain
1908	Colin	J. R. Keene	J. Rowe	J. Notter
1909	Joe Madden	S. C. Hildreth	S. C. Hildreth	E. Dugan
1910	Sweep	J. R. Keene	J. Rowe	J. Butwell
1913	Prince Eugene	H. P. Whitney	J. Rowe	R. Troxler
1914	Luke McLuke	J. W. Schorr	J. F. Schorr	M. Buxton
1915	The Finn	H. C. Hallenbeck	E. W. Heffner	G. Byrne

Year	Horse	Owner	Trainer	Jockey
1916	Friar Rock	A. Belmont	S. C. Hildreth	E. Haynes
1917	Hourless	A. Belmont	S. C. Hildreth	J. Butwell
1918	Johren	H. P. Whitney	A. Simons	F. Robinson
1919	Sir Barton	J. K. L. Ross	H. G. Bedwell	J. Loftus
1920	Man o' War	Glen Riddle Farms	L. Feustel	C. Kummer
1921	Grey Lag	Rancocas Stable	S. C. Hildreth	E. Sande
1922	Pillory	R. T. Wilson	T. J. Healey	C. H. Miller
1923	Zev	Rancocas Stable	S. C. Hildreth	E. Sande
1924	Mad Play	Rancocas Stable	S. C. Hildreth	E. Sande
1925	American Flag	Glen Riddle Farms	G. R. Tompkins	A. Johnson
1926	Crusader	Glen Riddle Farms	G. Conway	A. Johnson
1927	Chance Shot	J. E. Widener	P. Coyne	E. Sande
1928	Vito	A. H. Cosden	M. Hirsch	C. Kummer
1929	Blue Larkspur	E. R. Bradley	C. Hastings	M. Garner
1930	Gallant Fox	Belair Stud	J. Fitzsimmons	E. Sande
1931	Twenty Grand	Greentree Stable	J. Rowe, Jnr	C. Kurtsinger
1932	Faireno	Belair Stud	J. Fitzsimmons	T. Malley
1933	Hurryoff	J. E. Widener	H. McDaniel	M. Garner
1934	Peace Chance	J. E. Widener	P. Coyne	W. D. Wright
1935	Omaha	Belair Stud	J. Fitzsimmons	W. Saunders
1936	Granville	Belair Stud	J. Fitzsimmons	J. Stout
1937	War Admiral	Glen Riddle Farms	G. Conway	C. Kurtsinger
1938	Pasteurized	Mrs W. P. Stewart	G. M. Odom	J. Stout
1939	Johnstown	Belair Stud	J. Fitzsimmons	J. Stout
1940	Bimelech	E. R. Bradley	W. Hurley	F. A. Smith
1941	Whirlaway	Calumet Farm	B. A. Jones	E. Arcaro
1942	Shut Out	Greentree Stable	J. M. Gaver	E. Arcaro
1943	Count Fleet	Mrs J. Hertz	G. D. Cameron	J. Longden
1944	Bounding Home	W. Ziegler, Jnr	Matt Brady	G. L. Smith
1945	Pavot	W. M. Jeffords	O. White	E. Arcaro
1946	Assault	King Ranch	M. Hirsch	W. Mehrtens
1947	Phalanx	C. V. Whitney	Sylvester Veitch	R. Donoso
1948	Citation	Calumet Farm	H. A. Jones	E. Arcaro
1949	Capot	Greentree Stable	J. M. Gaver	T. Atkinson
1950	Middleground	King Ranch	M. Hirsch	W. Boland
1951	Counterpoint	C. V. Whitney	Sylvester Veitch	D. Gorman
1952	One Count	Mrs W. M. Jeffords	O. White	E. Arcaro
1953	Native Dancer	A. G. Vanderbilt	W. C. Winfrey	E. Guerin
1954	High Gun	King Ranch	M. Hirsch	E. Guerin
1955	Nashua	Belair Stud	J. Fitzsimmons	E. Arcaro
1956	Needles	D. & H. Stable	H. L. Fontaine	D. Erb
1957	Gallant Man	Ralph Lowe	J. A. Nerud	W. Shoemaker
1958	Cavan	J. E. O'Connell	T. J. Barry	P. Anderson
1959	Sword Dancer	Brookmeade Stable	J. E. Burch	W. Shoemaker
1960	Celtic Ash	J. E. O'Connell	T. J. Barry	W. Hartack
1961	Sherluck	J. Sher	H. Young	B. Baeza
1962	Jaipur	George D. Widener	Burt Mulholland	W. Shoemaker
1963	Chateaugay	John W. Galbreath	J. P. Conway	B. Baeza
1964	Quadrangle	Paul Mellon	J. E. Burch	M. Ycaza
1965	Hail to All	Mrs B. Cohen	E. Yowell	J. Sellers
1966	Amberoid	R. N. Webster	L. Laurin	W. Boland
1967	Damascus	Mrs E. W. Bancroft	F. Y. Whitley, Jnr	W. Shoemaker
1968	Stage Door Johnny	Greentree Stable	J. M. Gaver	H. Gustines
1969	Arts and Letters	Paul Mellon	Elliot Burch	B. Baeza
1970	High Echelon	Mrs E. D. Jacobs	J. W. Jacobs	John Rotz
1971	Pass Catcher	October House Farm	E. Yowell	W. Blum
1972	Riva Ridge	Meadow Stable	L. Laurin	R. Turcotte
1973	Secretariat	Meadow Stable	L. Laurin	R. Turcotte
1974	Little Current	Darby Danfarm	Lou Rondinello	M. Rivera

Futurity Stakes

Year	Horse	Jockey
1888	Proctor Knott	S. Barnes
1889	Chaos	G. Day
1890	Potomac	A. Hamilton
1891	His Highness	J. McLaughlin
1892	Morello	W. Hayward
1893	Domino	F. Taral
1894	The Butterflies	H. Griffin
1895	Requital	H. Griffin
1896	Ogden	F. Turbiville
1897	L'Alouette	R. Clawson
1898	Martimas	H. Lewis
1899	Chacornac	H. Spencer
1900	Ballyhoo Bey	T. Sloan
1901	Yankee	W. O'Connor
1902	Savable	L. Lyne
1903	Hamburg Belle	G. Fuller
1904	Artful	E. Hildebrand
1905	Ormondale	A. Redfern
1906	Electioneer	W. Shaw
1907	Colin	W. Miller
1908	Maskette	J. Notter
1909	Sweep	J. Butwell
1910	Novelty	C. H. Shilling
1911–2	(no race)	
1913	Pennant	C. Borel
1914	Trojan	C. Burlingame
1915	Thunderer	J. Notter
1916	Campfire	J. McTaggart
1917	Papp	L. Allen
1918	Dunboyne	A. Schuttinger
1919	Man o' War	J. Loftus
1920	Step Lightly	F. Keogh
1921	Bunting	F. Coltiletti
1922	Sally's Alley	A. Johnson
1923	St James	T. McTaggart
1924	Mother Goose	L. McAtee
1925	Pompey	L. Fator
1926	Scapa Flow	L. Fator
1927	Anita Peabody	C. Lang
1928	High Strung	L. McAtee
1929	Whichone	R. Workman
1930	Jamestown	L. McAtee
1931	Top Flight	R. Workman
1932	Kerry Patch	R. Walls
1933	Singing Wood	R. Jones

Year	Horse	Jockey
1934	Chance Sun	W. D. Wright
1935	Tintagel	S. Coucci
1936	Pompoon	H. Richards
1937	Menow	C. Kurtsinger
1938	Porter's Mite	B. James
1939	Bimelech	F. A. Smith
1940	Our Boots	E. Arcaro
1941	Some Chance	W. Eads
1942	Occupation	G. Woolf
1943	Occupy	G. Woolf
1944	Pavot	G. Woolf
1945	Star Pilot	A. Kirkland
1946	First Flight	E. Arcaro
1947	Citation	A. Snider
1948	Blue Peter	E. Guerin
1949	Guillotine	T. Atkinson
1950	Battlefield	E. Arcaro
1951	Tom Fool	T. Atkinson
1952	Native Dancer	E. Guerin
1953	Porterhouse	W. Boland
1954	Nashua	E. Arcaro
1955	Nail	H. Woodhouse
1956	Bold Ruler	E. Arcaro
1957	Jester	P. J. Bailey
1958	Intentionally	W. Shoemaker
1959	Weatherwise	E. Arcaro
1960	Little Tumbler	R. Broussard
1961	Cyane	M. Ycaza
1962	Never Bend	W. Shoemaker
1963	Bupers	A. Gomez
1964	Bold Lad	B. Baeza
1965	Priceless Gem	W. Blum
1966	Bold Hour	J. L. Rotz
1967	Captain's Gig	W. Shoemaker
1968	Top Knight	M. Ycaza
1969	High Echelon	J. L. Rotz
1970	Salem	J. L. Rotz
1971	Riva Ridge	R. Turcotte
1972	Secretariat	R. Turcotte
1973	Wedge Shot	J. Vasquez
1974	Just The Time	M. Castaneda

Kentucky Derby

Year	Horse	Owner	Trainer	Jockey
1875	Aristides	H. P. McGrath	A. Anderson	O. Lewis
1876	Vagrant	William Astor	James Williams	R. Swim
1877	Baden-Baden	Daniel Swigert	Ed Brown	W. Walker
1878	Day Star	T. J. Nichols	Lee Paul	J. Carter
1879	Lord Murphy	Geo. W. Darden & Co	George Rice	G. Schauer
1880	Fonso	J. S. Shawhan	Tice Hutsell	G. Lewis
1881	Hindoo	Dwyer Bros.	Jas. Rowe, Snr	J. McLaughlin
1882	Apollo	Morris & Patton	Green B. Morris	B. Hurd
1883	Leonatus	Chinn & Morgan	R. Colston	W. Donohue
1884	Buchanan	W. Cottrill	Wm. Bird	A. Murphy
1885	Joe Cotton	J. T. Williams	Alex Perry	E. Henderson
1886	Ben Ali	J. B. Haggin	Jim Murphy	P. Duffy
1887	Montrose	Labold Bros	John McGinty	I. Lewis
1888	Macbeth II	Chicago Stable	John Campbell	G. Covington
1889	Spokane	Noah Armstrong	John Rodegap	T. Kiley
1890	Riley	Edward Corrigan	Edward Corrigan	I. Murphy
1891	Kingman	Jacobin Stable	Dud Allen	I. Murphy
1892	Azra	Bashford Manor	John H. Morris	A. Clayton
1893	Lookout	Cushing & Orth	Will McDaniel	E. Kunze
1894	Chant	Leigh & Rose	Eugene Leigh	F. Goodale
1895	Halma	Byron McClelland	Byron McClelland	J. Perkins
1896	Ben Brush	M. F. Dwyer	Hardy Campbell	W. Simms
1897	Typhoon II	J. C. Cahn	J. C. Cahn	F. Garner
1898	Plaudit	J. E. Madden	J. E. Madden	W. Simms
1899	Manuel	A. H. & D. H. Morris	Robert J. Walden	F. Taral
1900	Lieut. Gibson	Charles H. Smith	Chas. H. Hughes	J. Boland
1901	His Eminence	F. B. Van-Meter	F. B. Van-Meter	J. Winkfield
1902	Alan-a-Dale	T. C. McDowell	T. C. McDowell	J. Winkfield
1903	Judge Himes	C. R. Ellison	J. P. Mayberry	H. Booker
1904	Elwood	Mrs C. E. Durnell	C. E. Durnell	F. Prior
1905	Agile	S. S. Brown	Robert Tucker	J. Martin
1906	Sir Huon	George J. Long	Peter Coyne	R. Troxler
1907	Pink Star	J. Hal Woodford	W. H. Fizer	A. Minder
1908	Stone Street	C. E. Hamilton	J. Hall	A. Pickens
1909	Wintergreen	J. B. Respess	C. Mack	V. Powers
1910	Donau	William Gerst	George Ham	F. Herbert
1911	Meridian	R. F. Carman	A. Ewing	G. Archibald
1912	Worth	H. C. Hallenbeck	Frank M. Taylor	C. H. Shilling
1913	Donerail	T. P. Hayes	T. P. Hayes	R. Goose
1914	Old Rosebud	H. C. Applegate	F. D. Weir	J. McCabe
1915	Regret	H. P. Whitney	Jas. Rowe, Snr	J. Nolter
1916	George Smith	John Sanford	Hollie Hughes	J. Loftus
1917	Omar Khayyam	Billings & Johnson	C. T. Patterson	C. Borel
1918	Exterminator	W. S. Kilmer	Henry McDaniel	W. Knapp
1919	Sir Barton	J. K. L. Ross	H. G. Bedwell	J. Loftus
1920	Paul Jones	Ral Parr	Wm. Garth	T. Rice
1921	Behave Yourself	E. R. Bradley	H. J. Thompson	C. Thompson
1922	Morvich	B. Block	Fred Burlew	A. Johnson
1923	Zev	Rancocas Stable	D. J. Leary	E. Sande
1924	Black Gold	Mrs R. M. Hoots	Hanly Webb	J. D. Mooney
1925	Flying Ebony	G. A. Cochran	W. B. Duke	E. Sande
1926	Bubbling Over	Idle Hour Stock Farm	H. J. Thompson	A. Johnson
1927	Whiskery	H. P. Whitney	Fred Hopkins	L. McAtee
1928	Reigh Count	Mrs J. D. Hertz	B. S. Michell	C. Lang
1929	Clyde Van Dusen	H. P. Gardner	C. Van Dusen	L. McAtee
1930	Gallant Fox	Belair Stud	James Fitzsimmons	E. Sande
1931	Twenty Grand	Greentree Stable	Jas. Rowe, Jnr	C. Kurtsinger

Year	Horse	Owner	Trainer	Jockey
1932	Burgoo King	E. R. Bradley	H. J. Thompson	E. James
1933	Brokers Tip	E. R. Bradley	H. J. Thompson	D. Meade
1934	Cavalcade	Mrs Dodge Sloane	R. A. Smith	M. Garner
1935	Omaha	Belair Stud	James Fitzsimmons	W. Saunders
1936	Bold Venture	M. L. Schwartz	Max Hirsch	I. Hanford
1937	War Admiral	Glen Riddle Farm	George Conway	C. Kurtsinger
1938	Lawrin	Woolford Farm	B. A. Jones	E. Arcaro
1939	Johnstown	Belair Stud	James Fitzsimmons	J. Scout
1940	Gallahadion	Milky Way Farm	Roy Waldron	C. Bierman
1941	Whirlaway	Warren Wright	Ben A. Jones	E. Arcaro
1942	Shut Out	Greentree Farm	John M. Gaver	W. D. Wright
1943	Count Fleet	Mrs John D. Hertz	G. D. Cameron	J. Longden
1944	Pensive	Calumet Farm	Ben A. Jones	C. McCreary
1945	Hoop Jr	F. W. Hooper	I. H. Parke	E. Arcaro
1946	Assault	King Ranch	Max Hirsch	W. Mehrtens
1947	Jet Pilot	Maine Chance Farm	Tom Smith	E. Guerin
1948	Citation	Calumet Farm	B. A. Jones	E. Arcaro
1949	Ponder	Calumet Farm	B. A. Jones	S. Brooks
1950	Middleground	King Ranch	Max Hirsch	W. Boland
1951	Count Turf	J. J. Amiel	S. Rutchick	C. McCreary
1952	Hill Gail	Calumet Farm	B. A. Jones	E. Arcaro
1953	Dark Star	Cain Hoy Stable	E. Haywood	H. Moreno
1954	Determine	A. J. Crevolin	W. Molter	R. York
1955	Swaps	R. C. Ellsworth	M. A. Tenney	W. Shoemaker
1956	Needles	D. & H. Stable	H. Fontaine	D. Erb
1957	Iron Liege	Calumet Farm	H. A. Jones	W. Hartack
1958	Tim Tam	Calumet Farm	H. A. Jones	I. Valenzuela
1959	Tomy Lee	Mr & Mrs Fred Turner, Jnr	Frank Childs	W. Shoemaker
1960	Venetian Way	Sunny Blue Farm	V. J. Sovinski	W. Hartack
1961	Carry Back	Mrs Katherine Price	J. A. Price	J. Sellers
1962	Decidedly	El Peco Ranch	H. A. Luro	W. Hartack
1963	Chateaugay	Darby Dan Farm	J. P. Conway	B. Baeza
1964	Northern Dancer	Windfields Farm	H. A. Luro	W. Hartack
1965	Lucky Debonair	Mrs Ada L. Rice	Frank Catrone	W. Shoemaker
1966	Kauai King	Ford Stable	Henry Forrest	D. Brumfield
1967	Proud Clarion	Darby Dan Farm	Loyd Gentry	R. Ussery
1968	Dancer's Image	Peter Fuller	L. C. Cavalaris	R. Ussery
1969	Majestic Prince	Frank McMahon	John Longden	W. Hartack
1970	Dust Commander	Robert E. Lehmann	Don Combs	M. Manganello
1971	Canonero II	Edgar Caibett	Juan Arias	G. Avita
1972	Riva Ridge	Meadow Stable	Lucien Lauren	R. Turcotte
1973	Secretariat	Meadow Stable	Lucien Lauren	R. Turcotte
1974	Cannonade	John M. Olin	Woody Stephens	A. Cordero

Preakness Stakes

Year	Horse	Owner	Trainer	Jockey
1873	Survivor	J. F. Chamberlin	A. D. Pryor	G. Barbee
1874	Culpepper	H. Gaffney	H. Gaffney	W. Donohue
1875	Tom Ochiltree	J. F. Chamberlin	R. W. Walden	L. Hughes
1876	Shirley	P. Lorillard	W. Brown	G. Barbee
1877	Cloverbrook	E. A. Clabaugh	J. Walden	C. Holloway
1878	Duke of Magenta	G. L. Lorillard	R. W. Walden	C. Holloway
1879	Harold	G. L. Lorillard	R. W. Walden	L. Hughes
1880	Grenada	G. L. Lorillard	R. W. Walden	L. Hughes
1881	Saunterer	G. L. Lorillard	R. W. Walden	T. Costello
1882	Vanguard	G. L. Lorillard	R. W. Walden	T. Costello
1883	Jacobus	J. E. Kelly	R. Dwyer	G. Barbee
1884	Knight of Ellerslie	T. W. Doswell	T. W. Doswell	S. Fisher
1885	Tucumseh	W. Donohue	C. Littlefield	J. McLaughlin
1886	The Bard	A. J. Cassatt	J. Huggins	S. Fisher
1887	Dunboyne	W. Jennings	W. Jennings	W. Donohue
1888	Refund	R. W. Walden	R. W. Walden	F. Littlefield
1889	Buddhist	S. S. Brown	J. Rogers	W. Anderson
1890	Montague	Preakness Stable	E. Feakes	W. Martin
1894	Assignee	J. R. & F. P. Keene	W. Lakeland	F. Taral
1895	Belmar	Preakness Stable	E. Feakes	F. Taral
1896	Margrave	Blemton Stable	B. McClelland	H. Griffin
1897	Paul Kauvar	T. P. Hayes	T. P. Hayes	Thorpe
1898	Sly Fox	C. F. Dwyer	H. Campbell	W. Simms
1899	Half Time	P. J. Dwyer	F. McCabe	R. Clawson
1900	Hindus	George J. Long	J. H. Morris	H. Spencer
1901	The Parader	R. T. Wilson	T. J. Healey	Landry
1902	Old England	G. B. Morris	G. B. Morris	L. Jackson
1903	Flocarline	M. H. Tichenor	H. C. Riddle	W. Gannon
1904	Bryn Mawr	Goughacres Stable	W. F. Presgrave	E. Hildebrand
1905	Cairngorm	Sydney Paget	A. J. Joyner	W. Davis
1906	Whimsical	T. J. Gaynor	T. J. Gaynor	W. Miller
1907	Don Enrique	August Belmont	J. Whalen	G. Mountain
1908	Royal Tourist	H. P. Whitney	A. J. Joyner	E. Dugan
1909	Effendi	W. T. Ryan	F. C. Frisbie	W. Doyle
1910	Layminster	E. B. Cassatt	J. S. Healey	R. Estep
1911	Watervale	A. Belmont	J. Whalen	E. Dugan
1912	Colonel Holloway	Beverwyck Stable	D. Woodford	C. Turner
1913	Buskin	J. Whalen	J. Whalen	J. Butwell
1914	Holiday	Mrs A. Barklie	J. S. Healy	A. Schuttinger
1915	Rhine Maiden	E. F. Whitney	F. Devers	D. Hoffman
1916	Damrosch	J. K. L. Ross	A. G. Weston	L. McAtee
1917	Kalitan	E. R. Bradley	W. Hurley	Ev. Haynes
1918	War Cloud	A. K. Macomber	W. B. Jennings	J. Loftus
1918	Jack Hare, Jr	W. E. Applegate	F. D. Weir	C. Peak
1919	Sir Barton	J. K. L. Ross	H. G. Bedwell	J. Loftus
1920	Man o' War	Glen Riddle Farm	L. Feustel	C. Kummer

Year	Horse	Owner	Trainer	Jockey
1921	Broomspun	H. P. Whitney	J. Rowe, Snr	F. Coltiletti
1922	Pillory	R. T. Wilson, Jnr	T. J. Healey	L. Morris
1923	Vigil	W. J. Salmon	T. J. Healey	B. Marinelli
1924	Nellie Morse	H. C. Fisher	A. B. Gordon	J. Merimee
1925	Coventry	G. A. Cochran	W. Duke	C. Kummer
1926	Display	W. J. Salmon	T. J. Healey	J. Maiben
1927	Bostonian	H. P. Whitney	F. Hopkins	A. Abel
1928	Victorian	H. P. Whitney	J. Rowe, Jnr	R. Workman
1929	Dr Freeland	W. J. Salmon	T. J. Healey	L. Schaefer
1930	Gallant Fox	Belair Stud	J. Fitzsimmons	E. Sande
1931	Mate	A. C. Bostwick	J. W. Healy	G. Ellis
1932	Burgoo King	E. R. Bradley	H. J. Thompson	E. James
1933	Head Play	Mrs S. B. Mason	T. P. Hayes	C. Kurtsinger
1934	High Quest	Brookmeade Stable	R. A. Smith	R. Jones
1935	Omaha	Belair Stud	J. Fitzsimmons	W. Saunders
1936	Bold Venture	Morton Schwartz	Max Hirsch	G. Woolf
1937	War Admiral	Glen Riddle Farm	G. Conway	C. Kurtsinger
1938	Daubet	Foxcatcher Farms	R. E. Handlen	M. Peters
1939	Challedon	W. L. Brann	L. J. Schaefer	G. Seabo
1940	Bimelech	E. R. Bradley	W. Hurley	F. A. Smith
1941	Whirlaway	Calumet Farm	B. A. Jones	E. Arcaro
1942	Alsab	Mrs A. Sabath	A. Swenke	B. James
1943	Count Fleet	Mrs J. Hertz	G. D. Cameron	J. Longden
1944	Pensive	Calumet Farm	B. A. Jones	C. McCreary
1945	Polynesian	Mrs P. A. B. Widener	M. Dixon	W. D. Wright
1946	Assault	King Ranch	M. Hirsch	W. Mehrtens
1947	Faultless	Calumet Farm	H. A. Jones	D. Dobson
1948	Citation	Calumet Farm	H. A. Jones	E. Arcaro
1949	Capot	Greentree Stable	J. M. Gaver	T. Atkinson
1950	Hill Prince	C. T. Chenery	J. H. Hayes	E. Arcaro
1951	Bold	Brookmeade Stable	P. M. Burch	E. Arcaro
1952	Blue Man	White Oak Stable	W. C. Stephens	C. McCreary
1953	Native Dancer	A. G. Vanderbilt	W. C. Winfrey	E. Guerin
1954	Hasty Road	Hasty House Farm	H. Trotsek	J. Adams
1955	Nashua	Belair Stud	J. Fitzsimmons	E. Arcaro
1956	Fabius	Calumet Farm	H. A. Jones	W. Hartack
1957	Bold Ruler	Wheatley Stable	J. Fitzsimmons	E. Arcaro
1958	Tim Tam	Calumet Farm	H. A. Jones	I. Valenzuela
1959	Royal Orbit	Est. J. Braunstein	R. Cornell	W. Hartmatz
1960	Bally Ache	Turfland	H. J. Pitt	R. Ussery
1961	Carry Back	Mrs K. Price	J. A. Price	J. Sellers
1962	Greek Money	Brandywine Stable	V. W. Raines	J. L. Rotz
1963	Candy Spots	R. C. Ellsworth	M. A. Tenney	W. Shoemaker
1964	Northern Dancer	Windfields Farm	H. A. Luro	W. Hartack
1965	Tom Rolfe	Powhatan	F. Y. Whiteley, Jnr	R. Turcotte
1966	Kauai King	M. J. Ford	H. Forrest	D. Brumfield
1967	Damascus	Edith W. Bancroft	F. Y. Whiteley, Jnr	W. Shoemaker
1968	Forward Pass	Calumet Farm	H. Forrest	I. Valenzuela
1969	Majestic Prince	Frank McMahon	J. Longden	W. Hartack
1970	Personality	Ethel D. Jacobs	J. W. Jacobs	E. Belmonte
1971	Canonero II	Edgar Caibett	Juan Arias	G. Avila
1972	Bee Bee Bee	William S. Farish, 3rd	Del W. Carroll	Eldon Nelson
1973	Secretariat	Meadow Stable	Lucien Lauren	R. Turcotte
1974	Little Current	Darby Danfarm	Lou Rondinello	M. Rivera

Triple Crown Winners (United States)

1919	Sir Barton
1930	Gallant Fox
1935	Omaha
1937	War Admiral
1941	Whirlaway
1943	Count Fleet
1946	Assault
1948	Citation
1973	Secretariat

Leading Jockeys (United States)

Year	Jockey	Wins
1895	J. Perkins	192
1896	J. Scherrer	271
1897	H. Martin	173
1898	T. Burns	277
1899	T. Burns	273
1900	C. Mitchell	195
1901	W. O'Connor	253
1902	J. Ranch	276
1903	G. C. Fuller	229
1904	E. Hildebrand	297
1905	D. Nicol	221
1906	W. Miller	388
1907	W. Miller	334
1908	V. Powers	324
1909	V. Powers	173
1910	G. Garner	200
1911	T. Koerner	162
1912	P. Hill	168
1913	M. Buxton	146
1914	J. McTaggart	157
1915	M. Garner	151
1916	F. Robinson	178
1917	W. Crump	151
1918	F. Robinson	185
1919	C. Robinson	190
1920	J. Butwell	152
1921	C. Lang	135
1922	M. Fator	188
1923	I. Parke	173
1924	I. Parke	205
1925	A. Mortensen	187
1926	R. Jones	190
1927	L. Hardy	207
1928	J. Inzelone	155
1929	M. Knight	149
1930	H. R. Riley	177
1931	H. Roble	173
1932	J. Gilbert	212
1933	J. Westrope	301
1934	M. Peters	221
1935	C. Stevenson	206
1936	B. James	245
1937	J. Adams	260
1938	J. Longden	236
1939	D. Meade	255
1940	E. Dew	287
1941	D. Mead	210
1942	J. Adams	245
1943	J. Adams	228
1944	T. Atkinson	287
1945	J. D. Jessop	290
1946	T. Atkinson	233
1947	J. Longden	316
1948	J. Longden	319
1949	G. Glisson	270
1950	J. Culmore	388
	W. Shoemaker	388
1951	C. Burr	310
1952	A. de Spirito	390
1953	W. Shoemaker	485
1954	W. Shoemaker	380
1955	W. Hartack	417
1956	W. Hartack	347
1957	W. Hartack	341
1958	W. Shoemaker	300
1959	W. Shoemaker	347
1960	W. Hartack	307
1961	J. Sellers	328
1962	R. Ferraro	352
1963	W. Blum	360
1964	W. Blum	324
1965	J. Davidson	319
1966	A. Gomez	318
1967	J. Velasquez	438
1968	A. Cordero, Jnr	345
1969	L. Snyder	352
1970	S. Hawley	452
1971	L. Pincay, Jnr	380
1972	S. Hawley	367
1973	S. Hawley	515
1974	C. McCarron	547

Acknowledgements

Colour

Barnaby's Picture Library, London 26–27, 40 top; Mike Cornwell Back cover; Fox Photos Ltd 40 bottom; Keystone Press Agency Ltd 38–39, 124 top, 172, 181, 183, 184; E. D. Lacey 122–123; Tom Parker 58–59; Pony and Light Horse 37 bottom, 171; Press Association Ltd 104; Mike Roberts 215; Peter Roberts 201; Solarfilma s.f. 101 bottom; Syndication International Ltd 124 bottom, 214, 216; Sally Anne Thompson Front cover, 25, 28 top, 28 bottom, 37 top, 57, 60 top, 60 bottom, 69, 70, 71, 72, 81, 82, 99, 100, 101 top, 102, 103, 121, 133, 134, 135, 136, 169, 170, 182, 202, 203, 204, 213.

Black and White

Sr D'Andrade 83 bottom; Associated Press Ltd 146 top; Australian News and Information Bureau 205 left; Austrian National Tourist Board 34 bottom, 118, 151 bottom right; Barnaby's Picture Library 142 top, 208; Belgian National Tourist Office 23; Black Star London 157 bottom, 185; Stefen Braun 91 top right; Caufield and Shook Inc. 43, 114 top, 175, 192, 205 right; Central Press Photos Ltd 13, 16, 151 bottom left, 166, 199 left; Jack H. Coote 48; John R. Corsan Back flap; Filimonov 173 left, 197 right; Finlay Davidson 29; Fotokhronika 199 right; Fox Photos Ltd 42 left, 93 bottom, 116 bottom right, 165 top left; Garrard & Co. Ltd 55 right, 115 top, 162; Daphne Machin Goodall 84 top; Hamlyn Group – Vic Stacey 12 top right, 14, 21 bottom right, 22 right, 62 left, 62 right, 84 bottom, 90, 94 left, 96 bottom right, 97 top, 147, 148 top left, 173 right, 177, 179 left, 180 right, 188 top, 189; Horse and Hound 33 top left; John Howard 20–21; Keystone Press Agency Ltd Title page, 11 bottom, 15 top, 18, 21 bottom left, 24, 30, 32–33, 108, 120 bottom, 128, 131, 160, 168 top, 211 top, 212, 217 bottom; E. D. Lacey 41 top, 126 bottom, 132, 137 top, 197 left; Keith Lambeth 97 bottom; Leslie Lane 12 left, 77 top, 95, 105, 144, 206; Mansell Collection 33 top right, 53 bottom, 86 top; Mary Evans Picture Library 167; Meteor, Copenhagen 112 top; Monty 46, 52, 91 top left, 139 bottom, 186 bottom, 190, 207, 209 top; John Nestle 10, 42 right; Norwegian Embassy 143 top right; Novosti Press Agency 112 bottom left; Desmond O'Neill 155 top, 156 bottom; Tom Parker 74, 158; Roy Parker 153 bottom; Paul Popper Ltd 113 centre; Barbara Pflaum, Black Star 107; Pony and Light Horse 49, 141 top, 179 right; Press Association Ltd 9 bottom, 17 left, 127 bottom, 145 top left, 145 top right, 159 bottom left, 198; Racing Information Bureau 8 top; Mrs Z. Raczkowska 210; Mike Roberts 53 top, 98, 155 bottom, 156 top; W. W. Rouch and Co. Ltd 31, 55 left, 68, 75, 83 top, 86 bottom, 106, 110 bottom, 130, 138 left, 159 top right, 174 bottom, 178, 191 bottom, 195 left; General Santa Rosa 33 bottom left, 51 top, 127 top; Sport and General Press Agency 91 bottom, 113 bottom right, 129 left, 141 bottom, 151 top; Peter Sweetman 140; Syndication International Ltd 8 bottom, 11 top, 17 right, 55 top, 61, 88, 88–89, 93 top, 109, 116 top, 145 bottom, 150, 164 top right, 191 top; John Tarlton 73, 79 bottom; Tate Gallery, London 54; Sally Anne Thompson 9 top, 12 bottom right, 15 bottom, 24 bottom, 33 bottom right, 44, 56, 79 top, 96 bottom left, 112 bottom, 113 top, 119, 143 bottom left, 218; United Press International (UK) Ltd 41 bottom, 137 bottom, 187; Velikzhanin 120 top; Lubomir Zaifert, Czechoslovakia 114–115.

The photographs on the following pages are reproduced from 'T.V. Vet Horse Book' by kind permission of the publishers, Farming Press Ltd: 21 bottom left, 22 bottom left, 34 top, 51 bottom, 76, 165 top right, 174 top, 188 bottom, 195 right, 211 bottom.

The line drawings on pages 61, 85, 87, 125, 126, 186 and 193 are taken from 'One Hundred Horse Drawn Carriages' published by Quartilles International Ltd, 67 London Road, St Albans, Herts at £1·00.